*For Michael Dov, my youngest grandson,
who will come of age when the issues dealt with herein
are being attended to and resolved.
He and his cousins Hillary, A.J., Erica, and Zach
will play a role in their resolution.*

Contents

Figures and Tables

Preface

This book had to be written. A quarter of a century of chaff passing for wisdom has been time enough. The new millennium need not be saddled with the baggage of the twentieth century. A modicum of reason is needed to level an inordinately uneven playing field.

For too many of us, the environmentalists and the media, the spinners and self-proclaimed arbiters of health affairs, were also the purveyors of the "facts" of our state of health. They were our fount of knowledge and repository of trust. But in their twenty-five-year hegemony they betrayed that trust. They turned the country into a culture of complaint and produced a population of paranoid hypochondriacs, abetting a great but baseless fear of the environment. Was it necessary? Was there merit to the many crises? *You've Been Had!* exposes the lie of the palpably groundless health scares of the past half-century and can be the anodyne for our time.

Too many of us can be told almost anything, and accept it. The spinners manipulated this incomprehension for their own ends. They linked environmental degradation—however it may be defined—with human health, serving the agenda of those who believe that if the public knew they were healthy and getting healthier—as the charts and tables clearly show they are—interest in things environmental would evaporate, along with financial contributions. Consequently, environmental pollution and health were inextricably linked, and the people were made to believe they were time bombs, ready to succumb to illness. Nothing could be further from the truth, yet a compliant public not only bought the sorry message, but clasped it to its breast.

It is also false to believe that the public would have dropped caring about the environment if they knew it had little, if any, connection with their health. Indeed, protection of water, air, soil, and food invites an on-going vigilance, but it requires neither the creation of a cancer epidemic nor a campaign of fear. Consequently, it is not surprising that so many are confused, uncertain, and scared.

Has our health declined with the demise of agriculture and the rise of industry? This is the essential question. Not only has it not declined, but it has markedly prospered. From 1900 to 1999, the data, the numbers, have increased favorably, including those for cancer and heart disease. By all indices, our health as a nation has improved significantly. But it is also evident that our lifestyles, not the environment, are responsible for most illnesses. Cleaning up the environment, whatever that means, will affect none of this, but attention to behavior could easily reduce our national mortality rate by as much as 50 percent, something medical intervention could not possibly achieve. Our goal must be to peel away the layers of misinformation and misunderstanding that have so encrusted the real issues of our physical and mental well-being. Paradoxically, we are at once needlessly worrying ourselves sick about our good health while killing ourselves and one another.

H. L. Mencken had it right. "The public," he wrote, "with its mob yearning to be instructed, edified, and pulled by the nose, demands certainties." But the only certainties are that the data, the numbers, the facts of life and death are fully in our hands; what we choose to do, or not do, is up to us. Consequently, the major issues of the twenty-first century will be issues we *can* control.

Though too many of us are confused, we find benightedness easy to live with. *You've Been Had!* seeks to make delusion more difficult by taking readers on a reality trek, stressing problems that properly need to be feared and those that do not, what is harmful and what is not. *You've Been Had!* will guide us through these minefields and on our journey we will face many essential truths. That cancer is not a modern affliction, but a risk run by all multicellular organisms, simply because we are multicellular, is one of them. The unpalatable fact is that it takes only a single cell, "one renegade cell," to strike out on its own and produce the billion cells needed to form an observable tumor. Given the trillions of cells that make up our bodies, it is inexpressively astonishing that tumors and cancers occur so infrequently.

We shall also dig into the environmental issues that have become icons of our time. Are they indeed the perils so many believe them to be, perils that have rocketed our anxiety levels into orbit? Can we lay the misguided anecdotal notions about infant mortality, aging, and longevity to rest, while placing blame where properly warranted, if prevention is to work? Indeed we can.

Throughout this book I deal with two questions: What do we really know, and what is only perceived? Perception is not unimportant, but reliance on our senses is simply inadequate in comprehending the panoply of risks that impact our lives. This book will show where we have been misled and why. *You've Been Had!* nudges readers down a new road, marching to a different drummer, seeking to return us to a less stressful, less anxiety-filled life while providing a firm basis to prevent past mistakes from recurring. I have tried to write a book that is readily accessible yet scientifically sound about a number of complex and emotion-tinged issues, a book that readers can lean on, rely on, and trust. Perhaps one day I'll know if I succeeded.

Most assuredly, the judiciously marshaled, lucidly laid-out, comprehensive evidence will be viewed as controversial, out of sync, with conventional wisdom, a "wisdom" that produced a nation of hypochondriacs, a culture of complaint and self-absorption. It is time to make waves and know ourselves and our country. "We shall not cease from exploration," T. S. Eliot wrote, "and the end of all of our exploring will be to arrive where we started, and know the place for the first time."

A book of this nature, ranging as it does across a panoply of turbulent issues, requires a good deal of help. I was fortunate to be able to consult Lester Levin, a friend and colleague off whom I could bounce ideas, secure in the knowledge that if I bounced too far, he'd reel me in. I was also fortunate to be able to call upon a bevy of outstanding librarians, those at Princeton University's Social Sciences Library, Princeton Public Library, Rutgers University's Library of Science and Medicine, and the West Windsor Public Library. Librarians are magical people, making things appear like rabbits from a hat. I suspect they'll be relieved that this project is over.

Carol May was a lucky find. Carol took my scribblings and turned them into typed, readable drafts, which she e-mailed to me for further work. It was a beneficial synergism, given that time is always a thief.

Helen Hsu, my editor at Rutgers University Press, must be accorded pride of place for believing in the book, its premise and substance, and believing, too, that its message was not only pertinent but overdue.

And then there are the many friends and family members whose encouragement I could not do without. Were it not for my daughter Dana, I suspect the completed, collated manuscript would have never gotten beyond my Mac. Dana is an organizer's organizer. When she took hold, the work blossomed and bore fruit—on time. She has my everlasting gratitude. I cannot thank my son, Scott, enough. While writing his own book, attending to his family and profession, he made time for commiseration and suggestions. My daughter Andi (Andrea) came up with the book's ingenious title. But there was also one who suffered in silence. My wife, Anita, cannot be repaid for all the lost weekends, holidays, and so many other times when she had to go it alone. Still, she was there for me when I needed advice, suggestions, and comfort. A place has been set aside for her—in heaven. Indeed, this was a family affair.

With all the help, all the suggestions extended to me, the interpretations, conclusions, errors, and omissions are mine alone.

MELVIN A. BENARDE, PH.D.
Princeton, New Jersey
September 2001

You've
Been Had!

Top of the Charts

It was one of the twentieth century's best-kept secrets. For a country as loose-lipped as ours, this was exceptional. If we're not careful, it could become one of the best-kept secrets of the twenty-first as well. Curiously enough, neither investigative journalists nor the media sought to exploit it. Actually, it need not be pried loose; many of us have known it for years, but after groundless health scares and crisis-filled years, the fact is: *we Americans are a healthy lot*. Not only are we healthy, but we're among the healthiest on the planet.

Years of reading and hearing about illness and adverse environmental effects on health have convinced far too many of us that everything is harmful and dangerous, and we're at risk for one dread disease or another. That's twentieth-century thinking. Indeed, through the decades of the seventies, eighties, and nineties, we were made to believe that we were sick, or about to be; that environmental pollution had exacted a devilish toll; that AIDS was the numero uno killer, and that cancer was of epidemic proportions and rocketing out of control. None of this is true. It never has been. Does thinking make it so?

Think of "Healthy People," Surgeon General Julius Richmond's annual Report to the President for 1979.[1] At the outset, and in bold print, Richmond told President Jimmy Carter that "Americans today are healthier than ever" and offered an intriguing number: "Seventy-five percent of all deaths in this country are due to degenerative diseases such as heart disease, stroke, and cancer." The document informs us that it is guns, anger, cigarettes, high-fat foods, alcohol, drug abuse, speed on the highway, a sedentary lifestyle, and overeating that substantially increase our risk of illness and premature death. Death now becomes an aggregate of cigarettes smoked, seat belts unfastened, glasses filled and emptied, and cheeseburgers devoured. The fact is, our bad habits slide irreversibly into disease and death.

Obviously, this is not the message that many of us want to hear. In fact, there are two messages: (1) we are a healthy people, and (2) illness and premature death are literally in our hands. The spinners prefer that neither message be disseminated widely. The first simply contradicts the environmentalists' message writ large over the past twenty-five years—one that is believed nationwide—that the *environment* is an agent of disease and the cause of our ill health. The second message flies in the face of our own best interests, because few of us want to hear that our well-being is our own responsibility. But choices must be made and lifestyles may need modification, calling for a bit more maturity than many care to shoulder. It's easier to believe that outside forces—environmental forces—are rigged against us. But that is exactly what environmentalists and the media would like us to believe.

One would have thought that our good health—nay, our *excellent* health—would be cause for rejoicing, shouting from the rooftops, and dancing in the streets. But there is not a sound. Not a whisper. Think *change*.

We are about to embark on a reality trek: to peel away layers of obfuscation and misinformation that has so encrusted the real issues of our physical and mental well-being that we have been unable to distinguish what is harmful from what is not. We begin with our country's ten leading causes of death. And we will ask which, if any, or any combination of them, is related to the environment. If the environment—we'll deal at some length with that fuzzy word—were squeaky clean, would any of the leading causes of death decline?

The numbers tell a remarkable story, far different from the twentieth-century stories we have heard. Corks should be popping for these numbers.

Causes of Death

The most complete and up-to-date set of numbers, from the National Center for Health Statistics (table 1.1), provides a mine of information, and the nuggets abound.

The table gives us the causes of death, followed by the total number of deaths that occurred in 1997, the death rate per 100,000, and the percentage or proportion of deaths from the particular illness compared to all other causes. It is almost immediately evident that coronary heart disease, CHD, is the sole and solid occupant of position one. Also apparent is that beyond CHD, the numbers fall precipitously, including cancer of all sites combined, and that AIDS is not among the top ten. Perhaps most illumi-

Table 1.1. Leading Causes of Death, United States, 1997

Rank	Cause	Number	Rate/10⁵	Percent of Total
	All	2,314,245	864.7	100.0
1.	Heart disease	726,974	271.6	31.4
2.	Cancer	539,577	201.6	23.4
3.	Cerebrovascular disease— stroke	159,791	59.7	6.9
4.	Chronic obstructive pul- monary disease (COPD)	109,029	40.7	4.7
5.	Accidents:	95,644	35.7	4.1
	Motor vehicle	43,458	16.2	1.8
	Other	52,186	19.5	2.2
6.	Pneumonia and influenza	86,449	32.3	3.7
7.	Diabetes	62,636	23.4	2.7
8.	Suicide	30,535	11.4	1.1
9.	Nephritis/nephrosis	25,331	9.5	1.0
10.	Chronic liver disease, cirrhosis	25,175	9.4	1.0
11.	All other	453,104	169.3	19.5

SOURCE: National Center for Health Statistics.
NOTE: Total population July 1, 1997 = 267,784,000.

nating is the fact that fully 62 percent of all causes of death can be attributed to CHD, cancer, and stroke (cerebrovascular disease). Recall Surgeon General Richmond's 75 percent figure back in 1979, and note that over the ensuing twenty years welcome declines have occurred. If chronic obstructive pulmonary disease, COPD, and accidents are added, the five leading causes account for 72 percent of *all* causes. Consider for a moment the reduction in overall deaths that would readily occur from lowering one, two, or three of the causes. If they are related to our behavior, reductions could occur relatively rapidly and would be greater than any medical intervention could possibly offer.

Pneumonia and influenza, in the sixth position, are the only infectious and communicable diseases among the ten. Pneumonia is primarily a problem of the hospitalized elderly, while influenza, "the flu," wreaks havoc among unimmunized young and old. From the total number of deaths, and from the U.S. population, which stood at 268 million on July 1, 1997, our overall death rate is 8.6 per 1,000, less than one percent. The fact that the great preponderance of us remain healthy most of our lives is the essential message.

Coronary Heart Disease

While some 31 percent of all deaths are due to CHD, it is also true that the death rate from CHD has fallen 6 percent since 1990, 17 percent since 1979, and 30 percent since 1930. That's a lot of people living longer, productive lives. Over the past thirty years, CHD incidence has declined by 2–4 percent per year. How, then, to account for these declines? Current consensus suggests a combination of primary prevention for incidence and effective patient management for prevalence. Primary prevention speaks directly to the question raised earlier: how can our national death rate be reduced? Would tipping the balance derive from our behavior or some external factor or factors? For primary prevention, the consensus of considered epidemiological opinion focuses on the following:

- Reduction in number of cigarettes smoked (lung cancer is only one of a number of illnesses that tobacco smoke affects adversely)
- Blood pressure reduction
- Dietary modification (to reduce cholesterol, increase HDL and homocysteine)
- Anger reduction

If these are the major risk factors for CHD, it would appear that we are our own worst enemies, and that lowering the 31 percent lies within our hands and can readily be accomplished.

In 1980, Dr. Reuel A. Stallones, professor of epidemiology at the School of Public Health at the University of Texas, concluded, in a review of the possible risk factors that might account for the substantial decline in CHD, with a prophetic observation: "We now have strong assurance," he wrote, "that programs based on our present knowledge can reduce the risk of death from ischemic heart disease. Unfortunately these programs require people to stop doing certain things they like to do, such as smoking cigarettes, or eating whatever they want to, or do things they do not want to do, such as taking anti-hypertensive drugs or exercising strenuously."[2]

As epidemiologic studies will be used to buttress claims made, this seems an appropriate point at which to define the subject. The definition I have long used in class maintains that epidemiology is the study of the *frequency* and *distribution* of an illness, event, or condition in a population, in an attempt to discover causal or etiologic factors, for the ultimate goal of control or prevention. Less formally, epidemiology seeks to determine why some people become ill at a point in time, and others do not.

As we shall see, the great benefit of epidemiology is its reliance on human rather than animal studies and its use of control populations for comparison with test subjects. Great care, however, must be exercised in interpreting data from epidemiologic studies. Accordingly, chapter 7 renders the essentials and caveats along with cogent examples.

Recently, a lifetime risk of developing CHD found that for a woman aged 50, the risk of developing a coronary episode (calculated as of age 85) was 1 in 3, or 31.1 percent, which is about three times greater than for her developing breast cancer—11.3 percent. Clearly, heart disease is a far greater risk for women than breast cancer. As figure 1.1 shows, this holds true for women generally. For men age 40, the lifetime risk is 1 in 2, but drops to 1 in 3 by age 70; it drops to 1 in 4 for women of that age.[3]

A research team at Harvard Medical School, challenging the notion that the older you get, the sicker you get, found that the older you get, the healthier you've been. "Compared with others in the older population, centenarians seem to either markedly delay, or, in some cases, escape life-threatening disease . . . had they not done so, it is unlikely they could survive to the practical limits of the human life span."[4] Primary prevention could just be the ticket to that destination.

Diabetes

Cancer, which looms so large on the body politic, and for which we have an uncommon dread, deserves our undivided attention, but we shall hold it in abeyance until we deal with the other less terrifying conditions of life. Diabetes, in the seventh slot, is diabetes mellitus (literally, honey-sweet diabetes), a disorder in which blood levels of the sugar, glucose, are abnormally high because the body doesn't release adequate amounts of insulin, an enzyme that normally metabolizes glucose, maintaining it at normal levels. We now know that at times our immune system's recognition apparatus falters, and the body begins manufacturing T-cells and antibodies against its own cells and organs. These attack the pancreas, knocking out the insulin-producing cells, thereby causing diabetes. T cells—produced in the thymus gland (hence the "T"), just behind the sternum, the breast

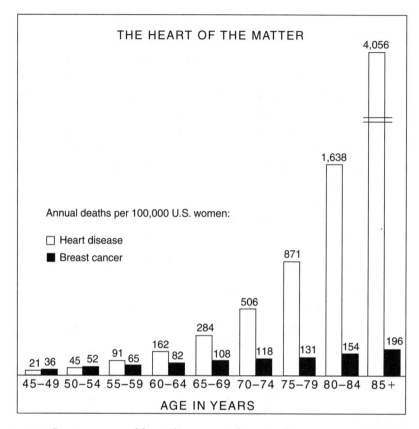

FIG. 1.1. *Breast cancer and heart disease mortality rates for women ages 45 to 85+. Clearly, of the two, heart disease is of far greater concern at all ages beyond 49. As the graph shows, heart disease kills at least six times more women in the postmenopausal years than does breast cancer.* (SOURCE: National Center for Health Statistics. Death rates are based on 1992 data, the most recent available.)

bone—are a type of white blood cell (lymphocytes) that normally is part of the body's defensive arsenal that directs and regulates immune responses.

Accidents

Is diabetes related to environmental pollution? In the same vein, are accidents?

Motor vehicle accidents, a major contributor to accidental death—which is hardly ever accidental—have been a part of our lives ever since that crisp September day in 1899 when H. H. Bliss stepped from a trolley car in New York City and was struck down by a horseless carriage. By

1990, 3 million people had been killed by motor vehicles. Should this level of carnage continue, we will see the fourth million by the year 2012. Motor vehicles, causing over 43,000 deaths in 1997 in the United States, contribute a continuing and violent threat to life. Millions are also injured every year, often severely. But this mayhem is not inevitable. Accidents, which I prefer to call "purposefuls," are in fact set in motion by a train of events in which our behavior plays a dominant role.

Although motor vehicle accidents have declined some 20 percent from the notorious 53,000 deaths in 1966, death rates for sixteen-year-old drivers have increased alarmingly. A substantial proportion of people killed or injured in car crashes have been caused by sixteen-year-olds.

According to the National Safety Council, vehicular accidents can be directly connected to alcohol consumption, impulsiveness, and poor judgment. Increasingly, poor judgment results in accidents in which drivers are distracted by the use of cell phones while driving. A new and highly creative development, the car office, replete with computer, fax, and copier, could drive the numbers even higher. Accidents, hardly. Purposefuls, absolutely.

Besides motor vehicles, what else contributes to the accident toll? Falls are the single greatest risk. Fifteen thousand deaths occurred from falls alone in 1997. Drugs, fires, poisoning, drowning, and firearms contribute additional thousands. Although accidents are the fifth leading cause of death for all races, ages, and sexes combined, accidents are in fact the leading cause of death for ages 1 to 44.

Homicide and Suicide

Cancer is the leading cause of death for the 45–64 age group, AIDS is the leading cause for those 25–44, but homicide leads the pack for 15–24-year-old black men. Indeed, buried within the total rates, and needing excision, are a number of chilling revelations. Trauma is an alarming killer lurking in our communities. Suicides, for one, while in the eighth position nationally, is both the third and fourth leading exterminator of the 15–24 and 25–44 age groups, respectively, with over 30,000 lives lost annually. There is something terribly wrong here. As a nation we are living longer, and with far less illness than ever before, yet suicide is increasing. Why? Have the suicidals been misled by the alarmist media into believing that it's all bad out there, that violence, illness, and abandonment await us all? This requires much consideration.

Homicide, at thirteenth position for all ages in 1997, was, quite remarkably, the fourth leading cause of death for 1–4-year-olds, second for those aged 15–24, and third for youngsters 5–14. A homicide epidemic affecting 15–24-year-olds took place between 1985 and 1995—a handgun-induced slaughter in which young men resolved disputes by killing one another over drug-dealing territory. The current lull appears to be due to strict and strong efforts by police to remove readily available guns from the street. With fewer guns, there were fewer fatalities. But the war over drug turf continues in other ways.

For the entire country, the homicide rate is 6.3 per 100,000 population—higher than any country in western Europe by a factor of two or three; thirteen times higher than Spain; and seven times higher than Norway and Canada, where homicide has always been low. The U.S. homicide rate among blacks is seven times that of whites. Still, we can take small comfort from the fact that we kill one another at a rate some three times lower than Russia's.

Six states—North and South Dakota, Iowa, New Hampshire, Vermont, and Massachusetts—have the country's lowest rates, and these appear to be related to gun ownership. Gun ownership and the availability of guns and homicide seem to be directly related. For example, Finland, with Europe's highest rate of homicide, also has its highest level of gun ownership.

The numbers indicate that over the past four decades, we have become a violent society. Through motor vehicles, suicide, and homicidal deaths, we are regularly and frequently killing one another and ourselves in alarming numbers. Environmentally related? Hardly. Unless our definition of environment undergoes major surgery.

Homicide among angry young men and women is one thing, but murder of *pregnant women* is quite another. Traditionally, *maternal mortality was understood* to mean death of a mother as a consequence of complications of pregnancy, physiological problems resulting in deaths that would not have occurred but for the pregnancy. Recently, however, researchers at the Maryland Department of Health and Mental Hygiene, delving deeply into records of pregnancy-related deaths, found that "a pregnant or recently pregnant women is more likely to be a victim of homicide than to die of any other cause."[5] They found that homicide was responsible for 20 percent of all pregnancy-associated deaths—more than any other cause of pregnancy-related deaths. This was strikingly in contrast to the fact that homicide was the fifth leading cause of death among nonpregnant women during the same five-year period. We are also informed however, that in

1998, homicide was the second leading cause of death among 15–24-year-old women, and sixth among women 25–44. Clearly, women between 15 and 44, no matter their reproductive condition, are at great risk of death from violent men. But it has now become evident that untold numbers of women who are either pregnant or have recently given birth are victims of extreme violence by husbands, lovers, and boyfriends. More than likely, this killing has been going on for some time, but not until now, with greater diligence for causes of death, has this chilling form of violence been revealed. With an entirely new wave of deaths to augment it, homicide's toll will increase markedly.

Traditional Medical Disorders

Cerebrovascular diseases (CVD), ensconced in third position for over twenty years, and chronic obstructive pulmonary disease (COPD) in fourth, nephritis in ninth, and chronic liver disease and cirrhosis in tenth, are all classic and traditional medical problems.

As a cerebrovasuclar disease, stroke occurs as a consequence of oxygen debt, when blood flow to the brain is disrupted. It is the most common cause of disabling neurological damage and death. Like water through a sediment-clogged pipe, a blood clot or fatty clump (an atheroma) can block blood flow anywhere if an infection inflames and narrows blood vessels to the brain. Drugs and low blood pressure can also restrict blood flow.

Whereas CVD is an obstructive condition of the circulatory system, COPD is the consequence of airway obstruction—obstruction of the respiratory tract. It is a tenacious obstruction often caused by either emphysema or chronic bronchitis. Our lungs consist of hundreds of millions of tiny air sacs—alveoli—whose walls are thinner than the thinnest tissue paper. The grapelike bunches or clusters of alveoli maintain a rigidity that holds the airways open. When the thin walls erode and after long-standing and ongoing irritation, most often from the result of immoderate cigarette smoking, the airways collapse and breathing becomes inordinately difficult. Death ensues from asphyxiation.

Nephritis is a kidney disorder, and the nephrotic syndrome is a collection of kidney ailments. Nephritis is most often the consequence of a bacterial—a streptococcal—infection, while nephrosis can result from a host of drugs, allergies, and diseases such as diabetes, cancer, and HIV infection, among others.

Cirrhosis appears to be the end-stage of a number of common causes of liver injury. It results in nonfunctioning and destroyed liver tissue that surrounds areas of viable, healthy tissue. Until the condition is advanced, many people remain asymptomatic and don't know they have it. The most common cause or risk factor is alcohol abuse. Among 45–65-year-olds, cirrhosis (Greek meaning "orange-colored") is the third most common cause of death.

So, here we have the third, fourth, ninth, and tenth causes of death, which between them are responsible for some 14 percent of what ails us. Are these environmental?

AIDS

AIDS struck the United States suddenly and explosively. Otherwise healthy young men were presenting with a rare, malignant tumor and an uncommon pneumonia. Once contracted, recovery was not possible. New cases and accompanying deaths piled up rapidly. From 319 cases and 121 deaths in 1981, the numbers rocketed to 78,834 new cases and 44,730 deaths in 1993. By the end of December 1999, over 730,000 cases had been documented along with 430,000 certified deaths. Early on, the unusual rare tumor, Kaposi's sarcoma, and the uncommon *Pneumocystis carinii* pneumonia, suggested a compromised immune system and alerted physicians. New York and San Francisco, with their large homosexual communities, were the first to reel under the onslaught. In fact, the initial epidemiological clues suggested a connection between homosexuality and the fatal disease. It wasn't until 1984, however, that a new virus was discovered, and with it the phenomenon of induced autoimmunity.

By attacking white blood cells, especially T cells, the virus HIV-1 was attacking the body's immune system, and defeating it, incurring an array of infectious diseases that normally would not occur, and causing death from diseases that normally are benign.

HIV tricks a T cell into switching on its copy machine, producing huge numbers of itself. This eventually destroys the cell, releasing the vast numbers of new virus particles to circulate, infect, and destroy additional lymphocytes. Over several months there is a profound loss of T-lymphocytes (CD4+ cells), which normally protect the body from microbial incursions besides destroying cancer cells. One feature distinguishing this virus from other retroviruses is the striking complexity of its viral genome. Most retroviruses are single-stranded RNA viruses that can replicate and contain only three genes. At this time, it is known that HIV-1 contains at least six additional genes. More than likely it is the concerted action of these six genes that contributes to its uncommon pathogenicity. Although incidence and mortality are impressive, neither has ever been high enough to rank near the top of the charts.[6] In 1995, its peak year during which some 50,000 AIDS deaths occurred, it thrust itself into eighth place ahead of suicide and homicide, but nowhere near the incidence of heart disease or cancer. Yet the public generally perceived it to be an unparalleled killer, at the top.

It has always been difficult to establish accurate and reliable case and mortality data because of the social stigma surrounding the behavior inherent in acquiring AIDS. The numbers could be higher, but to dislodge heart disease or cancer from their top positions, say in 1993, when AIDS first made the list, for each AIDS death there would have had to be an additional twenty and fourteen deaths, respectively. In 1995, each AIDS death would have had to increase 15-fold to nudge heart disease out of top place—a horrendous and unlikely prospect. Nevertheless, it is not likely that AIDS will dislodge heart disease as the nation's prime killer, though among 25–44-year-old black and Hispanic men, AIDS is the indisputable primary cause of death.

The public perception of AIDS's prominent position may well have been engendered by the media's constant reporting of AIDS cases and deaths as cumulative or aggregate figures. Consequently, readers and listeners are (still) regularly and frequently confronted with large numbers, such as 733,374 AIDS cases and 433,000 deaths as of December 1999. These numbers do make an impression. Few realize that they are the aggregate of twenty years of counting. By similar reckoning, heart disease and cancer have carried off 15 and 10 million citizens, respectively. It has never been suggested, as far as I have been able to determine, why AIDS data are uniquely brought to the public as aggregate totals. But numbers do impress.

Although the initial threat has abated in the United States, AIDS continues to be viewed as a major killer. With the arrival of the drugs Ritonaver and Indinovir in 1996, protease inhibitors used in combination with Zidovudine-AZT, the virus appeared to be immobilized. Protease inhibitors blocked the production of a protein needed for HIV replication. Euphoria set in: AIDS was curable. The drugs worked. Case fatality rates dropped over 50 percent, and deaths from AIDS dropped to fourteenth place in 1997.

Unfortunately, the virus became resistant to the drugs. By 2000, a magic bullet was nowhere in sight; neither a cure for the disease nor a preventive vaccine. Effective treatment can be expected but remains a distant promise, and it must be understood that effective treatment is not

Table 1.2. Estimated Incidence of Sexually Transmitted Diseases (STDs), United States, 1996

STD	*Incidence*
Chlamydia	3 million
Gonorrhea	650,000
Syphilis	70,000
Herpes	1 million
Human papilloma virus	5.5 million
Hepititus B	120,000
Trichomoniasis	5 million
Bacterial vaginosis	No estimates
HIV	20,000
Total	15.4 million

SOURCE: Adapted from *Sexually Transmitted Diseases* 26, no. 4 (1999), suppl.: 52–56.

synonymous with control. It is worth recalling that penicillin was hailed as the magic bullet that would eradicate both syphilis and gonorrhea. Rates reached all-time lows and eradication seemed entirely possible. However, social mores changed and the ready availability of antibiotic therapy clearly affected sexual decision-making. In the 1960s, syphilis and gonorrhea infection rates were rising once again, and forty years later they continue to be a significant public health concern.

On a worldwide basis, where AIDS has attained truly pandemic proportions, changes in personal behavior among adults offer the most rapid and cost-effective means of stemming this plague. Time is the enemy. Waiting for the development of appropriate drugs is tantamount to consigning literally tens of millions of people, including children, to grievous illness and premature death.

If the World Health Organization's estimate of fifteen hundred new cases daily is correct, the world is looking at 27 million new cases in five years and some 54 million in ten. Is it possible to wait for a magic bullet? Behavior change is the preferred approach for heart disease and lung cancer, so why not for AIDS?

If the most recent estimates of 10–20 million new cases of sexually transmitted diseases per year are correct, we are faced with a colossal public health problem when we include the other diseases as well. These numbers stand as ample testimony to the difficulty of changing people's behavior.[7] I may be overly pessimistic since in eight of the nine diseases noted in table 1.2, death is rarely an outcome. HIV, however, cannot make that statement.

Cancer

We have arrived at the number 2 cause of death: cancer. Waiting for us are two questions: Is there a cancer epidemic? and, Are cancer numbers and rates soaring? Figures 1.2 and 1.3 fulfill the adage that a good picture is worth many words; they are at the top of the good picture chart: not too many numbers, much substance. For example, figure 1.2 describes the male death rate for six major cancer sites for the years 1930–1996. Three ideas quickly suggest themselves. Between 1930 and 1996, lung cancer soared, and then began to fall. Soaring and falling are germane to the perception of a cancer epidemic. During the same period, stomach cancer declined steadily. The remaining four major sites—liver, pancreas, prostate,

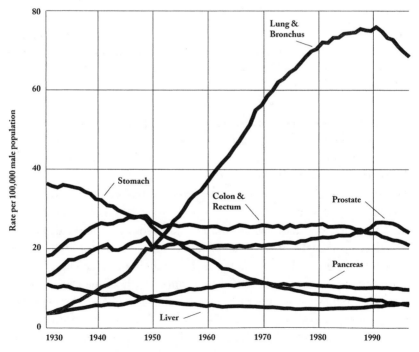

FIG. 1.2. *Age-adjusted cancer death rates for males, by site, 1930–1996.* (SOURCE: Reproduced by permission of the American Cancer Society.)

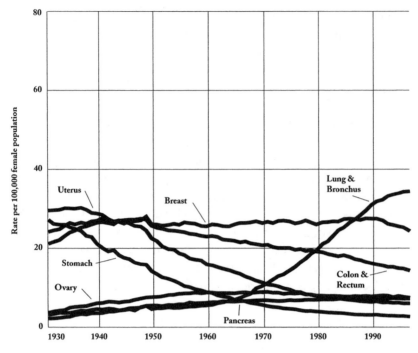

FIG. 1.3. *Age-adjusted cancer death rates for females, by site, 1930–1996. Clearly, cancer of six of the seven sites have remained constant or declined over the past six decades. Lung cancer alone has risen substantially during this time.* (SOURCE: Reproduced by permission of the American Cancer Society.)

and colon/rectum—remained remarkably constant. Figure 1.3 shows that cancer death rates for females are similar. From 1965 to 1996, lung cancer rose precipitously but breast cancer remained remarkably stable over the entire period. Prior to World War II, the United States was an agricultural society, and the dramatic shift to being an industrial giant had not yet occurred. Yet in these undeniably different environments, breast cancer rates remained virtually static, while uterine, stomach, and colon cancers declined. Cancers of the pancreas and ovary remained constant. If there is an epidemic, it is an epidemic of lung cancer—smoking-induced lung cancer. The only soaring cancer in sight is lung cancer, for both men and women.

What we have been experiencing is a "raising all boats" phenomenon. Lung cancer is not only the leading cause of cancer death, but by its prodigious numbers it distorts or skews the rates for all cancer sites combined—a good reason for not combining them. The skewing falsely implies that cancers of all sites are rising. If ever there was a numerical artifact, this is it. From 1950 to 1996, with lung cancer included, the combined cancer rate increased 6.5 percent—all boats rising—over forty-six years, while the overall, combined rate excluding lung cancer declined 17.7 percent. That's the story the American public should have received. That's the message that needs wide distribution.

How could the media let that one get away? Cancer is declining. *Cancer*, of all sites! Unfortunately for all, the media preferred to trumpet the overall increased rate rather than explain the distorting influence of lung cancer on all rates combined. Figure 1.4 unambiguously shows this disparity. National Cancer Institute figures also show that the overall cancer incidence—new cases—declined on average 0.7 percent annually from 1990 to 1996. Over this period, lung, prostate, breast, and colorectal cancers accounted for over 50 percent of new cases and were the major causes of death. The expectation is that if women eschew or reduce cigarette smoking, the declines will accelerate further. Unfortunately, lung cancer mortality may turn up sharply again due to increasing use of both cigarettes and morphine by teenagers.[8] That's another message requiring wide dissemination, but it remains unattended.

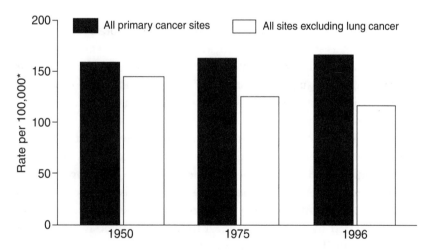

*Age-adjusted to the 1970 standard population.

FIG. 1.4. *U.S. cancer death rates for all anatomic sites, with and without lung cancer, 1950–1996. With lung cancer removed from calculation of rates, the cancer mortality rate for all sites combined has dropped 17.7 percent since 1950.* (SOURCE: Reproduced by permission of the *Journal of the National Cancer Institute* and Oxford University Press.)

Excluding skin cancers, breast cancer is the most common cancer among women, accounting for almost a third of all diagnosed cases. Breast cancer incidence rates increased some 4 percent per year from 1982 to 1987, but have since stabilized. This increased incidence appears to have been the result of increased use of mammographic screening, which detects early, asymptomatic breast tumors. Increased use of screening increases the numbers of "cases" detected over a specific period, which will force rates to rise. Much of this detection is early-stage disease. When screening levels off, the rate of disease will level with it, as long as other causal factors do not change. If they do, then the increase cannot be ascribed to screening.

Between 1990 and 1996, breast cancer mortality declined 1.8 percent per year. Age is a major risk factor. Seventy-five percent of new cases and over 80 percent of deaths occur in women aged 50 and older. For all races combined, 20–24-year-old women have an incidence rate of 1.3 cases per 100,000 women, while women 75 and older have the highest: 483 per 100,000. Even so, for women of all ages, heart disease is by far a greater risk than breast cancer. Another look at figure 1.1 can bring that reality into appropriate perspective. From a Gallop poll we learn that too few women realize the magnitude of this disjunction—another message that requires wide dissemination.[9]

Although a number of potential risk factors have been identified for breast cancer, as shown in table 1.3, at this time there are no known preventive measures. However, given the quickening pace of the Genome Project and increasing gene studies worldwide, knowledge of the role genes play in this cancer cannot be far away. Once it is known, preventive measures will surely follow.

A blip in the prostate cancer trend line now draws our attention. Between 1989 and 1993 prostate cancer incidence increased sharply. But the rate peaked in 1993 and has since declined. This rise in rate appears also to have been driven by increased screening, in this instance with the Prostate Specific Antigen (PSA) blood test. Again, the increase was an artifact generated by advanced medical technology, which must be dealt with cautiously if we are to avoid misinterpretation.

Ultraviolet light, especially "B," is the cause of over a million cases of skin cancer annually, surpassing all cancer sites combined. Skin cancer comes in three types depending upon the skin cells involved: basal cell, squamous cell, and melanocytes. Malignant melanoma, of the melanocytes, is far and away the most lethal and fortunately the least common. Never-

Table 1.3. Risk Factors for Breast Cancers

Strong Risks

    Inherited genetic mutations

    Two or more first-degree relatives with breast cancer diagnosed at an early age

Moderate Risks

    Nodular densities on mammogram (75% of breast volume)

    One first-degree relative with breast cancer

    High dose ionizing radiation to the chest

    Ovaries not surgically removed, < age 40

Weak Risks

    Never married

    Late age at full-term pregnancy (> or = to age 40)

    Late menopause (> or = 55 years)

    Early menarche (< 12 years)

    Urban residence

    Northern U.S. residence

---

theless, it is increasing at about 4 percent per year and was expected to be diagnosed in approximately 48,000 people in the year 2000. Non-melanoma cancers, the basal and squamous cell types, are the most common by far among the nation's white population.

Skin cancer is increasing for two dangerous reasons: we're taking off more clothing, exposing more epidermis than ever before, and we're spending more time in the sun in those damaging hours between 10 A.M. and 2 P.M., when the sun's rays are directly upon us. A third reason has recently been suggested: the use of presumably protective sunscreens that we think will allow us to spend more time in the sun, safely. This could be a mistake. At greatest risk are the fair-skinned among us, those with light eyes and hair and with the least amount of melanin in their skin. They burn easily, especially the children. The danger is not exaggerated. Researchers at the Queensland Institute for Medical Research in Brisbane, Australia, having followed 1,383 people—not mice—for five years, found that sunscreen use reduces the risk of developing squamous cell carcinoma by 40 percent.[10] But using sunscreen was not protective against either basal cell carcinoma or melanoma. This raises another formidable problem: light.

Light, or energy, travels in wavelike motion. Characteristically, waves extend from the shortest, tightly packed high-energy waves to the longer, low-energy waves. Variation in wave proximity imparts specific singularities such as colors of visible light, destructiveness of gamma rays, and the sunburn caused by ultraviolet rays, the light beyond violet. Beyond violet are UV-A, UV-B, and UV-C. Their wavelengths are measured in nanometers (a nanometer is equal to 10^{-9} meters). UV-A is approximately 400–320 namometers; UV-B, 320–290; and UV-C, 290–200. As the wavelengths decrease, they become more tightly packed and possess greater energy— and greater destructive potential.

Although UV-C has the potential for great harm, it never makes it into our world, as its energy is completely absorbed in the atmosphere, never arriving at street or beach level. UV-A and UV-B, with little penetrating energy, are limited to skin damage. However, their low-intensity, nonionizing radiation is unable to break chemical bonds, which means they do not produce mutant strands of DNA. Nevertheless, it's the A and B that can burn skin, even when it's cloudy, because these relatively high-energy packets readily pass through the clouds. That's worth bearing in mind. Most sunscreens have been formulated to deal with UV-B, that is, the creams contain chemicals that are supposed to keep B from skin. There is little or no built-in protection against the longer A wavelength, which appears, if the data are solid, to induce a majority of both the basal cell carcinomas and the melanomas. Consequently, reliance upon sunscreens for protection against UV-A is not possible at this time. That's important to know! For the protection needed, try the Australian technique: slip, slop, and slap. Slip on a shirt, slop on cream, and slap on a hat. If stripping down continues, remember that the sunblock numbers have yet to be standardized by the industry. One company's SPF-15 may be another's 12. Gary L. Kantor, chairman of the Department of Dermatology at the MCP/Hahnemann Medical School in Philadelphia, is adamant about sunblock. "Sunblock," he cautions, "must be applied at least 45 minutes before assuming a place in the sun, if it is to be effective." And he further maintains that "at least two ounces per application must be used. Thin smears will not do it. And it must be repeated after each swim." Unfortunately, this type of information is not found on containers of sunblock. It should be. So, caution is the name of the game, and the higher the number the better.

How important is this? Recent evidence obtained by medical researchers at George Washington University Medical School and the National Cancer Institute suggests a direct relationship between childhood sunburn and adult melanoma. They subjected both transgenic and wild-type mice to skin-reddening doses of UV light (15 minutes at UV-A and UB-B) at ages 3.5 days and six weeks and found that a single dose at 3.5 days was sufficient to induce melanoma. Similar doses at six weeks were not tumerogenic. The skin lesions produced in newborn mice were similar to the lesions seen in human skin cancers. Although it is too early to extrapolate these results directly to children, this mouse model adds strength to the proposed relationship of early sunburn/skin cancer. And it may well aid in developing real protection against sunburn and consequent cancer formation in susceptible individuals.[11]

Malignant Cell Growth

The malignant growth of tissue cells proceeds from the activation of oncogenes and the deactivation of tumor suppressor genes. Cancer is a disease of damaged genes. TP53 is a tumor suppressor gene (TSG), the opposite of an oncogene. Oncogenes can cause runaway cell division if they are switched on. With oncogenes on and TSGs off, cancer is almost a foregone conclusion.

TP53 can signal switched-on oncogenes to kill themselves: cell suicide, termed *apoptosis*, from the Greek, a falling off, as leaves fall from a tree. TP53 codes for a protein, P53, which circulates in the blood stream seeking cells running out of control, and in effect has them kill themselves. This works well in most of us. But for those who inherit a defective TP53, the switch is locked and oncogenes have nothing that can stop them.

Cancer is a disease of old age. The trend line, plotting increasing age versus increasing cancer deaths, from age 1 to 100, rises inexorably because the longer we live, the more genetic errors will accumulate. Cells must replicate their genes exactly when they divide so that each new cell receives a complete and intact set. Without a complete set, the cell could malfunction and die. As errors or mistakes accumulate, it becomes easier for the out-of-control cells to avoid being switched off by P53 and other TSGs. In his elegant and brief book, *One Renegade Cell*, Robert A. Weinberg, director of MIT's Whitehead Institute, informs us that "one fatal malignancy per one hundred million billion cell divisions does not seems so bad at all."[12] He isn't saying that any individual's cancer is okay; he is making the salient point that, given the staggering number of cells in our bodies and the continuing addition of new cells as we live and grow, it is nothing short of remarkable just how few cancers actually develop. Given the tremendous number of cells available, it is additionally remarkable that we don't get cancer soon after we are born. This requires reflection. It's a new paradigm. It's what's going on inside us, not what's out there.

This may be cold comfort to anyone with cancer, but others must take comfort from the fact that cancer is a relatively rare illness, even though it is our second leading cause of death. Because we have dealt so effectively with infectious diseases early in the twentieth century, so many of us live on to the older ages, leaving us with the diseases of old age. Success in dealing with the infectious diseases has given us length of days wherein mutated, broken genes can take their toll. But this too will yield, as knowledge of our genome's structure yields its secrets. I predict, even though scientists are not in the business of prophecy, that by the year 2042 the steps, the pathways leading to cancer, will be known, along with the means of their prevention. Why so long, why forty years? A great deal of difficult work remains to be done. For example, in the haste to complete the Genome Project, errors were inevitable. Remember that the human genome is a "book" of 3-billion-plus words. Even with the best computers, editing takes twelve to eighteen months. Then there are gaps in the sequences to consider. Apparently the gaps exist in stretches of short sequences repeated many times over. They will be challenging to get right. We are still a long way from finding all the genes that code for proteins. Between 35,000 and 40,000 genes have been verified. Perhaps another 25,000–30,000 remain, requiring another large chunk of time. However, the most demanding amount of time will be given to identifying gene functions. That's the key for all of us, and will require every bit of fifteen years, because one gene can make several proteins, and each can perform more than one function. The numbers are mind-boggling. However, as this great work moves along, information will become available, and new ideas will create ways of speeding up the process. As information becomes available, it will allow prevention and control to begin. We need only live long enough.

There is a conundrum here. Cancer, as we have said, is a disease of runaway cell growth, cells growing endlessly, out of control. But cells need to grow, otherwise we would never make it beyond fetal life or infancy. Our bones need to elongate, our skin must grow to cover the growing bones, our internal organs must enlarge, and we all know that cells are replaced as cuts, lacerations, and wounds are repaired and replaced and scars are formed. The replacement of peeling sheets of sunburned, destroyed, blistered skin has been a universal experience. So, cell growth is essential, which is stimulated, signaled, to occur by genes—oncogenes. But a balance is required: a balance between normal cell division and runaway cell division. That's the trick of life. When we learn that, we will have won the game. Maybe.

The Environment

For oncogenes to be turned on, a switch is needed. This switch, or switches, can be said to be the cause, or causes, of cancer. For most people over the past quarter of a century, the switch has been called the environment. It is altogether fitting and proper that we consider what this means, what it entails.

Misinterpretation and misrepresentation, whether accidental or purposeful, lead directly to misinformation and misunderstanding. This quartet has given "environment" a bad name, as in "environmental pollution," "tainted environment," "contaminated environment," and "environmental risk." Unrelenting misrepresentation over the past twenty-five years of "environmental risk factors" has made many of us fear the world. Air, water, food, and soil are presented as polluted and responsible for whatever ails us and as our leading causes of death. A quarter of a century's head start and a quarter of a century's stranglehold on the American mind may make it difficult, but not impossible, to extirpate this "cancer" on the body politic. But eliminate it we must, if prevention is ever to work. Misinterpreting what environmental risks are has a long tradition. As far back as 1964, the World Health Organization (WHO) issued its report declaring that the common fatal cancers occur in large part as a result of lifestyle and are preventable. Here are its words:

> The potential scope of cancer prevention is limited by the proportion of human cancers in which extrinsic factors are responsible. These factors include all environmental carcinogens, whether identified or not, as well as modifying factors that favor neoplasia of apparently intrinsic origin (e.g., hormonal imbalances, dietary deficiencies, and metabolic defects). The categories of cancer that are influenced by extrinsic factors including many tumors of the skin and mouth, the respiratory, gastro-intestinal, and urinary tracts, hormone-dependent organs (such as the breast, thyroid, and uterus), haematopoietic and lymphopoietic systems, all of which, collectively, account for more than three-quarters of human cancers. It would seem, therefore, that the majority of human cancer is potentially preventable.[13]

The misinterpretation occurred in the United States, where "extrinsic factors" was deleted and "environmental factors" was substituted. And if that wasn't slippage enough, "environmental factors" was translated once again, becoming "man-made chemicals." Even a cursory reading makes one realize that this interpretation was never WHO's intent, which was clear: extrinsic factors are synonymous with lifestyle, our behavior, or what we choose or don't choose to do. Because many people prefer blaming everyone but themselves, it is understandable that few complained about the transformation of the English language as it moved from Europe to the United States.

Nevertheless, for the first time, a value was enunciated: 75 percent of all cancers were attributed to extrinsic factors. That was the beginning. At a conference in Canada in 1969, John Higgenson, founding director of the International Agency for Research on Cancer, a WHO affiliate, stated that 60–90 percent of all cancers were environmentally induced. That remark was to haunt him and the world for decades. He had no inkling that his use of "the environment" would be so bent out of shape. The floodgates opened wide. Soaring cancer rates could hereafter be attributed to a polluted environment.

In 1979, Higgenson was interviewed by an editor of *Science* to further clarify his 60–90 percent attribution, and to deal with the seemingly intractable fact that so many Americans "believe that cancer-causing agents lurk in everything we eat, drink, and breathe." That such a perception is wrong is evident from Higginson's responses. He began by noting, "A lot of confusion has arisen in later days because most people have not gone back to the early literature, but have used the word *environment* purely to mean chemicals." Further along the interview he declared, "Environment thus became identified only with industrial chemicals." Then he said, "There's one other thing I should say that has led to the association of the term *environment* with chemical carcinogens. The ecological movement, I suspect, found the extreme view convenient because of the fear of cancer. If they could possibly make people believe that pollution was going to result in cancer, this would enable them to facilitate the cleanup of water, of the air, or whatever it was"—a remark not calculated to win friends or attract converts. "I think," he continued, "that many people had a gut feeling that pollution ought to cause cancer. They found it hard to accept that general air pollution, smoking factory chimneys, and the like are not the major causes of cancer."[14] For all the good it did, that interview might well have never occurred. Dynamic denial, on the one hand, and the power of the press to shape opinion prevailed, and this false thesis perseveres. The media and environmentalists are determined to hold their ill-gotten ground, no matter how wrong the association. But the facts will emerge!

In their now classic publication, "The Causes of Cancer: Quantitative Estimates of Avoidable Risks of Cancer in the U.S. Today"[15] ("Today" being 1981), R. Doll and R. Peto placed numbers and percentages on twelve categories of potential risk factors. Their list, shown in table 1.4, is worth contemplating.

For Doll and Peto, tobacco and diet were so intimately tied to cancer deaths that their estimates of their importance, their contribution to the disease, ranged from 55 to 100 percent. The uncertainty factor was apparent, but for them this dynamic duo were unmatched cancer risks. At the opposite end of the risk spectrum was pollution, to which they assigned a value of less than one. Recalling that these estimates were made at the beginning of the 1980s, it is reasonable to ask, Have they stood the test of time?

A research team of Harvard University's School of Public Health took up the challenge, and in 1996 produced its own estimates (table 1.5). This list has a familiar look.

Table 1.4. Proportions of Cancer Deaths Attributed to Different Risk Factors, 1981

	Percent of All Cancer Deaths	
	Best Estimate	*Range of Acceptable Estimate*
Tobacco	30	25–40
Alcohol	3	2–4
Diet	35	10–70
Food additives	<1	<0.5–2
Reproductive and sexual behaviors	7	1–13
Occupation	4	2–8
Pollution	2	<1–5
Medicines and medical products	1	0.5–3
Industrial products	>1	<1–2
Infections	10?	1–?

SOURCE: Doll and Peto 1981.

Table 1.5. Proportions of Cancer Deaths Attributed to Different Risk Factors, 1996

Cancer Risk Factor	*Percent Contribution*
Tobacco	30
Diet	30
Hardcore*	25
Alcohol	3
Microbial (viral, bacterial)	1–2
Pollution	1–2

SOURCE: Harvard School of Public Health.
*"Hardcore" are those cancers that would develop even in a world free of external influences simply because of the production of carcinogens within the body, and the occurrence of unrepaired genetic mistakes.

The Harvard list echoes that of Doll and Peto. Tobacco, diet, infectious agents, and sexual behavior are the primary culprits, while pollution, food additives, and ionizing radiation contribute little if anything to cancer risk or death. Both results state emphatically that any contribution by the ambient environment must be too small to be measured, and thus is of little or no consequence to our health. They show, too, that the public has overestimated the risk posed by low levels of radiation,[16] obviously encouraged by the constancy of the media and environmentalist mantra.

An objective observer could be forgiven her lack of comprehension, wondering out loud how it is possible that misunderstanding of "environment" and its risks has become so entrenched. But there's even more. Yet another Harvard group, this one from the Department of Medicine and the School of Public Health, has taken up the cudgel. The researchers introduced their recent study, "Environmental Risk Factors and Female Breast Cancer,"[17] with this caveat: "It is unfortunate," they write,

> that there is confusion as to what constitutes an 'environmental' exposure. Epidemiologists often label as 'environment' any risk factor that is not genetic, including diet, body size, exogenous estrogen use, reproductive factors, and medical treatment. Using this definition most breast cancer is thought to be due to 'environment,' as only a small proportion is due to inherited mutations in breast cancer susceptibility genes. The general public, however, often interprets this as evidence that much of breast cancer is due to 'environmental' pollution. In this review we restrict the definition of environmental exposures

to those which a person experiences passively, due to pollution or other characteristics of the outside world.

Their investigation concerned the possible risk of breast cancer from exposure to ambient environmental chlorinated hydrocarbons (pesticides), ionizing and electromagnetic radiation, and passive cigarette smoke. And their findings? "Based on current evidence, with the exception of ionizing radiation, no environment exposures can be confidently labeled as a cause of breast cancer." The echoes grow louder. But where are the media? Shouldn't women know this? Shouldn't everyone know this?

Most recently, an analysis of some 45,000 sets of twins from Sweden, Denmark, and Finland, led by members of the Department of Medical Epidemiology at the Karolinska Institute in Sweden, found that inherited genetic factors could account for only a fraction of major cancers, including breast cancers, and that environment was the insulting risk.[18] For them, however, environment was "shared" environment, the sum of the *common family experiences* and habits of the twins. They go on to inform us that "risk factors in the environment shared by a family could include human papillomavirus infection for cervical cancer, smoking (passive or active) for lung cancer, and diet and Helicabacter pylori (bacterial disease) infection for stomach cancer." Curiously enough, this is remarkably different from the environmental risks reported by *Newsweek* in its coverage of the Swedish report. For *Newsweek,* environment harkened back to the twentieth century's air pollution and chemical exposures. Among the quite dramatic photos accompanying the article were darkly polluting smokestacks and mounds of ground beef. These may be what *Newsweek* prefers to believe are causes of cancer, but it doesn't square with what the publication suggests.[19] Things can and do get twisted, unfortunately, for an already confused public. The idea of "environment" has had a long and misleading paternity. It's time to give it up.

The leading causes of death have been stable for at least twenty-five years: heart disease, cancer, and stroke have occupied the same top three positions, and suicide, homicide, cirrhosis, AIDS, and accidents switch a position or two every so often. Even Inspector Clouseau would look askance upon the ambient environment as the source of these conditions. The assault on the environment, which in fact was an assault upon us all, was entirely misplaced and unjustified. Neither evidence nor proof supported such a claim, while there was mounting and supportive evidence for the lifestyle and behavior paradigm. What will it take to convince and unshackle the American mind?

If better health for all were in fact the nation's goal, the first priority would be modification of our self-destructive behavior. The public, however, is not concerned with the self. Why? It has been led to believe that a soup of synthetic chemicals has been loosed upon them by an uncaring military-industrial complex and that this chemical fouling of the environment is responsible for what is perceived as our generally poor state of health. The environment, as commonly understood, does require vigilance, but for reasons other than human health. Consequently, we are flailing at windmills that pose minuscule risk and consume our energy, our time, and our taxes, whereas the major risks, the real killers, languish for lack of individual and institutional concern, support, and self-control. If we clasped the lifestyle model to our breasts, our country could follow a path to wholesale reductions in illness and death that no manner of medical intervention could ever hope to match. Are we ready for this message? Are we ready to strike out on the real road to personal well-being? It is time to deal with the facts.

There is yet another issue that should be of national concern: obesity. According to Peter G. Kopelman of St. Bartholomew's Hospital and the Royal London School of Medicine, "Obesity is now so common that it is beginning to replace undernutrition and infectious diseases as the most significant contributor to ill health." As Kopelman describes it, obesity is associated with diabetes mellitus, coronary heart disease, certain forms of cancer, and sleep-breathing disorders, and should no longer be regarded as a cosmetic problem affecting certain individuals; it should be seen as an epidemic that threatens global well-being.[20] This message also requires wider dissemination.

Life Expectancy

The National Center for Health Statistics has provided us with numbers that should elicit a smile and a measure of satisfaction. Before World War II, life expectancy stood at 62.9 years. At the inception of Social Security, most people were not expected to collect their checks. By 1990, however, 12.5 percent of the U.S. population was 65 or older, and by 2000, it was gaining on 13 percent. The biblical injunction of "three score and ten," seventy years, had already been attained and passed in 1969. By 1997, life expectancy had climbed to 76.5 years, which means that, on average, a person born in 1997 could be expected to live 76.5 years—that's a net gain of 13.6 years, or 18 percent, since 1940 (table 1.6). And since 1900,

Table 1.6. Life Expectancy, All Races, Both Sexes, United States, 1950–1997

Year	Life Expectancy
1950	68.2
1979	73.9 (8.3 years gained, an increase of 12.2%)
1990	75.4
1997	76.5

NOTE: The years 1940 to 1997 had an increase of 18%, a gain of 13.6 years.

when life expectancy stood at 47, the gain has been a tremendous gift of three additional decades! The gains are not universal or consistent because gender and race, not environment, make a substantial difference, as table 1.7 makes evident. Still, an unprecedented increase in life expectancy has occurred among all segments of the population. Furthermore, the U.S. Census Bureau recently estimated that the number of persons aged 85 and older—currently about 3.1 million—will grow to 19 million by 2080. Not only are the so-called elderly who are entering retirement healthier than past generations, but the absolute number has increased. Between 1990 and 1998, the over-65 age group increased 9.2 percent, from 31 million to 34 million. But the most telling statistic may be that the proportion of elderly reporting no disabilities rose from 76.3 percent to 78.5 percent in the same period. That more than three-fourths of older Americans are disability free must not go unremarked.

Infant Mortality Rates

And what about the youngest among us? Infant mortality rates (IMRs) have been no less remarkable in their downward trend. In 1900, for every

Table 1.7. Life Expectancy by Gender, United States, 1997

White women	79.9 years
Nonwhite women	74.3 years
White men	74.7 years
Nonwhite men	67.2 years

1,000 live births, approximately 100 babies died before their first birthday. By 1950 only 28 would do so, and by 1997, just 7.2. Astounding is not an excessive description of this singular public health achievement. When the subject of infant mortality is broached, Sweden is generally trotted out front and center as the "class act" of infant survival. True, 7.2 is not as low as Sweden's 4.0, but it may be all the more remarkable given the size and polyglot nature of the U.S. population. It is not appropriate to compare Sweden, which has a shade more than 8 million people—only half that of New York State—and an almost totally homogeneous white, Lutheran population living in three major population centers, with the United States. Note that in 1997, the last complete year for which statistics are available, the numbers fairly leap off the page: the United States' 7.7 IMR broke down as follows: white females, 5.4; white males, 6.7; black fe-males, 10.7; black males, 12.8. These numbers represent a uniquely American tragedy. No other developed country has this painful dichotomy, which so patently distorts the overall IMR. Reducing this disparity should be a high priority for the Bush administration and anyone else concerned about improving the health of the nation. Nevertheless, our attainment of a single-digit IMR, which is continuing to decline, is cause for acclamation. Simply put, the difference between the world's acknowledged best (i.e., lowest) IMR and that of the United States is less than three deaths per thousand live births per year. That is a prodigious statistic given the nature of our population and the complex causes of infant mortality. That the

Table 1.8. Infant Mortality Rates per 1,000 Live Births, United States, 1997

All races, both sexes	7.2
Female (all races)	6.5
Male (all races)	8.0
White, both sexes	6.0
Female	5.4
Male	6.7
Black, both sexes	11.8
Female	10.7
Male	12.8

numbers continue to fall is seen in the provisional IMRs for both 1998 and 1999, which indicate a rate of 6.9 per 1,000 live births. Furthermore, there is a wide variation across the country, a north and south dichotomy, aggravated by minority and economic conditions as shown in tables 1.8 and 1.9.

That the District of Columbia, so close to the halls of political power, has the nation's highest IMR, as well as one of the highest in the Western

Table 1.9. U.S. States with Lowest and Highest Infant Mortality Rates per 1,000 Live Births, 1997

States with the lowest rates	Rate
New Hampshire	4.3
Maine	5.1
Massachusetts	5.2
Washington	5.6
Utah	5.8
Wyoming	5.8
Oregon	5.8
Arizona	5.8
Minnesota	5.9
California	5.9
States with the highest rates	
Georgia	8.6
Arkansas	8.7
Alabama	9.5
Louisiana	9.5
North Carolina	9.2
West Virginia	9.6
South Carolina	9.9
Mississippi	10.6
Puerto Rico	11.3
District of Columbia	13.2

world, is at once startling and depressing. Income levels below the poverty line ($12,000 per year), along with exceedingly high teenage pregnancy rates accompanied by late or nonexistent prenatal care, difficult and premature labor, and resulting low-weight infants are good and sufficient reasons for the higher U.S. rate. Furthermore, the steep decline from 29.2 to 7.2 over the past four decades should also suggest that "the environment" is not the ticking bomb the spinners have led us to believe it is. It is noteworthy and well documented that since the 1970s, sexual activity has increased markedly among adolescents while unwanted pregnancies and HIV infections increased as well. But sales of contraceptive devices, especially condoms, have lagged far behind. Neither those who practice safe sex nor those favoring the reduction of teenage pregnancy appear to have a large constituency.

Nevertheless, with life expectancy rising to unprecedented levels, and with infant mortality rates falling to their lowest levels, along with decreasing heart disease and dropping cancer rates, is it reasonable to believe that our environment—the ambient environment—is toxic to children and other growing things? The media have been making much of very little, and not enough of the public's general good health. Why have they not gone public with what must be one of the most successful accomplishments of our time—accomplishments that mitigate the notion of an environment inimical to the health of the people? Most people not only do not know this, but worse, they believe otherwise, which in my view is a national scandal.

James Madison informed us that "knowledge will forever govern ignorance: a people who mean to be their own Governors must arm themselves with the power which knowledge gives." But how are they to get it? Remembering this idea as we move on may serve us well.

CHAPTER 2

Our Microbial World

Whoever wishes to investigate medicine properly, should proceed thus: in the first place to consider the seasons of the year, and what effect each of them produces (for they are not at all a like, but differ much themselves in regard to their changes). Then the winds, the hot and the cold, especially such as are common to all countries, and then such as are peculiar to each locality. We must also consider the qualities of the waters, for as they differ from one another in taste and weight, so also do they differ much in their qualities. In the same manner, when one comes into a city to which he is a stranger, he ought to consider its situation, how it lies as to the winds and the rising of the sun; for its influence is not the same whether it lies to the north or the south, to the rising or to the setting sun. These things one ought to consider most attentively, and concerning the waters which the inhabitants use, whether they be marshy and soft, or hard, and running from elevated and rocky situations, and then if saltish and unfit for cooking; and the ground, whether it be naked and deficient in water, or wooded and well-watered, and whether it lies in a hollow, confined situation, or is elevated and cold; and the mode in which the inhabitants live, and what are their pursuits, whether they are fond of drinking and eating to excess, and given to indolence, or are fond of exercise and labor, and not given to excess in eating and drinking.

From these things he must proceed to investigate everything else. For if one knows all these things well, or at least the greater part of them, he cannot miss knowing, when he comes into a strange city, either the diseases peculiar to the place, or the particular nature of common diseases, so that he will not be in doubt as to the treatment of the diseases, or commit mistakes, as is likely to be the case provided one had not previously considered these matters.[1]

The above may sound like nineteenth-century prose and belief. It isn't. These are the thoughts and beliefs of an ancient physician. The place, the island of Cos in Greece. The time, 2,500 years ago. The oldest-known account of the effects of environment on health belongs to Hippocrates, the Father of Medicine (460–377 B.C.), who believed that disease arose from natural causes. Illness was a consequence of environmental risk factors. How and where people lived could determine their state of health. This idea sat well with physicians for some two thousand years. Until the 1870s, no physician worth his frock coat and gold-headed cane practiced any other form of medicine, but there were stirrings. With the availability of high-power microscopes in the mid-nineteenth century, the unseen world became visible, and the connection was made between microbes and disease. It was revolutionary. In the history of medicine, nothing has been so spectacularly and rapidly accepted as the germ theory of disease, which holds that for every disease there is a specific microbe. The proof of this theory became the single most powerful force in the development of medicine during the nineteenth and early twentieth centuries. And with it, environment as a cause of disease came to a crashing halt. The devotion to and general cleansing of the environment was all but abandoned with the ascension of germs, disinfection, and vaccination. So powerful and so certain was the germ theory that Charles V. Chapin, health commissioner of Rhode Island, declared that "it mattered little hygienically whether the city's streets were cleaned or not, provided microbes were kept under control and people were protected against infection by the proper vaccines."[2] However, and nevertheless, by the mid-twentieth century, it was evident that the golden age of microbiology and its driving theory could neither explain nor deal with the leading causes of illness and death afflicting our communities today.

Today's leading causes of illness and death have been shown to be heart disease, cancer, stroke, accidents, suicide, homicide, AIDS, and cirrhosis. It appears equally evident that these are manifestations of how we live, what we do, and where we live and work. Hippocrates understood people and their motivations. At some point, individuals and society must realize that the threats and risks to our health are primarily of their own creation.

The treacherous effects of our personal environment, our behavior with respect to the prevalence and severity of degenerative and chronic disease, are perhaps nowhere better exemplified than among the Mebane, a primitive and isolated Sudanese tribe. Its several thousand tribe members live in and around the dismal swamps of the White Nile. Tests performed by Western physicians found them virtually free of obesity, coronary heart disease, duodenal ulcer, ulcerative colitis, allergies, bronchial asthma, and dental caries. They also enjoy low blood pressure from childhood to old age. By comparison, all these afflictions are common among members of the tribe who have left the swampy lands for Khartoum and other large African cities.³ Thus far they have not achieved our levels of harm, but as they learn more about the world beyond and gain access to guns, drugs, alcohol, fatty diets, tobacco, motor vehicles, and TV, they will more than likely follow.

While we have been seeking solutions for the noninfectious complications of our complex society, which have been referred to as the pathology of inactivity and the occupational hazards of a sedentary life, there has been a slow, but steady emergence or reemergence of infectious disease—more than likely brought about by the way we are rearranging our environment.

New Avenues of Transmission

Nowadays we have opened avenues of contact with organisms that are new even to our textbooks. As we consider examples of these, bear in mind that most microbes are not pathogens, nor are most arthropods (e.g., insects, ticks, fleas, crustaceans, and centipedes) vectors of disease. Nor are most mammals a source of human illness. Thus, a reasonable person could conclude that our environment is, for the most part, benign. With each example that follows, ask yourself: Why now? Why not in the nineteenth century? What has changed?

Let us consider an example of how technology brings us together with a microbe we would not normally encounter.

Legionnaires' Disease

Legionellosis is a respiratory infection caused by the bacterium *Legionella pneumophila*. It acquired its name and notoriety in 1976, when it caused an outbreak of atypical pneumonia among war veterans attending an American Legion convention in Philadelphia. *Legionella pneumophila* is unique among bacteria in that it is a ubiquitous aquatic organism, found in low numbers, but thriving in warm-water environments of 32°–45° C. Microbiologists refer to these bacteria as thermophiles. With the right amount of heat, they multiply profusely, but other than in hot springs, water at this temperature is unusual. Cooling towers and evaporative condensers are used to provide air conditioning for large buildings and to cool water for a range of industrial processes without the use of chemical refrigerants. Cooling towers have large reservoirs within which water temperature is maintained at between 25° and 35° C. Whirlpool spas also maintain water temperatures within *Legionella*'s preferred range.⁴ Is it any wonder, then, that a fair proportion of the 15,000 annual cases of *Legionella* pneumonia come from whirlpool baths? Cooling towers are open to the air and to the environment, and therefore contain sufficient organic matter for microbial nutrition and multiplication. Plumbing systems in homes, office buildings, and hotels also provide the warm to hot water for thermophilic growth. Cooling towers, evaporative condensers, whirlpools, spas, and showers produce mists of tiny water droplets containing *Legionella* that are certain to be dispersed within the droplets. The cooling tower at the Bellevue-Stratford Hotel contained large numbers of *Legionella*, which were dispersed throughout the hotel via its air-conditioning system. When inhaled, pneumonia resulted in veterans who were susceptible to it. Similar contamination and inhalation of aerosolized mists occur in home showers and whirlpool baths, which accounts for the continuing cases. Elderly people, cigarette smokers, persons with chronic lung disease, and those receiving immunosuppressive medication are at increased risk. Prevention is straightforward: improved design and maintenance of cooling towers and plumbing systems to limit the entrance of organic matter and the growth of microorganisms.

Did the *Legionella* microbe cause the pneumonia, or was it the cooling tower, or the source of water for the towers, or the susceptible individuals? Would the bacteria have gotten to the veterans, or to people in showers or whirlpools, without the towers, showers, or whirlpools? Would there have been pneumonias without susceptible people? Surely there is a complex series of events at work here. Epidemiologists would call this a multifunctional cause, a confluence of events and circumstances resulting in an illness. Think of this as a chain of events. That kind of thinking offers points of interdiction, or the means of breaking the chain and of controlling or completely preventing the problem. This kind of epidemiological thinking no longer has the microbe in the catbird seat.

Lyme Disease

Acorns. Lots of acorns. That's the key to Lyme disease. It's the number of acorns that are responsible for setting a train of events in motion that eventually led to Lyme disease, currently the most common arthropod-borne illness in the United States. Since 1982, when first reported, there have been 128,000 documented cases.

During the eighteenth and nineteenth centuries, forests were destroyed in New England to make way for farms, and deer were hunted almost to extinction. The emergence of Lyme disease is believed to have occurred as a consequence of conditions favorable to deer. As farmland reverted to woodland and with few predators at their heels, deer thrived. And with the new ease of travel, rural areas became populated with city folk susceptible to microbial attack, and with it, the beginnings of a conflict between humans and nature.

In 1977, Old Lyme, Connecticut, became nationally known for an outbreak of arthritis that was subsequently found to be due to a previously unrecognized corkscrew-shaped bacterium of the genus *Borellia*. The bacterium was named *burgdorferi* after its discoverer, William Burgdorfer.

For Lyme disease to exist in an area, a series of closely related elements must be present simultaneously: bacteria, ticks, mice, deer, and people. An abundance of acorns every three to four years accounts for the fluctuation of new cases, when the white-tailed deer, the white-footed mice, and the ticks thrive.

Adult ticks piggybacking on deer drop off to the forest floor, where female ticks deposit their eggs, which hatch the following spring and summer, just in time for the larval ticks to partake of a blood meal from a nearby mouse. It is during this meal that they may imbibe the spirochete. These larvae grow into a larger nymph, which over-winters on the forest floor. In spring, a mature tick readily finds a deer on which to hop. People entering the forest or woodland at the height of tick-deer activity are also entering a stable relationship that has been cycling for millennia, but had been restricted to wildlife.[5] Now, hikers and hunters are fair game for the black-legged tick, which can take a blood meal from either deer or human, but when the tick is given a preference, it's the human who becomes the depository of *Borrelia*. If susceptible, the victim may show the telltale bull's-eye rash, known as *erythema migrams*, along with one or more flulike symptoms, such as fever, chills, muscle aches, or lethargy. If Lyme disease remains untreated, *B. burgdorferi* can persist in human tissue and migrate to the brain, spinal cord, or joints and induce more severe symptoms, such as arthritis, memory loss, and disorientation.

With thousands of cases occurring annually, primarily localized in the East and Southeast, it is reasonable to wonder why our Western cousins escape this illness when venturing into the woods. The answer may be a lizard—the western fence lizard, *Sceloporous occidentalis*. Rather than feeding on white-footed mice, the black-legged ticks of the Western states feed on the fence lizard, which appears to have a borreliacidal protein in its blood that is death to *Borrelia*.[6] In addition, entomologists have found that only about 5 percent of Western ticks harbor *Borrelia*, while upwards of 50 percent do so in New England and in the East generally. These numbers speak volumes for the risk of disease in each area of the country.

Unfortunately, the tick's bite is painless, so that most people do not know they've been bitten. It is when feeding on exposed skin that the tick salivates profusely and passes the spirochete. Until a preventive vaccine becomes available, the only reasonable preventive measures are not to keep one's skin exposed and/or to avoid deer-tick habitats. Dare I ask what is the cause of Lyme disease?

Hanta Virus

Rain. Lots of rain. Piñon nuts. Lots of piñon nuts. Mice. Lots of mice. Sudden respiratory failure and death: also the fatal complex of HPS—Hantavirus pulmonary syndrome.

Americans thought they had seen the last of Hanta virus at the Hantaan River during the Korean War, where three thousand immunologically unprepared GIs contracted Hantavirus and three hundred of them died. Hanta virus disease begins with fever, muscle and abdominal pain, diarrhea, cough, and later difficulty in breathing, which becomes severe within hours. At the Hantaan River, the virus took a different tack, playing hob with kidneys. A drastic, life-threatening drop in blood pressure (shock) can occur from loss of fluid into the lungs. Death almost invariably follows shock.

In the Four Corners area of the United States, shared by Arizona, Colorado, New Mexico, and Utah, an outbreak in 1993 among otherwise healthy young Navajo men and women was rapid and fatal.

After six years of persistent drought, heavy rains—the consequence of an El Niño event—deluged the area, causing an abrupt change in the region's ecological balance. Piñon nuts grew everywhere, providing abundant food for the virus-carrying deer mice, whose number skyrocketed because its predators had fallen victim to the drought. Then, summer and fall's complex of environmental events accounted for forty-two cases and twenty-six HPS deaths. From 1993 to July 2000, 260 cases with one hundred deaths have been reported from thirty-one states. Viral transmission begins with dried mouse urine and excreta, which become aerosolized and can be inhaled. A rodent bite can also transmit the virus through a break in the skin.

The complex chain of events that culminates in HPS was solved in record time—in a matter of months—thanks to scientists who for years had tracked and learned the ways of mice, and to virologists who quickly found the link between the Hantaan River and the Four Corners viruses.[7]

Ebola Fever

Ebola hemorrhagic fever, named for a river in the Democratic Republic of the Congo, formerly Zaire, is another member of the notorious clique of hemorrhagic fevers.

Given its array of devastating and gruesome symptoms, Ebola can be frightening. Within days of becoming infected, victims respond with massive bleeding from nose, ears, mouth and bloody diarrhea, in addition to high fever and chest, head, and muscle pain. Death follows in some 50 percent of cases.

Ebola first gained international prominence in 1976 as it infected some thousand people, with five hundred deaths. Many of them were nurses and physicians treating the patients in hospitals. At the time, it was not known that contact with blood was a means of viral transmission. When Ebola occurred again in 1995, the outbreak was quickly contained. Although both outbreaks stemmed from hospitalized patients, Ebola defies all efforts to unravel its origin, locations, and natural habitat. In September 2000, Ebola struck again, this time in Uganda. The outbreak occurred in the Gulu region, some 200 miles north of Kampala, the capital, and the first person to succumb was a thirty-six-year-old woman. But given Ebola's means of transmission, new cases and new death tolls rose quickly. Family members caring for the body before burial were the next to succumb, after they follow the ritual of washing their hands in a common basin, thereby spreading the virus. Within days of the first victim's funeral, her mother, three sisters, and nine-month-old son were also dead, and the virus had spread beyond her village. By mid-November, the toll of dead had reached seventy-eight, but this time seventy-five had recovered. Health officials had no qualms that containment of the infection, the virus, would pose no problem: it was clear that person-to-person contact was the essential and sole means of spreading and that simple measures would be effective. In fact, transmission can be stopped in its tracks by the simple expedient of hand-washing with soap or rinsing in a chlorine solution. But in Uganda's small villages, neither soap nor bleach solutions are available. The way to stop this horrific virus would take only a small amount of money to buy these products.[8] Although outbreaks of Ebola have occurred half a dozen times in West Africa, it has and continues to elude all attempts to track its primary host and habitat. It is interesting that this last outbreak produced no shrieking headlines about a bloody killer on the loose. This time around, Ebola had lost its mediagenicity. Nevertheless, what is known and certain is that no case has ever been reported in the United States. A close relative, however, Korean hemorrhagic fever, KHF, was discovered in Baltimore, Maryland, in 1989. Rats carrying the KHF virus were found in slum areas and were believed to be responsible for deaths among the urban poor.

Marburg Fever

Marburg hemorrhagic fever was first recognized in 1967, when thirty-seven scientists in virology laboratories in Marburg, Germany, and Belgrade, Yugoslavia (Serbia), became ill and six died. The World Health Organization traced the sudden outbreak to a batch of fresh monkey cells the scientists used to grow the polio virus. The cells from the imported Ugandan monkeys had been infected with the virus, which later became known as Marburg viral HF. Here, too, the virus wreaked havoc with the human body: liver dysfunction, bleeding, and blood clots. Nevertheless, most victims recovered. Marburg HF has not been seen anywhere since 1970.

Lassa Fever

Lassa hemorrhagic fever was first reported internationally when two missionary nurses died in Lassa, Nigeria. Lassa HF is endemic to Nigeria, Guinea, Liberia, and Sierra Leone. In these countries, the combined annual number of cases is estimated at 100–300 thousand, with some 5,000 deaths. This, too, is another disease transmissible by rats to humans. The virus is shed in urine and excreta, which often contaminate food and individuals directly, via dried aerosolized particles. The close living conditions between the human population and the rats readily accounts for the high number of cases. In this instance, however, the rats were normally forest dwelling but came into the huts when the larger, more vicious rats left.

All of these HFs are zoonotic infections and are transferable from feral animals, usually rodents, to humans under appropriate conditions. All are prevalent in areas where the disease is a constant presence, with their home base in Africa. Furthermore, because they kill so swiftly and transmission is via direct contact, the illness runs a short course. Yet all can be highly frightening, especially because the media dramatize the symptoms and high fatality rates but conveniently fail to mention the usually small numbers, confined to local outbreaks, and of brief duration. It is noteworthy that none have leaped out of their endemic areas.

Tuberculosis

Tuberculosis (TB) offers a cautionary tale because the disease agent is in constant circulation to the United States.

TB is a contagious, potentially fatal infection "caused" by the bacterium *Mycobacterium tuberculosis*. In 1882, Robert Koch proved that the bacterium and the disease were inseparable. Although people have been contracting tuberculosis since ancient times, it became epidemic during the industrial revolution in the nineteenth century, in both Europe and the United States, when overcrowding in cities gave the bacterium ready access to large, susceptible, and often malnourished populations living in close proximity. Sneezing, coughing, even talking spreads the microbe in air via infected droplet nuclei. With the availability of a formidable collection of chemotherapeutic agents, from the 1950s through the 1970s, TB declined precipitously. Public health officials were then of the opinion that TB could be vanquished forever, but the mid-1980s were to prove them wrong. TB began to rise in parallel with AIDS, especially in such closed communities as prisons and homeless shelters, and the ease of long-distance air travel provided a new avenue for spreading TB from endemic areas to crowded, susceptible communities.

TB is one of the world's most serious infectious diseases, killing well over a million people annually. Eight million are known to be infected worldwide, particularly in Africa. More than half of the countries in Africa have the world's highest infection rate, with over 250 new cases per 100,000 people per year, compared to the United States, Canada, Australia, Sweden, and Finland, with fewer than 10 per year.

The organism, readily spread in air via droplets, can be inhaled into the lungs and establish a primary tubercle in a susceptible individual. Most people who contract a primary infection show no immediate symptoms. Pulmonary TB becomes apparent over weeks or months, which is part of the problem, as asymptomatic carriers can continue to spread the infection.

Recent immigrants have arrived from home countries, where TB is endemic, to their newly adopted country and city, where it is not and helped spread the disease. Transmission of the bacterium can also occur aboard crowded airplanes using recirculated air, which provides an excellent opportunity to pass and spread infectious organisms. To dilute and flush out airborne microbes, minimum ventilation standards have yet to be developed. Given the increase in movement between countries and the passenger density per plane, standards are long overdue.

West Nile Fever

Illegals crossing our long border with Mexico, and illegals coming in at any number of entry points form China, Pakistan, India, the Middle East, and Africa, have become another vehicle of disease transmission. West Nile encephalitis, or fever, a mosquito-borne viral disease, is an ideal example of this route of transmission. The West Nile virus was first isolated in 1937 from a woman in the West Nile region of Uganda. It took sixty years for the virus to reach and produce illness in New York City and environs. Before the ready availability of rapid international airline flights, this virus, and its winged messenger, remained in their natural habitats.[9] Not only do mosquitoes move freely in and out of airplanes, they also hitch rides in baggage and on clothing. Passengers harboring the virus may not manifest the illness, but they can be carriers from whom indigenous mosquitoes can pick up the virus when biting, and pass it along the line of transmission. Recently, a new theory has suggested that the West Nile virus, a natural resident of birds, arrived in the United States on birds migrating from the Middle East, where West Nile virus is endemic. Although it will be impossible to prevent birds from landing here, cases can be kept to a minimum by judicious attention to the reduction of the mosquito populations.[10]

Leishmaniasis

There is yet another illuminating example of how our defenses are penetrated.

Leishmaniasis, also known as *kala azar* (black fever) *espundia*, Dumdum fever, Aleppo boil, *uto*, and Chiclero ulcer, is a group of illnesses caused by the protozoan parasite *Leishmania*. A nasty biting sand fly (*Phlebotemus*) serves as the winged hypodermic to get around and into people, producing disfiguring scars and other unsightly cutaneous lesions. Fortunately, it is rare in the United States, since few, if any, physicians, including dermatologists, would recognize the symptoms.

But in fact, a new canine leishmania epidemic is in full flower among foxhounds in the United States and Canada. During the winter of 1999–2000, foxhounds began to die. These elegant beasts became haggard and lethargic, losing weight and hair, "developing enlarged joints, crusty skin lesions, and ropelike knots under their skin."[11] Thanks to veterinarians at North Carolina State University, the parasite was rapidly identified, but not before it had been reported in kennels in twenty states and Canada. Thus far, neither the protozoan nor the illness has been found in other dogs, other mammals, or in people. As sand flies are indigenous to the southern states, the yet unanswered question is, Where did they pick up their hitchhiking protozoans? And of the four types of leishmaniasis, why *donovani*, the one which produces visceral leishmaniasis, the enlargement of the liver and spleen in humans? Earlier, I noted that the best defenses can be penetrated if people are determined. For example, someone can carry contraband from an endemic area to areas free of the condition. Persian Gulf War soldiers were diagnosed with visceral leishmaniasis, a condition endemic in the Sudan, parts of China and India, and in Mediterranean countries. It is entirely possible that a returning G.I. carried an infected dog stashed in a duffel, undetected. At this time, evidence does not suggest that canine leishmaniasis can be passed to humans. Again, we have to wait and see.

What Now?

Industrialization, urbanization, technological advances, migrations—legal and illegal—and ease of travel have created a worldwide market for disease.

What conclusions can we draw from these "new" diseases? Clearly, the twentieth century has witnessed remarkable changes in our way of life. The speed and ease of travel has been one of the most prodigious changes. Remarkable changes have also occurred in food preparation, agriculture, animal husbandry, and technology. Population gains and shifts have required the opening of land previously left to wilderness and its diversity of animal, insect, and microbial species that have inhabited them for millennia. With this opening, we have insinuated ourselves into settings that afford these varied species new pastures. At some point, we must come to the realization that the "new" threats to our health are primarily of our own devising. Since we cannot slow the pace of change, and prefer not to, we will endure whatever risks come our way, and our health will continue to be at risk.

René Dubos reminded us that "progress" always implies the risk of encountering new dangers, and disease ensues whenever man fails, as he usually does, in making rapidly enough a perfect adaptive response to the new environments in which he elects to live and function.[12] We should not be surprised when bold headlines inform us of a "new" microbe in our midst. Pogo had it right: "We have met the enemy and they is us." Indeed, if the airlines and the feds were serious about preventing the virus of foot and mouth disease from entering the United States in 2000–2001, they would not have asked deplaning passengers if they had visited farms, and if they had, to have their shoes disinfected—assuming, of course, that the shoes being worn were the same as those worn while visiting a farm. No, a more serious approach would have offered no options, no exemptions. It would have been more effective for the Immigration Service to have placed disinfectant-containing mats throughout the passageway, from planes to immigration booths. That way, everyone, pilots and crew included, would have been disinfected. Without this all-inclusive procedure, quarantine will continue to be interdicted. Prevention of microbial spread cannot brook exceptions.

Chronic Conditions Revisited

Emergence comes in yet another guise. Diseases previously unsuspected of any microbial involvement are currently suspect and are being reconsidered as infectious agents.

Ulcers

For generations, gastroenterologists had lectured medical students that stress causes the stomach to produce excess acid and that the corrosive acid produces duodenal and gastric ulcers. Everyone knew it. As far back as 400 B.C., Hippocrates wrote that "a spare diet and water agree with ulcers, and with the more recent rather than the older." In 1596, Edward Spenser in *Faerie Queen* wrote "that my entrails flow with poisonous gore, and the ulcer groweth deadly more and more."[13] In 1920, Karl Schwarz, at the Merciful Brothers Hospital in Agram, Germany, wrote, his mantra: "Keine Saur, Keine Geschwur" (No acid, no ulcer). The words stuck and became medical lore for the next eighty years, until two Australian pathologists in Perth found in 2000 that it was a bacterium, *Helicobacter pylori* (*H. pylori*), that produces the characteristic inflammation, acidity, and chronic superficial gastritis.[14] Although it has low mortality, ulcer disease is high on the list of human suffering. For the 10–20 million adults who have this ailment, a microbial etiology must come as welcome news, as it appears that the great majority of cases can be alleviated by appropriate antibiotic treatment.

Most recently, a team from the Departments of Gastroenterology and Clinical Pathology at Kure Kyosai Hospital (Kure City, Japan) and the Department of Internal Medicine at the Fukuoka University School of Medicine found that "gastric cancer develops in persons infected with *H. pylori* but not in uninfected persons."[15] Although earlier studies had documented an association between the bacterium and the development of gastric cancer (in 1994, the International Agency for Research on Cancer, a WHO affiliate, declared *H. pylori* a class I carcinogen), the Japanese team prospectively studied (cf. chapter 7) 1,526 patients for an average of eight years and found a strong positive association for the presence of the organism and gastric cancer. *H. pylori* infection appears to trigger the neoplastic transformation.

Because of the ease of detecting the microbe, it should now be possible to reduce, perhaps even eradicate, stomach cancer with appropriate antibiotics. Japan will doubtless be the prime target of eradication attempts, as stomach cancer is the leading cause of cancer deaths in Japan. Given its apparent clustering in families, and among institutionalized individuals, person-to-person spread appears a likely means of transmission.

How do we know an illness, a condition, is infectious and microbially related? The first direct demonstration of the role of microbes, germs, and bacteria as agents of disease came from the study of anthrax, an infectious disease of sheep and cattle that is transmissible to people.

Robert Koch, a young German physician practicing medicine in Wollstein, a small country town in northern Germany, using criteria suggested by Jacob Henle, a former professor and friend, sought to establish a causal relationship between *Bacillus anthracis* and anthrax. He injected healthy mice with the blood of diseased sheep. The mice sickened. Placing bits of spleen from ill mice into sterile beef serum, he was able to obtain luxuriant growth of the bacillus. Koch then inoculated the new growth of organisms into a number of healthy mice, which also became ill. From these he was able to retrieve the bacillus. This series of experiments produced the Koch-Henle postulates that have become the gold standard for determining causality of microbially related conditions. Formally stated they require the following:

a. The organism must be found in all cases of the disease, but absent in healthy individuals.
b. The organism must be isolated from animals or humans with the same disease and be grown in pure culture.
c. When the pure culture is inoculated into healthy animals, it must produce the same disease.
d. The same organism must be recovered from diseased individuals and grown out in pure culture.

These criteria serve only for infectious diseases, and only those for which there are appropriate animal models. Helicobacter and gastric ulcer have satisfied the Koch-Henle postulates as far as possible in human volunteers. Fed to healthy young men, *H. pylori* was recovered from their inflamed stomachs, then grown in pure culture and recovered. Successful antibiotic therapy further demonstrated the accuracy of the proposed cause-effect relationship.[16]

Mad Cow Disease

During 1996, a fatal degenerative brain disorder was diagnosed among younger men and women in Great Britain. It has been suggested that these people had eaten or handled contaminated beef, and that the beef was the cause of their illness. Creutzfeld-Jakob disease (CJD) belongs to a family of human and animal diseases known as the transmissible spongiform encephalopathies, or TSEs. Spongiform refers to the characteristic appearance of infected brains, which become filled with holes, so that under a microscope the tissue resembles a typical household sponge. There is growing evidence that Bovine spongiform encephalitis (BSE), or Mad Cow disease, may have passed from cattle to humans. Just what type of organism induces the brain's spongelike appearance?

Since 1985, an epidemic of BSE has raged in the United Kingdom. Cases have also occurred sporadically in France, Germany, and Switzerland. Over 180,000 cows have been slaughtered to prevent its spread. The first suspicion of a possible risk for people suggested Creutzfeld-Jakob disease, a fatal disease (one in a million cases worldwide) producing muscle spasms and progressive loss of mental function, which has common characteristics with BSE.

All spongiform encephalopathies are slowly developing infectious diseases with strikingly similar lesions but with no other organ involvement. What type of organism can do this, and why did this illness not appear until the 1980s?

Intensive shoe-leather detective work disclosed a change in the rendering process used to produce nutritional meat and bone meal for livestock. This change involved discontinuation of a hydrocarbon solvent/steam treatment step to extract fat used for meat and bone meal. Solvents and steam reduce the infectivity of agents causing TSEs.[17] Although the British government banned the new process in 1988, it may be a case of locking the barn a bit late. We are staring directly at a striking and unfortunate example of the law of unintended consequences.

Whereas infectious agents—microbes—run the gamut from bacteria, fungi, Rickettsia, protozoa, yeast, and viruses, the TSEs do not harbor any

of these. If not these, what then? Something entirely new and unimaginable. The cause appears to be infectious proteinaceous particles, which have been dubbed protease-resistant proteins (PrPs), or prions—pronounced preeon—that possess the ability to convert normal brain protein into dangerous proteins simply by forcing normal proteins to change shape. How this modified or altered shape induces changes in the brain is unclear. Currently, the challenge is to find ways to affect the proteins' dangerous shape. Nevertheless, thus far, experimental studies have shown that BSE (the cow disease) and CJD (the human disease) can both be transmitted by injecting extracts of diseased brain into healthy animals. The clue came from *kuru,* the "laughing death disease" of the Foré tribe of .
Papua, New Guinea. Carlton Gajusek of the National Institutes of Health first described this illness in 1957. Only the men of the tribe were involved: they developed ataxia, or dementia, and died with a kind of grimacing smile as a consequence of ritual cannibalism—honoring their dead (men) by eating their brains. With the renunciation of cannibalism, *kuru* has disappeared, providing formidable evidence for the presence of an infectious agent. At this time, all evidence points to PrP as both necessary and sufficient to be considered the infectious agent of BSE and CJD. "By all available criteria, NvCJD and BSE are the same when passed in Tg (BoPrP) mice."[18] Dr. Koch would be pleased.

Prions are a protein-folding disorder, a thoroughly unique vehicle and concept for infection and transmission. They normally exist as protease-sensitive, metabolizable cell surface proteins. Illness occurs when an abnormal, protease-resistant form accumulates in the brain. The prion's ability to survive ultraviolet irradiation and other physico-chemical procedures designed to destroy nucleic acid support the theory. Each of us has a gene that codes for the prion protein. The mechanism that switches on the abnormal PrP remains to be elucidated. Given the quickening pace of genetic research, and the number of research teams investigating the BSE/CJD disease, expect the switch to be identified by 2004, if not sooner.

What is BSE's future in the United States, and why has it not yet visited among us? If the recent report of the Council on Scientific Affairs of the American Medical Association has it right, risk of transmission of BSE is minimal (no scientist can ever say absolute or never) for the following reasons:

1. BSE has not been shown to exist in this country.
2. Regulations are in place to prevent entry of foreign sources of BSE.

3. Regulations exist to prevent undetected cases from uncontrolled increases.
4. Appropriate guidelines exist to prevent high-risk bovine materials from contaminating products intended for human consumption.[19]

From the current evidence an objective observer could conclude that in the United States the public is protected. Not a hint of BSE has appeared over the past seventeen years, since it was first discovered in cattle in the U.K. in 1984. Furthermore, the National Prion Disease Pathology Surveillance Center was established in 1997 at the Division of Neuropathology at Case Western Reserve University in Ohio, with the support of the Centers for Disease Control (CDC) and National Institutes of Health (NIH), to monitor brain tissue and spinal fluid of individuals dying of encephalopathy for evidence of new variant Creutzfeld-Jakob disease, and to investigate possible cases of human-to-human as well as animal-to-human transmission. Not a case has thus far occurred in the United States.

Nevertheless, in one stroke, *Newsweek* brought BSE across the ocean and into our markets and homes. Mad Cow was here. That was their horrific message. *Newsweek*'s March 12, 2001, cover was explicit: "The Slow Deadly Spread of Mad Cow Disease" across the top; and below: "How It Could Become an Epidemic." And what more egregious way to dramatize the story than with a full page of a slab of beef wrapped in yellow tape declaiming: "Caution, Do Not Eat!" Chicken Little and *Newsweek* had become one. A national publication was spreading panic, generating wholesale fright that our meat was unfit to eat.

Everything about the article, especially the photos, was meant to impress readers that Mad Cow was here among us. To what purpose? Panic for panic's sake? To sell magazines? Here was an opportunity to educate readers, to show why the United States is free of BSE, and that our food supply is safe. But *Newsweek* instead became the Piper, leading the people over the cliff of fear, pandering to their worst apprehensions. The traditional media axiom, "If it bleeds, it leads," is alive and well at *Newsweek*. Shame on them.

Chronic Diseases

Although coronary heart disease is strongly linked to life-style and genetic susceptibility, another potential risk factor has recently come center stage. *Chlamydia pneumoniae*, a common respiratory bacterium that causes a form of pneumonia, may be a new risk factor for heart disease. A well-done

British study divided male heart attack survivors into three groups on the basis of their blood levels of *Chlamydia* antibodies. All were tracked for 18 months to ascertain the number of new coronary events. Men with the highest antibody levels had a four times greater risk of a coronary event than those with no antibodies. But the men with the highest antibody levels who were treated with antibiotics had a lowered risk equal to those with no antibodies in their blood.[20] While not conclusive, this type of study offers strong support for *Chlamydia* as a CHD risk factor. Additional studies with larger patient populations and longer treatment regimens are in the pipeline and are expected to be concluded by 2003. Final demonstration must await successful completion of the Koch-Henle postulates.

Microbiologists are also looking for microbiological causes for arthritis, diabetes (which is rising substantially in the adult population), inflammatory bowel disease—Crohn's disease—various cancers, and Guillain-Barré syndrome. An infectious etiology is also being considered for Bell's palsy, the most common cause of acute neuromuscular paralysis. Data on hand suggest it may be related to infection with a Herpes virus.[21]

Although it is known that human papillomavirus infection is a cause of cervical cancer, it was not known until recently that infection with *Chlamydia*, a gram-negative coccoid bacteria, and especially *Chlamydia trachomatis*, serotype G, was strongly associated with cervical squamous cell carcinoma. A study in Finland obtained an adjusted odds-ratio (relative risk) of 6, an inordinately high strength of association.[22] Convincing evidence now exists to add cervical malignancy to the list of sexually induced chlamydial infections, along with pelvic inflammatory disease and infertility.

Vasculitis, an inflammation of blood vessels of unknown cause but associated with the hepatitis virus, is another condition to take up residence in microbiology laboratories. These intriguing possibilities should keep microbiologists busy well into the night.[23] Stay tuned.

Come Clean!

Created fear and unnecessary fear combine to create a wall between us and microbes. This "wall" of separation is a two-edged sword. We need to protect ourselves from pathogenic organisms, but by drumming on that fearsome adjective "deadly," as in deadly microbes and deadly germs, the media have created unnecessary fear and hysteria, which fear-mongers exploit for pecuniary gain.

In fact, prevention, safety, and health remain in our hands. Other than AIDS, none of the diseases noted above ever came close to the "Top of the Charts" (chapter 1); they never even got close to the charts. Indeed, although the viruses of the many hemorrhagic fevers are virulent, contact is infrequent and passage difficult; the fatality rate is high, but the actual number of individuals involved is low. Ebola virus is a prime example. Its gruesome symptoms, with massive bleeding, gives it a power to frighten far beyond what it deserves. It cannot be transmitted by inhalation or shaking a hand. Direct contact with infected blood or other body fluid is necessary. Compared to automobile deaths and injuries, these exotic "new" diseases are almost nonexistent. The obverse side of that germ-fear coin is the inculcation of fear of all microbes. The fact is, most microbes are not only harmless, they are beneficial, and we do not live in a sterile, germ-free world. We can't, and we shouldn't want to.

Sterility is okay for canning tuna and niblet corn. But we humans have built-in defenses, immune systems that require contact with microbes to mature and develop the panoply of antibodies—the immunoglobins, proteins, circulating in our bloodstreams—with their exquisite specificity to protect against all foreign invaders. These antibodies are produced following exposure to foreign agents, for example, germs (antigens) not normally found in our body.

Our bodies provide an ideal environment for microbes—a complete food supply, warmth, and moisture—in which they can thrive. And, in turn, it is the function of the immune system to keep us relatively free of them, either by preventing their entrance or by destroying them. To achieve this level of protection, we need regular and frequent contact with microbes in order to develop a critical mass of antibodies. Should microbes manage to pierce the skin's protective shield, the immune system's scavenger cells and antibodies within the skin await them. Canny microbes that manage to evade defenses are confronted by additional cells and antibodies tailored specifically for them. But this depends on, and requires, steady and regular contact with the environment.

An inexperienced, immature, or disabled immune system can unleash a cascade of ailments, AIDS being an outstanding example. Arthritis and allergies are other less deadly but insufferable consequences.

In AIDS, the HIV virus enters and destroys immune T-cells, which normally regulate the immune system, thereby rendering the body ready prey to life-threatening infections and rare cancers. Immune cells can also become hideouts for the virus, where it can remain unaffected by circulating antibodies. The virus can also trick the T cell into becoming virtual virus copying machines, constantly increasing the numbers.

In the case of an immature system that has had little experience with microbes, similar responses flow from lack of available antibodies. Lack of adequate natural immunity can place the unprotected at risk of opportunistic infections. Opportunistic infectious or opportunistic organisms are those that are normally harmless but become harmful in defenseless individuals. Malnutrition can lower immunity, as can alcohol abuse; immunosuppressive drugs can do it, as can genetic deficiencies; and being too clean can do it, too. In our acquired fear, we appear to be marching inexorably in the too-clean direction, nudged along by scaremongers seeking to profit from our fear: not a new idea.

In his recent book, *Twenty Ads That Shook the World,* James Twitchell lays out Listerine's fascinating history. "Here is one of the first times," he writes, "that advertising really did create a 'cure.' But, of course, to make the cure, they first had to create the disease. Listerine didn't make mouthwash as much as it made halitosis. Or in advertising terms, you don't sell the product, you sell the need."[24] That "need" was created again when Bristol-Myers Squibb, the makers of Keri, an antibacterial skin lotion, decorated New York subway cars with ads purporting to cleanse you of germs picked up while riding the subway. Ads read: "You're the 423rd person to touch that pole today. Enough said." Of course you are expected to fill in the blanks, connect the dots. Touch the poles, and you pick up and take home other people's germs, and you will somehow become infected or ill. The fact is, your immune system will gain from the experience. Another ad held that "the turnstiles have at least 11,700 germs. (Have a nice day.)" Each of a half-dozen placards carried the notice: "Keri, the first and only antibacterial hand lotion for softer, safer hands." Yet another placard read: "The last guy holding this pole was named Sal Monella." Not only another anxiety-generating piece of nonsense, but it didn't sit well at all with Italian pole-holders.

Those ads brought a knowing smile to my face when I saw them. I recalled an earlier time, my years at James Madison High in Brooklyn. There, warnings were passed around in locker rooms and men's rooms to the effect that gonorrhea and syphilis could be lurking on toilet seats. That was a long time ago, but from what I see and hear today, the myth is hard dying, and scare tactics do sell.

Writing in an immunology journal, two British physicians stated that "recent newspaper articles reveal that there are now people, particularly in the USA, who are so obsessed with the concept of germs that they will no longer touch the hand rails in subway stations." They further note that "these individuals believe they are protecting their health, but are probably wrong. In order to function correctly, the immune system, like the brain, must learn from the environment."[25] How does one learn from the environment? Recent studies suggest an answer.

A prospective cohort study (see chapter 6) done by the University of Arizona's Department of Pediatrics followed 1,035 children from birth to ages 6 to 13 to determine the incidence of asthma. They found that exposure either to older children at home or to the children at day-care centers protected against its development as well as frequent wheezing later in life. "A young child's exposure to other children in or out of the home," they tell us, "leads to more frequent wheezing during the first few years of life. However, such exposure protects against the development of Asthma and frequent wheezing later during childhood."[26]

A recent study in Germany adds strength to this concept. Pediatricians at the University Children's Hospital, Munich, and Charité at Humboldt University, Berlin, followed 1,314 children from five German cities from birth to age 7 to determine if a relationship existed between early childhood infections and subsequent development of asthma. This study, as well as the Arizona study, proceed from the earlier work of David Strachan of the London School of Hygiene and Tropical Medicine, who collected data on 17,000-plus children over a twenty-three year period and found that allergic diseases were prevented by infection early in childhood, "transmitted by unhygienic contact with older siblings or acquired prenatally from a mother infected by contact with older children." He learned, too, that declining family size, improvements in household amenities, and higher standards of personal cleanliness reduced the opportunity for cross-infection in young families. Strachan is usually credited with originating the hygiene hypothesis, which suggests that common viral infections induce production of interferon, a protective host response. Interferon is more effective in eliminating virus than the alternative interleukin response. Children are born with a strong interleukin response, but quickly mature to the interferon response when given early contact with common childhood infections. Thus, having brothers and sisters, attending a day-care center at an early age, or growing up on a farm with frequent animal contact helps in developing immunological maturation and preventing allergic-type diseases. By contrast, living in small family groups, in hygienic conditions, and taking antibiotics early in life promotes development of allergic conditions.[27]

The German researchers obtained results similar to that of the Arizona group and concluded that "repeated viral infections other than lower respiratory tract infections early in life reduce the risk of developing asthma up to school age."[28] These studies are admirable examples of the immune system on a learning curve. Not too far down the road we should know just how much dirt is essential for our good health. In the meantime, how clean do we think we need to be? Should all microbes be removed from ourselves and our surroundings? In fact, we may be using too many antibacterial cleansers, soaps, bleaches, powders, and lotions in our homes. If there are health benefits from using the many "cleansers" currently touted and available, none of them have been published. Removing every last vestige of dirt and microbe from our bodies and homes may well leave us and our children open to opportunistic attack, allergies, and more. Simply put, fear of germs and obsession with hygiene are depriving the immune system of the information input upon which it is dependent. Antibacterials are excessive. Soap and water are more than adequate. A protective mantra for the twenty-first century might well be: "Give us this day our daily (dose of) germs."[29]

Dermatologists know that most of us bathe or shower too often, sometimes more than once a day. By doing so we wash away our skin's protective oils, causing excessive drying and scaling, requiring the need for lotions to deal with the dryness. Listerine made us gargle to rid the world of halitosis; Lifebuoy soap created body odor, and we've been scrubbing it away ever since.

Perhaps Ernie Pyle, in *Here Is Your War*, deserves the last word on cleanliness: "For a lifetime I had bathed with becoming regularity, and thought the world would come to an end unless I changed my socks every day. But in Africa I sometimes went without a bath for two months, and I went two weeks at a time without even changing my socks. Oddly enough, it didn't seem to make much difference." Two months without a bath, well, maybe; but the same pair of socks for two weeks, I'd have to pass on that one, antibodies or no antibodies.

Microbes, Microbes, Everywhere . . . Can Live with 'Em, but Not without 'Em

A germ-free world is of course a contradiction. No matter how hard we try, we cannot avoid or rid ourselves of microbes. It isn't required that we love the beasties, but it should be possible to appreciate the good they do and the benefits they bestow. We do need them, and they need us.

Consider that milk and milk products have been used as important foods since the walls of Jericho came tumbling down. Fermented milks, bacterially fermented buttermilk, acidophilus, yogurt, *leben, kumis, kefir*, as well as butter owe their unique flavors and texture to members of the unseen world. And where would butter be without bread, which owes its leavening of dough to yeast cells, another microbial species. Without yeast we'd all be eating matzoh, unleavened bread, all the time. Rye and pumpernickel are sourdough breads, as is buttermilk bread, the products of combinations of microbes. All our crackers are microbially cultured, and those crackers go exceedingly well with Camembert, Limburger, Roquefort, Brie, Gouda, Edam, and cheddar cheeses, none of which would exist were it not for molds (fungi) and bacteria. And what of those Spanish, Greek, and Italian olives, black and green, all microbially fermented. Can anyone imagine a world bereft of bacterially fermented pickles (kosher dills!), sauerkraut (I'm salivating worse then Pavlov's dogs), fermented cauliflower, and other veggies? Our banquet table would not be complete without an array of sausages: kielbasa, lebanon, genoa, cervelet, thuringer, and salami owe their singular tastes to our many bacterial friends.

To help wash all this down, wine, beer, vodka, sherry, champagne, and cider, the hard kind, cannot be made without abundant help from a variety of bacterial flora. And don't forget the Mexican *pulque* (*maguey*) the fermented wine of the agave; and bringing up the rear, as it were, are coffee, tea, and cocoa. Fermentation of coffee cherries occurs during drying, as it does for cocoa beans and tea leaves. Vinegar, ginger, and Tabasco all come to us via microbial flourishes, and could bakers and ice cream makers live without vanilla, from the fermented and dried pods of several species of orchids of the genus *Vanilla*? Not possible. But our table, already groaning under the delicious weight of all the goodies microbes made for us, needs the final touch of soy sauce, miso, tempeh, and MSG, fermented soybeans all.

Before we entered kindergarten, we had close and enduring contact with a host of microbes, and as our palates matured, that contact grew. Life without microbes is not only unthinkable, it would be dull and boring, and worse, inedible. But this is local contact. There is yet another, larger microbial world. It deserves top billing but is rarely, if ever mentioned.

All living things are organic, which means they are composed of compounds of carbon. All green things—plants, trees, and grasses, including those under the seas—use carbon dioxide to make carbohydrates via the process of photosynthesis.

The green things are a major source of food for grazing animals, fish, and us humans. The end product of all animal and human metabolism is carbon dioxide, which is returned to the atmosphere, and when all mammals die, the carbon in their bodies is returned to the soil. Soil microbes are the primary decomposers of dead organic matter in all human and animal waste, dead plants, and other organic things. This circular event goes by the name "carbon cycle" and is microbe driven.

For protein to be made, amino acids are needed. To make amino acids, nitrogen is needed. The protein of dead organic matter, plants, animals, and humans, decomposed by microbes, deposits nitrogen in the air and soil. Additional nitrogen reaches the soil in the form of urea from urine, and the microbial decomposition of urine releases ammonia, which is then metabolized into nitrogen. Soil bacteria convert nitrogen to nitrates and nitrites, which plants convert to amino acids, which become protein when eaten by all animals or humans. A substantial amount of nitrogen rises into the air, but neither humans nor plants can use it. Almost 80 percent of the air we breathe is nitrogen, but we can't use it. But microbes in the soil can, and do. They convert or "fix" it to ammonia, and then back to nitrates, which plants can use to make amino acids, which will become protein again. This circular event is the nitrogen cycle and is also microbe driven.

At least three amino acids contain sulfur (methionine, cystine, and cysteine) and are essential components of protein. A third cycle, the sulfur cycle, works to release sulfur from decaying protein's amino acids, which yet another group of bacteria can attend to, while others convert sulfur to sulfates that plants can use to make the sulfur-containing amino acids. Around and around it goes, forever cycling, ever since animals, plants, and the microbial world formed their unseen, intimate bond millions of years ago. Clearly, a world without microbes is unimaginable—worse, unworkable. Without decomposition and recycling there is no life, no growth, and no renewal. Microbes and humans are linked, forever. And bear in mind that the great majority of microbes work *for* us. Full time.

Still, all microbes are not benign, nor beneficial. A few can do harm, irreparable harm. It is not required that we love them, but neither is it necessary to fear and avoid them. What is needed is proportion. We need to place all that has gone before in a context. Numbers can help do that. Consider the following.

Sixty million years ago, an asteroid some 7 miles in diameter, traveling at 1,800 miles per second (100,000 miles per hour), slammed into the Earth at Chicxlub, near Progresso, in the Yucatan peninsula. The resulting fire, smoke, and airborne debris obliterated the sun for months. The Earth became as night, and a great dying ensued. Dinosaurs went extinct. That was our planet's last great extinction. But life went on. Sixty million years is a long time ago. More recently, life has been taken in other ways. In the year 1346, bubonic plague, the Black Death, a rat-flea-microbe triad, took hold in Europe when a ship carrying sick and dying sailors dropped anchor at Caffa, a port on the Black Sea; in its four-year pestilential rage, 20 million people died. Some six hundred years later in 1918–1919, influenza, the Purple Plague, swept in from the Far East, killing another 20 million. And in the 1980s, AIDS burst upon an unsuspecting world, and over two decades has taken another 22 million lives worldwide. Another 3 million plus, and AIDS will have exceeded the Black Death toll, which claimed 25 million lives. These events are writ large on our collective memories.

What accounted for these epidemics? After six-hundred-plus years, whatever it was that triggered the sudden movement of rodents and their fleas still remains a mystery. But we've gotten a handle on influenza: apparently, ducks, pigs, and farmers in China live in close proximity and exchange viruses, which facilitates genetic shift in the viral genome. It is this shift or mutation that results in increased viral virulence and leads to greater numbers of illness and death in populations. Influenza or flu (from the Italian, to be under the influence of) is a disease of the respiratory system. The virus enters the lung via virus-contaminated respiratory secretions (saliva) by means of person-to-person spread of infected droplets exhaled while coughing, sneezing, and talking, generally under crowded conditions, allowing the airborne droplets from one individual to be inhaled by others. A form of salivary togetherness. Similarly, the AIDS epidemic can be stopped in its tracks by a change in behavior on the part of those at high risk.

Shrieking headlines inform us that thirteen people died in Chile from a virus; 113 cases of Hanta virus occurred in the United States between 1993 and 1997; horses are dying in Australia; seventy-eight people died in the Congo from an Ebola-like virus; and the West Nile virus caused seven deaths in New York, a city of 8 million. Proportion is needed. The journalistic stitching together of these disparate conditions and events engenders and heightens unnecessary fear. The plague, the flu, and AIDS have been the three major killers over the past two thousand years. Over the same two thousand years, we humans have prospered and have had minimal problems with microbes.

The take-away idea is that health is the norm. Very much so. Microbial threats require vigilance, attention, and concern, not fear. For the most part, microbial risks are self-limiting and involve small numbers of susceptible people. Absolute safety, total freedom from illness, is not of this world. Proportion and the numbers should be our guide, and will help alleviate fear. A final glance at table 1.1 reminds us that in the United States, the annual death rate from every manner of affliction is less than one percent per year. Again, it is the numbers that serve us, not the news media.

Food, Glorious Food

Dietary Supplements

Dietary supplements are creatures of the nineties, bursting upon us like Topsy. We've made them into a $15 billion industry. But why? Why do we need to supplement our diets? We are among the best-fed people on the planet. In fact, too many of us are obese. So why supplements? We use supplements of vitamins, herbs, minerals, amino acids, and other chemical substances, not for their taste or aroma, not as food, but as medicine. Dietary supplements loom as the over-the-counter nonprescription drugs of the new millennium. Are we looking at beneficent nature or *caveat emptor?* Beneficent is clear enough, but *caveat*, from the Latin *caveo*, informs us to "be on one's guard," "to take care, lest," and *caveat emptor* tells us that "he alone, she alone, is responsible for making a bad purchase," thus, let the buyer beware.

If the rapidity with which supplements are flying off the shelves is a bellwether, the answer appears to be beneficent nature. In 1999, $31 billion was shelled out for dietary supplements and "functional foods" such as vegetable soup with echinacea, cornchips with kava, claiming to have health benefits beyond the foods themselves. Sales of supplements alone climbed from $9.8 billion in 1995 to an estimated $14.7 billion in 1999. During the same period, sales of functional foods increased from $11.3 to $16.2 billion and are expected to reach $50 billion over the next ten years. This speaks volumes about the public's willingness to part with its coin. What other industry has had so phenomenal an increase in so short a time? We must ask at least three pungent questions:

1. How do we account for so remarkable an increase? Was there some extraordinary event behind it?
2. What are dietary supplements used for?
3. What is being sold to us? What are we getting for our money?

For a food, food ingredient, or drug to enter the marketplace, manufacturers have to prove to the Food and Drug Administration (FDA) that their products are both safe and efficacious. Efficacy is the ability to produce an intended result claimed for a food or drug. As for safety, we expect that anything we put into, or on, our bodies will cause no harm. We obtained that security in 1938 with the passage of the Food, Drug, and Cosmetic Act, and again in 1960, when Congress mandated that manufacturers prove both safety and efficacy to the FDA's satisfaction before their products can enter the marketplace—a reasonable requirement that worked well. But it was too good to last. In its infinite wisdom, Congress turned around and removed that security by enacting Public Law 103–417, the Dietary Supplement Health and Education Act (DSHEA) of 1994. At the outset, we are told that "Congress finds that the importance of nutrition and the benefits of dietary supplements to health promotion and disease prevention have been documented increasingly in scientific studies." In fact, the opposite is true. The studies on supplements have been found wanting. And the following are the fateful words that left us vulnerable in the marketplace: Section 403 B (c), Burden of Proof, says: "In any proceeding brought under subsection (a), the burden of proof shall be on the United States to establish that an article or other such matter is false or misleading."[1] Short, definitive, absolute. The tables were turned. Why? Why give away our sole source of protection? The act did it. It created a new product class—a class of untouchables. Under the act, supplements are now *presumed* to be safe and efficacious until the FDA proves them otherwise. Under DSHEA, herbal products and supplements generally are not required to be proven safe before marketing. With this piece of legislation, the gates opened and the marketplace was flooded with products, and buyers have literally cleaned them off the shelves.

Along with the swiftness of their removal, supplements now have what I call "the 4 un's": buyers are grabbing supplements that are *un*regulated, *un*tested, *un*standardized, and have *un*known effects. We are paying the supplement industry to be their guinea pigs. Why? Because the manufacturers have not done the necessary studies, do not know what they are selling, and we have no idea what we are purchasing. Under the act, the FDA cannot compel manufacturers of herbal remedies to provide the public with evidence of scientific support for claims made, and it is the FDA that must now prove a product unsafe or lacking in efficacy before it can be removed from the marketplace—an all but impossible task.

Food ingredients and additives, not generally recognized as safe, must proceed through the FDA's approval process before becoming part of a food. This premarket approval requires manufacturers to conduct appropriate studies establishing efficacy and safety of the ingredients, with the results submitted to the FDA for review. Based on the outcome of its review, the FDA can accept or reject the data and the food product. Dietary supplements are exempt from this traditional premarket approval process. Was there a major force behind the explosion of supplements in the marketplace? The only possible response is: indeed there was.

A great nutrition debate took place at a conference sponsored by the Department of Agriculture in February 2000. It was Secretary of Agriculture Dan Glickman's way of attempting to shine the light of reason on a confusing and conflicting subject—diet. The public contributes $50 billion a year to the major players who were in attendance: Drs. Sears, Atkins, and Ornish. Each doctor maintained that the other didn't have a clue as to how one's weight could be reduced. Each maintained the other's diet was nonsense. Obviously, the public, parting with billions of dollars a year, believes otherwise. It was particularly ironic that Dr. Atkins complained that he has not been able to obtain government funding for studies to prove that his diet works. Imagine: the man has sold 10 million books, has large real estate holdings, and hawks a full product line; he's a millionaire many times over, yet he laments that we taxpayers are remiss in not funding his study. Neither his nor the others' diets have been tested, yet they are promoted as though they have been. People buy into the claims, believing that the diet plans have been tested and can do what the doctors say they can do.[2]

Use of Supplements

How are supplements being used? Here are some revealing data: colds, 59%; burns, 45%; allergies, 22%; rashes, 18%; insomnia, 18%; PMS, 17%; depression, 7%; diarrhea, 7%; and menopause, 4%. This cluster of conditions shares a common feature: they are common medical problems. Supplements—foods—are being used as medicine to treat illness. The public is doing what Congress believes they should do: make their own medical decisions and choose whatever remedies and therapies they prefer in a marketplace unfettered by government regulation. In doing so, we are becoming our own medical practitioners. Do we have the necessary experience and knowledge to make the difficult and appropriate decisions? Do we need to know only what the labels tell us, or is there more to know? What, in fact, do the labels tell us—or not tell us?

For many supplements, the Food and Drug Administration (FDA) has authorized the use of health claims such as "to reduce the risk of disease" when such a claim is used in conjunction with accepted practices. So, for example, a product containing a soy protein can carry the statement, "Using this product daily, as part of a diet low in saturated fat and cholesterol *may* reduce the risk of heart disease." The potential purchaser does not know whether it is a diet low in saturated fat and cholesterol or the soy protein that conveys the benefit, or if it's the combination. Also note the hedge word, *may*, which should be seen for what it is and not translated as *will*. How then can an informed choice be made? Not easily. Furthermore, safety cannot be assured because current food and drug laws do not contain defined safety standards for the individual ingredients that together constitute the supplement. Nor do supplement labels indicate any safety information, such as contraindications for those who may be using any number of medications for preexisting conditions that could exacerbate a problem. Consider the following. Cases of metabolic interaction between St. John's wort (*Hypericum perforatum*) and the immunosuppressive drug Cyclosporin were recently reported by a team of cardiologists and pharmacologists at the Clinic for Cardiac Surgery at the University Hospital in Zurich, Switzerland. Two patients in stable condition after heart transplants a year earlier required treatment at the hospital. In the first case, a sixty-one-year-old man had self-medicated himself with St. John's wort for a mild depression three weeks before his hospitalization. In the second case, a psychiatrist prescribed St. John's wort to a sixty-three-year-old man for his depression.

The singular untoward finding on admission was depressed Cyclosporin levels in both patients. After use of the St. John's wort was stopped, the Cyclosporin levels returned to their normal values. The researchers found that St. John's wort contained at least ten different chemicals that could contribute to its pharmacological effects: flavinoids, xanthones, and naphtodiantrons, which are enzyme inducers and can break down Cyclosporin, thereby reducing its bioavailability.[3] Herbs contain collections of chemicals, none of which is listed on labels. Ronald Evans of the Salk Institute in La Jolla, California, found that when the body in its wisdom senses the presence of potentially dangerous chemicals, it increases the production of the enzyme CYP3A, which can cleave and dispose of harmful chemicals. However, herbs such as St. John's wort can also trigger activation of CYP3A, which accelerates the destruction of Cyclosporin as well as drugs such as Indinavir, a protease inhibitor, and anticlotting and antiasthmatic agents. Molecular biologists believe that St. John's wort is not alone in possessing such chemicals. Similarly, a research team at the National Institute of Allergy and Infectious Diseases in Bethesda, Maryland, found that St. John's wort seriously depresses Indinavir. They advised that HIV-infected individuals avoid St. John's wort, as reduced Indinavir levels are a cause of antiretroviral resistance and treatment failure.[4]

The FDA has neither the manpower and budget to investigate all reports of negative effects of supplements, nor the means to determine if supplements are adversely affecting consumers. In the case of functional foods, the manufacturers marketing them are not required to apprise the FDA of their intent to bring their products into markets. The FDA learns about the product's presence only when a complaint is filed. The presence of herb supplements such as St. John's wort, echinacea, and gingko biloba in a functional food are adulterants under the law, as they have not been declared GRAS, "generally recognized as safe." To remove such products from commerce if the manufacturer does not voluntarily do so, the FDA must go to court. Because there is no guarantee of success, given the ill-defined state of current regulations, the FDA is reluctant to do so.

The reporting of adverse effects of supplements is spare, anemic, and poorly organized. Therefore, the FDA has no true idea of the extent of any problems. In 1999, however, a nationwide consumer survey found that 12 percent of herbal supplement users, or some 11.9 million people, experienced an adverse reaction.[5] Among those reported for St. John's wort were difficulty breathing, throat constriction, headaches, dizziness, rash, convulsions, and vomiting.

As for health claims such as "may reduce risk of some cancers, and risk of heart disease," a perusal of Section D of the Burden of Proof is in order. Claims such as "cleanses the blood" are vague and thoroughly lack clear purpose or meaning. There is no evidence as to how that cleansing occurs or what the blood will be cleansed of. Unfortunately for users and potential users, there are no standards or regulations governing or clarifying such statements. In effect, companies are free to say what they please, taking comfort in the assumption that neither the states nor the federal government will bother them.

Nevertheless, there is one consolation. Although Congress declared war on the FDA and won, the FDA managed to win one battle: the battle of the disclaimer. The 1994 act prohibits supplement manufacturers from making specific health claims without an accompanying asterisk. Thus, it is in the consumer's interest to look for the asterisk and search out the accompanying disclaimer. Just about all supplements carry the disclaimer, although most often it is neatly tucked away: "This statement (or these statements) have not been evaluated by the Food and Drug Administration, and is not meant to diagnose, treat, prevent, or cure disease." Look for it. Too often it is made to resemble a decoration. It isn't. Don't be misled.

Botanicals

What we commonly refer to as drugs are single-chemical substances that are biologically active, formulated to bring about a specific response in tissues and cells. Are supplements in fact drugs?

Just what supplements are being sold in the marketplace for medical purposes? Botanicals, or herbs, roots, leaves, stems, and flowers—in powder, gel, or liquid form—are mixtures of many chemicals. When ground and roasted coffee beans are mixed with boiling water, we get a brew with great odor, taste, and color. At last count, over nine hundred distinct chemicals had been identified in a cup of coffee. Tea and cocoa are much the same: loaded with chemicals. And vegetable soup—well, the number of chemicals would *bowl* you over. That's the nature of all plants—of all living things. They don't just *contain* a great number and diversity of chemicals, they are nothing *but* chemicals—some benign, some harmful, some deadly. Because they are natural does not mean they are safe. Safety and naturalness are not necessarily bedfellows. Bear in mind that chemicals obtained from plants were made by plants, for plants, for the many and varied reactions required of the plant to function. Indeed, it has been documented that food plants and herbs naturally account for 99.99 percent of the pesticides we humans ingest. These natural pesticides are manufactured by plants in part to defend themselves against an array of microbes, insects, and animals that crave their succulent tissues. Thus, with the ever-increasing consumption of herbs, regular herb users are among the greatest consumers of dietary pesticides, paralleling the pesticide consumption of vegetarians. It has been estimated that "Americans consume about 1.5 grams of natural pesticides per person per day, which is about 10,000 times more than they eat of synthetic pesticide residues."[6]

It is unquestionably a benefit that many plants and plant chemicals are used safely and beneficially, but caution must be exercised. Any chemical, natural or synthetic, that has an effect on some bodily function is, ipso facto, a drug. It is simply a misunderstanding to think that herbs are an alternative to drugs. They are in fact *alternative drugs,* a different way of taking a drug—a crude and untested drug, at that.

Taxol, a chemical and highly effective anticancer drug, was originally obtained from the bark and needles of the Pacific yew tree. Unfortunately, there are not enough yews for all the Taxol cancer patients need because the demand is so great. So Taxol, like so many other drugs originally obtained from plants, was chemically analyzed to produce a synthetic Taxol, indistinguishable from the original, thereby leaving the trees undisturbed. Such a procedure produces chemicals, drugs, whose identity and purity are known, and whose quality and potency are assured in the quantities needed.

Botanicals, with their crude mixtures of a variety of chemicals, have highly variable potency. Supplement manufacturers scrupulously avoid even a hint that their products be called or thought of as drugs. To do so would place them squarely in the FDA's purview and require full disclosure of efficacy and safety for the purpose intended prior to marketing. Supplement manufacturers would sooner pet a cobra than put themselves in that position.

With all the St. John's wort, saw palmetto, gingko biloba, and echinacea flying off the shelves in the United States, Canada, Mexico, Europe, South America, and Asia, is there really enough to go around? Tests show that many supplements do not contain what they say they do.[7] Potency of pills and capsules vary markedly within the same box or bottle. In September 1998, the *Los Angeles Times* tested ten brands of St. John's wort: seven of the ten lacked potency. Of fifty-four ginseng products recently tested, thirty-two were found worthless, and twenty-five contained no active ingredient at all. As already noted, supplements contain a host of undeclared chemicals. Some have caused lead, arsenic, and mercury poisoning; kidney failure; hepatitis; respiratory distress; allergic reactions; and hypertension. Angelica, *dong quai,* contains photosensitive chemicals that can induce severe sunburn, besides containing the terpenoid alcohol Borneol, which can produce mental confusion, dizziness, convulsions, nausea, and vomiting. None of these are listed on the label.

Chinese Herbals

There is currently a fascination with Chinese herbal medicine. Yet it is also widely recognized that the Chinese are no healthier nor longer-lived than those in Western European countries and the United States. In fact, the opposite is true. Why then the desire for many of the several hundred Chinese herbs? An answer may lie in the false notion that because they are natural, they must be harmless and without side effects.

For example, the Chinese herb *Aristolochia fangchi* has been shown to contain the nephrotoxin aristolochic acid, which is known to have caused an outbreak of progressive interstitial nephritis.[8] This type of kidney damage can require transplants and dialysis. Urinary tract cancers have also been documented. Reports of kidney damage have come from France, Britain, Spain, Japan, and Taiwan. In the United States, this herb is being sold as *Aristolochia sertenaria*, or Senega snake root, to treat snakebites. Capsules of *Aristolochia* are available on the Internet. However, in an unusual action, the FDA has moved to ban importation of *Aristolochia*, urging anyone having an adverse reaction to contact their MedWatch Program (1–800–332–1088) or report the problem on their Website (www.fda.gov).

Two herbs used to treat rheumatism, arthritis, bruises, and fractures— the root of *Aconitum kusnezoffei*, and *chuanwa*, the root of *Aconitum carmichaeli*—cause widespread poisoning and death, as they contain toxic alkaloids.[9] Similarly, the flowers of datura, used to treat asthma, chronic bronchitis, stomach aches, and tooth aches, induce anticholinergic poisoning. Cigarettes containing datura for asthma induce tachycardia (rapid heartbeat), dry mouth, dilated pupils, and an array of other symptoms. Datura and *Rhododendri* are known to contain the alkaloids hyoscyamine, atropine, and scopolamine, which have analgesic, sedative, and anticholinergic properties. Stephania and magnolia used in weight-loss diets have also produced nephritis. Licorice extracts contain glycyrrhizic and other acids that can cause sodium and water retention, resulting in diarrhea. And Chinese black balls, used in self-medication for joint pain and sleeplessness, can contain diazepam, indomethecin, phenylbutazone, as well as the heavy metals lead and cadmium and other nonprescription-type drugs. But you'd never know it. None of them ever appear on the label, because most have not been analyzed for the actual contents, and there is no requirement that they be listed.

From 25 to 50 percent of Chinese infants are given *chuenlin* by their mothers to clear them of the "toxic products of pregnancy." One of *chuenlin*'s alkaloids, berberine, can readily displace bilirubin from its serum-binding protein, causing a rise in free bilirubin, which can cause brain damage, along with icterus, or jaundice. Placing total faith in Chinese herbs or proprietary medicine is unwarranted. Complications are increasing with increasing use among both Asians and Westerners. In a recent review of the use of Chinese herbal medicines in Hong Kong, researchers of the Department of Clinical Pharmacology at the Chinese University of Hong Kong inform us that of the 150 most-often used herbs, ten are out-and-out toxic.[10]

Unfortunately, supplement manufacturers imply that their products are medically beneficial, will bring about a cure without using "drugs," and they hope that few read the small print or pay attention to the asterisks on the label.

Glucosamine

Glucosamine offers yet another cautionary example. In a recent review in *The Journal of Rheumatology* considering the value of glucosamine therapy for osteoarthritis, rheumatologists at the Rheumatic Diseases Unit at Queens University in Ontario, Canada, inform us that the mechanism of action of glucosamine in osteoarthritis (OA) remains to be established, as does the metabolism of the ingested glucosamine—information essential for understanding its effects. Furthermore, still to be obtained is the appropriate route of administration and the correct dosage. Furthermore, there are other questions to be answered. Are the different forms of glucosamine, the hydrochloride and the sulfate, equally effective? Does it work in all joints? What is the long-term safety of this therapy?[11] For some, less may be more, but so little is known about this cure that those prescribing it, and those using it, are doing so on a wing and a prayer, and both are flying blind.

Genistein

Genistein, a phytoestrogen, 4, 5, 7, trihydroisoflavone, suggested to play a protective role in breast cancer, offers yet another instructive tale. It offers, too, a window into how sloppy thinking and advice misinform concerned readers.

Genistein, naturally present as a beta-glucoside, is readily metabolized by intestinal bacteria to produce genistein, which exhibits estrogenic activity. However, after a critical review of the published literature on genistein, oncologists at Georgetown University Medical School in Washington, D.C., remind us that "although the evidence of the range of genistein's effects is far from conclusive, it is tempting for some in the scientific community to tout genistein as a potential chemopreventive agent or alternative to hormone-replacement therapy. However, studies indicating a potential cancer-promoting effect should not be taken lightly. Further studies must be done before the true scope of genistein's actions can be understood."[12]

In a recent essay on the benefits of soybeans, the author informs us that soybeans contain high concentrations of isoflavones, particularly genistein, and that "those phytoestrogens can alleviate the symptoms of menopause, and their consumption has been linked to reduced risks of breast cancer in East Asia. Soy proteins also lower levels of blood cholesterol, and some, though not all epidemiological studies link their intake with a reduced risk of cardiovascular diseases. Greater enthusiasm for the subtle taste of tofu could thus have highly cost-effective health benefits."[13] A cheaper means of treating disease is promoted here, although, while *some epidemiological studies suggest a protective benefit,* others do not. So, the article suggests that we go with those that do, and with a chemical that's cheaper. This is the type of article to be wary of. The word "links" has to be handled like the proverbial hot potato.

Nevertheless, in October 1999, the FDA permitted soy protein manufacturers to use claims of reduced heart disease on their product labels. This appeared to provide the requisite imprimatur and impetus for believing that soy products, containing isoflavones in whatever form, can alleviate coronary artery disease and also serve as a substitute for estrogen replacement in postmenopausal women. But, again, caution comes from yet another group of researchers. This time, endocrinologists at the Mayo Clinic in Minnesota reported that not only was there no evidence for an isoflavone-stimulating effect on the endometrium, nor a positive or negative effect on cognition, but also the "the administration of purified isoflavones in pill form resulted in no effect on plasma lipids." Their conclusion is clear. "It is premature to draw definitive conclusions regarding the use of isoflavones as an alternative to estrogen for hormone replacement in postmenopausal women." They further maintain that "randomized, placebo-controlled clinical trials are necessary to address these important issues."[14]

Obviously, we have a problem here. Far too many individuals who lack rounded knowledge of the subject are extending advice to an unsuspecting public, but such lack neither deters nor precludes offering advice. Then again, we live in a democracy where free speech is protected as an inherent right. Doesn't the public have an equal right of protection against nonsense and abuse of their health?

Testing Effectiveness

In chapter 4, we will see that Vitamin C, normally considered an antioxidant, had been found to be a pro-oxidant, depending upon its concentration.

Unfortunately, many of the antioxidants are not yet fully understood, nor are the issues simple or straightforward. We must use caution before we decide to self-medicate or allow physicians, who may assume some benefit, to do so. For example, in a recent in-depth review of the efficacy of herbal medicines for psychiatric disorders, psychiatrists at the Martin Luther King, Jr.–Drew Medical Center in Los Angeles examined four of the twelve most commonly used herbs for psychiatric symptoms: St. John's wort, kava, ginkgo biloba, and valerian. They concluded that the results of efficacy studies into effective treatments for patients are hampered by the chemical complexity of the products, the lack of standardization of commonly available preparations, and the paucity of well-controlled studies. They maintain that "it is premature for psychiatrists to recommend herbal remedies over established conventional treatments."[15]

Another great battle was fought over product labels. One brand of *dong quai* root states that it is "for women's special needs," and another, to "normalize women's system." Harmonex, a manufacturer of herbal products, promotes St. John's wort "for emotional and physical harmony" and "to give your mood a lift." How should one interpret these statements?

These are all structure-function claims. Supplements are permitted to say a product may affect the structure and/or function of the body, but they cannot say "alleviates constipation"; they can say "promotes regularity." They cannot say "prevents PMS," but they can say "for women's special needs." If a product states "cures cancer" or "treats arthritis" without the asterisk and disclaimer, it has crossed the line and is illegal. Currently, the onus is on the buyer to make the assumption that the product will cure, prevent, or treat. For example, Garlipure, a garlic product, states that it "helps maintain a healthy cholesterol level," but it carries the asterisk because "helps maintain" is just a fudge for "maintains," which is disallowed, because it is a healthy cholesterol level that prevents illness. Another garlic product says "supports heart health" and "helps maintain healthy cholesterol levels." Tiny to be sure, and buyers are being lured by the expectation that substituting garlic for higher-priced drugs such as Zocor and the other statins, Lipitor, and Mevicor, will give them equal protection. Not only does the asterisk say not so, but currently there is no scientific or medical basis for such claims for garlic (*Allium sativum*). It has, however, traditionally been recommended and accepted over-the-clothesline, as it were, as a natural remedy for heart disease, even though its efficacy has never been established.

In a randomized, double-blind, placebo-controlled trial, done at the

University of Bonn in Germany in an outpatient lipid clinic, two groups of men and women with cholesterol levels between 240 and 348 mg/dl (deciliter) ingested daily doses of steam-distilled garlic for twelve weeks. Their daily dose corresponded to eating 5 grams of fresh garlic twice a day. Analysis of their lipid levels, LDLs, HDLs, total cholesterol, and triglycerides over the course of three months showed no decreases, nor any differences between the groups. Lipoprotein levels were virtually unchanged at the end of the treatment periods. Their conclusion is unambiguous: "Based on the results of the present study, there is no evidence to recommend garlic therapy for lowering serum lipid levels."[16]

A recent meta-analysis (a statistical technique of pooled analyses in which groups of studies on a specific topic are analyzed as one in an attempt to improve clinical decision-making) appears to corroborate that conclusion. The methodology employed was rigorous. To be included in the analysis, a published study had to satisfy the following criteria: it must be randomized, double blind, and placebo controlled; it must use only garlic monopreparations; cholesterol levels in test subjects must be at least 200mg/dl; and total cholesterol levels had to be repeated as an endpoint. Thirteen trials satisfied these criteria. Six of the trials with the highest scores for methodological quality found no difference between the garlic group and placebo group. For the remainder, the researchers concluded that "garlic reduced total cholesterol significantly more than the placebo; however, the size of the effect is modest. . . . The use of garlic for hypercholesterolemia is therefore of questionable value." Furthermore, in clinical practice garlic "is not an efficient way to decrease total serum cholesterol level." They suggest that physicians advise patients who inquire about garlic that any effect is small and may not be clinically meaningful. An equally illuminating finding of the analysis was that none of the thirteen trials directly addressed the implication of lowering lipid levels via garlic. Modification of risk factors such as lipid level may not translate into a lower incidence of heart disease. The researchers speculate that perhaps there are other types of benefits, such as decreased blood pressure or increased blood flow.[17] But such studies have not been done, and will remain unanswered until large-scale, long-term investigations are mounted. This is the message to be passed over the clothesline.

The presence of parsley in some garlic supplements, ostensibly to mask the odor of garlic, is also surprising, as parsley contains psoralens, which can induce rashes and itching. Little media publicity has been given to the fact that between January 1993 and October 1998, the FDA received 2,621 reports of serious side effects with herbal supplements, along with 101 deaths.

The FDA lost yet another battle regarding the asterisk's type size and placement. The disclaimer can be anywhere manufacturers prefer, and the size is also unregulated—often no more than 7 points, and generally out of sight. Many go the extra mile trying to repudiate the disclaimer. For example, a container of Ginkoba tells us: "The statements presented here have not been evaluated by the Food and Drug Administration. This product is not intended to diagnose, treat, cure, or prevent any disease. Pharmaton Natural Health Products affirms that the statements presented here are supported by well-controlled clinical studies." As required, the disclaimer is there, but it is quickly followed by another reaffirming statement seeking to nullify the disclaimer. They mean to have it their way, and they do.

Supplement users must also ask how the suggested dose was determined. How many pills or capsules should they take a day, and how much active ingredient is in each tablet or caplet? Again, a close reading of the back of labels informs the reader that "the daily value has not been established." In fact, not a single product has an *established dose*! Users must determine it themselves.

Ginseng offers another cautionary tale. Packages of ginseng reveal that they contain *Panex ginseng* (Chinese/Korean), *Panex quinquefolius* (American), or *Eleutherococcus senticosus* (Siberian) ginseng. Each is botanically and chemically different, and the so-called Siberian does not contain the active chemical found in the Chinese. The wild-grown Chinese is different from the field-grown. The wild sells for up to $1,300 per pound. Is it any wonder that these products vary in potency?[18]

In Germany, a different set of criteria is used to judge an herb's benefit. The German E Commission, one of several responsible for overseeing drugs, is responsible only for herbs, which are regulated as drugs, not as supplements. It is noteworthy that German physicians know as much or as little about supplements as their U.S. counterparts. German physicians rely on the E Commission for their information, but they write prescriptions for herbs because of the pressure applied by their patients. German law requires that herbs be tested only for safety, not efficacy. Thus, approval by the commission says nothing about a supplement's ability to do what its label says it will do. If a supplement claims the product will have a beneficial effect, irrespective of its approval by the E Commission, it is meaningless. But E Commission approval is important to American supplement manufacturers who use it as a potent marketing gimmick.[19] The U.S. FDA requires stringent proof of efficacy. Testing and standardization in the United States can cost millions of dollars for a single product, and they can take years to accomplish. Is it any wonder that the German E Commission is preferred and recommended by purveyors of supplements even in the United States?

In January 2000, Congress struck again. Not satisfied with giving the supplement industry unbridled freedom from FDA oversight, a new amendment opens the gates ever wider. We learn that although pregnancy, aging, and menopause are natural processes, certain conditions associated with them, such as morning sickness, memory loss, and hot flashes, which were once considered diseases, will no longer be considered as such, and supplements marketed to alleviate these conditions will no longer be required to prove either safety or effectiveness prior to entering the marketplace. Out to lunch? You betcha!

Given the huge pot of gold at the end of the supplement rainbow, we can anticipate an exponential expansion of this industry, and with it equally increasing harm to the unsuspecting. The DSHEA is far from Congress's finest hour, and Senator Orrin Hatch, the original sponsor of this overly generous legislation, has much to answer for. What's a person to do? Given the 4 un's—unregulated, untested, unstandardized, and of unknown effects—and given the disclaimer "not meant to diagnose, treat, prevent, or cure," why in the world would anyone choose to use these products? Given the choice, beneficent nature or *caveat emptor,* well, the choice is . . . yours.

Foodborne Disease

Some of us live to eat, and some eat to live. Whatever our predilection, all of us prefer to believe that our food is safe to eat. And why not? Our food supply is one of the safest in the world. But food is not sterile, and eating, like everything else, is not risk free.

Among the 281 million of us, 76 million, or 27 percent, will experience a foodborne illness in any given year. Most are mild, with stomach aches for a day or two. Others are more serious. Estimates suggest that over 300,000 individuals are hospitalized, and 5,000 die.[20] The most severe cases occur in the very young, the very old, and the immunosuppressed. Although the number of deaths and hospitalizations never make it to the top of the charts, they are unnecessary and entirely preventable. If so, to what can they be attributed? For the first fifty years of the twentieth century, foodborne illness was a fairly benign event. Most food was prepared locally, and if it was microbial-contaminated the disease-causing organism was usually staphylococcus or salmonella transmitted by cooks or other food handlers. The illness generally involved nausea, vomiting, and diarrhea, as the body attempted rapidly to rid itself of the ingested toxins. Today, the risk of foodborne disease depends on the type of food, where it was produced, its preparation and distribution, and the consumer's innate resistance to infection. Consequently, an array of exotic germs currently compromise our food, but because raw food has a natural content of microorganisms, we must distinguish between microbial food poisoning and food spoilage. Indeed, these are neither synonymous, nor are the differences subtle.

Spoiled food is usually produced by bacteria called pseudomonads and coliforms that feast upon poultry, red meats, fish, and cheese and thereby impart to these foods the typical off-odor, taste, color, and feel with which every homemaker is familiar. Many would consider a fruit spoiled and unfit to eat if it is partially or wholly covered with mold or yeast. Although it may be esthetically unattractive, it is not poisonous and would not evoke gastric or neurological distress if eaten. Many people simply pare away the moldy areas to savor the winey flavor imparted by microbial conversions of fruit sugar to alcohol. Cottage cheese and hamburger, two highly proteinaceous foods, are readily perishable and spoiled. For some, they become unfit to eat after a week of refrigeration. Yet others accept and eat them with equanimity. When is food unfit to eat? An appropriate reply might be: when its appearance and odor make it unappealing. Fortunately, or unfortunately, depending upon individual and cultural differences, little universal agreement exists as to what is and isn't edible.

Some people prefer their meat "high." Many, and I number myself among them, would call such meat spoiled and not fit to eat. To others it is sheer delight. "High" or "gamy" meat with its strong odor and taste is the result of bacterial metabolism. Titmuck, an Eskimo delicacy, is fish buried to allow bacterial fermentation. Eskimo dogs refuse to eat this semi-liquid, foul-smelling snack that most of us would label putrid. Yet it is putrefaction that gives Limburger cheese its gourmet qualities and distinguished price. These examples of "spoilage" are the result of increased growth in the numbers of bacteria and mold, along with the by-products of their metabolism, but they will not cause food poisoning. We may avoid and dislike the off-odor and taste of "spoiled" milk, meat, fish, poultry, or cheese, but they are not illness-producing. Food poisoning, also the result of increased microbial activity, is a different and subtly insidious process. In most instances, the presence of bacteria is wholly unsuspected. Off-odors, taste, color, and a mucid feel are absent, leaving us with no hint of suspicion. That's part of the problem: spoiled food smells but doesn't sicken, but poisoned food looks and smells benign yet can cause illness.

Most foods are subject to some degree of deterioration with time. Considering their ease of spoilage, foods can be ranked as nonperishable, semiperishable, or perishable. The degree of perishability simply refers to the ability of microbes to use our food for nourishment. Grains, sugar, flour, and beans are relatively nonperishable. Without adequate moisture, microbes cannot metabolize them or use them for food. Potatoes and apples, which contain more moisture, are semiperishable; while meat, fish, poultry, and milk—high protein, high moisture, highly perishable comestibles—are desirable sources of nutrients both for the microbes and for us. The pithy remark that "sanitation is nothing more than a race between man and lower forms of life to determine who gets to the food supply first" is easily digested. We don't always win this race.

A comment about ptomaines, another form of "poisoning." Ptomaine poisoning is an old idea that is hard dying. Although it has been established that ptomaines (from the Greek *ptoma*, meaning cadaver) produce a class of foul-smelling chemicals, they are not involved in food poisoning, microbial or otherwise. Chemically, ptomaines are aliphatic diamines, nitrogen-containing compounds, formed through the breakdown of proteins by our microbial friends. Actually, the well-named ptomaines, putrescine and cadaverine, are formed from the amino acids ornithine and lysine, respectively. With the further breakdown of amino acids to amines and ammonia, obvious odor, taste, and color changes occur along with surface film, or slime, from bacterial growth. That's the "feel" we've come to know from two-week-old hamburger, uncooked chicken, and steak. These changes are typical of spoilage, but do not cause food poisoning. Neither putrescine nor cadaverine is harmful when swallowed. If a large dose were introduced directly into the bloodstream, illness would occur, but not the food-poisoning variety.

So, what has changed in our lives to place us at risk of exotic microbes? How we diet, for one, has been changing radically. What and where we eat, where the food comes from, and how it is grown can determine if we are at heightened risk. Because we are concerned about cardiovascular disease and cancer, we've moved away from fatty foods to fruits and vegetables. This switch has so increased plant consumption that domestic production cannot slake the demand. The need for additional sources of supply has opened our borders to semitropical and tropical areas of the underdeveloped world: Mexico, Central and South America, the Caribbean, Africa, India, and Pakistan, where gastrointestinal illness is endemic.

To cater to our changing dietary requirements, restaurants have opened salad bars, which require extensive and continued food handling. Because of labor shortages and low wages, food handlers and kitchen personnel are often illegal immigrants who bring their diseases with them. The microbes enter kitchens and, too often, the food supply.

Fruits and vegetables can become microbially contaminated during growth, harvest, distribution, and preparation. In the field, contamination occurs via soil or feces of either domestic or feral animals and even humans. Pathogenic microbes on the hard, seemingly impenetrable surface of a melon, for example, can be carried to the moist, meaty interior when one slices into it. Since 1990, foodborne outbreaks have been associated with cantaloupes, onions, unpasteurized cider, apple juice, orange juice, lettuce, raspberries, blackberries, alfalfa sprouts, and sliced tomatoes.

Those who gravitate to unpasteurized milk and milk products, as well as those who dote on raw oysters, clams, ceviche (marinated, chopped raw fish), raw eggs, and raw and rare hamburger place themselves at increased risk. Shellfish filter bacteria from the gallons of water they imbibe daily. If pathogens are present, these uncooked clams, oysters, and mussels will become ready sources of infection. One raw hamburger may contain meat from hundreds of animals. An omelet made from frozen liquid eggs can have eggs from hundreds of chickens. If one animal is pathogen free, another may not be. The mixing of meats or eggs ups the ante.[21]

Although we live mostly in harmony with a microbially dominated world, opportunities abound for food to become contaminated. Those bugs need a food supply just as we do. And they find it—given a little help. For example, meat and poultry carcasses can become contaminated during slaughter by contact with intestines containing a trove of microbial flora. Similarly, fruits and vegetables, if washed or irrigated with water contaminated with human or animal manure or sewage, will readily become sources of infection. Canned food is not immune if water used in cooling tunnels is drawn from fecally contaminated waterways. As cans proceed from cookers to cooling tunnels, the still-hot cans expand in the heat; and, with their double-clinched seams still open, drops of contaminated water can seep in. When the cans cool and seams close tightly, the bacteria will have an opportunity to grow. Bacteria can even slip into a hen's ovary. A normal-looking egg can hold explosive surprises for an individual who sucks raw eggs.

In the food industry, unwashed hands of food handlers have been the source of hepatitis from infected workers. Cooked, microbial-free food can be recontaminated by infected workers and by contaminated utensils, slicing equipment, and cutlery.

Many microbes have a generation time of approximately half an hour; that is, they double their numbers every half-hour given the proper conditions. At low numbers, most do not induce illness, but given the right combination of room temperature, moisture, and food, and doubling in number every half-hour, a single bacterium can become over 20 million bacteria in half a day. Count them: 1, 2, 4, 8, 16, 32, 64, 128 ... and on and on. Doesn't sound like much, but you could garner a good deal of money this way. The next time you're asked what you'd like for a birthday present, humbly say: "Only a penny, but double it every half-hour from 8 A.M. to 8 P.M." Food that is initially contaminated with only a few bacterial cells, if left unrefrigerated overnight, could be highly infectious by morning. Refrigeration and freezing do not shut down bacterial growth; they merely slow it. But there are always exceptions. For example, high salt, sugar, and acid content prevent bacterial growth, which is why foods such as corned beef, pickles, pickled veggies in general, and jam have a long shelf life.

The Villains

Having discussed the conditions and the environment in which they operate, it is appropriate to turn to the villains in the drama of food safety.

E. coli. *Escherichia coli,* named for a German microbiologist, is commonly referred to as *E. coli.* Because it has figured so prominently in the news, *E. coli,* more specifically *E. coli* serotype O157:H7, obtains top billing. *E. coli* is part of the common normal flora inhabiting human and animal intestines. Most coliform are harmless, even beneficial, but several are toxin producers, which when ingested induce diarrhea and accompanying discomfort. Fewer yet are enterohemorrhagic, the cause of bloody diarrhea, the hemolytic uremic syndrome (HUS). This offensive group is known by its numbers: *E. coli* O157:H7. This combination of letters and numbers refers to specific markers—surface antigens—which enables it to be distinguished from hundreds of other *E. coli* strains. The

"O" refers to a site, an antigen on *E. coli*'s surface, and 157 refers to the 157th such site identified. Additional O's continue to be identified. *E. coli* is a motile bacterium. It swims, propelled by a thicket of flagella, the whiplike structures on its surface. It is these flagella that contain the site of the "H" antigen.

Although Escherich discovered the first *E. coli* in 1879, the first confirmed isolation of O157:H7 in the United States did not occur until 1975 in a California woman who had bloody diarrhea. That seemed to be a singular instance, but it wasn't to last: O157:H7 made a dramatic public reappearance in 1982, with two such outbreaks. Now, the National Centers for Disease Control and Prevention (NCDCP) have estimated that 73,000 cases occur annually in the United States. It is also known that 85–95 percent of all cases of HUS in North America are due to O157:H7, which has also been responsible for over sixty deaths a year. In an outbreak, the cases can follow a similar pattern. Among patrons of a multistate food service chain, for example, 731 cases occurred in four states: 629 in Washington; 13 in Idaho; 57 in Nevada, and 34 in southern California. Of the 731, mostly children, 195 were hospitalized, 55 developed HUS, and 4 died.[22] A pattern that has become all too familiar.

E. coli victims experience acute bloody diarrhea and abdominal cramps, with little or no fever. The bout is over in a week to ten days. For those with the HUS, kidney failure accompanies the diarrhea and often requires dialysis and blood transfusions. Some few develop kidney failure and neurological deficits—seizures and blindness. Death can occur in as many as 3–5 percent of cases and the remainder recover. But O157:H7 does get around. It can reside in the intestines of healthy cattle and consequently can be found on cattle farms. Meat can become contaminated during slaughter and the bacteria can be mixed into beef when ground.

E. coli present on cow udders or on milking equipment can get into raw milk—another reason for avoiding unpasteurized milk. The infectious dose of this organism is small. The hamburger patties implicated in the four-state outbreak in 1993 had fewer than seven hundred bacterial cells prior to cooking and far less than that after. Unlike the microbial mainstream where more is better, this *E. coli* is capable of causing a panoply of disagreeable symptoms with low numbers. Remember, too, that there are no off-odors or tastes and the food looks and tastes just fine. The 25 percent of our population who prefer their hamburgers rare to medium rare are placing themselves at increased risk of ingesting viable cells from the center of the patty, which remains uncooked.

Drinking or swimming in fecally polluted water can also be high-risk activities in terms of contracting *E. coli*. The bacteria can also be transmitted through direct contact if hand washing is not practiced regularly and frequently.

O157:H7 is unique in that it did not emerge in an underdeveloped country and come upon us via imported foods. Although is appears to have arisen here, whatever triggered its appearance remains unknown, which is discomforting from a preventive public health point of view. However, the Food-borne Diseases Active Surveillance Network, Food-Net, affords a measure of protection. It is the primary foodborne disease component of the NCDCP's Emerging Diseases Program (EDP). FoodNet is also a collaborative project of the NCDCP, of nine states—California, Colorado, Connecticut, Georgia, New York, Maryland, Oregon, and Tennessee (all in the EDP program)—the Department of Agriculture, and the Food and Drug Administration.[23] This national network actively scrutinizes new and emerging diseases and monitors and identifies the community burden of foodborne diseases. Its nine-state catchment area includes over 29 million people, some 11 percent of the entire U.S. population. This is a sea change from the former passive surveillance in which local health departments reported new cases—if they did, at all—to the state.

The core of FoodNet is laboratory based. Over three hundred laboratories in the nine states regularly test stool samples of reported diarrhea cases for *E. coli, Salmonella, Campylobacter, Cyclospora, Cryptosporidium, Yersinia*, and *Toxoplasma*, providing a comprehensive, up-to-date database. FoodNet also monitors each of the labs in the entire catchment area to assure their performance and to survey physicians' stool culturing practices for validation. It also surveys the population directly within an area by random interviews, permitting calculation of estimates of diarrheal diseases, and provides information on those foods most likely to be risks for illness. If people will pursue a more risk-averse lifestyle—drinking only pasteurized liquids, avoiding raw meats and raw shellfish, and washing fruits and vegetables, especially those coming in from exotic areas—the case rate will continue to fall.

Recently, the Department of Health and Human Services informed us that FoodNet surveillance data from 1997 to 1999 found that illness from the common foodborne pathogens had declined nearly 2 percent, almost

900,000 fewer sufferers. While such sizable reductions are welcome news, that still leaves 75 million foodborne cases annually. A lot of sick and unhappy campers. More effective preventive measures are needed.

Campylobacteriosis. Campylobacteriosis is yet another gastroenteric infection and is the province of *Campylobacter jejuni*: *Campylo*, from the Greek meaning *bent* or *curved*; and *jejuni*, from that portion of the small intestine between the duodenum and ileum, meaning *empty* or *fasting*. In ancient times the jejunum was believed to be empty after death. Another disposable myth. Nevertheless, there is much in a name.

Currently, *C. jejuni* is the most frequently isolated pathogen in Food-Net sites. While it is among the most important enteric pathogens, little is actually known about how this organism produces disease. This germ is unique: although it causes the most common of diarrheal illnesses, 95 percent of its isolations are from sporadic events, not part of outbreaks among large aggregations of people. Yet over 10,000 cases are reported annually, which comes down to about six cases per 100,000 people. However, it is but the tip of the campylobacteriosis iceberg; estimates of its actual numbers run to well over 2 million, or almost one percent of the population. It is seasonal, occurring mostly in June, July, and August, and is primarily a disease of youngsters, more often male than female. Rough estimates suggest some five hundred deaths per year among those affected.[24]

Most cases have been associated with the handling of raw poultry or the eating of raw or undercooked poultry. Investigations have also found that infections have occurred when raw vegetables were prepared on unwashed cutting boards that were previously used to cut poultry. Drinking unpasteurized milk and consuming unpasteurized milk products are other sources of *C. jejuni* infection, as is contact with fecal matter from infected pets such as cats and dogs.

It appears that poultry are asymptomatic carriers of this bacterium. When the meat is prepared for marketing, the bacterium can be transferred from its intestines to the meat. Giblets, gizzards, livers, and hearts are readily contaminated. Unpasteurized milk becomes contaminated from udder infections as well as itinerant manure. Even mountain streams, normally thought to be pristine, can be contaminated by the droppings of wild birds.

The major preventive measures are to avoid unpasteurized milk, raw and undercooked chicken, both at home and away, and to wash one's hands vigorously with soap after contact with pet feces.

Salmonellosis. Vanilla ice cream. Imagine. The largest outbreak of salmonellosis in U.S. history was caused by vanilla ice cream containing the intestinal pathogen *Salmonella enteritidis.* This was a highly unusual occurrence because large companies that distribute ice cream nationwide (that's another major change that can engulf huge numbers of people) use nothing but pasteurized milk, and the heat of pasteurization kills all Salmonellae. It's the home-made ice cream and ice cream made from unpasteurized milk that is the usual and common source of salmonellosis. So, how could commercially made ice cream lay low so many thousands of people? Yes, thousands. Hundreds of thousands!

Tanker trailers hauling thousands of gallons of ice cream made from base premix had hauled nonpasteurized liquid eggs to processing plants before taking on the ice cream. That would have been O.K. had the tanker drivers not broken established work rules, which required tankers hauling unpasteurized liquid eggs to be thoroughly washed and sanitized before loading the ice cream premix. In this instance, tanker after tanker was found to have bypassed the protocols. The salmonella-containing liquid eggs contaminated the premix, which was not repasteurized after transportation, and 224,000 vanilla ice cream lovers became unwilling half-steppers.[25] Can this happen again? Will it happen again? Yes to both, but for the second "yes" I suspect it will be some time before that human error crops up again. The only way to prevent it is to take control away from drivers and maintenance personnel. Either liquid eggs cannot be delivered in trucks that also carry premix, or trucks that have discharged a load of liquid eggs are automatically sealed when their contents are emptied and cannot be opened until they are in a cleaning station, or some such unit. But that's asking too much of the trucking industry personnel, as it prevents rapid turnaround time. So expect it to happen again.

These salmonella organisms are named for Dr. Daniel Salmon, an American veterinarian, who isolated the microbe in 1885. Microbiologists have since identified over 2,300 serologically separate strains from all over the world. These are truly global germs. In addition to causing salmonellosis, salmonella are responsible for typhoid fever, which is primarily a waterborne malady and the domain of the microbe *S. typhimuriem.* This can be a serious illness with a persistent, spiking fever of 103°–104° F for weeks. Alternating sweats and chills, weakness, and head and body aches are typical. Recovery is usually complete, but individuals may become asymptomatic carriers, showing no signs of the disease. They can continue to pass on the organism, which means that other people can become infected from contact with feces or urine.

Salmonellosis is a typical foodborne illness having an onset 12–36 hours after eating a food containing the organism and its toxin. Typical symptoms include nausea, vomiting, diarrhea, mild fever, and abdominal pain. Symptoms are most severe in the very young, the elderly, and the immunosuppressed. Those with the milder symptoms recover in 3–7 days without treatment. A minority may develop Reiter's syndrome with symptoms of joint pain, eye irritation, and painful urination, which can last for an extended period.

The name to remember is *S. enteritidis*, the salmonella most often associated with the 40,000 confirmed cases annually. Because the milder cases go unreported, estimates of the total number must run well over a million. As *S. enteritidis* and related strains are normal intestinal flora of animals and birds, the microbe is ordinarily transmitted to people via fecally contaminated poultry, the most notorious contributor, along with eggs, milk, beef, and vegetables. All salmonella are stopped in their tracks by the heat of cooking and pasteurization. Drinking unpasteurized milk, sucking raw eggs, eating raw or rare meats, especially chicken, turkey, duck, and other game birds, should be viewed as an extreme sport, an exceptionally high-risk activity. It is well to recall that Salmonellae need only a few cells to induce typical symptoms, and that contaminated foods look fine, having no off-odors or tastes. Prevention is further enhanced by thoroughly washing hands with soap and water after handling turtles, iguanas, and lizards, which harbor salmonella and unfortunately have become household pets.

The incidence rate (new case rate) of salmonellosis among individuals with AIDS is far greater than among the public generally. Given the low doses of organisms needed for a frank clinical infection, the immunosuppressed are at far greater risk.

The Bhagwan Shree Rajneesh Incident. The Dalles, Oregon, a small community of some 11,000 people and located near the Columbia River on Interstate 84, is the county seat of Wasco County. Because of its natural beauty, it is a favorite stop for travelers. It is also the headquarters of the Rajneesh religious commune.

Between September 9 and October 10, 1984, at least 751 people were laid low by *Salmonella typhimurium*, a highly unlikely foodborne pathogen. Members of the Rajneesh commune had deliberately contaminated salad dressing in at least ten self-service salad bars in order to poison voters in an election year. It took the NCDCP's medical detectives over a year to finally crack the case. They could not believe that anyone would purposely contrive to poison a community. In subsequent criminal proceedings, two members of the Rajneesh cult were sent to prison. The candidate they had supported didn't get elected.[26]

Ground Beef. Ground beef is yet another microbe carrier, exacting a heavy toll of illness and death upon the unsuspecting, especially when it is not fully cooked and salmonella or *E. coli* is on site. Cooking ground beef to "well done" raises the possibility that the heat of cooking may form heterocyclic amines, chemicals such as 2-amino-3, 8 dimethylimidazo (4, 5-f quinoxaline) (MeIOx), 2-amino-3, 4, 8-trimethylimidazo (4, 5-f quinoxaline) (DiMeIOx), and 2-amino-1-methyl-6-phenylimidazo (4, 5 f pyridine) (PhIP), from chemicals naturally present in ground muscle tissue: creatinine, amino acids, and sugars. Would any right-thinking burger eater want to chomp into any of these jaw-breaking brutes? Certainly not. Nevertheless, these heat-induced amines can be present in nanogram quantities (10^{-9})—extremely low—yet test-tube studies suggest they are potent carcinogens. Therefore, in order to kill off salmonella and *E. coli* and other fellow-traveling pathogenic microbes but to prevent the formation of amines, imaginative cooking is called for.

Recently, a creative team of researchers at the Biology and Biotechnology Research Program at the Lawrence Livermore Laboratory in Livermore, California, studied this tantalizing culinary conundrum. For them, the heated question was: Can there be hamburger that is at once devoid of pathogens—as a result of cooking to their appropriate killing temperatures—yet simultaneously be carcinogenically safe, containing a low level or no heterocyclic amines, formed from precursor chemicals by the heat of cooking?

To their surprise, this adventuresome band of researcher-chefs found that turning ground beef patties every minute prevented the formation of DiMeIOx and PhIP at 160°C and 180°C (320° and 356° F, respectively). MeIOx formed readily at all temperatures, but at far lower levels when patties were turned every minute. Veteran burger flippers will surely latch on to this technique, as they will no longer be seen as pretentious exhibitionists, but rather as health-care specialists. Briefly stated, the procedure requires preheating a pan to 160° C (320° F), then frying to an internal temperature of 70°C (156° F), and flipping the patties every 60 seconds.

This constant flipping eliminates microbes and reduces the amines to safe levels. The guiding physical principle is worth listening to: "The upper surface of the meat loses heat to the air because of convection and evaporation of water from the surface, which cooks the meat faster with more frequent turnings." And they continue, "Some of the precursors (creatinine, amino acids, and sugars from the tissue) would be less likely to reach the lower meat surface and become hot enough to begin forming heterocyclic amines before the patty is turned and the fluid reverses direction. The faster cooking rate due to frequent turning, the repeated cooling of the upper surface, and the movement of the precursors inside the patty create conditions that are less favorable for heterocyclic amine formation."[27] The number of flipped and unflipped hamburgers that were required to obtain this revealing information was not reported. A startling omission.

Listeriosis. It is uncharacteristic for *Listeria monocytogenes* to be included among recognized foodborne pathogens. Consequently, it has only recently been deemed to be an important public health and foodborne problem. The illness, listeriosis, is a rare but serious nonenteric condition, especially for pregnant women, infants, and immunosuppressed adults. For most foodborne pathogens, gastrointestinal symptoms are the principal complaints. Listeriosis and *L. monocytogenes,* its inducing microbe, do not fit the mold, as the organism can be fearfully invasive. Its affinity is for the central nervous system, especially the brain. Settling in the meninges, the membrane covering the brain and spinal cord, it initiates inflammation (meningitis), with symptoms ranging from stiff neck and headache to confusion, loss of balance, convulsions, and death. Pregnant women may show only mild, flulike symptoms, but infection during pregnancy, especially in the third trimester, can lead to stillbirth, abortion, or premature delivery. Unfortunately, pregnant women are many times more likely to become infected than women generally. Fully 30 percent of all cases occur during pregnancy. Why this is so remains to be unraveled. On the other hand, immunosuppressed individuals, those with impaired T-cell immunity, as in AIDS cases, are hundreds of times more likely to become infected than the general population. The mystery is heightened because pregnant women do not have this T-cell, or other immune deficiency. In the United States, Listeria sickens some 2,500 people and kills about 500 people, annually.

Listeria has become not only a public health concern but also a food-business concern because of its ability to survive for long periods in soil, water, and food. Also disturbing is the germs' ability to grow and multiply excessively at temperatures below 5° C (41° F). The bacterial cells gain entrance to food processing plants via soil on workers' shoes, trucks, and animal hides, and on other surfaces.[28] Vegetables become contaminated from soil or manure used as fertilizer. Here, again, unpasteurized milk and foods made from raw milk are also likely sources.

Of the half-dozen listeria-induced outbreaks between July and September 1994, in Illinois, Michigan, and Wisconsin, the villain of the piece was commercially pasteurized chocolate milk. In one of the six outbreaks, it was the strange taste of the chocolate milk that was noted. It was found, however, that in this singular instance, the outbreak "was most likely caused by post pasteurization contamination due to poor sanitation practices at the milk company and exacerbated by holding temperatures in transit to the picnic that allowed the rapid growth of Listeria."[29] Of additional concern in these outbreaks was the fact that the organism caused gastric distress in some and invasive neurological symptoms in others. Obviously, Listeria cannot yet be counted on to follow a textbook prescribed course of action. Consequently, with this organism's many talents, it is absolutely essential that the two high-risk groups, the immunosuppressed and pregnant women, avoid raw milk and milk products as well as raw and rare meats.

Of more than passing interest is the fact that recent studies have shown *L. monocytogenes* to be easily killed by low doses of irradiation, a take-away point to bear in mind.

Yersiniosis. Yersinia enterocolitica is another relatively new addition to the mélange of organisms that have a proclivity for the human gut. Although human yersiniosis has been recognized for over half a century, foodborne infections are comparatively new. Given its close relationship to farm animals, especially pigs, this is a surprising circumstance. *Y. enterocolitica*, a close relative of *Y. pestis*, the germ that brought us the plague, is most often transmitted by eating raw or rare pork products. Chitterlings—raw pork intestines—may be the most risky of all. Infants can be readily infected by anyone handling raw chitterlings and failing to adequately wash their hands before picking up and holding a baby or its toys. Drinking raw milk can also give you yersiniosis, plus about half a dozen other impressive diseases.

FoodNet's database estimates some 2,700 cases of this infection per year. Children under five are at greater risk than adults, and transmission is greater in winter than summer, which is somewhat perverse given the fact that its optimal temperature for doubling its numbers is 28°–30° C (82°–86° F). Yersinia has the uncanny ability to reproduce at temperatures ranging from 0° to 44° C (32° F–111.2° F). With such talent, caution is obviously called for. Fortunately, most cases appear to be uncomplicated and enjoy rapid recovery. The diarrhea is usually mild, as is the abdominal pain. The acidity of the gastric contents is protective as the microbe succumbs readily to high acidity, which places individuals with low stomach acid at increased risk. A small proportion of children can sustain bloody diarrhea, lasting a few days to weeks. Some women have responded to the organism's presence with erythema nodosum, a rash on their legs and body, which can persist for weeks.

Prevention is based on avoidance of raw and rare pork and unpasteurized milk products. Not to be forgotten is the washing of hands after handling chitterlings and before touching children, their toys, bottles, and pacifiers.[30]

Toxoplasmosis. Toxoplasmosis has been among us long enough for 30–50 percent of all adults to have developed antibodies to *Toxoplasma gondii,* the infecting organism, a parasitic protozoan. This means some 60–140 million of us have been exposed to the organism. But our intact immune system keeps us disease free. Here again, two groups are at risk: pregnant women and immunosuppressed individuals. Estimates indicate that about three thousand children are born transplacentally infected each year. The majority of congenitally infected infants are asymptomatic at birth. But later in life, a cascade of symptoms such as loss of hearing and vision, mental retardation, and premature death can occur.

The ongoing AIDS epidemic has also provided a large and steady susceptible population for this protozoan. In a compromised immune system, the organism has little to prevent its passage to the brain and spinal cord, causing convulsions, paralysis, coma, and eventual death.

Cats are the culprits. Outdoors, cats eat birds and mice that are normal, healthy carriers of *T. gondii,* bringing the parasite inside where it can be shed in feces. Careless handling of litter is a well-documented means of infection. Indoors, the source of the germ is uncooked pork, lamb, and venison. Simply touching raw meat, then touching hands to lips, is sufficient to set an infection in motion. These meats can be safely eaten after cooking to an internal temperature of 155°–160° F (67°–70° C).

Like people, cats rarely exhibit symptoms when first infected. Cat owners have no idea that their cats may be carriers, and there are no tests to determine possible infection. To prevent exposure, cat litter should be disposed of in sealed bags. Pregnant women should have someone else deal with the litter, and when gardening, they should wear gloves, especially when handling soil. They should thoroughly wash hands before preparing food, and also carefully wash homegrown vegetables. If they must handle raw meat, they should wear plastic gloves, and they should not taste meat before it has been well cooked. And remember that microwave cooking does not necessarily destroy all *T. gondii* cells.

Finally, handling stray cats is a high-risk activity for pregnant women and for the immunosuppressed. Both groups should think carefully about bringing new outdoor cats into their homes.[31] Pregnant women are at far greater risk than their nonpregnant sisters because their cell-mediated immune response is decreased—a normal response during pregnancy to protect the developing embryo from the body's foreign tissue rejection response. Information such as this may enhance preventive measures.

Cyclosporiasis. Is there a better way to transplant a foreign parasite than bringing it home with you? That's how *Cyclospora cayetanensis* and its illness, cyclosporiasis, entered the United States, via Americans with diarrhea returning home from Nepal, Haiti, and Mexico. A study of the U.S. Embassy community in Katmandu, Nepal, including expatriates, found that 7 percent of family members were infected. Before 1996, cyclosporiasis was seen only sporadically and limited to foreign travelers. But in the spring of 1996, some 1,500 cases were reported around the United States and Canada, and another 1,000 in 1997, all attributed to eating fecally contaminated raspberries from Guatemala, where the diarrhea is endemic, mesclun lettuce, and basil. The basil and lettuce were from gourmet food stores in Virginia, Maryland, and Florida, and their paternity remains to be determined.

Cyclospora is not your typical garden-variety microbe. It is not a bacterium but a near relative of *Toxoplasma*. Both are known as coccidian protozoan pathogens whose presence and illness have been reported worldwide, but not in the United States until recently.

Transmission of the reproductive cells occurs via direct ingestion of fecally contaminated food and water. Infected individuals typically have explosive, watery diarrhea, abdominal bloating, cramps, and nausea. Flulike symptoms with muscle and bone ache often precede the onset of diarrhea.

For the immunologically competent, the illness is self-limiting but does last several weeks. Loss of appetite and weight loss are common.

Although blackberries, raspberries, and vegetables were implicated in the massive outbreaks, sporadic cases have found the parasite present in undercooked meat and poultry. An airline pilot recently became ill when he brought food on board that had been cooked in a Haitian kitchen. Unfortunately, wastewater in sewage lagoons has been used to irrigate pastureland, corn and berry fields, and vegetable crops.[32] Unless and until it is amply demonstrated that imported fruits and vegetables have been grown by standards deemed appropriate in the United States, consumers should stay with domestic produce, a reasonably preventive strategy. Rinsing fruits and vegetables does not reliably remove *Cyclospora*'s reproductive cells. Only irradiation accomplishes that. That's worth thinking about.

Food choice and food consumption in a global-village world places a vast array of new and exotic foods at our fingertips and on our tables. It also brings us closer to new and exotic diseases with which our medical community has had little experience. Even when all is done preventively, far too many of us will remain at risk, and foodborne illness will persist.

Protecting Our Food Supply

Insight into the degree of difficulty required to protect our food supply from inferior imports may be illuminating. From the U.S. General Accounting Office (GAO) we learn that the FDA and Customs have historically had problems stopping importers from distributing unsafe foods under the FDA's jurisdiction. Investigations by Customs confirm that the problems not only continue, but the procedures for controlling suspect shipments are easily circumvented. The GAO informs us that rather than requiring that detained suspected shipments be destroyed or returned, the FDA allows them to present lab test results as evidence that the shipments meet U.S. standards. But all is not as it seems because—and this borders on the unbelievable—the FDA does not have the authority to require importers to use designated laboratories: importers are free to choose their own labs for tests. As if that weren't trouble enough, the FDA does not certify the private labs chosen by the importers, who may also select the samples to be tested. Discrepancies between the FDA's test results and those from private labs are common, and importers are known to substitute shipments that have been tested as safe. It gets worse. In some instances, when the tested products failed lab tests, importers substituted other products for destruction rather than those the FDA wanted destroyed. It is also believed that the suspected products were sold on the U.S. market and consumed. Such evasions are seldom if ever punished. How bad is this laxity for consumers? Here's an example: in 1997, the FDA detained 7,874 import shipments. GAO found that most of these were released after importers presented their private laboratory results.[33] How many continents are on your plate tonight? We're eating out of a global garden—30 billion tons of it. Not all gardens are meant to be eaten out of. This is something to worry about. When the choice is between the cheaper Mexican or Central American strawberries and the American, choose the homegrown. Not for chauvinistic reasons, nor because of disapproval of the North American Free Trade Agreement. No, you choose the homegrown goods because they're inherently safer. We should be rejecting much of the "exotic" food coming in from Asia, Africa, and South America until the many exporting countries of these regions literally clean up their act. Until then, the only safe supply is the homegrown one.

Domestic food production can also be of concern. For example, under current federal law, federal inspectors must examine each meat and poultry carcass slaughtered, about 7 billion annually, and visit each of the approximately 5,900 meat and poultry processing plants at least twice during each operating shift. For other foods, the frequency of inspections is not mandated. According to the GAO, the inspection rate for foods other than meat and poultry has slipped from an average of once every three years in 1992, to once every eight years in 1994, to once every ten years more recently. Inspecting a food-producing plant once in ten years is simply ludicrous—another example of the fox guarding the hen house. Obviously, the food processors are telling the government how often they prefer to be inspected, if they have to be inspected at all. And you can bet that unannounced inspections have also been terminated. If government regulation doesn't protect us, what can?

It is both shameful and scandalous that every year millions—repeat, millions—of us become ill from microbially contaminated food, and literally thousands die. And, as we have seen, most are children and the otherwise healthy elderly. Ensuring the safety of domestically produced foods is sufficiently daunting, but ensuring the safety of imported foods, which are being consumed in ever greater quantities, especially from underdeveloped countries, borders on the impossible. The economic losses—the annual costs of medical care and lost productivity—are estimated to range from $7 to $37 billion.[34] The shame and scandal are especially egregious because the means to reduce illness and death by as much as 90 percent have been available for more than two decades. Food irradiation must take its place among the pantheon of accepted food preservation procedures. Until the public views food-borne illness and death as both unnecessary and unacceptable, the losses will continue. In the new millennium, it is time to cast off the regrettable baggage of the past.

There is also much to be concerned about regarding foodborne pathogens such as *E. coli* O157:H7. During a 1982 investigation of two outbreaks of severe bloody diarrhea, or hemolytic uremic syndrome, originating at the same fast-food chain, the Centers for Disease Control (CDC) identified a strain of *E. coli* O157:H7 that heretofore had not been recognized as a human pathogen. Commonly, *E. coli* is part of our normal gut flora, but not O157:H7, a verocytotoxin-producing strain, also referred to as enterohemorrahagic *E. coli* because it attacks the colon, producing bloody diarrhea. *E. coli* O157:H7 resembles the Shigella dysentery organisms, the known toxin producers, rather than the normally benign *E. coli* family. Whatever triggered the appearance of this "new" microbe remains elusive.

Cattle are the main source of infection, and most cases have been associated with the consumption of undercooked hamburger or raw milk. It does appear that meat becomes contaminated from intestinal contents at the time of slaughter. Indeed, hamburger can be a problem. Although there has been no increased consumption of ground beef in the United States over the past twenty years, the proportion eaten outside our homes, particularly in the fast-food sector, has increased substantially.

When hamburger is eaten rare or medium rare, as is the preference of some 25 percent of our population (bad, bad, bad), the ground meat contains living organisms. And because the infectious dose of O157:H7 is exceedingly small, it doesn't take more than a mouthful to produce an infection. Again, it's the behavior thing.

Food Irradiation

A solution to food contamination is irradiation. We've dallied overly long on the topic. The irradiation process has been demonstrated to be safe for the public in forty-one countries around the world. It's time to prevent the many deaths and illnesses we currently endure. With a safe and sure method of preservation available, it is unconscionable to keep the procedure from the marketplace. But hamburger is not alone.

Treating raw meat and poultry by irradiation at processing plants could eliminate *E. coli* O157:H7, salmonella, and *Campylobacter,* all commonly found on raw meat and poultry. Irradiating prepared ready-to-eat meats like hot dogs and deli meats could eliminate the risk of listeriosis and kill parasites like *Cyclospora* and the bacteria *Shigella* and salmonella. The benefit also applies to dry foods such as spices and grains that require extended storage and transportation over great distances. Because animal feeds are often contaminated with salmonella, irradiation would prevent the spread of salmonella and other pathogens to livestock. With capabilities of this magnitude, irradiation preservation should have taken its place alongside canning and freezing years ago. Furthermore, these microbes cause millions of unnecessary infections and thousands of hospitalizations in the United States every year. Irradiation can eliminate them entirely.

What is radiation preservation, or food irradiation, as it is often called? Radioactivity, a phenomenon accidentally discovered in 1896 by French scientist Henri Becquerel, is the key. Radiation is simply energy traveling through space, and radioactivity is the emission of radiation from the nucleus of atoms. Becquerel also discovered that during radiation the element uranium emits radiation steadily in all directions. Microwaves and radar are forms of radiation. But we shall see that not all atoms are radioactive.

By 1900, three types of radiation had been identified: alpha, beta, and gamma, named after the first three letters of the Greek alphabet. These three are distinguished by their penetrating ability. Alpha, with limited penetration, can be stopped by a thin film of water, a sheet of notebook paper, or light clothing. Beta is stopped by a sheet of cardboard and household aluminum foil. Gamma can be stopped only by several inches of lead or concrete: it alone has deep penetrating power.

Radiation is also divided into ionizing and nonionizing types. Ionization, used in processing and preserving food, and sterilizing medical instruments and single-use medical items such as surgical gloves, burn dressings, needles, cotton, and scalpels, has the requisite energy to change atoms into ions, that is, atoms that have lost electrons. Alpha, beta, and gamma rays can accomplish this and are forms of ionizing radiation. Other natural sources of ionizing radiation are our common building materials, cinderblock and brick, and the foods we eat, many of which contain small amounts of radioactive elements. Of course, we are bombarded daily by cosmic radiation—high-energy particles speeding in from outer space. These sources contribute to our natural background radiation levels. A household smoke detector contains a radioactive element. If held 20 centimeters—8 inches—from our bodies for one year, we would receive a dose of 2 millirem of radiation. Barely worth mentioning. Chest and dental X-rays contribute 10 millirem, but a two-packs-a-day cigarette smoker could be exposed to as many as 10,000 mrem/year because tobacco grows in soil.

One additional concept ends this short course in physics: radioactive isotopes. All atoms of a given element are not identical. Some elements have both lighter and heavier atoms. Atoms of greater or lesser masses are the isotopes, which emit alpha, beta, or gamma radiation. Well over a thousand isotopes emit radiation spontaneously. It is the highly penetrating gamma that is the choice for irradiation food preservation, the process of exposing food to controlled amounts of ionizing energy.

Food is passed through a field of ionizing energy either from machine-generated electron beams or from gamma rays from the element cobalt-60. The ionizing radiation passes through the food, generating large numbers of short-lived free radicals, which kill microorganisms and inhibit chemical processes, such as those that induce sprouting and ripening. At no time during the irradiation process does the food come into contact with the radiation source, and by using cobalt-60 or electron beams, neutrons are not produced so that it is not possible by either process to induce radioactivity in the food. That's a point that needs to be remembered. All energy passes through the food. There are no radioactive residues, nor can there be chain-reactions or meltdowns. The length of time food is exposed to the ionizing energy and the strength of the emitting source determine the irradiation dose the food receives.

Furthermore, radiation preservation is a "cold" process; only a slight temperature rise occurs in the food during the irradiation process. Thus, the procedure is especially attractive for normally heat-sensitive nutrients. With only a minimal rise in temperature, changes in flavor, color, odor, texture, and nutrient level are avoided. Consequently, the treated food retains its normal appearance, taste, and quality. Another benefit is flexibility. Irradiation can be used to preserve a variety of foods in a range of sizes and shapes: crates of potatoes; flour in 50- or 100-pound sacks; entire roasts of meat, whole turkeys, and/or sandwiches of sliced meat, fish, or chicken. The essential purpose of irradiation is to destroy indigenous microorganisms—bacteria, molds, yeast, worms—and thereby extend useful shelf life. The insurance of a safe food supply is of utmost importance.

In some studies, irradiation was found to reduce the Vitamin C level in oranges, but not as much as the natural variation between any dozen oranges taken from the same tree. Similarly, the reported loss in thiamin (Vitamin B_1) and riboflavin (Vitamin B_2) in irradiated pork was no more than the normal differences between a dozen slices of pork chops. In taste tests, trained experts consistently find no differences between irradiated and nonirradiated pork, beef, and meat patties.

That food irradiation is both safe and efficacious has been attested to by a plethora of concerned national and international organizations. So, for example, the World Health Association, Food and Agriculture Organization, Institute of Food Technologists, American Medical Association, American Dietetic Association, and an Expert Committee of the American Gastroenterological Association approved and advocated the use of food irradiation over a decade ago. And rightly so. Well over thirty years of investigation in half a dozen countries, producing hundreds of published studies, established the safety and usefulness of this procedure, one that could take its place at the table along with canning, dehydrating, freezing, smoking, pasteurizing, and pickling.

Over the past thirty years, the hope of finding something eerie, weird, or malign about irradiation has remained unfulfilled. Nevertheless, resistance persists, by those of the same ilk who have resisted pasteurization of milk, chlorination and fluoridation of water supplies, and the addition of iodine to salt. Radiation of food can save lives, which is the reason so many professional associations approve of it.

Irradiating food does produce radiolytic products, but they are identical to those produced by cooking, steaming, toasting, dehydration, and canning. So far, no one has demanded that we stop cooking and toasting. Hospitalized patients requiring the safest food—those receiving bone marrow transplants—eat irradiated food: the highest testimonial available. The FDA's Final Rule is clear: "In general," they tell us, "the types of products generated by irradiation are similar to those produced by other food processing methods."

At the doses of radiation specified in the FDA's Final Rule, 4.5 to 7.0 kiloGy microbes will be substantially reduced—but not totally eliminated. The Gray, Gy, is the unit of absorbed dose of radiation, a measure of the energy that is transferred. One kiloGy is equal to 1,000 Gy. Thus, the process is a pasteurization, not a sterilization. However, because different types of microorganisms have greater or lesser sensitivities to gamma radiation, the microbial profile of the food item will be altered. So, for example, bacteria such as the pathogen O157:H7 will be totally removed, as will salmonella, staphylococci, and listeria. Clostridial species, spore formers all, are hardier and will remain in small numbers. The spoilage organisms, *Pseudamonas, Lactobacilli, Leuconostoc,* and *Carnobacterium,* will also survive in small numbers. Over time, the small numbers will increase and the typical rising odors of spoiled meats, poultry, fish, and dairy products will advise that it is time to discard them. This is a far cry from having pathogens, the illness-provoking bacteria, on our dinner plates, rolls, or sandwiches. Indeed, two vastly different types of microbes are in competition with us for our food supply: the spoilage organisms that produce only off odors and taste but not illness, and the pathogens, the nasties, the illness producers, which play no part in spoilage but offer no clue of their lurking presence. Irradiation will readily dispose of them.

Pasteurization and sterilization may need another dollop of delineation. Think milk. Or beer. They're both heat treated for shelf life and safety. Milk as our model will do nicely. The heat treatment milk receives is based on the need to rid it of all mycobacteria, the organisms responsible for tuberculosis. In the process, the accompanying spoilage organisms are substantially reduced, but not totally eliminated. That could be easily accomplished, but the additional heat and time required would raise the temperature to boiling and surely ruin the milk for most people. Reduction but not total elimination of microorganisms is pasteurization. It provides a highly acceptable, safe product with a reasonable shelf life. The surviving beasties, enjoying all the available protein, carbohydrate, and fat, take about ten days to attain numbers sufficient to produce the noisome odors we call spoilage.

Think canned tuna, niblet corn, or corned beef hash. These are heat-treated in pressure cookers, which attain temperatures well beyond that of boiling water (212° F/100° C). To push sufficient heat through tuna, corn, or hash and attain indefinite shelf life, at least 250° F (121° C) is needed for as much as 20–30 minutes. That level of heat will kill all living things, including the most resistant bacterial spores, while cooking the hash, tuna, and corn to the right tenderness. Sterilization, then, is the complete destruction of all life. An all-or-none phenomenon. However, attention must be paid to the length of time that heat is applied. Overcook, and the products are inedible. It is the same with irradiation.

To sterilize beef, poultry, or fish, doses well above 10kGy would be required. At such levels, gamma rays slamming into tissue would induce unacceptable changes in texture, color, and odor. Consequently, the FDA, food processors, and food distributors agree that doses up to 7kGy are optimum, and that sterilization offers no practical or beneficial results that can't be achieved by pasteurization.

The FDA's salutary concluding remarks to its Final Rule are noteworthy. They tell us that "based on all the evidence before it, FDA concludes that irradiation of these products under conditions set forth in the regulation (below) will not present a toxicological hazard, will not present a microbiological hazard, and will not adversely affect the nutritional adequacy of such products. Therefore, the Agency concludes that irradiation of meat, meat byproducts and meat food products under the conditions set forth in the regulation below is safe."[35]

How safe is it? Irradiation treatment has been used routinely for more than thirty years to sterilize medical, dental, and household products, and it is also used for radiation treatment of cancer. Radioactive substances emit gamma rays continually. When not in use, the radioactive "source" is stored in a pool of water, which absorbs the radiation harmlessly and completely. To irradiate food, the source is raised out of the water into a chamber with massive concrete walls that prevent any rays from escaping. Medical products or foods to be irradiated are brought into the chamber and are exposed to the radiating source for a defined period of time. After use, the source is returned to the water tank. These types of facilities have been operated in this country for more than three decades without a fatal accident. Over one hundred such facilities are currently licensed, along with an equal number of medical radiation and bone marrow treatment centers around the country, which also use cobalt-60 to irradiate patients.

The safety of irradiated foods has been extensively investigated. Studies include feeding mice, rats, dogs, and other animals over several generations. No evidence of adverse health effects have been found in these well-controlled trials. In addition, NASA astronauts eat foods that have been irradiated to the level of sterilization—substantially higher levels than that approved for the population at large.

If we were to assign a value for the increased safety imparted by the cool gamma energy, the data on in-use experience in other countries, along with hospitals in the United States and NASA's use, suggest a 90 percent improvement level. Recall, too, that no other food processing method has had the long years of research and testing that irradiated food has had. Its forty-five-year history began in 1955, when the Department of the Army's medical department began its research at their facility in Natick, Massachusetts.[36] And in 1970, NASA adopted irradiated food for meat products eaten in space by astronauts.

An additional benefit to food derives from irradiation. The few bacterial cells that survive the radiation are destroyed at lower cooking temperatures than bacteria not so treated. Given these many benefits, it's understandable to learn of Wal-Mart's recent announcement that it will bring irradiated meats into its superstores. Irradiation may, in the beginning, increase the cost of fruits and vegetables by 2–3 pennies, and meats by possibly 5 cents per pound.

One of the key issues in determining consumer acceptance of food irradiation is the demand that treated foods be appropriately labeled. And they should be. People should know what they are purchasing. Accordingly, a distinctive label, the radura, an internationally agreed-upon standard and symbol, as shown in figure 3.1, bearing the notation "Treated with radiation," will be affixed to every package of irradiated food.

And what of radioactive waste—is there any? The food irradiation facilities themselves do not become radioactive, and do not create radioactive waste. That is another essential message to take away. Cobalt has a five-year half-life, which means that 50 percent of its total energy, its gamma radiation, decays, or is lost in five years, and another 50 percent in the ensuing five years, and on and on. Before totally decaying away, it requires periodic replacement. To accomplish this, the small "pencils" containing radioactive cobalt are reshipped to the original nuclear reactor, to be recharged for further use. There is no radioactive waste or residue. The shipment occurs in specially hardened steel canisters that have been designed and tested to survive crashes without breaking. Cobalt is a solid metal, and even if something should break, it will not spread through the environment. Given its relatively short half-life (five years) and its stable metallic form, the material is not a problem waste.

As 1997 passed into history, the FDA banned imports of raspberries from Guatemala. This unusually harsh action came on the heels of President Bill Clinton's initiative to improve the safety of imported produce and fruit. Why so harsh? As noted earlier, more than thirteen hundred cases of cyclosporiasis, a new illness in the United States, were reported in 1997.[37]

Twenty percent of all fresh raspberries sold in 1996 were from Guatemala, whose farmers planted their first vines only in 1987. The United States was being swamped by unsafe fruit. As someone remarked, "One does not have to leave home to contract traveler's diarrhea."[38] *Cyclospora cayetanensis,* the causative microbe, was crossing our border with impunity. Although President Clinton's new initiative to improve the safety of our nation's food supply was surely welcome, the means of virtually

FIG. 3.1. *Radura. The radura is an internationally agreed upon symbol of food treated by irradiation. The statement, "Treated by Irradiation," required by the FDA, will accompany the radura.*

eliminating cyclosporiasis is at hand and in place: irradiation. Those 1,300 cases should never have occurred.

There is a bevy of additional deserving reasons to promote irradiation. We are in an unrelenting race with a bewildering array of ravenous microbes and other parasites in our food supply. As much as one-fourth of the world's food supply is lost annually to microbial and pestilential spoilage. We're talking billions of dollars a year. Irradiation can easily cut that in half. Furthermore, irradiation is an energy-efficient form of food preservation. That's another plus. If that isn't recommendation enough, note that it also totally precludes the use of chemical preservatives. The irradiation process occurs after the food is packaged, which means the risk of recontamination is essentially zero. Adding all this to the fact of retention of freshness, retention of original nutritional status, no loss of flavor or appearance, and a return to medium and medium-rare hamburgers, we are left to conclude from such a calculus that we are indeed in thrall to a band of vocal, misguided Luddites opposed to the procedure. Shameful, and much to be concerned about. Change is overdue. But how is this to happen?

The American Medical Association's Council on Scientific Affairs published its Report No. 4, *Irradiation of Food*, in 1993. After a lengthy discussion of the process of food irradiation, it informed its membership and *Journal* readers that irradiated food was not only safe and efficacious, but a desirable addition to the pantheon of food preservation processes. It concluded by stating: "The Council on Scientific Affairs recommends that the AMA affirm food irradiation as a safe and effective process that increases the safety of food when applied according to governing regulations."[39]

Similarly, the American Dietetic Association, a national and international professional association of thousands of dieticians and nutritionists, published its position on irradiated foods. It had this to say: "The ADA encourages the government, food manufacturers, food commodity groups, and qualified food and nutrition professionals to work together to educate consumers about this additional food safety tool and to make their choice available in the marketplace."[40]

In addition, the Food and Agriculture Organization and the World Health Organization, both United Nations affiliate organizations, have endorsed food irradiation without reservation, as has the American Gastroenterology Association, thousands of physicians with professional expertise in the gastrointestinal tract. The list of endorsements is long and honorable.

U.S. Government Agencies
    Food and Drug Administration
    Public Health Service
    Centers for Disease Control and Prevention

U.S. Scientific Organizations
    American Veterinary Medical Association
    Council for Agricultural Science and Technology
    Institute of Food Technologists

National Association of State Departments of Agriculture
International Organizations
    International Atomic Energy Agency
    Codex Alimentarious Commission
    Scientific Committee of the European Union
    United Nations

They must be given high marks for their efforts. They're on the record. Unfortunately, that is not nearly enough. All of these efforts are passive. Not one has gone the extra mile to bring its recommendations to the public, where it would have an effect, change opinion, and with it, initiate more irradiation programs.

Unless and until each of these organizations or combinations of them actively reach out and bring their message to the people, nothing will change: illness and death will continue to pile up. In the United States, estimates suggest from 6 to 30 million cases of food poisoning annually. For *E. coli* O15:H7 only, with its devastating uremic hemolytic syndrome, a bloody diarrhea that wreaks havoc at both ends of the age spectrum, the CDC suggests there are 7,000–20,000 cases, with hundreds of deaths. These numbers, these *people*, appear to have little to no meaning or effect on environmentalists who are irrevocably opposed to food irradiation.

To oppose food irradiation today, after almost half a century of testing and proof that it is safe, is not just scandalous, it is criminal. The position that illness and death are preferable to food irradiation is pathologic. To overcome this neurosis, to silence the mischievous minority that presumes to speak, with authority, for the public and sow fear among legislators and food retailers, a new paradigm must emerge. While I gave high marks to those national organizations who went on record in support of food irradiation, I now rescind those high marks and in their place award F's for failure. Their on-the-record statements were feel-good statements, but they go nowhere, accomplish nothing. Has anyone ever read or heard of them? Has the media given voice to them? To regain their positions of excellence, they must become active and inform consumers—directly. How? By taking half- and full-page ads in newspapers across the country. These advertisements will bring the message of irradiation's safety and nutritional quality to the public. And for their part, radio and TV commentators must pick up on this effort and bring the message to their local communities. In our huge country, none of the media can reach all families. Only local efforts can succeed.

Radio and TV announcements must bolster that effort. The supermarket chains—the Winn-Dixies, Pathmarks, ShopRites, Krogers, Piggly-Wigglys, and others—will develop some stiffening in their spinal areas and stock their shelves with irradiated foods for their customers, who will respond positively once they obtain the correct information. The supermarkets have had a quarter-of-a-century to dwell upon this procedure. It's time for them to resist the heat applied by the antis.

Support should be enhanced by display posters provided by state and local chapters of the many professional organizations supporting food irradiation. These posters should be given to libraries, Y's, and supermarkets, and be augmented by handouts that people can take and share with family, friends, and neighbors. In addition, speakers can be provided for local businesses, garden clubs, and Y's, and state and local health departments can join the effort as another means of preventative health education. The public will be served. These educational materials and programs will have a profound effect on state legislators, such as in my own state of New Jersey, which has a sorry record of pandering to environmentalists on this issue. In 1992, the New Jersey state legislature proposed a total ban on irradiated food. Governor Thomas Kean, with a cooler, calmer head, managed to fend them off with a two-year moratorium. Currently a five-year moratorium is working its way through the Assembly, again under the aegis of the same sponsor, John Kelly, who has remained impervious to the mounting toll of illness and death.

It is also time for the thousands of members of professional organizations to realize that they, too, are citizens and voters, that bad decisions affect them as adversely as everyone else. Passivity is no longer acceptable. The means to deal effectively with microbial pathogens, to rid our food of them, is at hand. Given the recent food irradiation approvals, food distributors and retailers will need all the help they can get to assure that items are there to be purchased. For example, on July 20, 2000, the FDA announced that it had approved the use of ionizing radiation for fresh shell eggs to reduce their level of salmonella bacteria. The new regulation permits a treatment dose of up to 3 kGy,[41] and the eggs will bear the required Radura. Given the huge numbers of eggs consumed in the United States, and considering that fresh eggs are among the top three vehicles for transmission of salmonella and human salmonellosis, this federal approval will add a needed level of safety to the food supply. Furthermore, there was also good news for alfalfa sprouters. On November 3, 2000, the FDA approved the use of irradiation on seeds for sprouting, including alfalfa, to reduce its levels of pathogenic bacteria such as salmonella and *E. coli* O157:H7. Here, too, a considerable reduction in numbers of microorganisms will be achieved by irradiation of up to 5 kGy.[42] Finally, the FDA has also been petitioned to approve a large number of additional foods, such as preprocessed meats and poultry, and fruits and vegetables. When approved, the numbers of foods having obtained clearance will have more than doubled.

The Titan Company of San Diego, California, a food-irradiating company using electronic beam treatment—electronic pasteurization—recently announced that Omaha Steaks, International, Inc., a privately held Nebraska company nationally renowned for its premium steaks, red meats, and other gourmet foods, has contracted with Titan to have its ground beef line electronically treated—irradiated. Electron-beam processing utilizes high-energy negatively charged particles (electrons) as its microbicidal agent. These electrically charged particles emerge from a linear accelerator at tremendously high speeds, with energies ranging from 3 to 10 million electron volts, sufficient energy to penetrate food products in their final shipping containers. As the electrons flash through a food product, they create secondary particles, ions and free radicals, which disrupt the DNA chain of microbes on or within the depths of the product, destroying most of them. As with cobalt-60 irradiation, electron-beam food processing is a pasteurization process, not sterilization. Food irradiation produces foods with an extended shelf life, but not an indefinite one.

Currently the major users of irradiated foods in the United States are health-care and food-service establishments. Nursing homes and hospitals serve irradiated foods to patients with weakened immune systems. Can there be a better endorsement?

Have you been had by the negative mess on food irradiation? You bet you have!

Food, Cancer, Heart Disease

The impact of diet on cancer incidence in Western countries has been variously estimated to range from 30 to 70 percent.[1] It has also been suggested that diet can protect *against* cancer. Given this knowledge, Americans have made widespread dietary changes: meat and dairy products have given way to fruits and vegetables, which are said to contain anti-tumorigenic ingredients in the form of chemicals. So certain was this linkage that in 1991 the National Cancer Institute initiated and promoted its "Five-a-Day for Better Health" program, which set a goal of thirty-five servings of fruits and vegetables per week for everyone. Does diet protect against cancer? At all sites? If not, at which? Is the evidence for such a relationship presumptive or conclusive? How was this presumed association determined? For prevention, it is reasonable to inquire what causes cancer and by what means or mechanisms. Understanding carcinogenesis is critical if rational approaches to prevention are to emerge.

Cancer is a collection of diseases sharing the common characteristic of uncontrolled cell growth. Essentially, an oncogene must be switched on and a tumor suppressor gene switched off for this to occur. The clinically observable condition we call a cancer or tumor is the result of a sequence of events requiring a succession of mutations (directed changes in a gene's content of information) that progressively alters a cell's genetic makeup in the direction of runaway growth. That progression includes initiation, promotion, proliferation, and lesion: a tumor.

Initiation is the stage in which a cell's gene or genes are impacted and altered, predisposing them to cancer. The rule, however, is that cells normally repair abnormalities. Otherwise, cancer would be a fact of everyone's life. So-called initiated cells are often destroyed as part of the body's normal defenses. Apoptosis, the term given to programmed cell death, is a process that selectively eliminates cells with damaged DNA, preventing the flourishing of neoplastic cells. But apoptosis can be blocked—circumvented; in effect, we have a kind of warfare in our cells, a give and take, a balancing act, and mutations can accumulate and tumors occur, but that is the exception to the rule. Recall that though some 20 percent of us will have a form of cancer at some point over a seventy- to eighty-year lifetime, *80 percent of us will not.* Nevertheless, we are continuously exposed to internally generated or externally imposed mutagenic risk factors. The cells' normal energy metabolism releases millions of highly reactive molecules— byproducts—minute by minute, the result of oxidative reactions. These include superoxide, hydrogen peroxide, and the hydroxyl radicals, all mutagens and potential carcinogens that can affect DNA by altering the information content of the DNA code, the message center. The great majority of dietary mutagens are more than likely natural components of our food, as are the potential anticarcinogens.

A number of chemicals are promoters, which can cause initiated cells to grow excessively and become cancerous. Proliferation is the final stage in which cells begin their uncontrolled growth. Again, however, at each of the four stages, the body's immune system can kick in and reverse the process. If proliferating cells do not invade surrounding tissue, the tumor is said to be benign. If it does invade, it is malignant.

With that as prelude, how, then, can diet cause cancer?

Food can be contaminated by preformed carcinogens. Aflatoxins are a group of related chemicals derived from the common fungi *Aspergillus flavus* and *A. parasiticus*, which, given adequate warmth and moisture, can grow profusely on corn and peanuts and have been linked to liver cancers. Nasopharyngeal cancer has been associated with consumption, early in life, of fermented foods and salted fish.[2]

Carcinogens may be formed in the body by bacterial action. Nitrites ingested along with preserved meats and fish can readily be converted to nitrates by intestinal bacteria, and then, in combination with amines, form potentially carcinogenic N-nitroso compounds. Over three hundred of these N-nitroso compounds are known animal carcinogens. Several of these may induce stomach, bladder, colon, and esophageal tumors in individuals with chronic gastritis, urinary and large bowel infections, as well as those with infections of the oral cavity.

Mutagens such as benz (alpha) pyrene, a polycyclic hydrocarbon, may be ingested along with charcoal-broiled meats. And high-fat diets can increase bile production (a steroid acid), which stimulates bacterial growth in the colon, and which in turn may produce carcinogens. This process offers an explanation for the observed association between high-fat diets and cancers of the colon, breast, and prostate. How factual an explanation it is remains to be resolved.

Overeating leading to obesity has been linked to endometrial and postmenopausal breast cancers. This is a possible example of tumor promotion through excess endogenous estrogen derived from androgens occurring in fatty tissue, which is exacerbated in obese women. In addition, early age at menarche, under 12, appears to be another risk factor for breast cancer, as is late menopause, which is also a risk for endometrial cancer. Both cancers have been linked to excessive fat and high calorie consumption. These examples suggest that diet may offer avenues for cancer causation.

On the other hand, other elements in our diets may protect against cancer. Anticarcinogens, chemicals present in our food, may neutralize the activity of potential carcinogens. Diets high in fresh fruits and vegetables have been associated with decreased risk of cancer of the entire alimentary canal, the respiratory system, and the uterine cervix. Foods rich in retinol (preformed Vitamin A) have been linked with reduced risk of epithelial cancers—stomach, colon, rectum, breast, kidney, and lungs. Currently there is a profusion of possible protective micronutrients, making it excessively difficult to isolate and identify if any are protective. Micronutrients may also function at different sites, which implies more than one protective mechanism. Accordingly, several possible mechanisms have been suggested: antioxidant activity is one.

Without oxygen there is no life. Oxygen is critical for cellular respiration as well as a host of oxidative reactions throughout the body. But oxygen can be toxic. Oxygen stress on cells occurs via accumulation of structural damage from the incessant bombardment by metabolically generated free radicals.

Chemical compounds consist of two or more elements bound together by a chemical bond. This bonding involves negatively charged particles, the electrons. The arrangement of these electrons determines the stability of the compound. A stable compound has paired electrons; an unpaired electron is trouble—unstable and highly reactive, seeking stability. A compound with unpaired electrons is called a free radical, and to stabilize itself, a free radical seeks to capture an electron from a stable compound. This type of seeking creates additional free radicals—oxidants—resulting in a chain reaction, a cascade, until the unpaired electron pairs up or is deactivated by an antioxidant, enzyme, or scavenger.

Free radicals, or oxidants, are formed minute by minute via normal body processes. Bruce Ames and his research team at UCLA have estimated the number of oxidant hits to DNA at about 10,000 per day in human cells—compared to 100,000 in rodent cells.[3] In addition to internal generation, free radicals can be generated by a variety of factors: cigarette smoke, radiation, and herbicides. Both the internal and externally generated radicals can induce cell damage and death. Free radicals have been linked to DNA breakage, destruction of endothelial cells lining blood vessels and other organs, the inflammatory response seen in arthritic joints, heart disease, and premature aging. But the body is not passive. Protective systems limit damage. Enzymatic DNA repair is highly effective at maintaining mutations at minimum levels. Damaged DNA is repaired by enzymes that excise the lesions, which are excreted in urine, and can be assayed. Antioxidant defenses play a dual role: prevention of free radical generation, and interception of those that are generated. Vitamin C (ascorbic acid) is well known for its quenching of oxygen radicals, and Vitamin E (tocopherol) is one of the most important free radical scavengers—a chain-breaking antioxidant intercepting and stopping lipid peroxidation chain reactions. The enzymes superoxide dismutase, catalase, and glutathione peroxidase deal effectively with oxidant byproducts: superoxide, hydrogen peroxide, hydroxyl radical, and the aldehyde products of lipid peroxidation.

The body has other defenses, too. Vegetables of the Brassicaceae, the mustard family (plants with pungent seeds)—cabbage, kale, broccoli, cauliflower, rutabaga, turnips, rape, and mustard—have been suggested as inducers of enzymatic reactions, which may detoxify ingested carcinogens. So, for example, chomping down on broccoli sprouts may release isothiocyanates in the form of their glucosinolate precursors such as sulforaphane, which made headlines in 1997 and gave the world phytochemicals, which were touted as the magic bullets for cancer prevention to dwell upon. Indeed, sulforaphane and other plant-derived chemicals are inducers of phase 2 enzymes, which appear to remove carcinogens from cells. When published, the Johns Hopkins research informed us that three-day-old broccoli sprouts had ten thousand times the level of sulforaphane as mature plants and were highly effective in reducing the incidence and rate of development of mammary tumors in rats treated with a known carcinogen.[4] But they also noted, and this is an important "but," *that little is known of the metabolism of the glucosinolates in humans,* that is, the metabolism and possible protective effects of sulforaphane in humans *is not known.* For the media, that caveat was simply ignored. Rockefeller University researchers reported that the phytochemical indol-3-carbinol (I3C), another glucosinalate metabolite

from crucifers, inhibits carcinogenesis in rodents, but "clinically relevant biochemical and cellular mechanisms for the anticarcinogenic effects of IC3,
however, remain unclear."[5] Translated, it means that we don't know and have
no data about its effects in humans. For *Newsweek*, however (April 24,
1994), sulforaphane's benefits for rats meant similar benefits for humans.
Never mind the fact that the authors of the published article made a clear
point of the fact that they had not done any human trials and could not predict effects in people. This, unfortunately, is the type of hype that confounds
and misleads the public and gives science and scientists a bad press. But the
caveat was there. For the scientists, it was essential. As Robert Koch reminded us years ago, "A mouse is not a man." We forget this at our peril. But
it does not mean that young broccoli sprouts and other crucifers do not contain protective chemicals. It does mean that if benefits are to be derived, they
are yet to be found. Again, we are in thrall to that distasteful uncertainty factor that must be lived with—at least temporarily.

Kristi A. Steinmetz and John D. Potter did yeoman work in reviewing
228 studies—206 human epidemiological studies—and 22 animal studies
on the relationship between fruits and vegetable consumption and risk of
cancer.[6] They found that evidence for a protective effect of greater vegetable and fruit consumption is consistent for cancers of the stomach,
esophagus, lung, oral cavity, pharynx, endometrium, pancreas, and colon.
And they reported that the types of vegetables and fruits that most often
appear to be protective are raw vegetables, allium vegetables (onions, garlic, red pepper), carrots, green vegetables (dark green vegetables, green
leafy vegetables, green and yellow vegetables), cruciferous vegetables
(Brussels sprouts, broccoli, cauliflower, and tomatoes). They noted, too,
the noncancer-related effects of increased vegetable and fruit consumption, including benefits against heart disease, diabetes, stroke, obesity, di-
verticulosis, and cataracts.

For the twenty-two animal studies, which showed remarkably strong
relationships, Steinmetz and Potter cautioned us that "extrapolation of results of animal studies to human beings is difficult given species differences, the use of administered carcinogens, the use of genetically
susceptible animals, and relative doses of vegetables well above those typically consumed by human beings." Massive doses of carcinogens fed to
animals will often mean massive doses of an anticarcinogen to counter the
effects, doses that no human could ever consume. This raises a red flag. In
their 1997 publication, Paul Talalay and his Johns Hopkins team stated
that it is the consumption of large quantities of fruits and vegetables that is

associated with the positive benefits obtained. What constitutes large amounts may or may not be drawn from the National Cancer Institute's Five-a-Day campaign, which exhorts us to eat five or more servings of fruit and vegetables every day—thirty-five per week. Five-a-Day may prove to be adequate. Then again, it may not.

Of the 206 epidemiological studies reviewed by Steinmetz and Potter, 20 were prospective cohort studies, the remainder retrospective case-control studies. Together they demonstrated a spectacular degree of consistency—a strong, positive relationship between cancer protection and consumption of fruits and vegetables. While consistency is an essential criterion for establishing a cause-effect relationship (refer to chapter 7), it is only one of seven essential criteria. For the most part, the cohort studies were based on small numbers of participants in hospital-based metabolic studies. Considering that all 228 studies were observational rather than experimental or interventional, a high degree of skepticism, caution, about their conclusions and interpretation is warranted.

Are large-scale, prospective, randomized intervention trials available for guidance? Indeed they are. Considering their complexity, their cost, and the number of years needed to conduct them, we are fortunate to have six such studies, in which participants were randomly assigned to receive vitamin/mineral supplements or placebos, to provide experimental tests of whether nutrient supplementation reduces cancer incidence. We are indebted to William J. Blot of the International Epidemiology Institute, for reviewing the six studies.[7]

Linxian, China, a rural area in north-central China, has one of the world's highest cancer rates. Their esophageal and gastric cancer rates exceed 25 percent of the population. Two trials were conducted. The esophageal trial randomly enrolled 3,400 adults with diagnosed esophageal cancer who received a twenty-six-ingredient vitamin/mineral supplement at dose levels up to four times higher than the U.S. RDA (Recommended Daily Allowance), daily for six years. They were compared to a placebo control group. The second study enrolled some 30,000 adults for a five-year trial of four vitamin/mineral combinations: retinol plus zinc; riboflavin plus niacin; Vitamin C plus molybdenum, and a beta-carotene, Vitamin E, selenium combination. Compliance was exceptionally high.

Results of the first trial showed no significant differences in cancer mortality between groups. However, at the end of the six years, those on the vitamin/mineral mixture had fewer esophageal tissue abnormalities, or dysplasia.

The second trial found no differences for the first three combinations. For the beta-carotene, Vitamin E, selenium group, there was both lower total mortality and cancer mortality. Lung cancer rates were 50 percent less among this group, but tumors were not common among either group.

In Finland, another 29,000 men participated in a 5–8-year trial evaluating the effects of Vitamin E and beta-carotene. All the men were cigarette smokers. At the trial's end, there were no significant differences in lung cancer between the Vitamin E and placebo groups. Among the beta-carotene users, compared to non-users, the total cancer rates were higher.

In the United States, about 18,000 men in the Seattle area and other regions of the country participated in a trial evaluating a beta-carotene/retinol combination and a placebo's effect on lung cancer. Most had been smokers. The trial, originally planned to run for six years, was halted after four. The trial was shortened when the data from the Finnish trial became available. Lung cancer rose significantly among the beta-carotene/retinol users. Later, 22,000 American male physicians participated in a twelve-year trial of beta-carotene's effect on lung cancer. After twelve years of supplementation, no significant effects on cancer mortality were seen. The beta-carotene users and the placebo group had equal rates of cancer.

The American Second Primary Skin Cancer Prevention Trials followed a first trial in which 1,700 patients with either basal or squamous-cell skin cancer were given beta-carotene daily for four years. The second trial was conducted to determine the occurrence of a second primary cancer. Reductions in skin cancer were not seen. In the second trial, 1,312 patients were randomly assigned to receive a placebo or 200 micrograms daily of selenium. After an average of four years (0–10), no differences in skin cancer were observed. However, there was a significant 40 percent reduction in non-skin cancer in the selenium group. Lung cancer, prostate, and colorectal cancers were reduced, but the greatest reduction among the supplemental group was for esophageal cancer.

As Blot noted, "The six trials sent a mixed message regarding the effects of vitamin/mineral supplementation upon cancer risk." No magic bullet has emerged that could be considered a definite cancer inhibitor, and the determinants responsible for the lower risks of cancer associated with fruit and vegetable consumption remain unclear. His conclusion: "The evidence, such as it is, that diets high in fruits and vegetables decrease cancer risk has been vigorously used to market vitamins. Yet there is little or no evidence that any one, or any combination is protective against specific cancer sites." Contrary to what the media have presented to the public, the value of added fruits and vegetables remains equivocal. But Charles H. Henekens and Julie E. Buring of Brigham and Women's Hospital, Boston, and Richard Peto of the Imperial Cancer Research Fund, Oxford University, are unequivocal. In reviewing the subject, they declared that "despite the lack of reliable evidence exaggerated health claims are increasingly being made for antioxidant vitamins."[8]

How did we attain this state of affairs? The convergence of two paths offers an answer. Animal experiments, in conjunction with a plethora of retrospective case-control studies, provided a shaky underpinning for the hypothesis that certain food ingredients could lower the risk of human cancer. It was natural. It fit—with the preferred beliefs. Cancer, according to conventional wisdom, was out of control and of epidemic proportions. Traditional medicine, with its harsh drugs unable to stem the tide, was being bypassed for alternative, natural protection. Fruits and veggies and supplements were literally everywhere, a marketing success if ever there was one. The media were ready, the public was receptive.

In April 2000, a dash of cold water fell upon this scene. The Institute of Medicine (IOM), one of the country's four National Academies, published its latest report: *Dietary Reference Intakes for Vitamin C, Vitamin E, Selenium, and Caratinoids.* This report, the third in a series of dietary recommendations, drew two major conclusions: the role of antioxidants in chronic disease remains uncertain, and huge doses are risky. For the first time, the IOM set a ceiling on daily consumption of selenium and Vitamins C and E, to reduce the risk of adverse side effects from *overuse.*

Because of widespread overuse, the IOM recommended 75 mg (milligrams) per day of Vitamin C for women and 90 mg for men. For smokers, an additional 35 mg per day was recommended. The upper limit has been set at 2,000 mg (2 grams) per day for adults; intakes above this level cause diarrhea. A recent study at the University of Leicester in Britain found that healthy volunteers aged 17–49, given supplements of 500 mg daily for six weeks, turned Vitamin C into a pro-oxidant, creating the mutagenic lesion 8-oxoadenine.[9] Researchers in Italy found that the antioxidant activity of the carotinoids shifted into pro-oxidant mode depending upon their biologic environment and concentration.[10] Such observations may require the IOM to reduce its upper limits for Vitamin C and other nutrients.

For Vitamin E, the Recommended Daily Intake, RDI, is 15 mg from food for both men and women, equivalent to 22 International Units (IUs) of natural-source Vitamin E. Alpha-tocopheral is the only type of Vitamin E the body can readily use. The recommended upper limit is 1,000 mg (1 gram). This is equivalent to 1,100 mg of the synthetic dl-alpha toco-pheral. Above this level, tocopheral acts as an anticoagulant, which means risk of hemorrhage.[11] This switch from benefit to a harm follows the ancient dictum, "Dose makes the poison."

The recommended RDI for selenium is now 55 micrograms for both men and women. Note that this is micrograms (mcg), a thousand times less than a milligram. Labels must be read carefully. The upper limit was set at 400 mcg per day. Higher levels can induce selenosis, which causes loss of hair and fingernails.

The IOM set no RDIs or upper limits for Vitamin A because human studies yield contradictory results. Vitamin A deficiency in the United States is exceptionally rare, so that ingesting high doses of carotene is redundant and wasteful and may even be harmful, as the Finnish and American randomized trials have indicated. Nor has a need for carotene been established. Healthy people cannot get healthier.

The advice of Gary E. Goodman of the Fred Hutchinson Cancer Research Center in Seattle makes good sense. "The development of a cancer chemo-preventive agent," he wrote,

> should be a logical sequence of studies, starting with preclinical epidemiological studies that show in-vivo and in-vitro activity, and leading to early clinic evaluation and, finally, to the testing of the effect on cancer incidence. This scenario took place for beta-carotene and vitamin A from the early 1980s until the late 1990s. Although the results with beta-carotene in high-risk cigarette smokers have proven disappointing a great deal has been learned about beta-carotene and its human physiology. The surprising results of increased incidence of lung cancer in cigarette smokers will hopefully lead to a better understanding of the mechanism of the carotenoids. It also shows the strength and importance of conducting careful clinical trials even for agents widely accepted as safe.

This is excellent advice. Its implementation would generate confidence in a public battered by conflicting and confusing pronouncements.[12] Media, take heed.

What of chocolate, tea, and wine? Europeans discovered cocoa in 1502, on Columbus's fourth voyage to the Americas. Chocolate begins with cocoa nibs, the kernels, ground into chocolate. Its seminal ingredient is cocoa butter, without which no chocolate can claim respectability. In addition to its high sugar content, chocolate has the alkaloids theobromine and caffeine; the amine, phenylethylamine, serotonin (5-hydroxytrypta-mine); and a rich source of flavinoid phenolics, to prevent rancidification of its cocoa butter but which may also be potent antioxidants for low-density lipoprotein oxidation—those pesky LDLs. Indeed, consumption of the flavinoids has been inversely linked to heart disease: the more flavi-noid, the less heart disease. The question is: Are dietary phenolics active antioxidants in the human body? First, the suspicion. A cup of hot choco-late containing two tablespoons of cocoa (7.3 g) has 146 mg of total phe-nol and 1.5 ounces of milk chocolate, 205 mg of total phenol. Five ounces of red wine contain approximately 210 mg of phenol. If dietary phenolics are active antioxidants, chocolate and wine together could contribute ro-bust activity and benefit.[13] The flavinoid antioxidant catechin is also found in chocolate, at a level four times that of tea. Studies have suggested that because tea is also high in catechin, it may be protective against coronary heart disease and possibly cancer. In test tubes, catechins exhibit strong antioxidant activity, which could explain its claimed protective effects. A cup of tea with a chocolate cookie or slice of chocolate cake, and a glass of wine with a bite of dark chocolate, are not only splendid ways to relax, but at the same time may be health promoting: a marriage made in heaven.

A recent study from the Netherlands, where tea and chocolate con-sumption are as common as ham and eggs in the United States, tested the possible association between black tea consumption and risk of stomach, lung, breast, and colorectal cancers. This four-year study enrolled 58,279 men and 62,573 women. No protective benefit was found for tea con-sumption at any of the four cancer sites studied. Neither was there any ev-ident carcinogenic effect.[14] Flavinoid binding to estrogen receptors blocking estrogen activity in cells was seen as a mechanism for reducing the risk of both breast and ovarian cancer. This still remains to be demonstrated.

Yet another Dutch study, the Zutphen Elderly Study, a prospective cohort study of 805 men aged 65–84 living in Zutphen, a town in the east-ern Netherlands, measured the content of five flavinoid antioxidants in an array of foods, then assessed the flavinoid intake of the enrolled men over a period of five years. At the culmination of the study, they found that high flavinoid consumption was associated with lower coronary heart disease mortality. The predominant flavinoid in food is quercetin, which yielded the same risk estimate as total flavinoid consumption. Tea consumption yielded the highest correlation, with decreased CHD mortality. But the au-thors suggest that other substances in tea, the polyphenols, may be the beneficial ingredients. By comparison, onions had little effect on CHD mortality.[15] A randomized intervention study with similar results would do wonders for both medical-scientific and public confidence.

In 1995, Prabbat Jha of the World Bank's Human Development Division, in cooperation with members of the Division of Cardiology, McMasters University and Hamilton General Hospital, and the Mayo Clinic, completed a critical review of both prospective epidemiologic studies and randomized clinical trials regarding the role of antioxidant vitamins (E, C, and beta-carotene) in the prevention of cardiovascular disease. The emphasis was on differences in the results obtained by these two types of studies. Case-control studies were omitted because of their inherent unreliability.[16] This type of review is essential if a consensus is to emerge from the widely disparate results of published studies and their unwarranted recommendations to the public.

The reviewers limited their inquiry to studies of one hundred or more participants, and to those studies which also provided quantitative estimates of antioxidant vitamin intake. They were particularly concerned with the eight studies involving more than one thousand middle-aged patients. Together, these studies tracked 126,000 women and men, 86,000 receiving primary prevention and 40,000 receiving secondary prevention. Their critique was limited to prospective cohort studies that were consistent with epidemiologic determination of causality (see chapter 7)

Their analysis found that in three large cohort studies, Vitamin E intake or supplementation was associated with a significant reduction in cardiovascular disease. Less consistent reductions were seen with beta-carotene and Vitamin C. They noted that "considerable bias in observational studies, such as different behaviors of persons using antioxidants, may account for the observed benefit." On the other hand, none of the randomized trials showed any clear benefit for CHD reduction for either of the vitamins or beta-carotene. Their conclusion highlights the difference in types of studies: "Epidemiologic data suggest that antioxidant vitamins reduce cardiovascular disease, with the clearest effect for vitamin E; however, completed randomized trials do not support this finding."

Richard M. Hoffman and Harinder S. Garewal of the Department of Medicine, University of Arizona Health Sciences Center, arrived at a similar verdict.[17] From their review of the published epidemiologic studies, they maintain that "antioxidant supplementation is not a substitute for tobacco cessation, a prudent diet, and regular exercise. If a role for antioxidants is established, it will be in addition to these measures." They pose a particularly pertinent question to physician readers of the journal. Given the fact that additional studies are in progress and others are being planned, and given the fact that for science, the books are never closed and new information is a constant, "How should physicians," they ask, "counsel patients about antioxidant supplementation?"

> Since the positives tend to be emphasized in the lay press, a reasonable approach may be to discuss the lack of strong evidence supporting antioxidant supplementation, pointing out the negative studies. . . . However, since antioxidant supplements are readily available, physicians will not be able to prevent patients from using them. Physicians can play an important role in educating patients about known modifiable cardiovascular risk factors and in emphasizing the need to wait for completion of the clinical trials. Results from these trials may allow more definitive recommendations on antioxidant supplementation.

This may be prudent advice, given the mixed test results, but not only is it swimming against the tide, but few individuals believe in the need to wait for final and definitive results. In the current climate, I doubt that patients, or anyone for that matter, will sit still for a rundown of negative results when friends and neighbors are popping pills, and when supplements on every supermarket shelf shout, "Save your heart; buy me, eat me." Furthermore, given the current climate wherein insurance companies drive medical practice, it is the odd physician who can spend more than twelve minutes with a patient. Insurance and HMO guidelines all but forbid physicians to sit with their patients and have the type of interactive discussions needed to impart salient health messages. Physicians need the kind of help only the media can provide: wide and constant dissemination of the facts. Given the overwhelming lack of positive results in clinical trials and the prodigious difficulty and complexity of pinning down risk factors and potentially protective foods, it will be difficult to get information and advice to those who could use it. The Institute of Medicine's Report could, at best, do no more than find that the hypothesis on antioxidant vitamins and heart disease protection is not proven. With the current available evidence, no jury could have found otherwise.

Bear in mind that it is not because a food contains a specific level of an antioxidant, or has a certain type and number of antioxidants that is important, but its ability to effect a decrease in adverse coronary events or the incidence of cancer. Consequently, when reading about a health food or so-called protective foods, we must ask: Has it been shown to effect a disease state? What type of study was conducted?

But folks are not getting the message, as if all the above information were meaningless. Moreover, I was surprised and dismayed to note that the October 2000 issue of the *Harvard Health Letter* devoted two pages to "Tea and Health" and another two to whole fruits and vegetables.[18] I had thought that they, of all publications, would place the antioxidant issue in appropriate perspective.

I asked four friends (three women and one man) to read those four pages. This was hardly a scientific survey, but I was mainly interested in obtaining some opinions. These four concluded, on the basis of what was written, that tea was protective of both heart disease and cancer. How could a reader not come away with that message when they read that "antioxidants are believed to play a role in cancer by preventing damage to DNA, so the antioxidant properties of tea's flavinoids are also relevant to cancer prevention. In addition, laboratory studies have produced evidence that flavinoids act on DNA in other ways, either preventing mutations or repairing the damage that could give rise to cancer." But not a word about the IOM's report, or a hint of the difference between observational studies and clinical trials. Is it any wonder that people are thoroughly confused? Is there some desperate need to believe that fruits and veggies, tea and chocolate, are beneficial? Indeed, hope does spring eternal, and hope is essential, especially for those already ill. But purveying false hope is not virtuous.

Obviously we cannot rely on the media for help. Help, I'm convinced, must come from ourselves. We must become knowledgeable, able to ask the pertinent questions. We'll deal with this at length in chapter 7.

Responding to the need for additional, ongoing, large-scale studies to help resolve the question of antioxidant effects on coronary heart disease, Klipstein-Grobush and colleagues of the Department of Epidemiology and Biostatistics at Erasmus University Medical School in Rotterdam, The Netherlands, mounted a community-based prospective cohort study consisting of 4,802 men and women aged 55–95 who were free of myocardial infarction at the study's inception. Those four-thousand-plus individuals were followed for four years, during which time 124 developed an infarct. The study investigated whether dietary beta-carotene and Vitamins C and E were related to risk of myocardial infarction. After four years of follow-up and analysis of dietary intake from food sources, supplement intake, smoking, and alcohol consumption, the authors concluded that neither Vitamin C nor E had any effect on preventing an infarct, but that high levels of beta-carotene did appear to offer some protection. But they tell us that "whether this association may be ascribed to beta-carotene exclusively, to a diet rich in beta-carotene-containing products, or to dietary patterns and lifestyle behavior closely linked to a diet rich in vegetables and fruits remains to be elucidated."[19]

When the full impact of the most recent prospective cohort study of the effect of fruit and vegetable consumption on the incidence of colorectal cancer receives the wide publicity it is certain to get, there will be many unhappy campers. Few would have predicted its stunning results, including the study's investigators.

In 1991, the National Cancer Institute established its "Five-a-Day for Better Health" program to increase fruit and vegetable consumption among the public. In 1997, an expert panel convened by the American Institute for Cancer Research unequivocally endorsed the concept that fruit and vegetable consumption would reduce the risk of colorectal cancer. But time has not been kind to this hypothesis; indeed, far too many retrospective case-control studies underpinned it. In 1999, commenting on their study "Dietary Fiber and the Risk of Colorectal Cancer and Adenoma in Women" (*New England Journal of Medicine*, January 1999), Dr. Walter Willet noted: "The hypothesis that fiber intake is important in reducing colon cancer risk was interesting, but the reality is that the data have not provided much support for it." A year later, the other shoe fell: fruits and vegetables also proved illusory as protective against colorectal cancer. In this most recent study, a ten-member team from Harvard University's School of Medicine and School of Public Health followed 88,764 women enrolled in the Nurses Health Study, and 47,325 men enrolled in the Health Professionals Follow-up Study. Among women, diet was assessed and updated in 1980, 1984, 1986, and 1990, and among men in 1986 and 1990. Colon and rectal cancer incidence were determined as of June or January 1996. This study obtained the equivalent of 1,774,645 person-years of follow-up, along with 937 cases of colon cancer. A remarkably huge undertaking.

What did the data reveal? "Little association of colon cancer incidence with fruit and vegetable consumption." And their conclusion: "Although fruits and vegetables may confer protection against some chronic diseases, their frequent consumption does not appear to confer protection from colon rectal cancer."[20] A blow to theory and widely accepted belief if ever there was one!

Does this settle the matter for fruits and vegetables? Is this final? Not really. This question is extremely difficult to assess and pin down, simply because epidemiological observational studies, retrospective or prospective, may not be sensitive enough to identify any benefits. Benefits may be there, but the studies are seeking the wrong condition: cancer may not be the one. Studies may need to be further refined. The self-administered questionnaire may be too crude. For example, in an earlier study of prostate cancer, it was concluded that cooked tomato products were protective against this cancer, but that tomato juice was not. Then it was learned that the respondents had not checked off tomato juice because, due to its cost, it was not part of their diets. Indeed, one can find good and sufficient reasons for the study's failure. However, there is also the real possibility that fruits and vegetables simply are *not* protective against cancer. Until randomized clinical trials are undertaken, the jury must still be considered as out. It would certainly be helpful for a battered public if commentators and writers refrained from offering us remedies, however natural, for which there is scarce evidence of benefit.

Which brings up the question: Why is it taking so long to demonstrate conclusively that fruits, vegetables, antioxidants, and other plant-derived chemicals can reduce the risk of heart disease or cancer? This is a fitting question because, after two decades and hundreds of studies and media hype, it remains unanswered. Has traditional medicine, with respect to prevention, reached a plateau? Is a natural remedy in fact a will-o'-the-wisp? Will it be gene therapy that will achieve the elusive results? Time will tell. In the meantime, being an inveterate fruit and vegetable, and tea and chocolate consumer, I intend to continue the practice, if only for the pleasure of the taste and comfort it affords.

The Future of Cancer

Will cancer continue unabated? Will it be eliminated? Is diet to be the magic bullet? Back to the future. In the best of all possible worlds, a world free of risks, cancer will still prevail. Why? Because we are dealing with a condition that arises from faulty information-processing within our cells. Mutations occur at a low but steady rate even without exposure to external mutagenic agents; they are spontaneous and intrinsic to life. A cell's vulnerability to genetic damage (the code of life-information) derives from its natural need to grow, to reproduce its genome (the complete set of genes contained in the 23 chromosomes we humans pass to our offspring). With each cell division, the duplication process endows each new cell with a genome exactly the same as the one from which it sprang. But the process is far from perfect. Every so often a cell will miscopy a sequence of its DNA just prior to cell division, with the result that one of the new cells receives a defective copy, a mutated copy. The longer we live, the more cell growth, the more cell divisions, and the distinct possibility of more errors. That's life. Agents that stimulate cell growth increase the number of mutations as cell division occurs more often. Worse yet, in the process of cell division, DNA is more vulnerable to copying errors and to greater DNA damage.

During a seventy-year lifetime, a body produces about a trillion cells, a heck of a lot of cell divisions. And, as noted, each division provides an opportunity for mistakes, mutagen formation. In his splendid, accessible book, Robert A. Weinberg tells us: "While ten humans leading virtuous lives will collectively experience 100 million billion cell divisions, cancer is likely to kill only one of them. One fatal malignancy per 100 million billion cell divisions does not seem so bad after all."[21] In fact, cancer is held in check, but not totally so, because tumor development depends on the convergence of a set of events that is unlikely to occur in an average lifetime. So, again, in a world free of environmental risks and of self-imposed risks, cancer will continue to share our lives. Bruce Ames has phrased it succinctly: "Metabolism, like other aspects of life, involves tradeoffs."[22] Currently, however, ours is a singular season, an unimaginable time, and as I predicted earlier in this book, by the year 2042 all major cancer-causing genes will be known, and humankind will be on its way to eliminating them. But for now, the question remains: Can fruits and vegetables, with their impressive content of biochemicals—antioxidants, alkaloids, proteins, alexins, and more—counter the runaway growth of a renegade cell? Until this is unequivocally demonstrated, fruits and vegetables should continue to figure smartly in our diets because the water solubility of their chemicals means they are readily digested and removed from the body; harmful buildups do not occur. In moderation, they can't be harmful, and they may yet turn out to be beneficial. That's the message that needs to be spread. The public needs to know what the facts are, not what some people think they ought to be.

If our diets are to change markedly to fruits and vegetables, there will be a need for sources of supply well beyond our domestic capability. As we have already seen earlier, this possibility can be troublesome. Food safety requires paying attention to two imperatives: (1) food irradiationm which will all but guarantee that, at the point of purchase, the food is safe to eat; and (2) in the field, pesticide use, to guarantee that we—not the microbes, rodents, worms, insects, or weeds—get the better part of our food supply.

As the U.S. EPA defines them, pesticides are any substance or mixture intended for preventing or destroying any pest. The EPA maintains that currently pesticide residues of any type, and on any fruit or vegetable, are well below safe and regulated limits. Of course, this declaration does not square with conventional wisdom; nevertheless, the data are readily available.[23] In addition, over the past two decades neither epidemiological nor toxicological data support the notion that synthetic pesticides are a cause of human cancer. So, for example, in their recent review, "Pesticides and Cancer," a team from the Karolinska Institute in Stockholm, Sweden, introduced their review with this observation: "Because the risk of cancer following pesticide exposure from foods appears negligible, this literature will not be reviewed," giving high marks for pesticide's lack of harm. But they go further, informing us that although many published studies linked or associated pesticides with a variety of cancer sites, "few if any of the associations can be considered established and causal."[24]

Earlier, I related the captivating tale of the successful marketing of Listerine mouthwash. Their ploy was to create a need where none existed. It worked, and in spite of its execrable taste, sold gobs of it. Similarly, environmentalists have sequestered the term "organic," which to the scientific world has always meant any substance containing carbon, and they redefined it to mean food grown without pesticides. Then they created "health"-food stores, where the new organic food could be purchased. To make this work, they created the myth that pesticides cause cancer, and, given the unrelenting taboo of pesticides/cancer, cancer/pesticides, pesticides/cancer, they made it stick. The public bought the myth. A pesticide/cancer cause-effect relationship has not been found for us humans.

In their seminal publication, "Environmental Pollution, Pesticides, and the Prevention of Cancer: Misconceptions," B. N. Ames and I. T. Gold had this to say: "The amounts of pesticide residues ingested are so small, relative to levels that have been shown to have toxicological effects, they are toxicologically implausible as health risks." And they further conclude that "of all dietary pesticides that humans eat, 99.99 percent are natural: they are chemicals produced by plants to defend themselves against fungi, insects, and other animal predators." It has been estimated, and I noted this earlier, that we "eat about 1.5 grams of natural pesticides per person, per day, which is about 10,000 times more than we eat of synthetic pesticide residues."[25] These conclusions should offer a degree of comfort to anxious citizens who have been fed, over many years, a surfeit of unverified, anecdotal information. At this moment, a second look at figures 1.2 and 1.3 may add to the comfort level. Until the year 2042, hearty appetite!

Genetically Modified Foods

Once again the Luddites are at the gates. It was only a matter of time. Environmentalists in the United States were lagging behind their "Green" opposite numbers in England and on the Continent when the Monarch appeared. They latched onto it as they would a life line in a raging sea. The elegantly colored butterfly was a gift. Potential harm to the Monarch by ingesting genetically altered crops roused the somnolent and became a cause célèbre. American seed companies had gone too far, the Greens felt. Red lines had to be drawn. "Bio-tech" foods became the latest chic environmental crises.

Are gene-altered plants the "Frankenstein Foods" they have been labeled by environmentalists or are they the foods of the future?

In 1989, in an earlier book,[26] I wrote that "crops, like people, are susceptible to disease and injury, which either destroy them completely or reduce their food-yielding capacity. Because plants can not yet be 'vaccinated' against disease (this may be possible in the year 2010), pesticides must be used to ensure their health and productivity." I was wrong. My prediction was off—by fifteen years. Genetically modified plants are the vaccines that can prevent crop diseases and predation, substantially increasing crop yield and profit. They became a reality in 1995.

Following established practice, environmentalists and their handmaidens, the media, failed to provide the public with a full measure of issues surrounding these new foods. Their agenda, rather than being educational, invariably calls for doing away with or preventing these foods from coming to market. Is that necessary? Do modified foods present untoward health or environmental risks? What, in fact are genetically modified foods, and what, if any, risks do they pose? And, most troubling, why are environmentalists and the media on a feeding frenzy against them?

It began with Bt, yet it is Bt that will unlock the key to our understanding. Bt has a history, a paternity that reaches back aways. It made its initial appearance as the bioinsecticide Thuricide, a pesticide whose active ingredient was the microbe *Bacillus thuringiensis*. Here at last was the environmentalist's longed-for nonchemical pesticide, a biocide, and the dream of organic farmers. A new era was in the offing.

Japan, 1901. The silkworms *Bombyx mori* were dying. Shigatone

Ishiwata, a microbiologist-entomologist at the Japanese National Institute of Sericultural and Entomological Science, found the microbe that was infecting and killing the lepidopteran larvae. He called the silkworm disease *sotto*, and the offending bacterium *Bacillus sotto*.[27]

Germany, 1915. Ernst Berliner was studying an infectious disease of the Mediterranean flour moth *Angasta kuehniella*. The infected insects were originally obtained from a mill in Thuringia. In his final report, Berliner described a spore-forming bacteria which he named *Bacillus thuringiensis* as the cause.[28]

As it turned out, *Bacillus sotto* and *Bacillus thuringiensis* were one and the same, but "Bt" (for the latter) stuck. Bt is actually a soil bacterium with the unique ability to produce a crystalline protein that is not only insecticidal, but selectively so. Neither Ishiwata nor Berliner knew the importance of what they had brought forth. But the Germans were quick to capitalize on this discovery. In 1927, the first biocides capable of killing caterpillars (Lepidoptera) became available. The French were not far behind. In 1938, Sporeine became commercially available. But World War II intervened and stopped biocides in their tracks. Chemical pesticides banished them completely. Twenty years would pass before Bt came off the shelf again, as Thuricide, a spray and powder, marketed by both Abbott Laboratories and Sandoz, Inc.

The as yet to be fulfilled insecticidal promise of Bt took flight in 1966, when Howard Dulmadge, a USDA scientist, isolated a more powerful strain of Bt that quickly became the basis for a number of commercial products. But 1981 was the pivotal year. H. Ernest Schnepf and H. R. Whitely of the University of Washington at Seattle cloned the Bt toxin gene, made a copy of it, and sequenced it; all the words of its four-letter alphabet became known. By 1989, forty-two genes were sequenced. If 1981 was the year of the Bt gene, 1987 was splicing time. Groups of scientists inserted Bt genes in cotton plants, and a new way to deliver Bt was created. That's the history of Bt: traditional, careful, creative science at work. Knowledge building upon knowledge.

In 1988, the first cotton plants containing Bt genes with its insecticidal crystalline protein expressed were harvested. And in 1995, the Bollgard gene—a Monsanto product—became commercially available throughout all cotton-producing states, as well as worldwide. For the first time in history, there was a crop that could defend itself against the voracious boll weevil, with not a synthetic chemical in sight.

The beauty of Bt is its uniqueness, a treasure trove of insect-specific toxins. Its 20,000-plus strains are found in soils around the world and have the ability to produce seemingly endless insect-destroying proteins. Each of the many subspecies produces a protein specific for only certain pests. The process is simple and direct. An insect bites a plant carrying the Bt gene and swallows a part. When swallowed, the protein is released and locks on to specific receptor sites in the insect's stomach. Locking-on is tantamount to fitting a key into a lock. The protein chemically opens a channel in the insect's stomach, flows in, and dissolves the intracellular cement. As the gut liquid diffuses between the cell, paralysis occurs, and bacterial invasion follows, with subsequent insect death. Each Bt protein has a narrow insect (host) range. The operational term here is *insect*. Bt protein has no effect on birds, fish, or mammals, including people. Recall that our stomachs and those of all vertebrates are acidic, unlike those of insects (arthropods), which are alkaline. Since Bt's crystalline protein is alkaline, it can function effectively at the higher pH range. Receptor sites for this protein are lacking in acid environments; therefore, Bt is harmless to all but insects.

Insects are no different than we humans in their susceptibility to microbial invasion and death. Viruses, rickettsia bacteria, fungi, and protozoa—the full spectrum of the unseen world—are nature's way of limiting insect populations. Bt has been lending a natural hand for eons. From Ishiwata to Berliner, between 1900 and 1915, the number of insect orders (groups of related organisms) that Bt could kill jumped from only the Lepidoptera to nine orders by 1990, adding mosquitoes, flies, beetles, worms, protozoa, flatworms, mites, and ants. Biotechnology and agriculture were wedded. In fact, thuringiensin, Bt's beta-exotoxin, the crystalline protein, possesses the following attributes of an ideal biopesticide:

- Resistance to it has not developed. (Since the toxic protein is a chemical, made of a string of amino acids, it is reasonable to speculate that, in time, insect genes will mutate and resistance will develop. Given the current ability to manipulate genes, that time is a long way off.)
- It is easily grown and made.
- Petro chemicals are not needed.
- It is nontoxic to vertebrates: mammals, birds, and fish.

Modification of crop plants is not new—it is not a twentieth-century invention. For at least seven thousand years, farmers have labored long and haphazardly seeking to improve their crops: increase the yield, improve taste, increase the size of fruits and vegetables, and prevent disease. Remember, growing crops is *not a natural process.* Today's crops barely resemble their wild ancestors, which did not originate on the North American or European continents. Thus, improving suitability for cultivation in our environment has been a long, arduous, hit-or-miss process. Early farmers produced better crops by selective breeding, saving the seeds of the most vigorous plants, as well as those that looked and tasted better, for planting at a later time. They could do that because random genetic variation occurs naturally in all living things and is the basis of evaluation of new species through natural selection. Even before its scientific basis was understood, farmers took advantage of this natural variation by selectively breeding wild plants and animals, and even microorganisms such as yogurt cultures and yeasts for fermented milks and wine, to produce domesticated variants better suited to their needs. But this took decades. It was this type of selection that so changed teosinte, the ancient, wild "parent" of modern corn, into an important food and animal feed crop. Similarly, our modern tomato bears little if any resemblance to its progenitor because of centuries of natural selection and natural DNA recombination.

You have but to wander the aisles of your local supermarket to see the many varieties of apples: the winesaps, fugis, Granny Smiths, Baldwins, Pippins, Romes, and others. There are also the peaches and tomatoes, including the new tasty grape tomatoes, which so many of us are popping like peanuts, and the potatoes and nectarines, the fuzzless peaches that didn't exist when I was a kid. None of these are natural. All are man-made, via traditional breeding techniques that can also produce hazardous chemicals that take years to breed out. Genetic modification of plants is faster and highly specific, producing few if any noisome chemicals because the process deals with single genes whose chemical constitution is known.

Spectacular increases in crop yields became possible as a consequence of the meticulous experiments by the Austrian monk Johann Gregor Mendel, crossing different varieties of peas, in the 1860s.[29] Our modern science of genetics flows directly from his garden and his detailed notebooks. Mendel gave us the gene and its heritability. We now know that individual characteristics such as the height to which corn and wheat can grow, the color of flower petals and their numbers, as well as the texture of peas—whether peas are smooth or wrinkled—(for Mendel, "wrinkled" actually meant "angular") are determined by their gene-carrying traits that are passed on from generation to generation. By use of Mendel's ideas, crop yields doubled. Gene manipulation was the logical next step. Farmers now have the ability to produce crops containing genes from either similar or un-related foreign species simply because the genetic code is universal.

The concept of universality of genes is not only of transcendent importance, but crucial to the entire undertaking of genetic modification. As more and more genes were sequenced and compared, it was found that the products of the genes that encode similar traits in very diverse organisms are also similar in their protein sequence. Most genes do not have characteristics unique to any specific organism or species. That's a major take-away point, one that environmentalists and the media have yet to understand. It is all but impossible to determine the organism from which a gene arises by inspection of the gene sequence alone. Consequently, there is no way to identify fish genes, tomato genes, or spinach genes. As the lady said, "A gene is a gene is a gene." A key discovery is that, in the course of determining DNA sequences, identical genes are regularly found in organisms that are only remotely related, clear evidence that genes have been naturally transferred during the long and continuing evolution of all living things. Now that's something to contemplate.

Furthermore, the opportunity to select and multiply a gene and introduce it into a crop plant was not simply the next horticultural development, it meant that the time barrier had fallen, and an era of directed genetic change was at hand. It was now possible to introduce a new gene into an accepted and adapted variety in a single step. No longer would there be the tedious and time-consuming process of teasing out the many inferior plants that are regular and frequent results of traditional breeding. By picking the best or most vigorous plants, farmers have enriched the genetic constitution of plants for such attributes as higher yields, increased resistance to pests, and greater compatibility with production and shipping requirements. This is the farmer at work: it has little or nothing to do with natural selection. Natural selection is fine for Darwin's finches and turtles on the Galápagos, but for us humans it has not been the mode since hunter-gatherers settled down to a less risky existence shortly after the last ice age, some 10–14,000 years ago. Breeding as it has been practiced worldwide by farmers for millennia involves selection for optimal growth for the needs of people, and it is entirely unnatural. Human intervention, because of our need for more and better crops resistant to pests, drought, cold, and disease, has been a dawdling form of genetic engineering for millennia. Currently, the pace is picking up. That's the major difference, and speed is the contemporary contribution to the food supply.

Genes will perform in a new plant provided that the right signals have been attached to the gene prior to transfer. As we already know, bacteria have been modified to produce human interferon, insulin, and growth hormone, all of which we use. We no longer need animals to do so. In exactly the same way, we can now modify plants and animals. This straightforward technical achievement goes by a number of names: genetic engineering, genetic modification of food, and recombinant DNA technology. There is nothing malevolent or Frankensteinian about it. It is essentially the natural progression of humans at work: biologists, geneticists, microbiologists, entomologists—men and women in dozens of countries contributing to the betterment of humanity.

The ways in which modified foods contribute to the betterment of humanity are many and varied:

- They allow a much wider selection of traits for improvement; e.g., not only pest, disease, and herbicide resistance is achieved to date in plants, but also, potentially, drought resistance, improved nutritional content, and improved sensory properties.
- Their laboratory development is faster, more precise, and lower in cost.
- The desired change can be achieved in very few generations.

The method allows greater precision in selecting characteristics that lead to a number of additional benefits:

- Improved agricultural performance (yields) with reduced use of pesticides.
- Ability to grow crops in previously inhospitable environments (e.g., via increased ability of plants to grow in conditions of drought, salinity, extremes of temperature, consequences of global warming), leading to improved ability to feed an increasing world population at a reduced environmental cost.
- Improved sensory attributes of food (e.g., flavor, texture).
- Improved nutritional attributes (e.g., combating antinutritive and allergenic factors and increased Vitamin A content in rice, helping to prevent blindness in Southeast Asia).
- Improved processing characteristics leading to reduced waste and lower food costs to the consumer.

Furthermore, genetic modification has a huge potential for mankind in medicine, agriculture, and food. In food, the real benefits are not the early products that have appeared so far, but the longer-term benefit to the world, especially the Third World: the potential to contribute to the elimination of hunger and malnutrition while helping to prevent the otherwise inevitable pressure to encroach on natural resources. Currently, there are 800 million people in the Third World who regularly do not receive enough food to alleviate hunger, and millions more who do not receive adequate nutrition. This problem will become increasingly worse due to the world's escalating population. That's reason enough to want to see this technology succeed.

With conventional breeding, traits can only be transferred between plants or animals of the same or related species and with crossing of hundreds of genes in unknown ways. Genetic alteration of a single known trait permits genes to be transferred between different species, and potentially between animals and plants. So, for example, Bt corn has been genetically modified to make it produce the Bt protein that kills the corn borer, a major threat to corn crops. Ishiwata and Berliner had no idea how their early discoveries would help feed the world.

These benefits notwithstanding, perceptions and unfounded fears have cast a shroud over biotechnology and genetic modification of food.

In May 1999, entomologists at Cornell University raised the question: Might insects, nontarget insects ingesting pollen from Bt corn that had been wind-blown to other neighboring plants, be adversely affected by the Bt toxin? Of particular concern were Monarch butterfly larvae. That was a reasonable question and deserving of study. In their tests, all of which were performed indoors in their labs, the researchers found that Monarch larvae reared on milkweed leaves dusted with pollen from Bt corn "ate less, grew more slowly, and suffered higher mortality than larvae reared on leaves without pollen."[30] The fact that this work lacked field trials made not a wit of difference to the researchers. Was it factual or artifactual? The work was published in one of the most reputable and respected scientific journals, and it generated international consternation. The "real" possibility that the Monarch could be adversely affected became a media event, a circus. Here was the proof, the evidence environmentalists had been hoping for. Biotech was a menace, and had to be stopped. They took to the streets.

For butterflies, 2000 was a vintage year. In January, University of Maine (Orono) scientists reported that the chance of cross-pollination between corn plants in the field, whether produced by traditional breeding practices or by genetic engineering, is small for plants in close proximity to one another and quickly drops to zero with increasing distance. Two varieties of corn, genetically modified Roundup Ready and an unmodified variety, were grown at the university's Rogers Farm. It was this

farm, with its genetically modified corn plots, that eco-terrorists deci-
mated in August of 1998.[31] Obtaining new information was obviously not
on their minds. Results of the study found that hybrid corn grown downwind of the Roundup Ready plots had about one percent cross-pollination
in the first six rows within 100 feet of the Roundup Ready corn. In the
middle six rows, the frequency dropped to 0.1 percent, and in the last six
rows the frequency dropped to 0.03 percent. Cross-pollination was not
found in corn 1,000 feet away. Only plants immediately downwind of the
Roundup Ready corn exhibited significant cross-pollination. This indicates that although cross-pollination is possible within 1,000 feet of the
modified crops, a 1,000-foot buffer or border rows can adequately protect
nongenetically modified corn crops from neighboring modified crops,
which would also protect insects' larvae from ingesting Bt toxin.

The University of Illinois at Champagne-Urbana contributed to the
expansion of information. From their study we learn that Bt corn grown
widely on university plots in east-central Illinois had no adverse effect on
black swallowtail caterpillars that thrive in weeds alongside cornfields.[32]
This, of course, contrasts sharply with the results obtained by the Cornell
researchers who managed only limited in-vitro studies, indoors. In their
field tests, University of Illinois researchers grew Pioneer variety 34R07,
which contains Monsanto Event 810, a genetic configuration of corn carrying the gene that encodes the *Bacillus thuringiensis* toxin fatal to European corn borers, which also ravage corn crops in North America. Pollen
from the Bt corn was carefully monitored and measured at a series of locations ranging from half a meter to 7 meters from the cornfield. The researchers report: "We found that many caterpillars died, but not, as far as
we can tell, due to anything connected to the corn or the corn pollen.
There was no correlation between mortality and distance from the cornfield or between mortality and pollen load." Some of the deaths were directly attributed to predation by spiders, carnivorous insects, and other
environmental factors. Black swallowtail females can lay up to eight hundred eggs during their two-week lifetime; overall life expectancies for
caterpillars in the field are invariably are low. And they noted, "We also
measured the weights of the surviving caterpillars, and we found no negative pattern suggesting a problem in their growth and development." In
the laboratory, the researchers exposed more caterpillars to Bt corn pollen
from the plants in the field, as well as pollen from nonmodified but genetically similar corn plants. The endotoxin from the same Bt corn again had
no effect on survival of the caterpillars, nor did the pollen from nonmodi-

fied corn. Pollen from another transformed variety, Novartis Max 454, however, did cause mortality in the laboratory. Antibody assays of the Novartis corn showed that it contained forty times as much endotoxin, on average, than did the 810 variety.[33]

From the University of Guelph in Ontario, Canada, we learn that researchers from the Department of Environmental Biology found that pollen from Bt corn is not present in high enough doses on most milkweed plants (the preferred food of Monarch caterpillars) to harm Monarch larvae. Mark Sears, chairman of the department and chair of the Canadian Corn Pest Coalition, stated that "the actual threat to the Monarch butterfly can only be determined by assessing the dosage that affects the larvae and their degree of exposure to Bt corn pollen in the field. Outside of cornfields, you probably wouldn't find concentrated dosages of pollen because wind and rain remove it from the surface of the milkweed leaves. This study focused on the distance Bt pollen travels. Examining milkweed stands in cornfields, at their edges, and at distances of 5, 10, 25, 50, and a 100 meters away, he found that within the fields, approximately 150 pollen grains/cm^2 were present on milkweed leaves. At the edges, 80–100 grains were found, and at five meters, only one grain. These numbers were compared to those obtained from a "dose-response assay," from which data of increasing doses are plotted against increased mortality rates to determine dosages with negative effects on Monarch butterfly larvae. Results show that 135 grains/cm^2 (the lowest dosage so far tested in the field) had no greater effect on Monarch larvae than non-Bt pollen. Sears is conducting a two-year study to determine the ecological impacts of Bt corn pollen on selected nontarget butterfly species, including the Monarch. So far, studies indicate that Bt corn is not as big a threat as environmentalists and the news media had anticipated.[34]

March 2000 was a particularly good month for the Monarch and for the protective effect of buffer zones. At Cornell University, another group of entomologists found that creating a refuge in a crop field reduces the chance of insects developing resistance to transgenic insecticidal plants. These investigators conducted field tests to find ways of reducing the likelihood that the diamondback moth develops resistance to Bt broccoli plants.[35] According to Anthony M. Shelton, "Bt transgenic plants can greatly reduce the use of broader spectrum insecticides, but there is concern that this technology may be short-lived due to insect resistance." To manage resistance to Bt-engineered plants, his group examined several planting options, including how the refuge was placed in the field. The findings are clear—a refuge is needed, but how that refuge was placed in the field is also important. Using a "20 percent mixed refuge," in which the Bt and non-Bt plants were mixed randomly, compared with a "20 percent separate refuge," in which a block of non-Bt plants was grown next to the Bt plants, they followed changes in the insects' level of resistance over the course of the season. Their results supported theoretical models that indicated that a separate refuge would be more effective in keeping the diamondback moth from becoming Bt resistant. Additional studies examined how to manage the insects in the refuge. Results demonstrated the importance of making sure sufficient insects are generated on the non-Bt plants to mate with any resistant insects that may have survived on the Bt plants. According to Fred Gould, a noted expert in the use of Bt transgenic plants, "Field studies like this one are essential for developing public confidence in resistance management techniques."[36]

So, a series of studies from four universities in widely separate areas of the country, with different experimental conditions, different weather conditions, obtained similar data. They are not absolute, but they do set a trend. The likelihood that other studies will contradict these is minimal, but possible. Studies such as these will breed confidence into what is degenerating into a politicized and emotional issue, in which perception and fear overwhelm reason. If the public is kept ignorant of these impressively consequential findings, the Cassandras of this world will have perpetuated their self-fulfilling prophecies, and vandalism and media frenzy will prevail.

As if to dot the i's and cross the t's, the U.S. EPA issued a report in September 2000 concluding that Bt corn is unlikely to pose a serious threat to Monarch butterflies. The report also held that persistence of Bt insecticide in soil was not a problem, nor was there concern for evolving resistance to the Bt insecticide by crop plants.[37] This was the last thing the Greens wanted to hear. They were furious. They had been pressing the EPA to disapprove Bt corn as well as other modified crops. That genetically modified crops do not pose a threat to human health or to the environment appears to be on its way to confirmation.

At the moment, crankiness is ascendant. Perpetual worriers see ill effects lurking behind anything "unnatural." Will gene-modified crops contribute to the increased use of chemicals now that it has been established that plants can tolerate them, and will this depress biodiversity? A recently completed field trial belies the latter claim. A ten-year study of four transgenic crops in twelve disparate natural habitats found that "population sizes of all crops declined after the first year as a result of competition from native perennial plants. In no case did the GM lines persist significantly longer than their conventional counterparts."[38] Given time, concerns will be tested and answers obtained.

Opponents of genetic modification believe that farmers will now use far more chemicals to completely clear their fields of weeds. However, early field trials indicate that herbicide-resistant cotton and corn require less chemical treatment for weed control, and insect-resistant plants require less chemical coverage, which means an increase in beneficial insects, which will mean additional food for birds. Opponents maintain that farmers will use more chemicals to control insects unaffected by Bt. What farmers actually will do in their fields remains to be seen. Nevertheless, chemicals are expensive, and farm profits are not so lofty as to be frittered away on unnecessary chemicals. Bacterial gene swapping, vertical transfer within similar species, is a natural phenomenon that occurs frequently. The idea that altered bacteria run amok, hopping around from species to species in horizontal transfer, creating Frankenstein-like creatures or foods, has all the makings of a sci-fi flick. From studies of bacteria in their natural habitats, microbial ecologists have learned that modified bacteria are unlikely to grow out of control. In fact, studies demonstrate that these modified bugs are less hardy than their unaltered counterparts, and die out relatively rapidly, which means their genes have little opportunity to spread. In addition, bacteria are being genetically altered to limit their DNA from moving to other (different) species and surviving. Entering a foreign species will destroy it. As research progresses and the knowledge base of horizontal gene transfer increases, environmental risks or, more precisely, assumed risks, should fade.

Unfortunately, only a casual reading of the spring 2000 issue of *Greenpeace* magazine, with its "truth" about GMOs (genetically modified organisms) and the false and misleading information given its readers, suggests otherwise.[39] If the many recent incidents of ecoterrorism that occurred from Oregon and California to Michigan, New York, and Maine are a bellwether, reason has taken flight. How else to understand the burning of an academic building on the campus of Michigan State University—a building housing offices and labs of faculty and students engaged in biotechnology research. The militant vandals of the Earth Liberation Front claimed responsibility for torching Agriculture Hall simply because biotechnology studies were being done there. Doing violence, without evidence that harm will occur to human health or to the environment if the research continues, is shocking enough, but when such violence is perpetuated by supposedly educated young people it is appalling. How different is this from book burning or the wanton destruction committed by the followers of Ned Ludd in the early years of the nineteenth century who could not abide the advance of technology? Modern-day Luddites are telling us they oppose advances in agriculture and nutrition simply because it is not done in the old way. The public must decide if this violent opposition is tolerable.

What do we know about the safety of genetically altered food? Does the new biotechnology create risks that traditional methods of breeding and cross-pollinating did not? Is the moving of genes by splicing somehow detrimental, more so than grafting and tissue culture? A recent report from the National Academy of Sciences informs us that "crops modified by molecular and cellular methods should pose risks no different from those modified by classical genetic methods for similar traits."[40] That was in 1989. In April 2000, the Academy spoke again, emphasizing that "there was no evidence that any foods on supermarket shelves made from those plants were unsafe to eat." And they declared also that "the process of inserting genes from one species into another was not inherently dangerous."[41]

Allergic Reactions

Unfounded perceptions and fears about safety of these foods linger. Some fear the possibility that allergic reactions could occur from unsuspected sources, as in the case of nuts. Pioneer Hi-Bred International of Johnston, Iowa, is the world's largest seed company. In 1992, Pioneer scientists transferred the methionine-rich 2S albumin gene from Brazil nuts to soybeans. Soybeans, prized for their high protein content, are widely used for oil and meal: oil for cooking and salads, meal for animal feed. But soybean seed protein is deficient in the essential amino acid methionine while, Brazil nuts have a high methionine content. Brazil nuts are also known to be allergenic for susceptible individuals. Although the risk is only about one in 100,000, the allergic response in affected people can be quite severe. Pioneer developed the methionine-rich soybean for use in animal feed, but it is well nigh impossible to separate soybeans destined for animals from those slated for human consumption. Soy protein, which is less allergenic than milk protein, is used in infant formulas, baked goods, dairy substitutes, and meat tenderizers.[42]

Early in the project, Pioneer learned of the potential allergenicity of Brazil nuts and took the problem to the University of Nebraska's Steven

Taylor of the Department of Food Science and Technology. The question was: Would eating transgenic soy protein containing the Brazil nut gene cause allergic responses, that is, release histamine with its ensuing symptoms? Human volunteers were challenged by skin-prick extracts of Brazil nut, soybean, and transgenic soybean. Blood serum from individuals with known allergy to Brazil nuts reacted strongly to both the Brazil nut extract and the methionine-enhanced soybean. A full account of this study was published in the *New England Journal of Medicine*.[43]

For Pioneer, the issue was whether to go forward with the enhanced soybean that provides both high-quality protein for hundreds of thousands of malnourished individuals as well as a high-quality animal feed, or to discontinue the project. An analysis of the human risk of death from the enhanced soybean found 1.25 potential deaths annually in the United States, less than two per year given the 1 per 100,000 risk of being allergic to Brazil nuts. Not only did they decide to terminate the project, but they made their decision public. Rather then praise them for their action, environmentalists and the media used the information to dramatize the dangers of biotechnology and corporate recklessness.[44]

An in-depth look at the concern for food allergy may be useful at this point. Food allergy derives from abnormal immunological responses to substances in foods, usually naturally occurring proteins in foods such as peanuts, milk, and seafood. Allergic responses run the gamut from mild skin rashes and gastrointestinal upset to life-threatening anaphylactic shock. Although all food allergens are proteins, natural proteins are rarely allergenic. As genetic modification introduces new genes into plants, and as those new genes produce new proteins in the modified plant, there is potential for allergenicity, and it must be assessed for. Currently, assessment follows a "decision tree" developed by the International Food Biotechnology Council in conjunction with the Allergy and Immunology Institute of the International Life Sciences Institute.[45] The first step of an assessment classifies the source of genetic material as either common, less common, or of unknown allergic potential. Eight food groups—eggs, milk, fish, shellfish, peanuts, soybeans, tree nuts, and wheat—are well known common allergens for some people. These eight account for 90-plus percent of all the world's food allergies.[46]

The most difficult assessment occurs with genes obtained from viruses, bacteria, or nonplant foods—sources with no previous history of allergenicity. Assessment here requires comparison of amino acid sequences of the introduced protein with the amino acid sequence of known allergens. This type of assessment can provide reasonable assurance of the introduced proteins' potential for allergenicity. So, is eating a foreign protein a hazard? In fact, everything we eat or have already eaten is foreign. That's another take-away point. Bear in mind that DNA is an intrinsic part of all living organisms. The DNA introduced via gene transfer is a minuscule fraction of the total DNA ingested when a food is eaten. The transfer of a gene from a modified plant to an individual consuming the plant (food) is entirely unlikely to precipitate an untoward reaction as the DNA is fully digested in the stomach and small intestine. Furthermore, the allergic potential exists only for foods eaten raw, as the heat of cooking inactivates the genes. Nevertheless, for the first time in the history of the use and regulation of food, for the first time in the history of this or any other country, zero risk, absolute safety, is being demanded of genetically modified food. Considering that absolute safety, zero risk, is an impossibility and nonexistent anywhere on earth, it stretches the bounds of reason for the U.S. EPA and the FDA to be leaning in that direction with modified foods, which are not all that different than traditional foods.

The sequence of identification and testing proceeds from the understanding that food safety is uncompromising. There are not, have never been, separate food supplies: for the most part, we all eat from the same table. No one wants to harm themselves or their families, yet the unrelenting war against taco shells, for example, suggests otherwise. You may recall that Kraft Foods, maker of taco shells that were sold in food stores around the country, announced a nationwide recall of its shells in September 2000. This was the first recall in the United States of a genetically modified food. The corn in question, Starlink, contained a new protein, Cry9c (cry for crystal), produced by the Bt bacterium. The Starlink corn had been approved for animal consumption by the Department of Agriculture. The FDA had not yet approved it for human consumption because of the possibility of human allergenicity to a bacterial protein. It had not been shown to be allergenic, and there was not a scintilla of evidence that anyone who had eaten the shells had been harmed by it. Nevertheless, the shells were made to look as though they had caused harm. As Cry9c had not previously been consumed in human diets, there were no people with a known allergy to it from whom blood for testing could be obtained. As previously noted, all allergens are proteins, but not all proteins are allergens, and because this is a bacterial protein, it would normally and automatically be ticketed for the testing process described. This did not occur. Instead, under enormous public pressure from Genetically Engineered Food Alert, a coalition of environmental groups critical of modified food, the FDA removed the shells from food stores as an adulterant. Under food and drug law, any substance in food not recognized as safe is classified as an adulterant. At no time, however, has either the FDA or the EPA stated or found it to be harmful or allergenic. In fact, members of the EPA Advisory Panel believed the risk, if any, to be extremely low. Given that Cry9c's string of amino acids did not match those of known allergens, that the shells had to be cooked, and that they had to pass through stomach acid, why were Starlink corn shells summarily removed? No one had absolute proof of its safety, and numbers are not fuzzy things. But 1 in 4 people are allergic the media proclaimed! Intuitively, you knew it was wrong. Was one person in every four really allergic? It had to be an error, a mistake. But that was what the media was trumpeting.

Speaking with scientists at both the EPA and FDA, I asked about such an alarming number. Think of it! Who among our families, friends, neighbors, and co-workers is allergic to food? If 1-in-4 is true, then twenty-five of every one hundred people in the country must be protein-sensitive and allergic. It would be the country's greatest epidemic. Every household would have someone unable to eat meat, fish, poultry, shellfish, nuts, milk, cheese, any protein-containing food.

Both agencies had similar responses. "Nonsense. When we read that number in the newspaper, we threw up our hands. The media did it again." So, I asked, "If it's not true, why hasn't someone said so?" That's when they stunned me. In both instances the reply was, "We are not supposed to give any suggestion of partisanship." Silence. I was speechless—an unusual trait for me. But not for long. "If you don't speak up," I asked, "who will?" "Yes, we realize that is a problem." So, the public remains ignorant of the facts, believes the media's nonsense, and fear of food increases. The government knows the press is misleading the public, but it can't or won't speak up for fear of being accused of partisanship. By whom? Surely not the general public. Who, then? Two possibilities remain: environmentalists and the media. The only thing that makes sense is that governmental agencies do not like noise directed at them.

But that 1-in-4 thought does not go away so fast. Hadn't the writers at the *New York Times* wondered about this figure—wondered if 1 in 4 wasn't inordinately high? Why so accepting? Why didn't they check it out by calling the FDA, the AMA, the ADA, or by speaking with an allergist at one of the four medical schools in New York City? It isn't as if the information is tucked away and difficult to pry loose. But what of the editor?

How could that number slip by him or her? Suppose a writer had written that 1 in 4 people on their way to work via the subway are carrying weapons, loaded .45 caliber automatics. Would that pass unremarked? Not possible. Intuitively, an editor would know it's far too high. That some people in the subway are carrying loaded weapons is reasonable given past experience, but 1 in 4 would never fly.

The American Academy of Allergy, Asthma, and Immunology estimates that 1–2 percent of the general population is at risk of allergy to foods *and* insect stings; that is, 1–2 people in any hundred. In a recent survey about the prevalence of peanut and tree nut allergy in the United States, researchers of the Division of Allergy and Immunology at the Mount Sinai School of Medicine in New York found that approximately 1.1 percent of the general population is affected by food allergies, and that despite the reactions, about half of those affected never seek evaluation by a physician.[47] Furthermore, pediatricians at three academic medical centers have shown that over 20 percent of children and adolescents, at least 1 in 5, who show an early allergic response to peanut protein lose that response as they mature. Peanut allergy need not be lifelong. Consequently, those who believe they are allergic might consider a "challenge" to determining if they have outgrown their original allergy.[48]

Considering that no federal agency had found the taco shells to be allergenic or otherwise harmful, why did the media move so forcefully to have the shells removed from markets? The function of the media is to present us with balanced information that allows us to make up our own minds about various issues, so why do they persist in making up our minds for us? We are aware that there are people who are allergic to nuts, eggs, fish, and shellfish; we are also aware that market shelves are chock full of peanuts, peanut butter, eggs, and all manner of fish and shellfish. Because people are allergic has never meant that nonallergic members of the eating public could not avail themselves of these foods. Those who are allergic know which foods to avoid. To have a food banned because a vocal minority prefers it that way is wholly inappropriate. If vegetarians had their way, meat would disappear from our tables. And if Zen practitioners had their way, we would be eating nothing but grains. It is difficult to understand why those who hew to unique diets are not content to eat those diets without attacking those with other preferences. The wholesale removal of taco shells was wrong.

Through the winter, into the spring and on to June 2001, Genetically Engineered Food Alert, a coalition of environmental groups, mounted an unrelenting campaign hammering away at the potential horrendous adverse allergic effects that the Cry9c protein contained in Starlink corn could engender. Their intention was nothing less than scaring us pantless. On June 9, the *New York Times* brought the allergy message to its readers front and center; front page, top right, with allegations in full bloom.

A week later, on June 14, buried deep at the lower left on p. C8 in its Business Section, well away from prying eyes, the *Times* had this to say: "U.S. Finds No Allergies to Altered Corn," and it noted that scientists at the NCDC had found no evidence that any people had had allergic reactions to Starlink corn. The CDC had checked individual blood samples for antibodies to the Cry9c protein. None was found.

But why hide the good news, the information that would make a profound difference to the many people who have been literally bombarded with predictions of dire consequences? Who benefits from such placement? The *Times* may not be helpful, but it is consistent. On July 11, 2001, it struck again. Deep in the Business Section, right at the fold, lower left (p. C8), was the headline: "No Altered Corn Found in Allergy Samples." Readers of the Business Section learned that all the Starlink corn-chip samples were *completely free* of genetically modified corn. Indeed, the people who had complained of allergic reactions had in fact *not eaten Starlink corn.* The plot sickens. Obviously the placement of these two articles was a considered editorial decision, hardly an accident. But the question remains: Why would the *New York Times* want to keep this important information from its many readers? Stay tuned.

What we are witnessing is an unrelenting war upon modified foods by antis such as organic farmers, who believe that bioengineered foods will put them out of business because pesticides will no longer be needed by farmers to protect their crops from a host of pests. Opposed, too, are those who believe that genetically modified foods are unnatural, and as such must be demonized. They are abetted by those who see a conspiracy by multinational corporations to control the world's food supply. These fringe groups have bonded in common cause. In a pluralistic society, innovations are normally readily embraced, but now a vocal minority has decided, a priori, to unconditionally oppose this one; in an open society, this turn of events should trouble everyone. Who anointed these antis to speak for the general public?

It is even more troubling that these groups have gotten the ear and attention of the media, and that newspaper accounts of modified foods call for the need of *absolute* safety. That the commentators do not see the absurdity of the idea must engender worry. If someone or some other group suggested that absolute safety, zero risk, be applied to automobiles, skateboards, plane travel, football, horseback riding, baseball bats, sunbathing, guns, ketchup, or ice cream, we would all be up in arms. Life would come to a crashing halt. No one can demonstrate or provide zero risk for any of these products, or anything else. Why, then, are we placing so great a burden on modified food? In this miasma, we have forgotten the words of Philippus Aureolus Theophrastus Bombastus von Hohenheim, the sixteenth-century Swiss physician also known as Paracelsus, who said it for all time: "Dosis sola facet veneum," or "The dose makes the poison." The mere presence of a protein does not convey toxicity—allergenicity. We've got to be careful lest the lemmings lead us over the brink.

The fact that Paracelsus's principle is being violated with modified foods suggests not only that we no longer believe that life has risk, but that the doctrine of reasonable certainty, which has guided our federal agencies since the passage and adoption of our food and drug laws, is being shunted aside. Taco shells have been summarily removed from markets because of a suspicion that Cry9c, a new insecticidal protein, may possibly be allergenic. There is no evidence to support that suspicion. Why are we not being guided by the probability and extent of harm, not its mere possibility?

The depths to which environmentalists, the Greens, will sink to achieve their ends has not been plumbed. For example, during the recent nationwide elections, our home phone rang one evening—during dinner, of course. An unidentified voice told us not to vote for the incumbent congressman, Rush Holt, because he was poisoning our food. Rush Holt was apparently unopposed to genetically modified food. "Keep the poisoner out of Congress," we were told, without further substance. Rush Holt won another term in Congress, but not by much.

Of even more concern is the Greens' preventing golden rice—yellow rice loaded with Vitamin A—from getting to the millions of people who desperately need it because it is allegedly unsafe. A newly developed strain of rice, devised by Ingo Potryus and Peter Beyer of the Swiss Federal Institute of Technology in Zurich and the University of Freiburg in Germany, respectively, languishes in a grenade-proof greenhouse because environmentalists consider it another Frankenstein food. Indeed, it is unlike any other strain of rice on Earth because its seeds contain genetic instructions to produce beta-carotene, a major source of Vitamin A. This set of instructions were borrowed from a daffodil and inserted into the rice's genetic code. The World Health Organization (WHO) maintains that an estimated 124 million children the world over lack sufficient Vitamin A, most of them living in areas of the world where rice is the main dietary staple. Vitamin A deficiency induces blindness in half a million children annually, and it is responsible for diarrheal diseases in many others. Another rice strain, this one with instructions to produce greater levels of iron, is in the development stage, but fear pervades the researchers while the needy are held hostage to cantankerous "environmentalists."[49]

The lack of outcry on the part of the academic community is depressing. Rather than step forward to write and speak on the issue, explaining why allergenicity, for example, is more than likely a fraudulent issue, and why zero risk in anything is wholesale nonsense, our university people seem to have faded into the background, and the public is left dangling in the wind.

How should modified foods be tested for safety? Would it serve to gather a thousand people and have them eat at least one ear of Bt corn a day, for a year, while another thousand ate non-Bt corn? I doubt that would provide a reliable answer. A better way would be to keep tabs on the hundreds of farm families that have planted their fields with modified corn, potatoes, beets, broccoli, and other vegetables, and have been eating them for years. They can be considered our vanguard. I suspect that these families continue to be as healthy a non-Bt eaters. They are a ready-made cohort for interested epidemiologists.

The Chinese Experiment

But in fact it is not necessary to follow several thousand people to see who eats and does not eat modified foods. Nor is it necessary to wait and see if adverse health effects occur among farm families eating modified foods. The Chinese government in mainland China has already embraced genetically modified crops and cattle and has presented us with an experiment-in-progress. The Chinese cultivate tens of millions of acres of cotton and had been spraying the plants with tons of organophosphate pesticides to kill the boll weevil grubs that feed on them so voraciously. Organophosphates contain chemicals similar to those in the nerve gases Sarin and Tabun, which means that the Chinese farmers and their families placed themselves at inordinate risk. The death rate among them has been so high that the government does not disclose the numbers. Now the Chinese government believes that Bollgard, Monsanto's remedy against the boll weevil, is the answer. The Bt toxin is built into the cotton plants and repels the weevils, eliminating the need to spray. In China, cotton plants had to be

sprayed 20–30 times during May and September, the height of the growing season, because the worms become ever more resistant to the pesticide. Ceasing to spray means not only saving the cost of the pesticide, but
also the intensive labor, which translates into additional profit for the
farmers. Most important is the fact that this change will also save lives, prevent illness, and increase crop yields by as much as 50 percent or more. Estimates suggest current and projected savings at some $100 per acre. This
level of savings will make China's cotton, as well as wheat, corn, and rice,
competitive with Western countries.[50]

Pest-resistant cotton is only one item on the Chinese government's to-
do list. Virus-resistant papaya, potatoes, tomatoes, and tobacco are high on
their agenda. In fact, China was the first country to grow genetically modified tobacco plants—as long ago as 1988. Since then, the government has
approved over one hundred modified crops, far more than any other
country. Already in markets and being widely eaten are slow-ripening
tomatoes (with longer shelf life, benefiting both storekeepers and consumers) and virus-resistant green peppers.

Rice, the world's single most consumed food, is in the process of
modification to increase its Vitamin A content as well as its stickiness.
The majority of Chinese prefer sticky rice to dry rice. Stickiness is a gene-
controlled trait. Rice's genome was completely deciphered by Monsanto
geneticists, and modifications are proceeding apace. For example, rice
plants with fewer stalks but double the number of kernels per stalk, meaning far higher rice yields, are well along the developmental process, as is
rice requiring less water, which means less susceptibility to drought. Rice
with higher protein content is yet another project in Monsanto's very active pipeline. But all this is not limited to rice. Soybeans are being modified
to increase their levels of protein and oil, which will mean better cattle feed
and tastier beef, which the Chinese are craving in ever greater amounts.

The Chinese are not suicidal people. They are not consuming genetically modified foods in ever-greater amounts because of some mystical
urge for a better life in the hereafter, nor is the government pouring huge
amounts of hard-to-come-by dollars into genetic research because they
have no other use for it. No, the Chinese have a vision—a vision of the future in which genetically modified crops and cattle will increase yields,
lower costs, and provide adequate food supplies for the world's most
populous country—regardless of what flood, drought, or cold may lie
ahead. Famine in China may become a thing of the past. Perhaps most important of all, as it becomes evident to all that the Chinese people are thriv-

ing and the wild predictions of genetic disaster by the Greens become but a distant thunder, it will make China the exporter to the world, increasing its balance of payments.

China has a controlled press, and as the Chinese government introduces genetically modified foods seeking to ensure adequate food for its 1.25 billion population, the people will not receive the type of prejudged, prepackaged views generated by a small but highly vocal and biased group that has co-opted the media in Europe and the United States. In China, genetically modified foods will make it or break it on their merits—a thoroughly democratic process. And right behind China are Thailand, India, Indonesia, and the Philippines: all are in need of the benefits that food modification promises to provide.

In another significant advance, a team of Chinese and Filipino researchers recently produced a variety of hybrid rice expressing the Bt endotoxin. This successful transfer made the rice resistant to two of its most notorious pests, the yellow stem borer and the leaf folder, without any loss of crop yield. Hybrid rice has shown that it can outproduce traditional rice by 20 percent. For China, this has meant millions of additional tons of rice. With the new, resistant rice, pest control will become a reality, as chemical control has been ineffective because the stem borer larvae remain on the outer surface of the leaf for only a short time before penetrating the stem. The expression of the Bt gene in this rice is expected to be a major pest-management tool for rice pest control not only in China, but in India, Vietnam, Indonesia, Malaysia, Thailand, and the Philippines as well.[51]

Other Products

Rice is not the only concern of farmers. *Xanthamonas campestris* is a bacterium with a voracious appetite for tomatoes. It is unrelenting in its predation, causing bacterial spot disease, which is devastating to tomato crops in areas of the world with high humidity and heavy rainfall, causing substantial losses to farmers and others involved with the crop. But it turns out that peppers have a gene, Bs2, which confers resistance to *Xanthamonas* and bacterial spot disease. A team of researchers at UCLA, San Francisco State University, and the University of Florida isolated Bs2 from peppers, cloned it, and successfully introduced it into tomatoes, making it a part of its genome. Farmers will no longer need to spray their tomato crops with chemical pesticides to protect them against *Xanthamonas*. Although this is another example of transgenic transfer—peppers to tomatoes—the tomatoes look like tomatoes, and taste and smell like tomatoes. Not a hint of peppers anywhere.[52] Transfer of a gene for a specific attribute transfers only that attribute. It is worth recalling that we humans share genes with fleas, flies, and flounder, but an objective observer would never mistake us for any of them.

Speaking of flounder, it won't be long before super salmon will be in our markets. Flounder, a cold-water fish, contains a gene expressing a protein that prevents the fish's freezing in extremely cold conditions. Researchers isolated and copied a part of the flounder's DNA that works like a genetic switch, turning on the production of this antifreeze gene. Normally, this process works only when the fish is exposed to cold. This switch was coupled to a growth-stimulating hormone gene from Chinook salmon, then inserted into fertilized eggs of Atlantic salmon. In the Atlantic salmon, the switch remains on, producing a continuous supply of growth hormone that accelerates the salmon's growth. Atlantic salmon can now grow to market size and weight in 18 months rather than the 24 to 30 normally required. For fish farmers, this means raising fish faster and cheaper.[53]

The Future

In a recent interview, Jane E. Henny, commissioner of the Food and Drug Administration, said: "As we have evaluated the results of the seeds or crops created using biotechnology techniques, we have seen no evidence that the bio-engineered foods now on the market pose any human health concerns or that they are in any way less safe than crops produced through traditional breeding." Asked if it was common for scientists to use antibiotic resistance marker genes in the process of bioengineering, and if she was concerned that their use in food crops will lead to an increase in antibiotic resistance in germs that infect people, she answered: "Antibiotic resistance is a serious public health issue, but that problem is currently and primarily caused by the overuse and misuse of antibiotics. We have carefully considered whether the use of antibiotic resistance marker genes in crops could pose a public health concern and have found no evidence that it does. . . . I'm confident of this," she continued, "for several reasons. First, there is little if any transfer of genes from plants to bacteria. Bacteria pick up resistance genes from other bacteria, and they do it early and often. The potential risk of transfer from plants to bacteria is substantially less than the risk of normal transfer between bacteria. Nevertheless, to be on the safe side, the FDA has advised food developers to avoid using marker genes that encode resistance to clinically important antibiotics."[54] Such comments get little media attention. The public surely wants and needs to hear them, but such news doesn't sell. For the media, public education is not a high priority: it appears only the bottom line is.

Marker genes and antibiotic resistance can use a dollop of elucidation. To transfer a gene to a plant cell, a means of inserting the gene is needed along with a means of identifying where the genes have landed. Several procedures can assure the transfer. One of the most efficient is a soil bacterium that routinely moves in and out of plant cells and carries the gene. As only a few plant cells incorporate the desired gene in transfers, a marker is needed to determine which plants contain it. The current procedure links the trait with a marker that expresses readily identifiable characteristics. The kanamycin resistance gene, a widely used marker, produces an enzyme that inactivates the antibiotics kanamycin and neomycin. Plant cells that do not express the kanamycin gene (do not contain it) are killed by these antibiotics, providing a means of rapid screening. The kanamycin gene is used as a marker because the chemical produced by the gene is easily digested in the stomach even under low acid conditions. It's harmless and doesn't effect antimicrobial resistance. Nevertheless, it raised this question: Could these marker genes be transferred from the modified plant to intestinal bacteria and spread resistance to therapeutic antibiotics? An FAO/WHO expert panel was convened to consider the implications a marker gene might pose. They concluded that the presence of marker genes in food did not compromise its safety for either human or animal consumption.[55] Following that panel, the FDA noted that marker genes held no threat of toxicity or allergenicity.[56]

How much more surety can be imparted? Not a great deal. Fieldwork will, of course, continue, and experience will provide assurance—or it will not. But human health and food safety are not the *real* issues at hand. We are, in fact, witnessing a popular movement in England and Western Europe against America's genetically modified foods. This movement is really a revolt of the masses against the power and wealth of the United States, which has emerged as the strongest, wealthiest country the world has ever seen. Modified food is a cover, a mask, allowing discontented people to vent deep-seated love/hate emotions. Genetic engineering is simply one more example of the creativity, intelligence, and level of American agriculture and science in an age of biotechnology. We pride ourselves on moving fast in a fast-moving world in which we are a few steps ahead of our cousins abroad. This does not sit well with many.

Genetic engineering is awash in politics and succumbing to the mob. But one thing is certain: genetically modified decaffeinated coffee. A team of geneticists at Ochanomizu University, Tokyo, and the University of Glasgow, Scotland, informs us that they have sequenced and cloned the gene encoding for caffeine synthase, a key enzyme in the biosynthesis of caffeine.[57] With the gene sequence known, it is but a step to developing transgenic coffee and tea plants entirely devoid of caffeine. It would be unimaginable to keep this bioengineered product from our supermarkets. Any such attempt would see my wife storming the barricades.

Robert Shapiro, the recently retired CEO of Monsanto, took the science from the laboratories and made genetic engineering a commercial reality. He had a vision: *feed the people of the world with food of high nutritional quality at costs they can afford, avoiding petrochemicals in the process by placing genes into plants so they do not require chemicals for insect control.* It seemed so right, so straightforward. He almost succeeded, but, as usual, visionaries are always ahead of their time. Nevertheless, genomics and genetic engineering offer solutions to old problems and open the future to greater health and prosperity. When the mob has spent its fury, the science will be waiting—to serve the people.

Have you been had? You bet you have!

Troubled Air

From the popular lyrics we learn that "love is in the air," but the words are silent about carbon dioxide, arguably the most notorious air pollutant of the twentieth and twenty-first centuries—and beyond, if we fail to heed the signs.

Carbon dioxide, a simple chemical in the air since time began, has only recently become a pollutant. But at its current and climbing levels, it may unleash untold adverse effects upon every aspect of our lives.

Of all the planets in our solar system, the Earth, our habitat, is remarkably unique in possessing a level of comfort provided by a generous climate unmatched anywhere. We have had a convivial, reliably stable climate since the last ice age, ten to fourteen thousand years ago. The average global temperature of 59° F (15° C), and its accompanying hospitable climate, has been eminently agreeable for the growth and well-being of all living things. Planet Earth has prospered.

Our nearest celestial neighbors, Mars, Venus, and the moon, have been less fortunate. Venus is far too hot, and Mars too cold. Mars is smaller than the Earth, and its exceptionally thin girdling gaseous blanket, its atmosphere, is 95 percent carbon dioxide, containing little if any moisture. So little, in fact, that it never rains on Mars. It is fiercely cold there; what little moisture exists is frozen solid in its −50° C (−122° F) temperature. By comparison, the carbon dioxide on Venus occurs in an exceptionally dense atmosphere, which prevents the escape of heat, sending its surface temperature soaring to a broiling 470° C (878° F). The moon, our nearest neighbor, has no atmosphere at all. With one-sixth of the Earth's gravitational pull, any naturally present carbon dioxide and water vapor have long since escaped into the far reaches of space. But sunlight does strike the moon. Without an atmosphere, however, some light (heat) is reflected, and a portion is absorbed. Without a heat-trapping mechanism, the absorbed heat quickly dissipates, and the daily temperature plummets to a chilly

−160° C (−320° F). Without an atmosphere, the moon is a barren, dead place. Of the other six planets in our system, Saturn, Uranus, Neptune, and Pluto are far from the sun and are virtually in deep freeze, while Mercury and Jupiter are too hot for comfort.

The Earth alone, just far enough from the sun, is comfortably livable, and in large measure owes its uniqueness to an encircling, shielding, beneficent atmosphere. Planet Earth is sheathed in an envelope of gases, a veritable protective cocoon, conveniently divided into layers. The *troposphere*, closest to the ground, is our world. Extending from sea level to just above Mount Everest, these six miles contain our clouds, storms, atmospheric gases, weather, dust, ice, and liquid water. The top of the troposphere mingles with the bottom of the *stratosphere*, a cloudless, stormless, cold region containing a protective layer of ozone.

Our climate is inextricably bound to the presence of carbon dioxide (CO_2) and water vapor in the troposphere. Sunlight, or radiation, when striking atoms and molecules of various chemicals, dust, and clouds, will either pass through, be reflected, or be absorbed. Those things through which light passes are said to be *transparent*; those things that hold light are *opaque*. Opaque materials absorb light (heat) and become warm. They can also reemit their heat. That's the key.

The atmosphere of our world is transparent to solar radiation. The sun's more energetic, shorter wavelengths of visible light readily pass through. A portion strikes the Earth, is absorbed, warming it. At this point, a cautionary note about light is called for. Light can alter its character from highly energetic shorter waves, to less energetic longer waves. That's another key. So, energetic light rays—waves—strike the Earth, warm it a little, then are reflected back to space as less energetic, longer infrared waves, which are not absorbed by carbon dioxide and other gases that are naturally present in the atmosphere. It is at this point that our current air pollution problem begins. And, as the crux of the carbon dioxide problem is approached, our concern must rise to the level of worry, as the current response engendered by this formidable issue does not match its gravity.

Over 98 percent of the air we breathe consists of nitrogen and oxygen, by far more of the former than the latter. The remaining 2 percent consists of some sixteen gases, including carbon dioxide, water vapor, and methane, along with nitrogen and sulfur oxides. More nitrogen than oxygen notwithstanding, ours is an oxygen-driven world. Nevertheless, neither nitrogen nor oxygen absorb in the infrared. But carbon dioxide, water vapor, ozone, methane, and the oxides of nitrogen and sulfur, all transparent to visible incoming light energy, are strong absorbers of thermal infrared. But they do not hold on to this absorbed heat. These gases, present at trace levels, reradiate their absorbed heat back to Earth. This added heat is responsible for maintaining the global mean surface temperature at a balmy 15° C (59° F), some 33° C above what it would be without these trace gases. These gases are exceedingly beneficial—a naturally protective life-support system, a system unique to the Earth and responsible for our success. The underlying element is the Earth's energy balance. If absorbed solar radiation is balanced by the range of reradiating sources, the global energy system will maintain the stable mean surface temperature that it has enjoyed over the past ten to fourteen thousand years. It is the total balance of energy that produces the 15° C global mean temperature.

To reiterate: as light waves pass into the Earth's atmosphere, a portion is scattered as the waves bounce off molecules of air, water, dust, and a host of gases. Another portion is scattered and re-reflected by clouds, while a substantial portion reaches the ground, striking everything in its path—trees, homes, people, animals, cars, lakes, and hills—to be absorbed and reflected, depending upon the type of surface. Much of the short-wave radiation is transformed by the cool Earth into the longer wavelength thermal infrared (IR), which excites molecules in its path to increased activity—warmth—which they in turn absorb and re-reflect toward Earth. A balance is struck. The essential facet of this balancing is that the Earth gives up heat and cools to a humanly comfortable and supportive temperature. Therefore, if incoming solar radiation should accumulate in the atmosphere beyond the point of balance, for whatever reason, global temperature must rise, unevenly to be sure, but it must rise.

The Greenhouse Effect

The sequence of events in which short-wave radiation is absorbed by the Earth and then reradiated as longer-wavelength IR that is trapped in the atmosphere by the specific absorbing gases is referred to as the *greenhouse effect*. Why "greenhouse"? Because the glass of a greenhouse permits the passage of visible short-wave radiation but absorbs a portion of the longer wavelengths. The incoming light falls upon soil, plants, tools, pots within the house, warming them. In turn, they reradiate part of that light. The glass allows no more than 10 percent of the warm IR to pass through, retaining 90 percent, maintaining the greenhouse warmer than its external surroundings. If, however, the temperature of the greenhouse is not adequately controlled and the greenhouse is not appropriately ventilated, the flowers and other living things will die of excessive heat. Early greenhouses had this problem.

The natural greenhouse effect is a most salutary condition found only on planet Earth. Venus, on the other hand, is a hothouse; an extremely hot house, and Mars is a veritable icehouse.

Anything that alters the radiation received from the sun or lost to space, or that alters the redistribution of energy within the atmosphere, can affect temperature and thereby the climate. A change in the available energy is a radiative forcing. With our excessively accumulating greenhouse gases, we are currently experiencing an *enhanced greenhouse effect* due to positive radiative forcing. Carbon dioxide, methane, the nitrogen and sulfur oxides, ozone, and water vapor are accumulating at unprecedented levels. Our atmosphere is becoming denser. Too much heat is being re-reflected Earthward. The energy balance is being upset.

The Intergovernmental Panel on Climate Change (IPCC), a committee of internationally renowned climatologists established by the World Meteorological Organization and the United Nations Environmental Program, recently declared, "We have clear evidence that human activities have affected concentrations, distributions, and life cycles of these gases." And they further noted that "carbon dioxide concentrations have increased by almost 30 percent from 280 ppmv in the late 18th century to 360 ppmv (parts per million by volume) in 1994."[1]

It's a cycle, an unpleasant cycle. With increased warming there is increased evaporation—moisture loss from soil and lakes—which means large reservoirs of water above us. Because water vapor also traps the IRs, it is another major greenhouse gas (GHG). It, too, reradiates its heat Earthward, and so our habitat becomes warmer, and our atmosphere is no longer a pleasant greenhouse, but an enhanced greenhouse. Heat to the Earth is becoming excessive and temperatures are rising, making for inhospitable surroundings.

Is it possible that we humans can overwhelm nature? Do we have such power? George Perkins Marsh (1801–1882) thought so. Marsh, author of "The Earth Modified by Human Activity," was certain that where man was concerned, "there is scarcely any assignable limit to his present and prospective voluntary controlling power over terrestrial nature." But Marsh, as prescient as he was, could not have foreseen that humankind appeared to be marching inexorably toward a denser atmosphere—in the direction of Venus. If we are, how are we doing it? And is there no braking, no slowing down, no prevention? Is it foregone?

Again, the IPCC has considered this prospect and concluded that a triad of sources is responsible for enhancing our greenhouse: combustion of fossil fuels, cement production, and land-use conversion.

Fossil fuels refer to oil, coal, and wood. Any naturally occurring carbon-containing material when burned in air produces CO_2, water, and heat energy. Coal and oil are naturally occurring substances that originated from over millions of years of decay, pressure, and heat on woody plants, trees, and ferns for coal, and dead plants and animals in marine sediments for oil. Both have great heat value. But the release of vast quantities of CO_2 from these fuels is at the heart of an enhanced greenhouse—that is, global warming.

Fossil fuels are used in our electric power–generating plants. In the modern era, electricity is the name of the game. The tremendous quantities of coal and oil burned to boil the water, to make the steam, to drive the generators that will produce the electricity needed, nay, demanded, for our homes, offices, businesses, and industry, release billions of tons of carbon dioxide—gigatons—into the air annually. Our thirst for electricity is limitless and unquenchable because it is people driven. Here again, the IPCC informs us that the United States is the world's foremost user of electricity, as well as the atmosphere's greatest polluter by carbon dioxide. Electricity, like water, has become the driving force of all nations. Those with only small amounts of it want more, anticipate the need, and will eventually obtain it. It is only a matter of time. This demand brings up the question of prevention, or braking the headlong flight toward increased warming. Demand for electricity is fueled by people—ever-increasing numbers of people. Due to our natural growth and unconstrained immigration, the U.S. population has literally mushroomed. Look at the numbers in table 5.1. They portend a warning.

Current world population is approximately 6,111,000,000, and in time is estimated to rise to 7–10 billion. Between 1900 and 1950, our population doubled. It will double again by 2010, only a few years down the road. With a population of over 300 million and no end in sight, our need for electricity must continue to increase, and with coal- and oil-fired power plants as the primary producers, additional gigatons of CO_2 must rise into the greenhouse, with additional radiative forcing.

Table 5.1. Population of the United States, 1900–2010

Year	Population
1900	75,994,575
1950	150,697,361
1980	226,545,805
1990	248,791,672
2000	281,421,906
2010	300,000,000 (estimated)

Electricity-Generating Plants

We demand the energy to power our electrically driven world. We cannot function without our computers, powerbooks, printers, scanners, hard-drives, modems, routers, zip-disks, TVs, radios, air conditioners, toasters, microwaves, vacuum cleaners, irons, mixers, toaster ovens, refrigerators, washers, dryers, pencil sharpeners, can openers, fax machines, telephones, battery chargers, electric clocks. To these add the larger and larger supermarkets with their tremendous demands for electrically driven refrigeration, and the ever-larger shopping malls and high-rises.

The demand for electricity is nowhere more evident than in the thousands of colleges and universities across the country, where the millions of students have a bewildering array of electric power–demanding appliances and conveniences. It is the odd student who does not claim ownership of a computer, radio, TV, VCR, popcorn popper, refrigerator, hair dryer, microwave, CD player, electric shaver, stereo system, coffeemaker, alarm clock, answering machine, and toaster. Most have not a clue how the electricity is generated and distributed, other than placing a plug into a wall socket, yet they will rail against excessive emission of CO_2. That they are flagrant and profligate users of fossil fuels is lost on them, and the schools obediently cater to their demands. But they are no different than society generally. Nevertheless, industry, including colleges, is by far the major user of electricity and emitter of GHGs, followed by transportation, residential use, commercial, and agricultural uses. Everyone shares responsibility.

The Automobile

The automobile is another notorious CO_2 emitter. The next time you take the family car for a spin, consider this. A car emits 19–20 pounds of CO_2 per gallon of gas. If the average car has a 20-gallon gas tank and uses a tankful a week, then 20 gallons times 20 pounds per gallon emit 400 pounds of CO_2 per tankful per week. At fifty tankfuls per year, that's 20,000 pounds per car per year. If we multiply 20,000 by the 218,300,000 registered vehicles on the road in 1999 (according to the National Safety Council), the air absorbs 4,366,000,000,000 pounds, or 2,183,000,000 tons, of CO_2 per year. With the increasing population, the number of cars also increases, as do the tonnages of CO_2. No matter how you slice it, it's a monstrous accumulation. And this is only for the United States. On a worldwide basis—with global warming, one must think globally—the contribution rises to tera and penta tonnages. Tera is a prefix meaning trillion, 10 with 12 zeros; penta is a prefix meaning quadrillion, 10 accompanied by 15 zeros. On a worldwide basis, we could be dealing with an additional three zeros, bringing emissions to atto: 10 with 18 zeros. We are not simply into huge numbers here, but numbers so large as to be incomprehensible, which may be another part of the problem. Although at these vast levels we already approach incomprehension, we have not yet added the contribution of coal and oil electricity-generating plants, the heaviest polluters of all. Their contribution alone could stagger the imagination. Indeed, we humans have become major players in what used to be solely nature's province.

Cement

But wait, there's even more. In their several reports, the IPCC has spoken of three major CO_2 contributors: fossil fuels, cement production, and "land-use conversion." Cement? How can so dense a material play a role in enhancing the greenhouse? Cement begins with limestone, one of the most common rocks on Earth and a veritable storehouse of carbon dioxide. It has been estimated that "the amount of carbon in sedimentary rock is more than 600 times the total carbon content of the plants, water, air, and living cells."[2] If all the carbon dioxide locked away in limestone over millions of years were to be suddenly released, it would be difficult to distinguish Earth from Venus. Although such a catastrophe is unimaginable, not possible, it is possible to release tremendous amounts of CO_2 from limestone in the process of making cement. In our high school chemistry classes we learned about decomposition reactions in which a compound such as limestone, calcium carbonate ($CaCO_3$), decomposes into simpler substances given the right heat treatment. For cement and limestone, calcining is such a treatment. Calcining is the process of heating limestone to high temperatures, 1100°–1600° F) (600°–900° C) but not high enough to cause melting. This heat treatment drives off moisture and decomposes the carbonate to form calcium oxide (lime) and lots of CO_2—gigatons of it. Cement production and concrete require limestone as their core ingredient and are often seen as a measure of a country's progress. There would be major battles over any attempt to reduce cement production in either developing or developed countries.

Deforestation

"Land-use conversion" is a euphemism for deforestation, or the replacement of natural woodland with roads, lumber production, cropland, and cattle ranches. The primary forests at issue are tropical, stretching in a belt along the equator from Brazil and the Amazon, through the Democratic Republic of the Congo to Malaysia and Indonesia. Along this forest primeval is yet another of the Earth's great carbon dioxide storehouses. The areas involved are immense. Here, too, the scale of deforestation may be incomprehensible. What does it mean, for example, to say that tens of thousands of square miles of forest disappear annually? In Peru, 500,000 acres of forest, 780 square miles, twelve times the size of Washington, D.C., was cleared for coca crops to satisfy the Western world's desire for cocaine. Since 1970, over 60 percent of the Lacondana Forest in the Mexican state of Chiapas has been lost. Lacondona, with some 5,000 square miles, is the size of Connecticut. Similar deforestation occurs around the world as a consequence of population pressure, corruption, and bureaucratic ineptitude.[3] Whatever the cause, deforestation changes climate as a result of the loss of trees, which are carbon dioxide absorbers. Trees scrub the air of CO_2 and store it until the tree is cut down and burned, which releases the stored CO_2 When trees are cut for lumber, the wood continues banking CO_2.

Deforestation plays a dual role. On the one hand, trees are no longer available as sinks, as absorbers of CO_2 from the air. But, having been cut and burned, or even cut and allowed to decay, their stored CO_2 is returned to the air to add to an already overtaxed atmosphere. Furthermore, as land is cleared, it becomes more reflecting, thereby adding more of the longer-wave IR radiation to the greenhouse to be reradiated Earthward, adding yet more heat.

Methane

Although CO_2 as an absorber of IR radiation is a potent GHG, other gases in the greenhouse add to its enhancement. Methane or marsh gas (what miners refer to as "fire damp"), a simple carbon compound (CH_4), is highly IR-absorbing. Unlike CO_2, methane's presence in the air was not revealed until 1948. Its concentration in air has been rising far more rapidly than CO_2. Although normally present at a level of 0.00022 percent (indeed a trace) and 700 ppbv (parts per billion volume) in preindustrial times, molecule for molecule it is as much as ten times more absorbing of IR than carbon dioxide. Methane is the primary ingredient of natural gas, found in all the oil and gas fields of the world and bubbling up from lake bottoms as marsh gas. It is also produced as a byproduct of microbial digestion of dead organic matter. But by far the largest additions derive from rice paddies of China and India, with some 10–14 percent of all methane produced there. This presents a conundrum. With the population growing exponentially around the world, now at 6-plus billion and counting and 7–10 billion anticipated by 2010, primarily in underdeveloped countries, rice production must at least double. With it, far more methane will drift into the atmosphere—unless new ways of growing rice are found. Researchers at the University of California at Irvine have found that unplanted, flooded rice fields produce as much methane as planted fields. Their data indicate that levels emitted vary with the growth cycle, soil content, and flooding conditions. It remains to be determined if methane arises from the soil and is emitted through the plant, or if the plant creates the methane.

Animals are yet another major methane source. Anaerobic bacteria in the guts of cattle, sheep, goats, buffaloes, and camels produce methane from fodder, which is released to the air from both ends of these cud chewers' digestive systems. Together, these ruminants account for some 15 percent of emitted methane. Until new and imaginative feed formulations are devised, methane levels from these sources will remain stable unless their populations also increase. Not to be overlooked are the termites of this world, whose tiny guts also house methane-producing microflora. Scientists are uncertain whether the vast number of termites on this planet produce 5 or 155 million tons of methane annually. While it might be nice to know the actual amount, nothing could be done to alter their methane production.

Finally, we have the contribution of landfills and biomass burning to the CO_2 levels, bringing the current level to 1,721 ppbv. Rice cultivation, animal husbandry, biomass burning, and landfills contribute as much as 350 teragrams of CH_4 per year. Recall that "tera" is 10 followed by 12 zeros.

Nylon and Nitric Acid

Would it have made a difference if nylon hadn't been invented? The atmospheric concentration of nitrous oxide (N_2O) has increased from about 275 ppbv in preindustrial times to about 313 ppbv currently. Three to eight tera grams (Tg) of nitrogen are added to the atmosphere annually. One of the major anthropogenic sources is adipic acid, without which there would be no nylon, the generic term for all synthetic polyamides that are fabricated into tubes, pipes, sheets, filaments, and coatings. Would you believe that 5 billion pounds are manufactured worldwide, yearly? But nylon can't take all the credit. Nitric acid production and nitrogen-fixing bacteria in the soil are additional contributors. The bacterium *Nitrobacter* converts nitrate (NO_3) in the soil to molecular nitrogen (N_2), a gas that rises into the atmosphere, where it reacts with oxygen to form N_2O, which has strong IR-absorbing properties. In fact, N_2O is some 250–300 times more IR-absorbing than CO_2. A little goes a long way, thus the mighty impact of agriculture. This problem will require a great deal of creative thinking to modulate.[4]

Ozone

"Ozone" comes from the Greek, meaning "to smell," which it does. But there is stratospheric ozone and ground-level ozone. Our concern is not with the ozone produced at sea level, where sunlight reacts with auto emissions such as hydrocarbons and nitric oxide, which can burn the eyes and irritate the throat and lungs. The ozone of the greenhouse is the ozone of the upper reaches of the stratosphere. Here, in a highly chemically reactive area, ozone is constantly destroyed and regenerated, naturally, in accordance with the grand plan. Accordingly, it is unique among the trace GHGs in having neither natural nor artificial reservoirs. It is constantly being produced and destroyed in a series of photochemically catalyzed reactions in which oxygen molecules, migrating up from the troposphere, react with ultraviolet light (UV), split into highly reactive oxygen atoms that combine with nearby oxygen molecules (O_2) to form ozone (O_3) and heat. With solar radiation being strongest above the equator, the photodissociation of oxygen is greatest there. From there, the newly formed ozone is swept around the Earth and across the poles by stratospheric winds. Its trace concentration notwithstanding, ozone is a formidable absorber of IR and plays a major role in atmospheric heat balance.

Considering that stratospheric ozone has no reservoirs or wellsprings, and that ground-level ozone never makes it to the stratosphere, its levels should remain constant. "Should" was correct until the 1930s, when the chlorofluorocarbons, the CFCs, the freons, were born in Dayton, Ohio. At the time, these newly hatched organochlorine compounds were thought to be the perfect chemical: inert, nonflammable, nonexplosive, and noncorrosive. Who could ask for anything more? They were perfect for refrigerators, where they substantially reduced electricity demands, and for air conditioning in homes and automobiles. Another use was as aerosol propellants and insulating material, and for plastic/foam cups, trays, and packaging materials, and much, much more. The CFCs were a great invention and a great advance—until 1971, when James Lovelock discovered their presence in the air over Ireland.[5]

Inherent in the CFC molecule was a fatal flaw. When escaping into the air, these gases pass unimpaired through the troposphere to the level of the ozone layer, and above. At the top of the stratosphere, or the bottom of the mesosphere, UV radiation is intense, striking the CFCs and splitting them, releasing energetic chlorine atoms. And therein hangs a tale. A tale of holes at the poles.

Chlorine atoms destroy stratospheric ozone molecules faster than they can be replaced. One chlorine atom can destroy 100,000 ozone molecules. For ozone, it's a losing game. And for the citizens below, not necessarily only on the beach, the risk of UV-induced melanoma increases, because the ozone layer is the natural barrier preventing potentially harmful UV radiation from penetrating the stratosphere and impacting the gentlefolk of the troposphere, particularly in countries of the Southern Hemisphere such as Australia and the southern tip of South America around Patagonia (Argentina) and Chile, and in the Northern Hemisphere over portions of Greenland, Iceland, Sweden, Norway, and Finland. CFC production has been dramatically reduced in response to international agreements, and their atmospheric concentrations are expected to diminish substantially during the twenty-first century.

Chemicals have a life of their own, however. Once released, they cannot be pulled back, and their die-off may be years in the making. CFC molecules take about eight years to reach the ozone layer. Consequently, their ozone-depleting activity doesn't even begin until years after they are released. That is another reason why their adverse affects cannot be anticipated until well into the mid-twenty-first century. The same UV radiation that splits the CFC molecule is also the radiation that directly destroys the ozone in the ozone layer. But in this normal and natural process, the Earth's protective ozone layer is continually regenerated by the ready availability of oxygen molecules.

Water Vapor

Water vapor is another major GHG. In 1963, Fritz Möller of the University of Munich in Germany advanced the idea that water vapor could well act as an amplifying or intensifying positive feedback mechanism.[6] If increases in CO_2 induced a warming effect, then increased evaporation from the seas and oceans would increase atmospheric water vapor, which in turn would absorb more IR, thereby driving temperatures still higher. A quarter of a century later, researchers at the University of Chicago demonstrated the fact of Möller's concept and lent credence to climate models. "The rate of increase," they reported, "gives compelling evidence for the positive feedback between surface temperature, water vapor, and the greenhouse effects. The magnitude of the feedback is consistent with that predicted by climate models."[7]

Changes in the climate system that are being more confidently predicted in response to the increasing levels of GHGs are increases in mean surface temperature, rising sea levels, increases in precipitation, and changes in the biosphere.

Other Culprits

As if the five principle GHGs were not enough, atmospheric chemists at the University of East Anglia in Norwich, England, recently reported that they isolated and identified trifluoromethylsulfurpentafluoride, not only an exceedingly difficult word and rare chemical, but, according to William T. Sturgis, its discoverer, molecule for molecule it is 18,000 times more IR-absorbing than CO_2. According to Sturgis, SF_5CF_3 was not present in the atmosphere before 1950. He estimates some 4,000 tons have been released to date, with about 270 tons emitted per year. Current opinion holds that this esoteric compound may be an unnoticed byproduct of industrial processes using fluorine. Obviously, the air, like the ocean, is viewed as a bottomless pit.[8] Until that idea is relegated to the trash bin of history, we will continue to have troubled air.

Were We Warned?

None of this information should come as a surprise. It was foretold, but few were listening. Is our current greenhouse dilemma "déjà vu all over again"?

As early as 1896, the Swedish chemist and Nobelist Svante August Arrhenius understood that carbon dioxide was transparent to incoming radiation, but opaque to the infrared. Calculating, without benefit of computers, the effect of added CO_2 on the Earth's temperature, he found that the doubling of CO_2 in the Earth's atmosphere would produce a 3.3° C (6° F) increase in mean global surface temperature.[9] Although his work was well known, it gathered little more than dust on library shelves. But there was little urgency until Roger Revelle and Hans Suess of the Scripps Institution of Oceanography in San Diego sounded the tocsin. "Human beings," they wrote, "are now carrying out a large-scale geophysical experiment of a kind that could not have happened in the past nor be replicated in the future." But it was the subsequent thought that grabbed our full attention: "Within a few centuries we are returning to the atmosphere and oceans the concentrated organic carbon stored in the sedimentary rocks over hundreds of millions of years."[10] That was the essential point. And it led directly to the massive scientific effort of the International Geophysical Year of 1957–1958, during which projects for the measurement of atmospheric CO_2 were undertaken.

Charles D. Keeling and Robert B. Bacastow of Scripps, in conjunction with the National Oceanic and Atmospheric Administration (NOAA), established CO_2-monitoring stations atop the summit of Mauna Loa, a defunct volcano, on the island of Hawaii. A second monitoring station was set up at the South Pole station of the U.S. Antarctic Program. Since 1958, Keeling's group has collected air samples and analyzed them for CO_2. His rendering of monthly mean CO_2 levels, which clearly show an ever-upward climb, as seen in figure 5.1, are among the most quoted, most reproduced pieces of scientifically and politically scrutinized data of the past two decades.[11] People were beginning to listen.

In its 1995 report, the IPCC concluded that "the atmospheric concentrations of greenhouse gases, inter alia, carbon dioxide, methane, and

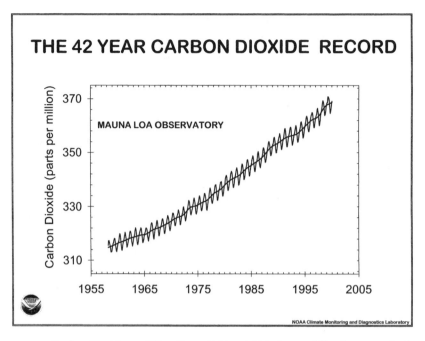

FIG. 5.1. *Carbon dioxide trend line. From 1958 to 2000, the trend line for atmospheric CO_2 has been steadily upward. The saw-toothed curve represents seasonal fluctuations due to uptake of CO_2 by trees and plants in spring and summer (photosynthesis), and an increase in atmospheric CO_2 in fall and winter, as plants and trees release their CO_2 via respiration.* (SOURCE: Courtesy of NOAA Climate Monitoring and Diagnostics Laboratory, CMDL, Carbon Cycle–Greenhouse Gases.)

nitrous oxide, have grown significantly (since about 1750): by 30 percent, 145 percent, and 15 percent, respectively. . . . These trends can be attributed largely to human activities, mostly fossil fuel use, land-use change, and agriculture."[12] It remained for James E. Hansen in the summer of 1988 to move the very real possibility of an inhospitable global warming to the front pages of the world's newspapers.

Global Warming

Hansen, director of NASA's Goddard Institute for Space Studies, testifying before a Senate committee, sounded the alarm with a force and authority rarely encountered in an established scientist. The Earth was getting warmer, "and he was 99 percent certain that the accumulation of greenhouse gases was responsible for the warming trend." Hansen's testimony came at a propitious moment. It was hot. Weeks of drought had parched the American grain belt, and the North and Southeast were in the throes of an extended hot spell. If Hansen's climate models were approximately correct, the probability of another blistering summer was as high as 80 percent. Hansen had not only the heat working for him, but also years of environmental consciousness raising. The media embraced the story, and the threat of a potentially overheated planet raced across the country and around the world. Suddenly, global warming moved directly from academic journals and conferences to the fast lanes of the electronic media.

Indeed, how does one project future temperature and climate using computer models? After all, there can be no laboratory experiments to test the Earth's response to increases or decreases of the GHGs. Models do have their place.

At one time or another, we all constructed models—planes, trains, cars, ships, houses—our attempts to portray or simulate reality in a manageable and inexpensive way. Manageable is the operative term. Marine engineers build models of ships and aviation engineers build models of planes; ships are tested in tanks of water and planes in wind tunnels. Waves can be generated and sent crashing against imaginatively designed hulls, and winds of gale force can be hurled at newly designed wings and fuselage. Will the hull list and capsize, will the plane lose a wing and crash? Models can tell us many things quickly, safely, and reliably. Mathematical models place numbers on variable ranges of values and attempt to determine rates of change over time. It becomes quantitative rather than simply descriptive, and as the model increases in complexity, it can provide information on the rates of change of several mutually dependent variables concurrently. The atmosphere and oceans, major elements in determining climate, are in constant motion, ever changing. But they should be amenable to mathematical statements providing descriptions of climate over time—over years. A hundred years.

As already noted, changes in radiatively active trace gases in the atmosphere produce radiative forcings, an energy unbalance resulting in the warming of the Earth's surface temperature beyond its normally stable level. As the warming and other climate effects will not be uniform over the Earth's surface, a model's role is to simulate possible continental- and regional-scale climate responses. Current models include the most important large-scale physical processes governing the climate system.

The principal models in use are called General Circulation Models (GCMs), which begin with a baseline atmospheric CO_2 concentration of about 300 parts per million volume (ppmv), which approximates the level during the eighteenth century, before the industrial revolution. The model is run with CO_2 concentrations at double this level until the simulated climate reaches a new equilibrium. The difference between the two results indicates the likely climate response to this level of CO_2. But doubling is only one among a range of CO_2 concentrations that must be tested, and an equilibrium climate would not be expected to occur at once over the entire Earth. Models that simulate the time-varied response of the climate to increasing greenhouse gases have been coupled with atmosphere-ocean global models. These models simulate the lag in climate change induced by deep-ocean circulation. And models have improved along with understanding of the unimaginable complexity of the climate system and the recognition of the need to frequently include additional processes.

When a model is used for climate projection, it is first run for many simulated decades without any change in external forcing in the system. The quality of the simulation can then be compared with what actually transpired over the same number of decades. But models are far from perfect. Among the major uncertainties in all models are the difficulties in representing the radiative properties of clouds—and their many different types—as well as the coupling between atmosphere and ocean. But perfection is neither necessary nor expected.

In 1988, the World Meteorological Organization (WMO) and the United Nations Environmental Program (UNEP) created the Intergovernmental Panel on Climate Change, IPCC, and an assemblage of the world's foremost climate scientists to provide the best available data to run the models as well as interpret their output. Working Group I (WGI) was given the task of assessing the climate-change issue; Working Group II (WGII) was to assess the impacts of climate change; and WGIII was assigned the task of formulating response strategies.

Working Group I developed four scenarios they believed encompassed the then possible temperature increases along with the CO_2 levels that would force these increases. Figure 5.2 deploys projections of both CO_2 levels and global temperature changes anticipated between 1990 and 2100, for four different scenarios, A, B, C, and D.

For CO_2 emissions, the trend line for the business-as-usual scenario (A) rises steadily as the countries of the world continue their profligate ways. Nothing changes. Energy generation continues to be coal and oil based. Only modest improvements in energy efficiency use are instituted. Deforestation and cement production continue unabated. In this scenario,

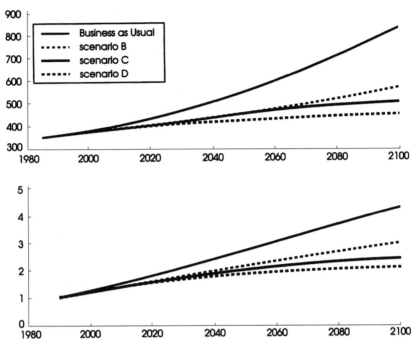

FIG. 5.2. *IPCC scenarios. Projected carbon dioxide concentrations (top) and tempera-ture change (increases) according to four IPCC emissions scenarios.* (SOURCE: *The Impact of Climate Change*, UNEP/GEMS Environmental Library No. 10, 1993. By permission of the United Nations Environmental Programme.)

CO_2 levels rise beyond 800 ppmv. Average global surface temperature increases steadily, rising to over 4° C (39.2° F) by 2100. By contrast, Scenario D projects temperature and CO_2 levels based on major shifts in fuel from coal and oil to nuclear power and renewable sources during the period 2000–2050, and foresees CO_2 emissions reduced to half of 1985 levels by 2050. Nevertheless, a temperature increase of 2° C appears a foregone conclusion. Scenarios B and C show the effects of more modest changes in energy efficiency and the benefits of shifting to nuclear power, respectively.

Computer models have shown that any warming trend will not occur uniformly over the planet. The warming is anticipated to be more intense at higher than lower latitudes, and greater in winter than in summer. In some areas in the high northern latitudes in winter, warming would be 50–100 percent greater than the global average, which in fact is nonexistent except as a calculated average obtained from thousands of values from around the world. The value, 15° C, includes the scorching 134° F (43° C) recorded at Death Valley, California, on July 10, 1953, as well as the impossibly cold −128.6° F of Antarctica reached on July 21, 1983, and everywhere in between. Disarmingly small increases in temperature may be disastrous for some areas and beneficial for others.

Since its 1995 evaluation, the IPCC has updated its projections. In its year 2000 Special Report, what some would have believed to be disarmingly small temperature increases may in fact not be all that small, for anyone.[13] Currently, they maintain that there is stronger evidence of human influence on climate, and they conclude that if emissions are not curtailed, average surface temperature could be expected to increase from 2.7° to almost 11° F (6.1° C) by the end of the twenty-first century. They found, too, that warming over the past one hundred years "is likely to be the largest of any century during the past 1,000 years, and that sea level rise has been 10 times greater in the past 100 years than the average rate over the past 3,000 years, and there has been widespread retreat of mountain glaciers in non-polar regions, and a decline in sea, ice, and snow-covered areas during the past fifty years."

What does this portend? It is not all bad, but a reasonable person could be forgiven for believing that the bad outweighs the good. As the impacts of climate change will intrude upon human health, agriculture, and the environment generally, it is fitting that we treat each in some detail.

Effects on Human Health

Climate change is expected to have broad and adverse consequences for human health. These would occur directly via exposure to thermal stress and indirectly via increases in other air pollutants, pollens, and mold spores. Of concern also are malnutrition and increases in the potential transmission of vector-borne and water-borne diseases.

As temperate regions such as North America are expected to warm far more than tropical and subtropical areas, the most direct effect of a warmer world would be the impact of the higher temperatures themselves. Accordingly, the numbers of very hot days in North America, temperatures well above 90° F (32.2° C), are expected to double, with a 2°–3° C rise in the average summer temperature. Should the IPCC's more recent prediction of far higher temperature increases prevail, this doubling could be tripled. Extremely hot temperatures increase the number of people who die on any given day. The very old, the very young, and the chronically ill may well succumb in excessively hot weather if adequate air conditioning is lacking. Air conditioning itself will be extraordinarily challenged as demand skyrockets. Deaths will increase as brownouts and blackouts occur, and occur more frequently. Those with heart problems are at greater risk because the cardiovascular system must work harder to keep the body cool during prolonged hot spells. Also, heat exhaustion and respiratory problems increase. This is not a conjecture or speculation, nor are computer models necessary to obtain potential numbers of expected excess deaths. The data are already available, as heat-related deaths have occurred every summer, especially during extensive hot spells. Prolonged exposure to high heat and humidity lead to fluid loss and exhaustion, a failure of the body's heat-loss mechanism, with consequent heat stroke. Dehydration, age, excessive sweating, vomiting, diarrhea, and debility predispose one to heat stroke; high humidity, strenuous exertion, poor ventilation, and heavy clothing contribute to dehydration or heat exhaustion.

Heat stroke can be the most serious health problem in a hot environment. It occurs when the body's thermoregulatory system ceases to function and sweating stops. Why this occurs remains a physiological conundrum, and most distressing is the fact that the individual has no idea it's happening. But when it does happen, the body's only effective means of ridding itself of excess heat is gone. The skin becomes hot and dry and reddens dramatically at this point; body temperature is at least 104° F and rising. Mental confusion is often another sign. If, at this point, a person is not quickly cooled, the end stages are unconsciousness, delirium, convulsion, and death.

A lesser degree of heat causes heat exhaustion, the result of excessive fluid and salt loss. Sweating continues, but muscular weakness, fatigue, giddiness, and headache are pronounced. Heat cramps, occurring at the far end of the heat-stress spectrum, are the pain of muscles in spasm. This is most often seen in those who sweat profusely, consume copious amounts of liquid, but fail to replace lost salt. Taking fluids without salt further dilutes the body's salt (electrolyte) balance. It is the loss of salt from muscle that induces the painful cramping. The elderly, who are more than likely on low-salt or no-salt regimens, should be aware of the non-sodium-based salts that are appropriate for their special needs. Indeed, anyone on restricted salt diets must be aware of this danger as a warmer world settles upon us all. Common sense notwithstanding, heat-related deaths could be expected to rise in a warmer world. We have already witnessed the July 1995 heat wave in Chicago, which was directly responsible for 765 deaths.

A warning system such as the Philadelphia Hot Weather-Health Watch/Warning System (PWWS), which alerts the public to the approach of oppressive air masses and their extended periods of extreme high temperatures, high humidity, moderate to strong southwesterly winds, and high pressure, could reduce heat-related mortality. The PWWS is a three-tiered system that produces a health watch, health alert, or health warning and then, depending on what is required, initiates a series of interventions, including media announcements, promotion of a "buddy system," home visits, nursing and personal care alerts, increased emergency medical staffing, and provision of air-conditioned facilities.[14] It is worth a moment's concern to wonder if available electric power will be the Achilles' heel of such programs.

Because few studies exist that assess implications of climate change on air quality, or of population exposure to ground-level ozone, to extreme weather events such as flooding and cyclones, and most specifically to vector-borne disease and the dynamics of their transmission in a warmer world, we are forced to rely on published laboratory studies and conjecture. So, for example, the severity of allergies may be intensified by changes in heat and humidity, thereby contributing to breathing difficulties. Ozone at sea level can cause lung damage among children and the elderly, reducing pulmonary function and sensitizing airways to other irritants and allergens. At relatively low exposure levels, even healthy individuals can experience chest pain, coughing, nausea, and pulmonary congestion. Hospital, fire, and police emergency facilities would be well advised to prepare themselves for such increases.

As for vector-borne disease carried by arthropod or rodent vectors, projected climate changes would likely make conditions less hospitable for the transmission of flea- and louse-borne plague, for example, and certain kinds of encephalitis. Others, such as St. Louis encephalitis and Western equine encephalitis, might extend their range. It is well established that infectious agents and their vector organisms are sensitive to humidity, soil moisture, wind, and changes in forest distribution and surface water. However, although projected changes in climate could provide opportunities for diseases to spread, the current U.S. and Canadian health infrastructure may prevent or at least control this effect. However, this will place increased demand on personnel and costs. West Nile virus encephalitis offers a current and cautionary example.

Malaria is yet another example of climatic factors encouraging the breeding activity of *Anopheles* mosquitoes in otherwise nonendemic areas.

This has already been observed in both New York and New Jersey.[15] On the other hand, GCMs suggest that in a warmer world, greater northward dispersion may not occur.[16] Malaria, by the way, usually thought of as indigenous to central Africa, was prevalent throughout the American colonies. By 1850, malaria had extended its range as far north as what is now Minnesota, Wisconsin, and Michigan. By the 1930s, malaria had disappeared from northern and western states but was still causing deaths in Louisiana, Mississippi, and Alabama. It wasn't until the 1970s that malaria was considered eradicated in the United States. A warmer world with increased precipitation could see malaria returning to its previous haunts. Not a propitious omen. Should a sustained warming trend occur, dengue fever (or breakbone fever, so called because of the awful pain it engenders), another mosquito-borne disease, is anticipated to extend its range to states above the Mason-Dixon Line.

Ticks, as we have seen, transmit Lyme disease, Rocky Mountain spotted fever, and Erlichiosis. Ticks are highly dependent on warm, humid environments, and a climate change for the warmer could be expected to alter their distribution in both the United States and Canada.

Diarrheal diseases can be induced by an array of bacteria, viruses, and protozoa. Climatic effects on the distribution and quality of surface water, including flooding or shortages, can impair local sewage systems and personal hygiene. In 1995, heavy rainfall in British Columbia contaminated a reservoir with oocysts from domestic and wild cats, resulting in an outbreak of toxoplasmosis. Cryptosporidiosis is the most prevalent waterborne disease in the United States and can be fatal to immuno-compromised individuals. Flooding and melting snow can wash fecal material from agricultural areas into water sources. In Milwaukee, 403,000 cases occurred in 1993, when unusually heavy spring rains did just that.[17] And in what has been described as the worst case of contaminated drinking water in North America, *E. coli* O157:H7, together with flooding due to heavy rains that lashed Walkertown, Ontario, Quebec, for days before the outbreak, were responsible for sixteen deaths and two thousand serious illnesses. The drenching rains flushed manure-laden farm runoff water into the public water supply system, and with it the verotoxin-producing coliform bacteria.[18] Indeed, experience does provide guidance.

Although climate models indicate an unevenness in global precipitation, it is clear that higher temperatures will increase the rate of evaporation of moisture from oceans, rivers, lakes, land, trees, and plants, which means more rain and more drought. Areas at increased risk of water losses are the already arid and semiarid areas of northern and southern Africa, India, Mexico, the southwestern United States, Brazil, and the Mediterranean countries. Drought can create economic and social problems, given the disastrous effects on crops and livestock and on hydroelectric power generation. In areas such as Sweden, Norway, Finland, and Denmark, increases in glacial meltwater to rivers can lead to flooding, landslides, and river sedimentation. The problems multiply.

Rising sea levels carry with them concern for coastal areas and wetlands. In its 1996 report, the IPCC informed us that "improved methods for filtering out the effects of long-term vertical land movements, as well as greater reliance on the longest tide gauge records for estimating trends, have provided greater confidence that the volume of ocean water has, in fact, been increasing and causing sea level to rise within the indicated range—10–25 centimeters."[19] It is further suggested that a doubling of CO_2 could cause sea levels to rise by up to a meter by 2100. Rising sea levels along with increased storms could imperil populations living in the low-lying coastal areas of the United States, Cuba, South America, India, China, Bangladesh, Egypt, Malaysia, and many Pacific islands. If, or more likely when, populations in these areas are forced to move to seek living space, their migration could aggravate existing population pressures, causing widespread social unrest. It is well to recall the Dust Bowl era of the 1930s, when thousands of "Okies" left Oklahoma for a better life in California, and California's response: armed state police, blocking the highway and entrance to California. Not a pretty picture.

Effects on Livestock

And what of the effect of increased temperature on livestock?

As a critical source of protein and other nutrients, livestock, cattle, sheep, goats, pigs, horses, and poultry must be given consideration in any global warming scenario. Adverse effects would likely present themselves either via the available food supply or through physiological effects of heat balance. Should food stocks dwindle as a result of climate shifts, animals would be compromised. Similarly, widespread drought would exact major losses. If heat increases occurred beyond an animal's capacity for internal cooling, its appetite would fall, which in male animals would affect not only their weight and thereby meat yields but reproductive capacity as well. Thus, unmanageable temperature increases could have far-reaching deleterious effects. Furthermore, warmer temperatures will require augmenting air-conditioning facilities to prevent decreases in egg-laying in poultry and to avert milk production decreases and weight loss in cattle. Added costs of energy use would be passed on to consumers in the form of higher prices for these items, unless energy costs could be maintained or reduced by more energy-efficient management. Finally, insect pests in cattle could exceed their ranges if regional weather patterns shift. Insect pests can so annoy cattle that they become malnourished, with all that portends.

How Do We Reduce Emissions?

That GHG emissions auger major changes for our Earth is certain. To be sure, some areas should benefit—increased warming can extend growing seasons and increase crop yields—but model projections suggest that the bad will outweigh the good. Time, as usual, is the enemy. The problem is the long lifetime of the GHGs in tandem with the climate's slow response to atmospheric changes. This means that time is not on our side, because even if in the next twenty-four hours it were decided to cut GHG emissions by 5 or 10 percent, warming will still occur—to a lesser extent, to be sure, but we Earthlings are sure to be in for a warmer world. How much warmer is the pivotal issue, one that requires our full attention and commitment. The degrees of warmth are in our hands. Few politicians and lawmakers live by the climatologists' 25-, 50-, and 100-year projections. For legislators 2, 4, and 6 years, the periods of congressional, presidential, and senatorial terms, govern their lives and the issues they choose to champion. It is the exceptional individual or individuals who are concerned with events geared to unfold a quarter or half-century down the road, when, more than likely, they will already have gone to their reward, and besides, memories are short.

Nuclear Power

How can emissions be reduced? Energy of course is the key. In the face of uncertainty in model projections and to avoid, as far as possible, major shocks to our economy, reasonable people would switch from fossil fuels to nuclear power.

In November 2000, representatives from 175 countries met for two weeks at The Hague, in the Netherlands, to try to hammer out an acceptable agreement on ways to reduce GHG emissions worldwide. The Hague conference had been set in 1997 in Kyoto, Japan, and the targets, timetables, and priorities agreed upon there were to be ratified at The Hague.

The 1997 Kyoto agreement, the Kyoto Protocols, called for thirty-eight industrialized nations to cut their emissions by an average of 5.2 percent from the 1990 levels by the year 2012. Of course everyone understood that these were minimal cuts, only the beginning; far larger reductions would be required, but they had to start somewhere. The United States, the world's leading emitter, with a quarter of the world's total, had agreed in Kyoto to work for a 7 percent reduction by 2012. The fifteen nations of the European Union committed themselves to an 8 percent reduction, and Japan had agreed to go for 6. At the same time, it was not lost on the participants that these first minimal steps could be swamped by China's and India's plans to increase their energy productivity by burning their huge reserves of coal. Be that as it may, however, at The Hague conference, the Kyoto Protocols met only with wrangling.

The protocols required that at least 55 percent of the participants had to ratify them to become binding. When the conference opened, these reductions had not yet gone into effect, and GHG emissions from the major developed nations had continued to increase along with economic expansion.

In a videotaped message to the opening session, U.N. Secretary General Kofi Annan told the gathering that "if we are going to bring greenhouse gas emissions down to a sustainable level we need to make radical changes in the world economy, and in the way we all live." He also noted that "measures to reduce global warming in industrialized countries will be in vain if meanwhile developing countries are following the same wasteful and noxious pattern of industrialization." Those were potent, emotion-generating words, fighting words.

After two weeks of often contentious negotiations, the Kyoto Protocols remained unratified. No agreements. The sticking point: fossil fuels. To stabilize emissions, fossil fuel use must be dramatically reduced or curtailed, which requires tremendous motivation and for which at this time there is a considerable lack. The United States would commit to no reductions. Paul Krugman, an economist and a columnist for the *New York Times*, sees a domestic political reality in the squabbling at The Hague. He believes that we cannot expect to see reductions in carbon dioxide emissions anytime soon. Writing in the *New York Times,* he had this to say: "The ultimate reason that the climate talks failed, that global warming will go unchecked, is the power of America's vitriolic anti-tax right." He was alluding to the fact that if carbon dioxide is damaging our atmosphere, the efficient way to effect a change is via market incentives to burn less carbon-based fuel. "Any economics textbook would provide the answer: a heavy tax on the use of fossil fuel—in this instance, gasoline. Since that is not in the cards, maybe future retirees won't have to move to Florida to find warm weather. It's looking like a long, hot century."[20]

Obviously the business-as-usual scenario is firmly ensconced on the front burner. Attempts at reducing GHG emissions will occur when pigs can fly, or when the public becomes committed. Until now, global warming has been the concern and province of scientists, the power-generating industry, and environmental groups. The public has remained on the sidelines. Until the apathy changes, the public will continue to be at the mercy of the coal and oil lobbies, as well as of environmentalists and the media, who resist considering clean energy from the atom.

According to the IPCC, the 1990s were not only the century's hottest decade, but also the hottest decade of the millennium. And the commission is unequivocal about the cause: human activity contributes an overabundance of GHG to the atmosphere. Yet the media were generally cool to this hot story. Here again, the problem appears to be that of certainty versus uncertainty. The media wants and understands certainty. Scientists cannot deliver certainty, certainly not on something as vast and complex as the planet's climate system. In addition to the media itself, writers and editors unable or unwilling to latch on to this multifaceted and urgent issue have dominated news coverage. Rather than reporting on the scientific consensus and the complexity of the problem, the focus has been on lack of certainty and, accordingly, little needs to be done right now. But in fact the public needs to be educated about the issue and prepared for the climatic shocks that lie ahead.

Furthermore, the environmentalists simply cannot seem to get their act together. At The Hague conference, the disparate environmental groups could not agree on an overall strategy for limiting carbon emissions.[21] Environmental groups are on the right track in their desire to see an end to the age of carbon, but are unalterably opposed to nuclear power, no matter how greenhouse friendly it may be. For them, wind, solar, hydro, and tidal power are the natural and only way to achieve the energy needed to run this country and other countries of the world. Because they are vocal, it is their message, *their impractical message*, that gets to the public. The media urgently need to learn to deal with the scientists' uncertainty as well as the fact of when, not if, warming occurs, and the country's tremendous need for electric energy and its source. This point was forcefully impressed upon the citizens of California through its severe power shortages in 2001. How many states will follow California's decision to shut down electricity to their customers because it was simply running out of electricity? At first, Californians were asked to turn off their Christmas holiday lights because of the dire shortage. That was followed by rolling, hour-long brown-outs in parts of the state. True, part of the shortage stems from the fact that a number of power plants cannot run because they are in violation of air-quality standards. Nevertheless, it is essential to recall that California, with well over 30 million people and boasting the seventh largest economy in the world, places ever increasing demands on its electric power–generating facilities, which simply cannot meet the demands. Therefore, it is foolhardy to expect that even in sunny California, wind and/or solar power can take up the slack.

Governments may not agree, but states and the people can. The people of the United States, and of the world generally, can agree to move away from fossil-fuel-derived electric power by accepting nuclear power, by realizing and understanding that nuclear power can provide the increasing demand for electricity across the country—and provide it without GHG emissions. In areas of the country where wind is available, windmills can also add to the local store of electricity; and wherever the sun is constant, solar power may also provide added local electrical energy until such time as it can be stored and transported to more distant locations. Our energy needs should manage more than adequately if all of these options are used.

Because our population will continue to increase—and with it the need for energy—electricity, coal, and oil cannot continue to be our primary sources of fuel. More oil means more imported oil, and more imported oil means continual shocks to our economy that OPEC nations can and will deliver. Excessively high costs of oil are causing unnecessary inflationary pressures. This country can become master of its own energy destiny, and foreign oil should play a minor role in our fuel requirements.

There are many issues that the media must lay before the public, including the safety of nuclear power plants, whose record of safety is far better than that of oil- and coal-fired plants. That story needs wide dissemination. Between the media and the environmentalists, who get undue media attention, the public, bandied from pillar to post, is left wondering who and what to believe, as time runs down. Given the appropriate information, the public will make the right decision.

Running the Engines

As for the infernal internal combustion engine, it has had an unparalleled hundred-year run. It is time to give way. Battery-driven vehicles, hydrogen fuel cells, and compressed air–driven vehicles all have a part to play in reducing the use of gasoline. Here as well, motivation will be the driving force. Edmund Burke, the Dublin-born British statesman, said it for all time: "The public interest requires doing today those things that men of intelligence and good will wish, five and ten years hence, had been done." Why wait until it's too late?

What about fuel cells and compressed air cars?

A fuel cell operates like a battery, but it isn't a battery. It doesn't run down or require recharging. It constantly produces energy, electricity, and heat as long as fuel is supplied, and the electricity is produced from a chemical reaction. No combustion here.

A fuel cell consists of two electrodes, the positively charged anode and the negatively charged cathode, separated by a thin, flexible polymer membrane electrolyte (the conductor of electricity). Each of the electrodes is coated on one side with a thin layer of platinum—the catalyst. The sandwich of electrodes, catalyst, and membrane forms the membrane electrode assembly—the cell.

Hydrogen (fuel) is fed into the anode, while oxygen enters via the cathode. Activated by the platinum catalyst, the hydrogen atom splits into a proton and electron, which take different paths to the cathode. The proton passes through the electrolyte. The electrons create a separate current that can be utilized before they return to the cathode, to be reunited with the hydrogen and oxygen in a molecule of water—H_2O. Figure 5.3 shows the relatively simple but efficient process.

Individual fuel cells producing about 0.6 volts each are combined into a fuel cell stack to provide the required level of electricity to power the motors at the wheels of trucks, buses, and cars. A number of automobile manufacturers have combined to develop cells appropriate for their vehicles. The Ballard Company of Vancouver, British Columbia, one of the earliest fuel cell developers, is working with Daimler Chrysler and the Ford Motor Company to develop efficient, fuel-cell–driven vehicles. Their vehicles are designed to meet the performance and refueling requirements of buses, automobiles, and trucks. They will be comparable to conventional vehicles in size, weight, operating life, acceleration, speed, range, and re-

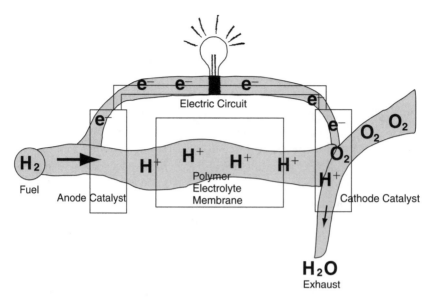

FIG. 5.3. *Conceptual rendering of the workings of a fuel cell. The cell consists of two electrodes sandwiched around an electrolyte. Oxygen passes over one electrode and hydrogen over the other, generating water and an electric current.* (SOURCE: Courtesy of Fuel Cells 2000.)

fueling time. The NECAR 4, based on the Daimler Chrysler A-class and powered by Ballard fuel cells, was unveiled in Washington D.C., on March 17, 1999. Using liquid hydrogen as fuel, this car emits only water vapor and meets California's standards as a Zero Emission Vehicle (ZEV). It can reach speeds up to 90 mph and travel some 280 miles (450 km) before refueling. The latest zero-emission bus is Xcellis, which has been in service in Chicago and Vancouver, and is expected to become widely available by 2004.

The Ford Motor Company has developed three fuel-cell cars: the sport utility vehicle P2000 SUV, the concept sedan P2000, and the latest, unveiled in January 2000, the Think FC5—a methanol-fueled vehicle. Methanol (methyl alcohol, wood alcohol) will supply the hydrogen to power this zero-emission vehicle. Methanol is also being considered for powering fuel-cell–driven lawn mowers, weed eaters, and other auxiliary power plants.

Commercialization of these developments is currently focused on mass production, with its attendant cost reductions. It is only a matter of time before these vehicles hit the road. With no moving parts in the cell, the road and the car should be essentially silent. Now that's a benefit to be applauded.

Given half a chance, the infernal combustion engine, which has presided over the twentieth century and played a prominent role in the development of our civilization as we've come to know it, earns a well-deserved furlough in the not-too-distant future.

If Guy Negre has his way, his two-cylinder zero pollution "motor" vehicle will be the savior of the twenty-first century. Negre's company, M.D.I. (Motor Development International) of Luxembourg, plans to build pneumatic vehicles powered by compressed air—4,350 pounds per square inch. According to M.D.I.'s marketing information, its five-seat, plastic-body car can reach 30 miles per hour in seven seconds, cruise at a top speed of 60 mph, and travel 120 miles on a tank of compressed air before requiring a recharge.[22] If this vehicle becomes a reality, the result of the type of imaginative thinking required for the twenty-first century, many engineers will be surprised.

Troubled Indoor Air

Troubled air is inside as well as outside. Evidence has accumulated and been documented that the air in our homes, offices, and other buildings can be far more seriously polluted than the outdoors—more polluted and a greater threat to our health. So much of our air pollution research was expended on outdoor air that indoor air hasn't received nearly the attention it deserves.

Would you believe these numbers? 93, 5, 2. It may be hard to believe, but most of us spend 93 percent of our day—a twenty-four-hour day—indoors, 5 percent in transit (cars, buses, trains), and only 2 percent outdoors. Believe it. Two percent outdoors! You need only keep a log of your daily activities from the time you rise in the A.M., to the time you call it a day in the P.M., to see how accurate these three numbers are. I did it for a week, and I'm a believer.

With that much time spent indoors, let's consider the factors that place us at potential risk for adverse health effects. Four sets of factors require consideration:

Physical, chemical, biological, psychological
(Physical: temperature, humidity, ventilation)

Acceptable comfort levels for homes and offices appear to fall within a narrow range, approximately 68°–75° F (20°–24° C). Below 68° F is too cool for most people, and above 75° too warm. However, in addition, temperature must be balanced by appropriate moisture/humidity levels. This too requires maintenance with narrow limits: 40–50 percent. Below 35 is too dry and above 50 too moist for comfort. But even with both temperature and humidity in balance, if the rate of ventilation, the number of air changes per hour, is inadequate, discomfort will set in. In fact, the National Institute of Occupational Safety and Health (NIOSH) found that the cause of illness in at least 50 percent of cases was due to inadequate ventilation. For ventilation to be suitable, it should not contribute odors or drafts.

Clearly, indoor air quality (IAQ) has a degree of complexity to it. It's a balancing act, but one that is achievable by paying attention to the systems. However, because ventilation and chemicals are inseparable, one cannot be discussed without the other, especially because chemicals are all around us. We live in a sea of chemicals. We are chemicals. Everything is chemical. The food we eat, the air we breathe, the ground we walk on, our clothing, furniture, toothpaste, mouthwash, mascara, lipstick, paper, pencils, chalk, books, inks, carpets, shoes, polishes, waxes, creams, sprays, soaps, detergents, hair spray, and shampoo. All are chemicals. Is it any wonder, then, that some of us—never all of us—will be sensitive, perhaps even hypersensitive, to "something in the air" in the home or office?

Environmental tobacco smoke heads the list. Some headway has been made as cigarette, cigar, and pipe smoking have been decreasing in both home and office, as smokers quit or are forced outdoors. Recall that it was in 1986 that the surgeon general reported that second-hand smoke could cause cancer in healthy nonsmokers, and it was in 1991 that the NIOSH determined that secondhand smoke (side-stream smoke) was a potential occupational carcinogen. So, yes, outside is where it belongs. But perhaps not even there.

Along with tobacco smoke, formaldehyde must be on anyone's short list of noxious indoor chemicals. It may be the single most important indoor pollutant because of ubiquity and toxicity. It is a colorless gas with an acrid, biting odor. Wood products, many of them used in homes, are among its important sources. Urea-formaldehyde resins are commonly used to manufacture particleboard, plywood, paneling, and ceiling panels. And because it is relatively inexpensive, it is the most common adhesive used to produce wood products. As if those weren't trouble enough, it is also contained in insulating foam, synthetic fabrics, and waterproofing. The list is long. And all can release their biting formaldehyde into the household and office air, which can be intensely irritating to the mucous membranes that line the eyes, nose, mouth, and upper airways.

Waxes, polishes, cleaning compounds generally, paints, varnishes, window cleaners, perfumes, deodorants, hair sprays, wood fillers, and a slew of substances emanating from building materials—all volatile organic compounds, VOCs—besiege indoor air. Indeed, we can be bathed in a veritable chemical stew that can induce acute and chronic adverse effects if ventilation is inadequate. Irritability, dizziness, blurred vision, and skin irritation are commonly recognized sequela of these emanations and are warning signs.

But it doesn't end there. Carbon dioxide, a gaseous byproduct of our metabolism that is expelled when we exhale and is also the final combustion product of the fossil fuels kerosene, gas, and wood, used in a variety of home heaters, can build up in poorly vented homes, especially in winter, becoming the source of stale, "stuffy" air, initiating headaches and drowsiness. But CO_2 is not nearly as dangerous as its relative, carbon monoxide, CO, a constant source of trouble that is dose related. Carbon monoxide is a colorless, odorless gas, also the result of the combustion of fossil fuels from cooking and heating units; it is especially worrisome because it has a unique affinity for hemoglobin, forming carboxyhemoglobin, which severely reduces the red blood cells' ability to carry oxygen to cells and tissues. Carbon monoxide can enter homes from attached garages, where it can originate from automobile exhausts. At low concentrations, fatigue and chest pain may be the only symptoms, but as the concentration increases, confusion, nausea, and death may ensue.

Strange, unfamiliar, out-of-place odors can lead to sensory discomfort and irritation, which can induce stress and anxiety, especially when the source of the odor remains unidentified. Unidentified sources of off-odors can set off alarm bells. It would not be an overstatement to say that proper ventilation can and does substantially reduce and remove these problems.

Adequate ventilation will also deal effectively with biologic agents. Microorganisms such as bacteria and fungi, and the larger beasts such as dust mites, find desirable living conditions in wet or moist walls, ceilings, carpets, and furniture, as well as in poorly maintained humidifiers, dehumidifiers, air conditioners, bedding, and yes in our house pets.

Biological agents can cause eye, nose, and throat irritation, shortness of breath, dizziness, and asthma, as well as infectious diseases via aerosols.

Dust mites have become a major source of complaints. The body parts and feces of these six-legged creatures, which are not insects but take up residence in carpets, bedding, furniture, and stuffed toys, can be the source of allergic and asthmatic attacks when inhaled by sensitive individuals.

The more chemicals we bring into our homes, and the more time we spend there, the more we will be at increased risk if we do not give adequate attention to ventilation, humidity, and temperature. If these are appropriately attended to, indoor air pollution will be minimal to nonexistent. HVAC—heating, ventilation, and air conditioning—is the trivium we must attend to if we are to keep our indoor air trouble-free. Consider the following questions to help you increase your indoor air quality.

1. Are you among those who block air supply vents? Barriers can disrupt airflow patterns of an entire floor, as can partitions or other barriers, if not done properly.
2. Are air supplies and return registers located close together?
3. Are building air intake vents too close to exhaust vents?
4. Is the intake supply located near loading docks, parking or heavy traffic areas, chimney, or trash bins?

A little checking, looking around, and a bit of redoing can accomplish wonders for indoor air. Consider, too, air filtering, humidifying, and cleaning units. These are notorious supporters of bacteria, mold, and mites. Take a look inside. Make sure they are properly maintained—regularly and frequently.

Remember that indoors we are not alone. There are formidable foes to be dealt with. And recall the key numbers: 93, 5, and 2. Because you spend 93 percent of your life indoors, you must keep it a healthy place. Neither your home nor your office should be killing you.

Troubled Outdoor Air

But what of polluted outdoor air? Isn't that consequential, too?

In 1974, researchers at the Harvard School of Public Health organized a prospective epidemiologic cohort study to determine if federal EPA standards for half a dozen air pollutants—suspended particulate matter, soot, sulfur dioxide (SO_2), nitrogen dioxide (NO_2), carbon monoxide, hydrocarbons, and photochemical oxides—were adequate as promulgated.

To resolve some of the insufficiencies of the many previous studies, and "to obtain comparable data from a variety of communities with differing levels of pollution," the Harvard team selected three pairs of cities: (1) Topeka, Kansas, and Portage, Wisconsin, as the clean cities; (2) Watertown, Massachsetts, and Kingston-Harriman, Tennessee, as the slightly less clean pair; and (3) Steubenville, Ohio, and Carondolet, at the southern tip of St. Louis, as the dirty cities.

This study had two components: first, measurement of the concentrations of air pollutants, especially SO_2, sulfates, and respirable particulate matter; and second, "determination of the effects of these concentrations of pollutants on the health of adults and children on a prospective basis." Specifically, the researchers were concerned with the effects of air pollution on mortality.

The sample population included 8,480 individuals ages 25–74, with at least 2,100 people from each of the six cities. In fact, the numbers ranged from 2,174 in Watertown to 3,583 in Kingston-Harriman. In addition to adults, the study included children. Initially, all first and second graders in each community, public as well as parochial, were enrolled. In Topeka, because it was large, half of the schools were selected randomly. All children were resurveyed annually. This study was designed to continue for a period of fourteen years. Assessment of health was accomplished by personal interviews using a standard questionnaire, a standard pulmonary function test performed by trained, nonmedical interviewers.

In the case of the children, questions were sent home to be completed by parents. Pulmonary function tests were also performed on them. Air quality monitoring was conducted in each community in an attempt to quantify both population and individual exposures. Smoking habits of parents, other adults, and children were accounted for.

After fourteen years of interviews, pulmonary function tests, air monitoring, and data collection and interpretation, the Six Cities Study, as it came to be known, was published as "An Association between Air Pollution and Mortality in Six Cities." It created nothing but controversy. What were the results? Mortality rates were most strongly associated with cigarette smoking, but there was another strong association: "Air pollution was positively associated with death from lung cancer and cardiopulmonary disease, but not with death from other causes considered together." The controversy that was to ensue and continue for seven wrangling years sprang from the conclusion that "mortality was most strongly associated with air pollution with fine particulates, including sulfates." Fine-particulate air pollution (soot) includes particles with diameters of less than 10 microns (a micron is 1/25,000th of an inch, not much larger than the largest bacteria) and as small as 2.5 microns (a human hair is approximately 60–65 microns wide), the type that can readily slip into and out of the bronchial tree. Here they can induce tissue damage because they can be breathed more deeply into the lungs, coming to rest in the alveoli and stimulating fibrosis, or scarring. Fine-particulate pollution was directly related to the combustion of fossil fuels—coal and oil—from trucks, buses, and automobile exhausts, from manufacturing, and from electric-power generation. With the publication of these results and the Environmental Protection Association's (EPA's) move to require further reductions in particulate emissions, the American Petroleum Institute, the oil industry association, immediately challenged the results, claiming they do not support the need for more stringent regulations and standards.

The published data showed increased emergency room visits due to asthma, increased hospital admissions, and increased mortality from lung cancer and heart disease. Meta-analysis suggested that there was no evidence of a threshold for the effects of particulates, and that the data were consistent with a linear dose-response relation. The *New York Times* reported that particulate air pollution in U.S. cities kills up to 60,000 people annually.[23]

Industry critics and critics within the scientific community took issue with what they called shaky science and with the EPA for imposing excessively costly regulations. To resolve the issue, an independent review was undertaken. The Health Effects Institute (HEI), an industry and EPA-funded nonprofit organization in Cambridge, Massachusetts, assembled a team of experts who essentially replicated the study from Harvard's original data sets, and obtained the same results. Tiny particles *can* kill. Although the increase was slight in each city, when all cities were aggregated the death toll rose substantially. As the man said, it's the fossil thing. But to keep the controversy in perspective, it is worth remembering that when the Six Cities Study was published in 1993, the major finding was that mortality rates were most strongly associated with cigarette smoking. In an overview of the epidemiological studies of lung cancer and air pollution, at the President's Cancer Panel Conference on avoidable causes of cancer (April 7–8, 1994), analysts at the HEI concluded their review this way: "The excess lung cancer associated with ambient air pollution is small compared with that from cigarette smoking. However, given the ubiquity of combustion-source ambient air pollution exposure, the contribution of this exposure across a population may be of public health importance."[24]

What does it all mean and portend? It is evident that fossil fuels—coal and oil—are responsible for all air pollution problems, for all the troubled air.

A portion of fossil fuel byproducts, carbon dioxide especially, flies to the stratosphere, while another set of chemical byproducts remains at ground level to induce respiratory and allergic problems. Both types of air pollution—GHG emissions and particulates—are the consequences of overuse of fossil fuels, and both pit the oil/coal industry against the American people, and against the people of the world. Neither problem will be solved or sufficiently reduced in the near future unless there is a major move away from fossil fuels. But the American public, which dearly wants cleaner air, is ambivalent. Americans love their cars and cheap gasoline: two very potent love affairs. Modifying cars and taxing gasoline appear to be nonstarters given the current political climate, in which President George W. Bush, only three months into his presidency, caved under pressure from the coal and oil lobbies and reversed his campaign pledge to regulate emissions of CO_2 in power plants. In addition, the public is ambivalent about nuclear power. Unless and until these contradictions and ambivalences are resolved, air pollution, both in the greenhouse and at sea level, will continue unabated into the much warmer twenty-second century, along with enough fine particulates to increase the community burden of lung cancer and coronary heart disease. Obviously, the business-as-usual scenario will prevail—unfortunately.

Clean Energy: Power from Atoms

Radiation is as natural as "little green apples in the summertime," as much a part of our world as sun, wind, and rain. It was an integral part of planet Earth long before we evolved from our hominid ancestors. With the appearance of *Homo erectus* 500,000 years ago, humankind has been living cheek-by-jowl with natural radiation. But it was not until the closing years of the nineteenth century that the presence of radiation was revealed. Wilhelm Konrad Roentgen, professor of physics at the University of Würzburg in Germany, discovered X-rays in 1895. He found that these invisible rays possessed the energy to pass through paper, wood, rubber, and aluminum, as well as his hand. In 1901, Roentgen received the first Nobel Prize in Physics for his discovery.

Four months after Roentgen's discovery of X-rays, Henri Becquerel, in France, demonstrated the presence of radiation. How did he do it? Cleverly. He placed a photographic plate inside a heavy paper envelope so that visible light could not expose it. He then placed a piece of uranium ore (a fluorescing mineral) on top of the envelope and placed them together outdoors. He did this on both sunny and cloudy days. Under both conditions, the photographic plate became completely exposed. The ore emitted rays—energy—that passed through the envelope and exposed the photographic plate. Sunlight clearly was not needed for the effect. Thus, natural radiation was discovered. Becquerel also found that the strength of the radiation was directly proportional to the amount of uranium present.

It was also in France that the Curies, Pierre and Marie, contemporaries of Becquerel, developed a method for quantitatively measuring the amount of radioactivity in a sample of uranium ore. It was Marie who discovered that the element thorium was also radioactive, and, as with uranium, the amount of radiation depended solely on the amount of thorium present, not on any specific thorium compound. But she and Pierre went further, finding that the amount of radioactivity present in pitchblende, an ore containing uranium oxide, was far greater than expected from the amount of uranium in the ore. Their continued testing and searching led to the discovery of two highly radioactive elements, radium and polonium. A gram of radium, 1/454th of a pound, emitted more than a million times the radiation of a gram of uranium.

We shall see how the immense energy locked in radioactive minerals can be released to provide almost unlimited sources of clean electric power. For their work on radioactivity, the Curies shared a Nobel Prize in 1903 with Becquerel. Marie Curie won a second Nobel in 1911, for the isolation of radium and polonium.

We humans are exposed to radiation daily from the sun and outer space. Naturally occurring radioactive minerals are present in the Earth, in the buildings we inhabit, and in the food and water we consume. There are radioactive gases in the air we breathe, and our bodies are radioactive. A major contributor is radon gas, a radioactive gas formed from the decay of uranium, which emanates from the soil, and which often concentrates in buildings. The level of natural exposure varies around the world, usually by a factor of about three. At many locations, however, levels of natural radiation exceed average levels by a factor of ten and, in some areas, by a factor of one hundred.

In addition to the natural radiation background, we are exposed to radiation through other sources: mining, the use of ores containing naturally radioactive substances, and from radioactive residues of nuclear weapons testing around the world. This exposure is augmented by the use of radioactive materials in agriculture, medicine, research, and industry, which is expanding globally, along with nuclear power plants and other nuclear installations that release radioactive materials into the environment. Nevertheless, however disagreeable these contributions may be, their radiation levels are but a fraction of the global average to natural exposure.[1]

The medical and dental use of radiation is the largest man-made source of radiation exposure, and it is growing. It includes diagnostic radiology, radiotherapy (treatment of disease), nuclear medicine, and interventional radiology. Large numbers of people, particularly in developing countries, cannot yet avail themselves of these procedures. Consequently, for the time being, these people receive less radiation exposure from medical diagnosis and treatment than those living in more developed countries. But this circumstance is expected to change in the near future. The average levels of radiation exposure due to medical and dental uses of radiation are equivalent to approximately 50 percent of the global average level of natural exposure. Computerized axial tomography (CAT) scans account for only a few percentages of the procedures, but for almost half of the exposure involved in medical diagnosis.

Radiation exposure also occurs as a consequence of occupational activities. Exposure is incurred by workers in industry, medicine, and research who use radioactive substances, as well as by passengers and crew during air travel. It is substantial for astronauts. The average level of occupational exposures is similar to the global average of natural exposure.

Hazards of Radiation

Given the low levels of radiation exposure around us, the relevant question is: Just how hazardous are these background levels, this combination of natural and man-made levels? The short answer is that if there is any hazard, any risk, it is so small as to be undetectable. Nevertheless, radiation exposure can have potentially harmful hereditary effects in the offspring of individuals exposed to it, though they have yet to be detected in exposed human populations. That said, it is time to place numbers on the contributions of both the natural and man-made sources of radiation, since numbers can augment or diminish perceptions. As you peruse tables 6.1 and 6.2, it will be helpful to know the units universally used to describe exposure levels. The universal quantity used to express radiation exposure to the human body is the "absorbed dose," the gray (Gy). But the biological effects per unit of absorbed dose vary with the type of radiation and the body part exposed. To account for these variations, a weighted quantity, the sievert (Sv), or the "effective dose," is used. A radioactive source is described by its activity, which is the number of nuclear disintegrations per unit time. The universal unit of activity is the bequerel (Bq); one bequerel is one disintegration per second. Table 6.1 gives the average annual radiation dose from natural sources, and table 6.2 shows the annual effective dose individuals receive.

It is clear that cosmic rays are a major contributor of radiation to the global natural background. In outer space they consist primarily of high-energy protons—the nuclei of hydrogen atoms—which generate showers of particles that reach Earth. Residents of Denver, the "mile-high city," receive approximately 0.5 mSv (50 mrem) per year, while their neighbors in Leadville, living at altitudes over 10,000 feet above sea level, receive annual doses of 125 mSv. Floridians by comparison receive only 0.25 mSv. Airplane passengers flying at seven miles above Earth receive some 15 mSv

Table 6.1. Average Annual Dose of Radiation from Natural Sources

Source	Annual Dose (mSv)*	Range (mSv)
Cosmic rays	0.4	0.3–1.0
Terrestrial gamma rays	0.5	0.3–0.6
Inhalation (radon)	1.2	0.2–10.0
Ingestion	0.3	0.2–0.8
Total	2.4	1.0–12.4

SOURCE: United Nations Scientific Committee on the Effects of Atomic Radiation.
*Millisievert equals one-thousandth of a sievert.

just during their time in the air, on average. The good citizens of Flagstaff, Arizona, receive more cosmic radiation than folks in New Jersey and New York. On the other hand, Iowans, Pennsylvanians, and Tennesseans have greater contact with radon. Areas of Brazil, China, Iran, and India have the world's highest natural exposures, with documented hot spots. How that has affected their health will be discussed shortly. From our two tables it is evident that the natural background is a far greater source of exposure than

Table 6.2. Annual per Capita Doses from Natural and Man-Made Sources

Source	Average Annual Dose (mSv)*	Range or Trend
Natural Background	2.4	1–10 mSv with sizable populations at 10–20 mSV
Diagnostic Medical Exams	0.4	0.04–1.0 mSv
Atmospheric Nuclear Testing	0.005	decreased from a max. of 0.15 mSv in 1963
Chernobyl Accident	0.002	decreased from a max. of 0.04 mSv in 1986
Nuclear Power Production	0.0002	increased with expanding activity, but decreased with improved practices
Approximate total	2.8072 mSv	(280.7 mrem)

SOURCE: United Nations Scientific Committee on the Effects of Atomic Radiation.

anything man-made. We see that the annual global per capita effective dose due to natural radiation is approximately 2.4 mSv. But the range is wide. In any large population, about 65 percent would be expected to have annual effective doses between 1 and 3 mSv; another 25 percent would have annual effective doses of less than one mSv, while 10 percent would have doses greater than 3 mSv.

When accidents occur, environmental contamination and exposures may become significant. The accident at the Chernobyl nuclear power station in 1986 is illuminating. Of course, the exposures were highest in the local areas surrounding the reactor, but low-level exposures took place in the European region and in the entire Northern Hemisphere. In the first year following the accident, the highest regionally averaged annual doses in Europe, outside the former Soviet Union, were less than 50 percent of the natural background. Subsequent exposures decreased rapidly.[2]

The generation of electricity by nuclear power facilities is ongoing. Assuming it continues for one hundred years, the maximum collective dose to the world's population can be estimated from the cumulative doses that occur annually. "The normalized 100 year truncated figure is 6 man-Sv per gigawatt year. Assuming the present annual generation of 250 gigawatt years continues, the truncated collective dose per year of practice is 1500 man-Sv to the world population, giving an estimated maximum per capita dose of less than 0.2 micro-sieverts (μSv) per year."[3] Clearly, after the natural background, it is the diagnostic medical examinations that contribute the highest doses by far. This is an interesting trend, reflecting the growing use of the many medical interventions. Most surprising is the contribution from the world's nuclear bomb test explosions. Even at their height in 1963, their annual contribution to man-made levels apparently never exceeded 7 percent of the natural background. This essential underpinning is our stepping-stone to nuclear power production.

The Physics of Nuclear Energy

Our universe, our planet, and everything in it, without exception, are made up of both stable and unstable elements. All elements are assembled from atoms, which have nuclei consisting of *protons* and *neutrons*. Circling the nucleus, like planets in our solar system, are negatively charged *electrons*. Extremely strong forces bind neutrons, which are electrically neutral particles, to the protons.

A stable atom has a balance of protons and neutrons. Most elements are stable, but a few are unstable, that is, the number of neutrons and protons are not the same. The unbalanced elements are radioactive. *Isotopes* are atoms with different masses as a consequence of having different numbers of neutrons in their nuclei. Thus, tin has 10 isotopes, oxygen, carbon and uranium each have 3. Tin, with 50 protons, has isotopes with 62, 64, 65, 66, 67, 68, 69, 70, 72, and 74 neutrons. Uranium, with 92 protons, has isotopes with 142, 143, and 146 neutrons. All isotopes of the twenty-three elements of atomic weight greater than Bismuth (208.9)—for example, Uranium-238, Radium-226, Thorium-232, Protactinium-231, and Polonium-209—are radioactive.

Early in the history of physics, it was discovered that radioactivity was a nuclear effect, and that radioactive elements emitted three types of radiation: alpha, beta, and gamma. As shown in figure 6.1, positively charged alpha rays could not penetrate a piece of paper. Beta, a negatively charged particle, could travel through air and pass through metal foil but was stopped by wood and most clothing. Massless gamma, electrically neutral and with the highest energy and speed, has the greatest penetrating power. This form of radiation can readily pass through the human body, clothing included. It penetrates tissue, organs, and bone, and, accordingly, it is the ray against which we must protect ourselves with shielding. Dense materials such as concrete and lead are the materials of choice. But all is not as it seems.

Although alpha, beta, and gamma radiation are high-energy particles, they lose their energy as they interact with the matter around them. During this interaction, alpha and beta particles cause atoms and molecules to lose electrons. In physico-chemical parlance, these alpha and beta rays lose their energy by causing atoms to ionize. The electron and positive ions produced are called *ion pairs*. The type and number of dislocations or aberrations produced within a cell depends upon the density of the ionizations, or the number of ion pairs produced along the particle's track as it streaks through cells. Gamma rays, because of their extremely high energy, penetrate deeply, but because of their speed generate few ion pairs per unit path traversed. Alpha particles, the least penetrating, produce a greater number of ion pairs than the gamma particles, and thus can do more damage to cells. The alpha particles' lack of penetrating power prevents their exit and thus they remain on site continuing to damage cell structures. Any radiation passing through matter (cell, tissue) deposits energy along its path, resulting in temperature increases, heat, and ionization, which together can produce hydroxyl radicals that can damage genes and chromosomes.

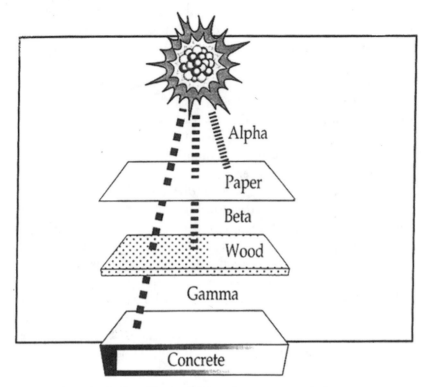

FIG. 6.1. *Types of radiation. The three main types of ionizing radiation are alpha, beta, and gamma rays. Alpha particles are the most energetic but can travel only a few inches in air. They lose their energy as soon as they collide with matter. Beta particles can pass through paper but are stopped by wood, glass, or foil. Gamma rays travel at the speed of light and are highly penetrating. A wall of concrete, lead, or steel stops gamma rays.* (Source: Courtesy of the U.S. Department of Energy.)

Radiation, however, refers to any substance or matter that emits rays at high speed. Consequently, all radiation can be classified as ionizing or non-ionizing. This classification is based on the wavelength of the specific radiation. Wavelength refers to the distance between the waves, peaks and/or valleys, as noted in chapter 1 in the discussion of ultraviolet light and sunburn. All forms of radiation are part of the electromagnetic spectrum. The shortest, the ionizing, and the most energetic include the cosmic, gamma, and X-rays, while the longest and least energetic are the radio frequency and microwaves. In between is visible light, made up of the colors of the rainbow and the only form of radiation our eyes can detect. Beyond violet is ultraviolet, and beyond red is infrared, neither of which can be perceived by the human eye. While visible light is not harmful, we have seen that ultraviolet rays can be. The sources of exposure to radio frequency (rf) and microwave (mw) radiation are radio and TV broadcasting, radar, cellular phones, towers, microwave ovens, and up-link satellite dishes. The few epidemiological studies of rf/mw-exposed populations are equivocal. None have been able to appropriately assess exposure levels. Here again, if there are untoward health effects, they are below current levels of detection.

Ionizing radiation has no such assessment problem. Given its rich energy levels, it is ionizing radiation that captures the imagination. It is the bond between proton and neutron in the nucleus of the atom that holds the key to power. That bond can be broken, or split, if a neutron manages to penetrate to the nucleus. When this occurs, the breakup releases the binding nuclear energy. This splitting is referred to as *fission*, and it is this fission that unleashes a string of fissions called a *chain reaction*, which in turn produces huge amounts of energy—heat—that will boil water, producing the steam needed to spin turbine blades connected to a generator that produces electricity. Consider for a moment that fission of one kilogram (2.2 pounds) of uranium-235 can produce as much energy as the burning of 2,600 tons of coal—without the particulate pollution or carbon dioxide residue that contributes so mightily to global warming. But is it safe?

Indeed, before we enter the realm of nuclear power generation, it is prudent not only to ask, but also to determine if the power, the energy, locked in the atom is safe for humankind to draw upon. With that body of information in hand, decision-making will be easier. But before sending neutrons flying into atomic nuclei, we shall also visit the question, of risk perception, and raise the question, What is safe?

Effects of Large-Scale Radiation

Given the widespread apprehension and concern about the health hazards of ionizing radiation engendered by Hiroshima and Nagasaki, continued by Three Mile Island, and culminating in Chernobyl, it can be useful as well as revelatory to reflect upon each of these events, from a distance, considering that over fifty-five years have elapsed since Hiroshima and Nagasaki, over twenty years since Three Mile Island, and over fifteen years since Chernobyl.

What in fact have we learned from the events that transpired in each of these places, and can the knowledge gained be useful for us today—and

tomorrow? What actually occurred 56, 21, and 16 years ago? "Actually" is
the apt and operative term, as there are striking differences between what
was believed to have occurred and what actually occurred.

It is essential to understand that nuclear power requires careful
decision-making at individual and community levels, and then at a national
level. How this country generates its needed energy—electricity—is a nationwide concern and cannot be made on the basis of poorly understood
past events. George Santayana didn't say it quite like this, but he'll understand: those who understand the past incorrectly are doomed to make a
mess of the future! Consequently, the goal here is to examine the facts as
they are currently known, thereby lessening confusion and fear, which have
had a long head start over factual information. Catching up may be next to
impossible. But the stakes are too important not to try. A clever fellow said
that "strongly held opinions often determine what kind of facts people are
able or willing to perceive." I suspect that for too many people, opinions on
nuclear power and radiation are firmly held. Too firmly held. I suspect,
too, that the genesis of this fear is predicated on an understanding of past
events that have been frozen in time, and in memory: Hiroshima and Nagasaki, Three Mile Island, Chernobyl.

The media have quite clearly distorted the risks, and the casualties are
people individually, and the nation collectively, including the media, who
often forget they too are citizens who must make informed decisions. It has
also been observed that "there is no point in getting into a panic about the
risk of life until you have compared the risks which worry you with those
that don't, but perhaps should." After all, most people accept and are
oblivious of the risks of driving a car. The documented fact of
40,000–50,000 deaths annually stops no one from driving. Yet the possibility of an estimated two deaths per year from all nuclear power generating plants combined—repeat, *estimated*—has been deemed unacceptable.
The effects of radiation, especially due to the atomic bombing of Hiroshima and Nagasaki, have been perceived as monstrous and devastating.
Therefore it is essential to at least consider the actual outcome of fifty years
of study of these two populations. What has been learned can be of immense benefit to humankind generally. At the same time, bear in mind that
the radiation doses experienced at Hiroshima and Nagasaki are far, far in
excess of anything anyone in the United States could conceivably experience. Accordingly, risks of cancer and other untoward health effects can
reasonably be expected to be far less, to nonexistent, but the facts can be
a guide for discussion and decision-making.

Of one thing we can be certain: what is about to unfold will be seen as contrary to conventional wisdom. Does that doom it to perdition? Perhaps, perhaps not. Nevertheless, shining the light of reason and understanding on this new information will surely play hob for the messenger.

Hiroshima and Nagasaki

Monday, August 6, 1945. 8:15 A.M.: The bomb-bay doors of the B-29 bomber *Enola Gay* opened. "Little Boy" tumbled earthward. A mushroom cloud arose. Within minutes, three-fifths of Hiroshima vanished. The shock wave, fire, and radiation claimed seventy thousand-plus lives.

Thursday, August 9, 1945. Midday: Bock's Car, a B-29 bomber, opened its bomb-bay doors. "Fat Man" tumbled earthward. A mushroom cloud appeared. Half of Nagasaki disappeared. Seventy-three thousand, eight hundred eighty-four people died.

In response to the Truman presidential mandate of November 1946, the Atomic Bomb Casualty Commission (ABCC) was founded. It remained in effect until 1975, when it was reorganized under its new name, Radiation Effects Research Foundation. It remains the foremost institution in the world conducting continuous systematic, large-scale studies on the long-term effects of radiation.

In 1949, at age twenty-nine, William J. Schull went to Japan to head up the Department of Genetics of the ABCC and remained one of its key researchers for the next five decades. *Effects of Atomic Radiation: A Half-Century of Studies from Hiroshima and Nagasaki,* his recent book, is an engrossing, enlightening, and sober account of the results of fifty years of following, testing, and recording the vital data of the survivors and their children.[4] At age eighty-two, Schull continues these studies at the Human Genetics Center, University of Texas Health Science Center, Houston. The ensuing discussion closely follows his account.

From Schull we learn that in the days shortly after the bombings, the print media worsened matters by publishing many ill-founded speculations. Allegations were trumpeted in national and international newspapers. "Hiroshima and Nagasaki would be uninhabitable for decades, if not centuries: an epidemic of misshapen monsters, animal and plant, would occur. Lingering death faced those individuals who had fortuitously survived the immediate aftermath of the detonation of those weapons." None of these occurred. In fact, within a few months, plants were sprouting and reconstruction of the cities was underway. Figures 6.2 and 6.3 show two views of Hiroshima today. Figure 6.2 is a view of Shukkeien Gardens, a

FIG. 6.2. *Shukkeien Gardens. This garden, a short walk from downtown Hiroshima, was originally designed in 1620. Today its islets, bridges, fish, and woods offer townspeople and tourists an ideal haven for quiet time.* (SOURCE: Courtesy of the Hiroshima Tourist Bureau.)

short walk from downtown Hiroshima. The gardens, with their islets, bridges, and fish, are a favorite relaxation area for townspeople and tourists. Figure 6.3 is a view of a mall in downtown Hiroshima, a bustling metropolis; Pacela Mall is as modern and active as any in the United States. In figure 6.4, we see the sweep and development of the bay area around Nagasaki Harbor, with a cruise ship in port.

Ionizing radiation is unavoidable, and a known cause of cancer. As we've seen, most human exposure is from natural sources. Radiation-associated human cancer is studied in population groups that have been exposed to doses such that cancer cases in excess of those normally expected may be identified. Estimates of risk can be obtained from populations for whom individual doses may be reasonably estimated. These populations include survivors of atomic bombings, medically irradiated patients, individuals occupationally exposed, as well as those exposed to elevated natural radiation. As cancer is a fact of life, that fact presented

FIG. 6.3. *Hiroshima Mall. Downtown Hiroshima is a bustling metropolis. Pacela Shopping Center is as modern and thriving as any in the United States.* (SOURCE: Courtesy of the Hiroshima Tourist Bureau.)

ABCC researchers with a unique difficulty: How many cases, from which sites, were radiation-induced, and which were not? Now here was a conundrum few would have expected. After all, Hiroshima and Nagasaki, it was assumed, were so totally irradiated, how could radiation not be the cause of all cancers? And there ought to be many. Unfortunately, a cancer is a cancer is a cancer. No tags or labels are present to indicate their cause.

While it is well known that ionizing radiation can induce cancer of almost any tissue or organ, some sites are more prone than others. And over the past decades it has been found that younger people are at higher risk than older, and this too varies by site.

The studies of the Japanese survivors are especially illuminating because this population includes a large number of men and women with a range of exposures and ages. So, for example, among the 86,572 survivors who formed the Life Span Study (LSS), there were 7,578 deaths from solid tumors over the forty years of 1950–1990. That's 8.6 percent of

Fig. 6.4. *Nagasaki Harbor. This view of the Nagasaki Bay area offers a sweeping panorama of the waterfront and environs. A cruise ship is berthed at a pier.* (Source: Courtesy of the Japanese Tourist Office, New York.)

the total number of survivors and approximately 190 cancer cases annually over forty years. It was from this group of cases that the ABCC's oncologists and geneticists had to determine which were radiation-induced. They did. Of the 7,578 deaths from solid tumors, 334 (4.4 %) have been attributed to radiation exposure. More than likely, this number requires a moment's reflection and digestion: 334! That's all! No, that's not all. There's more. During the same forty years, 87 of 249 leukemia deaths were found to be radiation-induced. A total of 421 cancer deaths. Unimaginable! A stunning revelation if ever there was one.

By the year 2000, 40-plus percent of the survivors were still living. Their vital experiences are being closely observed for additional significant information. While it can be argued that even one radiation-related death from malignancy is one too many, there is obviously no epidemic of cancer deaths among the radiation-exposed in either city. That, too, should give pause to consider, or to reconsider.

Statistically significant risks were not observed for either incidence in new cases or deaths from cancers of the rectum, gall bladder, pancreas, larynx, uterine cervix, uterine corpus, prostate, kidney, or renal pelvis. And, while most types of leukemia (acute or chronic neoplastic diseases of the bone marrow) are associated with radiation, lymphoma and multiple myloma appear not to be. Chronic lymphocytic leukemia has been observed but does not appear to be radiation-related. Analysis of solid tumors individually and in combination found no appreciable differences between Hiroshima and Nagasaki. But the ABCC's analysis did reveal a twofold greater risk for females than males, as well as a trend for decreasing risk with increasing age at exposure. The lack of difference in tumor type and number between Hiroshima and Nagasaki is revealing, as it has been widely accepted that although both bombs dropped were gamma and neutron emitters, "Little Boy," the bomb dropped over Hiroshima, was a greater neutron emitter and thus more energetic and harmful than "Fat Man," the bomb released over Nagasaki. However, demonstrating such difference in overall health effects has been unavailing.

Stomach cancer normally is the most common of all cancers among the Japanese, accounting for over 30 percent of all cancer deaths. In Hiroshima, among those postnatally exposed, doses up to 5 Gy produced radiation-induced stomach cancer, but in Nagasaki the only stomach cancers observed were among those who received doses in excess of 5 Gy. As for thyroid cancer, between 1958 and 1987, 225 cases were found among 79,972 survivors: 162 in Hiroshima and 63 in Nagasaki. There was striking radiosensitivity among those under age ten at the time of exposure. Only 3 percent of cases occurred in those age twenty or older at the time of the bombing.

The ABCC's concern was not limited to cancer. Although the average survivor received doses in the range of 0.2–2.0 Gy, other aberrations were considered. Fertility, for example, was measured in several ways: chance of fertilization, successful reproduction, time between beginning of cohabitation and first pregnancy, and first live-born delivery. Interestingly enough, none of these was altered by radiation exposure. This is worth additional reflection.

What of chromosomal abnormalities? Realizing that the chromosome is the vehicle by which genetic information is transmitted from generation to generation, this was of critical concern. As chromosomal abnormalities are frequently found in association with malignant tumors, it was anticipated that there would be a number of fatal malignancies given the observed chromosomal aberrations. There were none, including no evidence of Down's syndrome or alterations in sex ratios. Given the stress induced by the bombing, an increased likelihood of abnormal outcome was anticipated but not found.

The investigators also looked at possible biochemical changes. Electrophoretic studies to identify abnormal proteins, if they had been created, were done using blood samples obtained from children of survivors. Both enzyme and nonenzyme proteins were studied for twenty-eight proteins of the blood plasma and red cells. After more than 1,256,000 tests, four mutants were found among children whose parents received more than 0.01Sv.

Twenty-one of the five hundred combined pregnancies in both Hiroshima and Nagasaki exposed to more than 0.01 Gy terminated with an infant with mental retardation, much higher than the 4–5 normally expected. A number of pregnancies terminated with infants with small heads, that is, two or more standard deviations below the average. Among 1,473 individuals on whom head size was measured between ages 9 and 19, 62 had a small head. Some were mentally retarded; some were not.

In utero exposure to ionizing radiation increases the frequency of mental retardation. Among those exposed to 1 Gy or more, there was a loss of approximately 25 points in IQ. Exposure to 1 Gy prenatally appears to imply a decrement in average school performance scores of about 1.6, which is tantamount to the shift of an average individual from a score of 3 to about 1.4, that is, from the middle 50th percentile of a class to the lower 5th or 10th.

Ocular damage was yet another concern. Of some 464 individuals exposed in utero, 309 were examined. Only one, a male, had any degree of opacity.

As for the cancer risk of those exposed prenatally, with respect to adult cancers, their risks appear to be slightly higher than those postnatally exposed. But this remains to be studied further as those born at the time are only now reaching the age when natural rates of cancer begin to rise appreciably.

A major concern of survivors was premature aging and premature dying. The determination of "aging" too rapidly, or more rapidly than naturally, was a challenge for the ABCC's researchers. After all, what are the normal signs of aging? Gray hair, loss of hair, wrinkled skin, coarser skin, losses of hearing and vision. The ability to walk and run as fast as one used to is another sign, as are loss of sense of smell and taste, loss of memory, and spots on the skin. Singly or as a cascade, these do give the impression to oneself and others that aging is occurring, as of course it is, from the day we are born. But premature aging and death usually refers to a time well before that which is considered normal. But that too varies by culture and

heredity. As life expectancy increases, so to does the age of premature death, which must also vary by time and country. As half the survivors are still alive, definitive answers will emerge only as that cohort passes from the scene.

For coronary heart disease, the effect of premature death was observed only above 1.5 Gy. But the numbers of excess deaths are far less in spite of the high exposure levels. There is evidence that among both heavily exposed men and women in Nagasaki the risk of a premature coronary event has been seen. Heavily exposed women in Hiroshima had excess deaths from coronary heart disease and stroke. Men in Nagasaki are now showing an excess. But Nagasaki women and Hiroshima men do not yet show these excesses. Nevertheless, Schull warns us that interpretation requires caution. Over the past fifty-six years, major changes have occurred, especially dietary. On the one hand, changes may decrease stroke, but increase heart disease. Cholesterol levels have risen over the past thirty years. Consequently, true radiation effects have been difficult to excise. The one reasonably clear finding is the excess deaths among those who received radiation at the younger ages and also received doses of 2 Gy and above—heavy exposures.

In summary, then, from the LSS we learn that radiation at any level is not a health risk. We also learn that congenital abnormalities did not occur following the bombing, "nor is there," Schull informs us, "evidence that the health or development of the children of survivors has been measurably impaired." Although there are excess cancers among the survivors, the numbers are far smaller than anyone would have believed or imagined. Given the stunning revelations Schull has made available, his few pages should not only be required reading, but re-reading. Finally, it is essential and also comforting to know that, unless an atom bomb were to explode above one of our cities, no one will ever experience the levels of radiation that were broadcast across Hiroshima and Nagasaki. At the same time, it is vital to recall that we are awash in radiation every moment of our lives.

Three Mile Island-2

The year is 1979. At 4 A.M. on March 28, Metropolitan Edison's Three Mile Island (TMI) Unit 2 nuclear power plant near Middletown, Pennsylvania, malfunctioned. It was to be the greatest power plant accident in American nuclear history.

A power generation plant, whether using coal, oil, gas, or nuclear fuel, is nothing but a huge boiler, a place to heat water to boiling to create the steam needed to spin the blades of a turbine connected to the shaft of a generator. With coils of copper wire on the generator and a huge magnet surrounding it, a spinning generator creates electricity. That's it. The difference between coal/oil-fired power plants and a nuclear power station is the fuel. As with naturally occurring coal and oil used in traditional power plants, the naturally occurring element uranium is the fuel for nuclear power plants. Uranium fuel doesn't burn: it fissions. The atoms that make up uranium are split, generating huge amounts of energy—heat. On March 28, 1979, a series of malfunctions, human errors, led to a partial reactor core meltdown and the subsequent release of radioactive iodine into the air. Faulty control room instruments along with inadequate emergency response training prevented a proper response to an unplanned automatic shutdown. Water to the reactor core was carelessly cut off. With lack of water, pressure in the core increased, causing a safety valve to open, which was set to automatically shut down the reactor. The plant operators could not fathom what was happening, confused as they were by readings on the display panel. During March 29 and 30, operators used a system of pipes and compressors to move the gas to waste-gas decay tanks. The compressors leaked. Radioactive gas was released to the outside air. At no time, however, was there a possibility of an explosion, for three reasons: (1) there was never enough oxygen in the system for an explosive mixture; (2) the uranium fuel had less than 3 percent of the isotope uranium-235; and (3) there was containment, an impenetrable steel-reinforced concrete housing, built especially to prevent the release of radioactive material in the event of a meltdown.

For the public, garbled communications reported by the media along with a steady drumbeat of an impending disaster, as featured in the heady, imaginative film, *China Syndrome*, caused thousands of fearful residents to flee the area. Actually, TMI was nothing more than a mouse that roared.

Although it had received little media attention, both the U.S. Department of Energy and the State of Pennsylvania Department of Environmental Resources had been obtaining hundreds of air samples around TMI-2 (reactor Unit 2) and found no unusual levels of radioactivity, especially of radioactive iodine-131. Yet, misinformation was generating communitywide anxiety, stress, and fear.

When the media circus finally abated and cleanup began, it was the Japanese government that paid for a large part of it. The cleanup operation would provide appropriate training for their engineers. Indeed, in spite of Hiroshima and Nagasaki, the Japanese government understood the need to free themselves from the vagaries of foreign oil and coal supplies, as well as their polluting effects. They made the decision to go nuclear. Nuclear power would provide their ever-increasing electric power needs. Currently, nuclear energy provides 36 percent of Japan's electricity. In February 1991, when cleanup was completed, TMI-2 was cited by the National Society of Professional Engineers as one of the top engineering achievements in United States.[5]

And what of the release of radioactive gases? What has been learned over the past two decades? Of overriding importance was the finding that the average whole-blood gamma exposure for individuals living within five miles of TMI-2 was 0.1–0.25 mSv. These values are a fraction of the average U.S. exposure of 0.8–1 mSv from natural background exposure. This is also something to be reflected upon.

At the request of the Three Mile Island Public Health Fund, a court-supervised fund was created to address public health issues of concern to residents of the area surrounding the TMI nuclear facility. The Division of Epidemiology of the School of Public Health at Columbia University sought to determine whether or not the pattern of cancer occurrence after March 28, 1979, was related to the radiation release from the facility.

Within a 10-mile radius of TMI lived a population of approximately 160,000 people. All nineteen hospitals within 30 miles of TMI agreed to allow Columbia University epidemiologists access to their patient records and to the new cancer cases occurring between 1975 and December 1985. During those eleven years, 5,493 new cases were diagnosed. What did the study determine? The authors of the published report "failed to find definite effects of exposure on the cancer types and population subgroups thought to be most susceptible to radiation. No associations were seen for leukemia in adults or for childhood cancers as a group." They reported too, that "rates of childhood leukemia in the Three Mile Island area are low compared with national and regional rates, and for leukemia in adults, there was a negative trend." And again, "Overall, the pattern of results does not provide convincing evidence that radiation releases from the Three Mile Island nuclear facility influenced cancer risk during the limited period of follow-up."[6]

They also found that exposure patterns projected by computer models agreed with data from the TMI dosimeters used at the time of the accident. With the level of gas released from TMI-2 and potential exposures of radiation less than the existing natural background, one must wonder if the epidemiologists were in fact searching for a virtual needle in a nonexistent haystack.

Shortly thereafter, the National Cancer Institute, concerned that questions continued to be raised about possible adverse health effects resulting from releases at TMI, from the reprocessing plant at Hanford, Washington, as well as from the routine operation of nuclear facilities around the country, conducted a survey of death rates among populations living near sixty-two nuclear facilities, industrial power generating plants, and weapons plants. Their published account informs us that "this survey has not shown that the operations of any of the 62 nuclear facilities have caused excess childhood leukemia in their vicinity." They reported also that "although public concerns have been raised with respect to Fernold, Rocky Flats, Hanford, Three Mile Island, and others, this survey has not detected excess mortality due to leukemia or other cancers that might have been caused by radioactive emissions from any DOE facility or commercial nuclear electric power plant." But they are not absolute, for, as they declare, "we can not conclude that nuclear facilities have not caused any cancer deaths in persons living near them. It can be concluded, however, that if nuclear facilities posed a risk to neighboring populations, that risk was too small to be detected by a survey such as this."[7]

But that is not the end of it. In June 1996, seventeen years after the TMI-2 accident, U.S. District Court (Harrisburg) Judge Sylvia Rambo dismissed a class action lawsuit alleging that the accident caused adverse health effects. Her finding is exceptional. "The parties to the instant action," she wrote, "have had nearly two decades to muster evidence in support of their respective cases. . . . The paucity of proof alleged in support of plaintiff's case is manifest. The court has searched the record for any and all evidence, which construed in the light most favorable to plaintiffs creates a genuine issue of material fact warranting submission of their claims to a jury. This effort has been in vain."[8]

Yet the search continued. In June 2000, a research team composed of members of several departments of the University of Pittsburgh's School of Public Health and the State of Pennsylvania Department of Health published their findings on the mortality among residents of Three Mile Island between 1979 and 1992. Their study shows that radioactivity released by TMI-2 has not caused an increase in cancer deaths. Listen to their conclusion: "The mortality surveillance of this cohort (32,135 people) to date does not provide consistent evidence that low dose radiation releases during the TMI accident had any measurable impact on the mortality experience." And they go on to say that "most notably, the increased risk of mortality from heart disease in males and females, observed over all, was no longer apparent after controlling for confounders and natural external background radiation."[9] So much for the greatest power plant disaster in U.S. history.

Chernobyl

Chernobyl was different. Chernobyl, located in the Ukraine about 12 miles south of Belarus, forms a triangle with Kiev and Chernigov. The nuclear reactor at Chernobyl was a pressurized water reactor designated RBMK, an acronym for a high output, multichannel facility.

During the night of April 25 to 26, 1986, the operating staff of reactor No. 4 was testing a turbogenerator prior to shutting the reactor down. Test procedures were poorly written and operating rules were disregarded. Unknowingly, they had disabled a number of safety systems and also withdrew control rods from the reactor core, producing a huge power surge that did not prompt an automatic shutdown. The surge could not be controlled manually. At 1:23 A.M., the reactor exploded, followed shortly by a second explosion that destroyed part of the building. This explosion threw hot and highly reactive pieces of the reactor core into the air. Burning graphite fell on nearby buildings, setting them on fire. Destruction of the reactor's housing, the attempts to put out the fire, and attempts to quench the fission reaction resulted in great plumes of radioactive particles hurled into the air. It has been estimated that the total radioactivity released was some two hundred times greater than the combined releases of the bombs that fell on Hiroshima and Nagasaki.[10] Now *that* is worthy of pondering, especially in terms of potential health effects. Given the type of crude power plant and the new generation of plants coming on-line, it is doubtful that the world will ever again see such levels. By comparison, although TMI-2 sustained damage to its reactor core, there was no steam explosion there. Had there been one, there would have been no releases to the atmosphere because of TMI's steel and reinforced-concrete containment building, which Chernobyl did not have.

Average doses to the people most affected at Chernobyl were about 100 mSv for 240,000 recovery operation workers, the early liquidators. By the time the numbers of liquidators had risen to 600,000, the doses had decreased markedly. But for the 116,000 evacuees, the 30 mSv doses were still high. Many people refused to leave their homes and continued to live in the contaminated areas for ten years after the accident. They received doses of 10 mSv.

Beyond the Ukraine, Belarus, and the Russian Federation, other European countries received windborne radiation doses of approximately 1 mSv, which then decreased over the years to levels of the natural background. Closer to Russia, Poland's population, for example, received an average of 8 mGy, with a range of 0.2–64 mGy. It has been estimated that as many as 5 percent of children received doses of 200 mGy. Throughout Europe, doses of Iodine-131 to infants' thyroids were as high as 25 mGy.

The accident produced severe, immediate effects. Of six hundred workers present at the site during the early morning of April 26, 134 received doses of 0.7–13.4 Gy and became acutely ill. Thirty died within the first six months: twenty-eight within three months, and two others three months later. During 1986–1987, some 200,000 liquidators received doses of between 0.01 and 0.5 Gy. They are currently being followed for possible late consequences such as cancer.

Among individuals exposed as children, approximately 1,800 thyroid cancers, with fewer than ten deaths, have been documented. If the trend continues, additional cases are anticipated over the coming decades. Other than these increases, evidence of a major public health impact attributable to radiation exposure does not appear to have occurred fifteen years after the accident. Most striking is the fact that the risk of leukemia does not appear to be elevated, not even among those who became acutely ill and the firemen and early liquidators. Chernobyl had gamma and neutron levels far greater then anything experienced at Hiroshima and Nagasaki, and far, far greater numbers of exposed individuals.[11]

Over the next ten years, those who were forty and fifty years old in 1986 will be in their sixties and seventies, the time when cancer rates are in their normal inexorable rise. As the exceedingly large cohort of exposed liquidators reaches these older ages, we could see a rising tide of adverse effects, cancers at a range of anatomic sites, along with vastly increased numbers of thyroid cancers among young adults. *Or we may not.* Chernobyl could well turn out to be an accidental "natural" experiment of the effects of a range of radiation doses to a vast human population, an experiment that no country could ever put to the test in any other way. It could mean that no longer would it be necessary to extrapolate effects at low doses from effects at high doses. We would finally know with a high degree of certainty if the current linear no-threshold theory is valid for human beings. This requires a brief explanation.

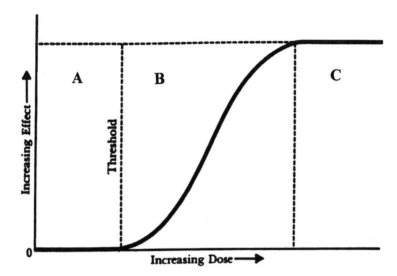

FIG. 6.5. *A typical radiation dose-response curve showing the classic response of increasing effect with increasing dose. A = No effect range; B = range of increasing effect with increasing dose; C = maximum effect range.*

The long-term, low-level effect of exposure to potentially (or actually) harmful chemicals is referred to as *chronic toxicity*. A dose-response curve, like Gaul, has three parts: (1) the initial flat portion showing, as seen in figure 6.5, that a number of increasing doses produce no (detectable) effects; (2) a rising curve, the beginning of which is the threshold *a,* or the point below which untoward effects are not observed or the point at which effects begin; with increasing doses, observable effects increase to a maximum, and by the time the curve arrives at its maximum effects level, it has described a classic S shape; (3) a flat final curve, showing increasing doses produce no observable effects. Thus, the term or concept of threshold is used in animal testing studies to denote the point between no effect and effects of exposure. It is generally accepted that thresholds exist, because there is verifiable, observable, experimental evidence that below a specific level of chemical X, in a particular species of animal, detectable responses do not occur, but as doses increase, effects appear.

On the other hand, radiation exposure lacks consensus as to the existence of a threshold. In the absence of conclusive animal-based test data, various federal agencies have assumed that even the smallest radiation exposure carries a risk. This assumption, referred to as the *linear no-threshold theory* or model, extrapolates (estimates unknown values by

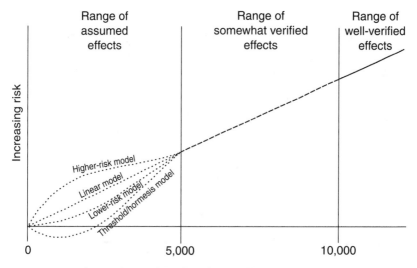

FIG. 6.6. *Four radiation dose models. These four models of low-level radiation effects appear to fit research data. The linear model is used by regulatory organizations. The threshold model is used by those who see the data as showing no effects below a certain level. The higher- and lower-risk models are preferred by those who interpret the data as showing higher and lower risks, respectively, than the linear model.* (SOURCE: Courtesy of the U.S. General Accounting Office.)

extension of known values) verified high-level radiation effects to lower exposure levels. Adverse effects are anticipated at every dose. This model extrapolates from the high-dose effects observed at Hiroshima and Nagasaki and projects backward to zero. This type of dataless projection may be no more than untutored guesstimates. Figure 6.6 shows four different models that could fit the available data. At the far right is an area well above 10,000 mrem (100 mSv), where the dose response has been verified. As the curve moves backward and below 10,000, it moves into a gray area, into a range of somewhat verified effects. Below 5,000 mrem (50 mSv), the annual standard set for worker safety, we enter a never-never land of assumed effects, for which a range of models has been suggested as fitting. Both the higher- and lower-risk models are preferred by those who interpret the data as showing higher risks and lower risks, respectively, than the linear model. It is well to recall that the natural radiation background in the United States averages 280–300 mrem, and that each chest X-ray contributes some 6 mrem. As a consequence of the many published studies of health effects of low-level radiation—as we shall see—the Biological Effects of Ionizing Radiation (BEIR) Committee of the National Academy of Sciences is issuing a reevaluation of the linear model in 2001. Its reassessment may well show that a threshold beneath which radiation is harmless does exist. Stay tuned.

A University of Pittsburgh study developed a compilation of average radon levels in houses for 1,729 U.S. counties, containing 90 percent of the U.S. population. It is interesting that a comparison of the radon levels with lung cancer mortality rates in these counties found that, with or without correction for smoking, a statistically strong tendency for counties with high radon levels had low lung cancer rates. After eliminating five hundred potential confounders, they concluded that the linear no-threshold theory grossly overestimates the cancer risk from low-level radiation.[12]

On Thursday, December, 14, 2000, reactor No. 3, Chernobyl's last working reactor, was shut down. Sergey Bastovoi, a young engineer, turned the on-off switch to off. An era ended.

Several months earlier, Patrick K. Tyler, a journalist for the *New York Times,* visited Chernobyl and its working reactor. His searching observations convey an illuminating message. His observations begin by noting that, "to any visitor, it seems more than unusual that thousands of people still come to work here every day." He tells us too that, "despite intensive medical investigations into the health effects of the huge amount of radiation released from the explosion and fire that ripped through reactor No. 4 in 1986, . . . the overall health of the plant workers remains good, though more questions than answers remain about Chernobyl's long-term effects." Walking about, Tyler found that "in man-made canals that once carried cooling water to and from the reactor, hefty carp and catfish have taken over. And in the nearby forests the swelling deer population has attracted poachers who ply the trails of the zone at night." Considering the large numbers of people working there, the deer population, whose venison people are obviously sampling, along with the available fish, Tyler's further observations are no less provocative. "In the aftermath of 1986," he wrote, "Chernobyl became a symbol of nuclear devastation that incited a numbing fear in the Ukraine and Belarus, a fear that researchers suggest has so far been more destructive to public health than the huge release of radiation." Sound familiar?

The realities of life were not lost on Tyler. He informs us that for the current six thousand workers, the power station represented a paycheck and a guaranteed apartment. Speaking with a young worker, she tells him that "I was a student in electrical engineering in Moscow and came here two years after the accident . . . and frankly, I came for financial reasons because living here on 1,300 rubles a month, with your own apartment, was better than living in Moscow on 130 rubles a month and no apartment."

Reading that "on the deck that overlooks the sarcophagus (the covering of the destroyed reactor) where Vice President Gore stood briefly during his visit to Chernobyl in 1997, the radiation goes from 4 to 10 times the naturally occurring level, still not necessarily dangerous but not recommended for extended exposure," I mused to myself about the real meaning of the linear dose-response, no-threshold model.

Tyler's reporting on health effects is most revealing and needfully assuring. He learned that "the health effects from other long-life radioactive elements, like cesium and strontium, have been difficult to measure. There have been no clusters of leukemia or other cancers in the fallout zones where the thyroid cancers have appeared, but the latency period for other health effects may be longer, experts say." He concluded his report with a telling bit of data: "A United Nations conference on Chernobyl concluded in 1996 that the only clear change evident in health to date was a 'highly significant' increase in thyroid cancer rates among people who were children in 1986 in the affected area. 'To tell you the truth,' said Dr. Mykola D. Tronko, director of Ukraine's Thyroid Cancer Institute, 'even 14 years after the accident, we have more questions than answers.'"[13]

By comparison with Chernobyl, Hiroshima, and Nagasaki, Three Mile Island, with its minuscule leak of radioactive gas, was a nonevent. Three Mile Island seared the American conscience as a great nuclear disaster but contributed far less radiation than the natural background. The media gave Pennsylvania and surrounding states agita, a far more serious problem.

Natural Background Radiation

As we shall now see, many areas around the world have natural background radiation far in excess of those of Denver or Leadville. For us, the question will be: Have the people in these excessively high background areas had patterns of cancer or other illnesses and death higher than those living in areas of normally low background areas? We shall also note the findings of other countries with respect to adverse health effects in populations living close to nuclear facilities, or working in them.

Epidemiologic studies have sought to ascertain possible adverse health effects of low-level radiation. Many studies have attempted to relate natural background levels, principally radon, with local cancer rates. A major premise has been that in areas with higher background levels, studies should show increasing cancer rates if there is a linear relationship between radiation dose and cancer induction: low cancer levels at low radiation levels, and increasing rates of cancer with increasing dose. Some studies have zeroed in on areas where natural background levels are ten to one hundred times higher than average U.S. levels. Other studies have investigated the pattern of mortality near nuclear facilities. As to be expected, results differ. Most show no evidence of elevated cancer risk. Some find slightly elevated risks. Some find lesser risks. Taken together, the studies suggest that low-level radiation effects are either small or nonexistent, and thus do not agree with the no-threshold theory.

As noted in table 6.1 earlier in this chapter, in most regions of the world natural background radiation varies by a factor of 3, but can exceed that by 10 to 100. Especially high concentrations of natural background radiation occur in Brazil, China, India, and Iran. Highly elevated levels exist along the coast of Brazil at Guarapari and in the state of Minas Gerais (Brazilia is its capital). Kerala, at India's most southern tip, has a long history of studies documenting its exceptionally high natural levels, as has Yanjiang county, southwest Guangdong Province, on China's southeast coast. Iran's Caspian coast at Ramsar, north of Tehran, is yet another area of exceptionally high natural radiation to which the population has been exposed for centuries.

So, for example, a study in Guangdong Province, China, among a rural, stable population of some 80,000, the radon-220 (Thoron) levels indoors and outdoors was 167.6 and 18.5 Bq/m^3, respectively. Those were the levels the people in the high background areas were inhaling daily for generations. In the low background areas, the levels were 2.3 times less for radon and 9.6 times less for Thoron. After fourteen years of continuous observation, the collaborative team from the Universities of Zhongshan (Guangzhou), the University of Salzburg (Austria), and the University of Nebraska found twenty-three lung cancer deaths in the high areas and twenty-seven in the low, a difference that was not statistically significant. They concluded: "There was no observable excess lung cancer risk."[14]

A team of researchers from the U.S. National Cancer Institute and the People's Republic of China conducted a study in Shenyang, an industrial city in China's northeast that has *the world's highest rates of lung cancer in women*. They placed alpha-track radon detectors in the homes of 308 women with newly diagnosed lung cancer and 356 randomly selected female "controls." The median household level of radon was 2.3 picocuries of air (pCi/L). Twenty percent of the homes had radon levels greater than 4 pCi/l. After a year, they found that levels of radon were not higher in homes of those women who had developed lung cancer than in the homes of those who did not. They also observed that lung cancer risk did not rise with increasing radon levels. They further inform us that the results suggest that exposure-response relationships at levels of typical indoor home exposures may not be as steep as suggested by risk models using data from underground miners.[15]

Yet another mixed team of U.S. and Chinese scientists studied thyroid nodularity and chromosome aberrations among 1,001 women aged 50–65 in a high-background area of south China where radiation levels were three times higher than areas of normal background. The women in the high-background areas were compared to 1,005 women of the same age group in the normal area. They concluded, "Continuous exposure to low-level radiation throughout life is unlikely to appreciably increase the risk of thyroid cancer."[16]

The coastal areas of Kerala state, where India meets the Indian Ocean and Arabian Sea, have deposits of radioactive, Thorium-containing monazite sands, similar to those in Brazil. Kerala is a diversely populated area that has been inhabited for over a thousand years. Alpha, beta, and gamma particles emitted by the high levels of Thorium, a radioactive metallic element, are regularly inhaled and ingested. Levels of total radiation reach as high as 70 mGy/yr, and on average they are over seven times the level observed in interior areas.

A research team of the Regional Cancer Center at Trivandrum recently surveyed the population for cancer levels and found "no evidence that cancer occurrence is consistently higher because of levels of external gamma radiation."[17] Another team from the Bhabha Atomic Research Center screened 36,805 newborn infants for congenital malformations. They inform us that from their observations, "the stratification of newborns with malformations, stillbirths, or twinning showed no correlation with the natural radiation levels in the different areas. Thus, no significant differences were observed in any of the reproductive parameters between the population groups based on the monitoring of 26,151 newborns from high-level natural radiation and 10,654 from normal-level natural radiation areas of the Kerala Coast."[18]

This coast has been intensively studied. Another group studied chromosomal aberrations in the lymphocytes of newborn infants. Cytogenetic studies using cord blood samples from newborns in high-level natural radiation areas of Kerala have been ongoing since 1986. During this time, 10,230 infants have been screened for a range of chromosomal aberrations. Comparing 8,493 infants from high-level areas with 1,737 infants from normal areas, they found that "within the limitations of sample size, the frequencies of total autosomal and sex aneuploids as well as structural anomalies were comparable between the high-level and normal level natural radiation areas."[19]

Oral submucus fibrosis (OSMF), a precancerous condition, is a crippling disorder that appears to be unique to the Indian subcontinent. It produces a progressive stiffening and thickening of the oral mucosa and deeper tissues, limiting the opening of the mouth and protrusion of the tongue. Kerala has a relatively high percentage of cases. A recently reported study by members of the Dental Division of the Medical College at Trivandrum found "no significant difference between the observed prevalences of OSMF in the study and control populations." They remarked also that "it appears highly improbable that the cases of OSMF encountered in the study area were induced by high background radiation alone. Our findings suggest that the observed prevalence of OSMF in the area sampled was on a par with that in other endemic areas: the high natural background radiation cannot be said to have a causal relationship with the disorder."[20]

Other Radiation-Induced Mortality

Four additional groups of people can contribute useful information on patterns of radiation-induced mortality: children born of parents treated for cancer; families living near nuclear facilities; employees of nuclear facilities; and people living in naturally high background areas in the United Kingdom and Europe. Perhaps after considering these groups, Americans will get a new message about ionizing radiation. Perhaps.

A collaborative study of residential radon exposure and lung cancer was conducted by the Norwegian Cancer Registry, the Norwegian Radiation Protection Authority, and the National Radiological Protection Board of the United Kingdom. The association was tested in 427 Norwegian municipalities. Radon detectors were sent to 10,000 homes; 7,500 were returned. Data on smoking habits and asbestos contact were obtained. They found a consistent increase in incidence of lung cancer with increasing numbers of cigarettes smoked, but no positive trend with increasing radon exposure. However, when the data were submitted for regression analysis, an increase in small-cell anaplastic tumors was calculated for women only.

Based on a total female population of 2.1 million, fifteen excess cases per year could be expected.[21]

Low-level radon background was the concern of the U.S. General Accounting Office. They examined eighty-two ecologic and analytic epidemiological studies, with the help of Dr. Thomas Gisell, professor of health physics at Idaho State University.

Of the eighty-two studies, forty-five were directly radon related. They looked at a range of cancer types; some looked at cancer in children, while others looked at genetic effects. Of sixty-seven radon-related cancer studies, twenty-two reported results indicating a statistically significant correlation between natural background radiation, radon, and cancer rates. Forty-five found no correlation. Eight of the forty-five found a negative correlation, and four were inconclusive. Others reported statistically significant chromosomal aberrations, but no cancer correlations. Following this, the National Academy of Science issued its BEIR IV Report in 1999. Of the thirty-nine studies the report considered, seventeen reported a positive correlation between radon and lung cancer, fifteen reported no correlation, and three found a negative correlation. None of the GAO eighty-two studies or the 39 NAS studies had background levels as high as those in China or India, which may account for the discrepancies. Nevertheless, it is curious that no direct cause-effect relationship between cancer and natural background radiation levels is found in extremely high background areas while only discordant results are forthcoming from areas of far lower natural levels. It gives one to wonder.

What of families living in close proximity to nuclear installations? For the past two decades, France has obtained 75 percent of its electricity from nuclear energy. Its first nuclear power station opened in 1962. Members of the Department of Biostatistics and Epidemiology of the Institut Gustave Roussy in Villejuif, France, studied six sites: four producing electricity, and two fuel reprocessing plants. Their study zones extended from less than three miles to ten miles around the sites. For each nuclear site, a control site of the same population size was chosen, and both the nuclear site and the control site were compared to national data. The period of observation covered ten years. Over that time, fifty-eight deaths from leukemia were documented around the nuclear facilities, compared to sixty-two in the control areas and sixty-seven expected from national mortality data. Although the fifty-eight and sixty-two leukemia deaths are comparable and not significantly different, the fifty-eight are slightly lower than the national data. In addition, there was a deficit of brain tumors around the nuclear sites compared to national statistics, but the nuclear sites had double the number of Hodgkin's disease deaths. However, after correction for different causes of death, both brain tumors and Hodgkin's deaths proved to be statistically insignificant.[22]

In England, an increased incidence of childhood leukemia had been reported near two nuclear installations: Sellafield, where spent nuclear fuel is reprocessed; and Dounreay, the site of a fast breeder reactor, where reprocessing is also done. Researchers of the Cancer Epidemiology and Clinical Trials Unit of the Imperial Cancer Research Fund in Oxford investigated the allegations. They identified each child under age 15 diagnosed with leukemia between 1972 and 1985 who had lived near these nuclear sites. They then compared the incidence of leukemia in children in the 143 electoral wards that comprise the Westshire, Baskingstoke, and North Hampshire District Health Authorities. Drawing circles of 10-kilometer (6-mile) radii around each of the nuclear stations, they were able to see which of the 143 wards contained a case of leukemia and its relation to a nuclear facility. In their publication, they inform us that the risk of leukemia in children within a six-mile radius of the nuclear facilities is not great. "About 60,000 children aged 0–14 were living at any one time within a 6-mile radius of the nuclear establishments. About two of these children would normally be expected to develop leukemia each year, but three have been registered, representing one extra case of leukemia among those 60,000 each year." They conclude, too, "that these findings weigh heavily against the hypothesis that the recent increase in childhood leukemia near Dounreay (a single case!) might be accounted for by radioactive discharges from nuclear plants."[23]

What about children of cancer survivors whose therapy included radiation treatments? Do they exhibit radiation-induced effects? A Canadian study suggests not. A team composed of members of the Department of Preventive Medicine, University of Toronto, Department of Pediatrics, McMasters University, the Ontario Cancer Treatment and Research Foundation, and Health and Welfare of Canada (the opposite number to our Department of Health and Human Services) designed a case-control study to investigate this. They focused on cancer diagnosed in either parent before conception and the radiotherapy treatments received by the pelvis and abdomen, or chemotherapy with alkylating agents. Their endpoint was congenital anomalies in the offspring. They found that the risk of having a child with congenital anomalies was not increased among parents who had been treated for cancer. In their words, "The risk of congenital anomalies among live-born offspring whose parents have had cancer or been treated for cancer is not higher than that in the general population."[24]

And what of cancer in children of nuclear industry workers? Do they have an increased risk? A group of epidemiologists from the University of Leeds, the London School of Hygiene and Tropical Medicine, and the Imperial Cancer Research Fund devised a cohort study to determine whether children of men and women occupationally exposed to ionizing radiation are at increased risk of developing leukemia or other cancers prior to their twenty-fifth year. Between the years 1993 and 1996, all employees of three nuclear facilities—the Atomic Weapons Establishment, the Atomic Energy Authority, and British Nuclear Fuels—were enrolled. The subjects of the study were 39,557 children of male employees and 8,883 of female employees. During the period of the study, 111 cancers were reported of which 28 were leukemia. Their conclusion: "Cancer in young people is rare, and our results are based on small numbers of events. Overall, the findings suggest that the incidence of cancer and leukemia among children of nuclear industry employees is similar to that of the general population."[25]

But then, in nuclear facilities, there are the workers themselves. What of their risks? Surely, if there is concern that radiation escapes the facility and exposes those around it, workers inside the facility should be at greater risk. Why would anyone work in nuclear power stations, or in any occupations where radiation is present? Several studies provide guidance.

A remarkable study was done by the Department of Epidemiology at the School of Public Health at the Johns Hopkins University in Baltimore. The Naval Shipyard Workers Study was designed to determine whether there was an excess risk of leukemia or other cancers associated with exposure to low levels of gamma radiation. This study included shipyard workers from six government and two private yards: Charleston, Groton, Mare Island, Norfolk, Pearl Harbor, Newport News, Portsmouth, and Puget Sound. The thousands of workers enrolled in this study provided an ideal population for studying low-dose radiation effects because they are similar demographically, perform the same tasks in overhauling nuclear submarines, and are exposed to the same occupational hazards, except for potential radiation risks: exposure to cobalt-60 radiation. The Johns Hopkins team was able to group workers by exposure levels from 0 to 1.0 rem (0.01 mSv). One group of 1,043 workers had exposures of 5 rem (0.05 mSv) or more. Many workers were exposed for as long as twenty years.

What did the study find? "The nuclear worker population does not show a significant increase in the risk of any cancers studied except for mesothelioma when compared to the general population." And they continue. "The population does not show any risk which can clearly be associated with radiation exposure." Furthermore, the data clearly indicate that both nuclear worker groups (those exposed to radiation above 0.5 rem, as well as those below) have a lower mortality from leukemia and lymphatic and hemopietic cancers (blood cell formation) than does the non-nuclear group. All three groups have lower rates than the general population.[26] Not only does this huge study appear to undermine the no-threshold theory, there are intimations of a protective benefit for low-dose exposure, although the researchers make no mention of it.

Rumor has it that this study cost taxpayers over $10 million, and rumor also suggests that this 450-plus-page study was never published in a peer-reviewed journal because of pressure from antinuclear advocates. The fact that the media never discovered the study and made its conclusions public is a greater mystery.

A collaborative team of epidemiologists and biostatisticians of the Life Sciences Center of the Pacific Northwest Laboratory, the Oak Ridge Associated Universities, and Los Alamos National Laboratory, analyzed mortality data on workers at the Hanford site (Washington), Oak Ridge National Laboratory (Oak Ridge, Tennessee), and the Rocky Flats Nuclear Weapons Plant (Denver). They were concerned about chronic (protracted) occupational exposure to low doses of ionizing radiation. For this study, white male workers who had worked at either of these sites for six months or more were enrolled, and their data on the employees included all documented deaths between 1944 (Hanford), 1943 (ORNL), 1947 (RFNWP), and 1981. After examining the data they state that "these combined analyses provide no evidence of a correlation between radiation exposure and mortality for all cancer or from leukemia."[27] In a follow-up study and publication, in which an additional five years of data were obtained (1982–1986), they again inform us that "for leukemia the combined excess risk estimate was negative, and for all cancers except leukemia, was almost exactly zero."[28]

We can all be certain of one thing and can take comfort from it: researchers from the most prestigious and productive universities and organizations around the world have provided the type of information needed to assist in decision-making as well as given us solid information on what formerly was an elusive subject. It should no longer be.

Regulatory Affairs

Nuclear power plants, whether in the United States, the United Kingdom, Japan, India, Canada, France, or elsewhere, do not set their own rules and regulations. Because there are potential risks to workers and the public, a number of organizations both regulate and establish operational standards.

The International Commission on Radiological Protection (ICRP), formed in 1928, provides worldwide guidance on radiation protection. The National Council on Radiation Protection and Measurements, the U.S. counterpart of the ICRP, was established by Congress in 1964. In 1974, Congress passed the Federal Energy Reorganization Act, giving the Department of Energy responsibility for promoting nuclear energy, and established the Nuclear Regulatory Commission (NRC), which has the responsibility for licensing construction and plant operation. It also licenses medical, industrial, and research projects involving nuclear materials, and is responsible for inspection and enforcement, which means it can fire users and revoke licenses for infractions. It also sets standards for use of radioactive materials and administers a research program dealing with reactor safety. Perhaps most important for the population generally, the NRC develops nationwide regulations on radiation limits. Its published standards limit the amount of both occupational and general public radiation exposure via air and water.

In addition to these, the BEIR Committee studies and publishes reports on radiation standards. UNCEAR is the United Nations Committee on the Effects of Atomic Radiation. Established in 1955, it tracks studies and reports on radiation levels around the world and attempts to interpret health effects and set standards. The International Atomic Energy Agency (IAEA), founded in 1957, an independent intergovernmental organization within the U.N. system and located in Vienna, has 128 member states that have agreed to abide by its objectives: to increase the contribution of atomic energy for peace, health, and prosperity throughout the world, and to ensure that the assistance, supervision, and controls it provides are not used in any way to further military purposes.

We know that we are continuously bathed in natural as well as man-made radiation, and that—as we have learned from our vast knowledge and experience, radiation is not the ugly duckling it was originally thought to be. Furthermore, we can be secure in the knowledge that numerous national and international organizations and agencies are ever watchful.

Therefore, it is natural to view nuclear power as a needed, an important, and a preferred source of clean energy.

Power Generation

How many people even know how electricity is produced by nuclear power stations, and how many people have been inside one? My information, limited as it is, suggests that the answer is few, too few. Working on that premise, let us consider how power/energy/electricity comes to us, and, indeed, let us enter a plant. Just what goes on there?

The function of any power plant is to convert a source of energy—coal, oil, wood, natural gas, or uranium—into electricity. In fact, the fuel, no matter what it is, is asked to do only one thing: boil water. Power plants can be thought of as huge water boilers and steam generators. Boiling water produces steam, which is piped to turbine blades and sets them spinning furiously. As electricity can readily be produced by a copper wire moving through a magnetic field, the turbine blades, connected to a copper-wired generator and surrounded by a huge magnet, are set spinning, producing electricity. In a word, mechanical, rotational energy is converted to the electricity needed to electrify our homes, offices, businesses, and industry. To accomplish this, large power plants are needed to house and spin huge generators. Fossil fuel plants burn coal and oil to create the heat needed to boil water. A condenser, containing cool water drawn from a nearby river, converts steam back to water and the cycle begins anew. Along with the heat energy, burning fossil fuels must produce particulate matter and carbon dioxide, both vented to the atmosphere, where they create adverse health and environmental problems.

A nuclear power plant uses steam to generate electricity just as a fossil fuel plant does, but with a difference. The difference is the fuel. In a nuclear power plant the fuel is not fossil; it is one of the Earth's other natural elements, uranium.

Uranium, a very hard, dense, silvery, radioactive metallic element, was discovered in 1789 by Martin Klaproth, a German chemist studying pitchblende, an impure uranite (uranium phosphate), and the principal mineral of uranium, occurring in black, tarry masses. He named this material Uran, after the planet Uranus. Its radioactive properties were not recognized until 1866. But it was not until the discovery of the phenomenon of nuclear fission by Otto Hahn and Fritz Strassmann in Germany in 1939 that uranium was vaulted from obscurity into international prominence.

Natural uranium oxide (U_3O_8) is a mixture of three isotopes. U-234 contains 0.00054 percent uranium; U-235 contains 0.72 percent, and U-238, 99.275 percent. (As noted earlier, an isotope of an atom contains the same number of protons but different numbers of neutrons in its nucleus.) It is the U-235, with 0.7 percent uranium, that is the reactor fuel. But it must be enriched to a level of approximately 3 percent (a number of more than passing interest and one to take with you as we move along) in order to sustain the chain reaction that will produce the heat energy needed to boil water. One ton of natural uranium oxide can produce more than 40 million kilowatt-hours of electricity, equivalent to burning 16,000 tons of coal or 80,000 barrels of oil. Those numbers are worth reflecting upon. But with uranium there is no burning, no particulates, and no carbon dioxide. This fuel releases heat by a process of fission.

It is vital to remember that an atom is the basic component of all matter. All matter. And an atom is the smallest part of an element that still contains all the chemical properties of the element. In size, an atom compares to an apple as an apple compares to the Earth. But small can be big. In turn, atoms are composed of yet smaller particles: protons, neutrons, and electrons. The atom is believed to resemble a solar system, with the electronegatively charged electrons orbiting a nucleus of electropositively charged protons and uncharged, neutral neutrons, as depicted in figure 6.7.

Uranium-235, with 96 protons and 139 neutrons in its nuclear core, for a total of 235 particles, holds the potential energy. It is the heaviest of all naturally occurring elements and thus has the largest number of protons and neutrons, a huge amount of energy waiting to be unleashed.

When uncharged neutrons are sent flying into uranium atoms, some manage to avoid repulsion by the outer shell of planetary electrons and penetrate to the nucleus, smashing into the proton/neutron cluster, and rupturing the gluons, the "strong force" holding them together. This bond cleaving releases a cascade of energy as the process is repeated and repeated. Such a self-propagating reaction, this fissioning, is called a *chain reaction*.

The release of heat from burning coal is the result of the interaction of carbon atoms with oxygen atoms from air. But the reaction is far less productive of heat than fission. As noted, one ton of uranium is the equivalent of 16,000 tons of coal, and it is noteworthy that no ash, CO_2, or other residue is produced by fission. Remember that anything made of carbon—wood, oil, plants, trees, animals, insects, anything living, anything described as organic—has the carbon atom as its basic structural building block. When burned in air, CO_2 is the final byproduct. And as we

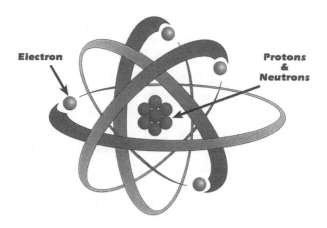

FIG. 6.7. *Electrons orbiting a nucleus. Current theory holds that all atoms are composed of protons, neutrons, and electrons. Typically, protons and neutrons in the atom's nucleus are held together by gluons. Electrons circle, or orbit, the nucleus.* (SOURCE: Courtesy of the Western Electric Company, Pittsburgh.)

now know, excessive CO_2 released into the air can destabilize the Earth's temperature and hence its climate.

Back to our nuclear reactor. If the amount of U-235 is small, as it usually is, too many of the fast-moving neutrons pass through without being absorbed. That's why 0.7 percent uranium requires enrichment to 3–4 percent. At that level, the chance of a neutron striking a nucleus is much increased. At 3–4 percent, the chain reaction will attain a critical mass and will continue uninterrupted. This may be the time to state unequivocally that *a nuclear reactor cannot be a bomb or become an atom bomb without far greater U-235 enrichment*: a bomb requires 80–90 percent enrichment. Again, it's the numbers. In addition, a nuclear reactor has water circulating through it, and water, you may recall, is not only a coolant, but also a moderator that slows down neutrons. Visions of a nuclear reactor as a potential bomb must be summarily dismissed.

Now, because of the positively charged protons in all atomic nuclei, and because like electric charges repel, nuclei in nature do not react with one another. If they did, we'd be awash in constant nuclear reactions. We would not *be*.

Once set in motion, a chain reaction continues, and heat is constantly produced. But the heat-producing fission process is controlled. That's a key. In nuclear reactors, neutrons are slowed down by collisions with such moderators as water, graphite, or beryllium.

In the United States, two types of nuclear power plants are in use: boiling water reactors (BWRs) and pressurized water reactors (PWRs). A BWR heats the water in the reactor core and allows water to boil directly to steam, which goes directly to the turbine connected to a generator, producing electricity before being recycled back into water by a condenser and reused. A PWR uses water under pressure so that it heats, but does not boil. The hot water is pumped from the reactor to a steam generator, where the heat is transferred to a second, separate water supply, which boils to make steam.

Both the BWR and PWR are light-water reactors, so called because their coolant is ordinary water—H_2O. Heavy-water reactors use heavy water, D_2O, two atoms of deuterium and one atom of oxygen. Design of the heavy-water reactor (HWR) is similar to a PWR to the extent that the primary coolant transfers heat from the core to a secondary coolant system by way of a steam generator. The similarity ends there. Heavy water is used to moderate the neutrons generated in the fission process. It is more effective at this than ordinary water, so the core can operate with less concentrated uranium, meaning it can use unenriched or natural uranium. However, heavy water is far more expensive than ordinary water. Economics does influence choices.

The essence of a nuclear power plant is its reactor, which contains the core, control rods, and coolant. The core contains the fuel, which is formed into ceramic pellets about three-eighths of an inch in diameter and a bit over half an inch in length. Each uranium-containing pellet releases about the same amount of energy as a ton of coal. These energy-rich pellets are stacked end to end in fuel rods, which are twelve to fourteen feet long and just over one-half inch in diameter. The fuel rods, shown in figure 6.8, are arranged in bundles or fuel assemblies in the core of the reactor. Within the assembly, rods must be carefully spaced to allow a liquid coolant to circulate freely between them. Approximately two hundred assemblies are grouped together to make up the reactor core. Where does the fission occur? Fission takes place within the fuel assemblies, in the core. Interspersed among the fuel assemblies are movable control rods, made of neutron-absorbing material—usually cadmium or a cadmium-zirconium alloy. The speed of the chain reaction depends upon the control rods. Heat production is moderated or augmented by lowering or withdrawing the control rods. The energy released by the chain reaction heats the water, the coolant, that flows between the fuel assembly rods, prevent-

FIG. 6.8. *Fuel assembly. View of a fully packed fuel assembly containing energy-rich pellets in the fourteen-foot-long fuel rods. This assembly will be placed in the core of a pressurized water reactor.* (SOURCE: Courtesy of the Western Electric Company, Pittsburgh.)

ing the core from becoming overheated while carrying heat away from the reactor to the generator.

Because the fission process produces radioactive products, barriers are built into every plant to protect against the release of radioactivity. Ceramic pellets seal in the radioactive uranium, and the pellets are packed into zirconium alloy rods, additional barriers against release of fission products. The core is placed in a shielded, 450-ton, eight-inch-thick steel reactor vessel. And the reactor is housed in the containment, an airtight building made of steel-reinforced concrete, some three feet thick. This containment, an essential secure barrier, is standard equipment on all U.S. reactors; it was lacking at Chernobyl. Had it been there, the accident would have been contained and Chernobyl would not have become a household word for fear. And because it was there at Three Mile Island, TMI was never more than a media event.

Augmenting the barriers noted, nuclear power plants have additional and independent backup systems, redundancies, designed to operate in the event normal operation is disrupted. One such system, an emergency core cooling system, is designed to pump thousands of gallons of water into the reactor to prevent the core from overheating. If the normal power supply is lost, a backup source kicks in. This suggests we give a moment's attention to meltdown.

What is a meltdown, and whence did it spring? Meltdown came into the culture via the film *China Syndrome*, which created the imaginative notion of a total meltdown of a reactor's core, such that the molten materials simply penetrate the reactor vessel and floor of the containment building and melt into the Earth all the way to Shanghai or Hong Kong. At Three Mile Island, about half the fuel in the core melted but was readily contained within the reactor vessel. Had it penetrated the reactor vessel, it would have collected in the lower part of the steel and concrete containment building. Nothing would have escaped from the building. With meltdown out of the way, this would have been the place to deal with nuclear power plant as a bomb. But that's been done. *It remains only to affirm the impossibility of such a consideration.*

In 1999, nuclear power plants around the country generated 728 billion kilowatt hours of electricity, enough to meet the needs of 67.5 million households. That 728 billion kilowatt-hours was 55 billion more than was generated in 1998.[29] The increase in efficiency is equal to approximately nine additional large power plants servicing an estimated 4.9 million more people. And this has been accomplished with the current generation of power plants. The new generation of Advanced Boiling Water Reactors

(ABWRs), Advanced Boiling Water Reactors (ALWRs), and Asea Brown Boveri (ABB) System 80+'s will usher in an era of safer, simpler, more economical nuclear power generation.

This era was ushered in when the world's first advanced nuclear plant began commercial operation in Japan. Kashiwazaki-Kariwa Unit 6, an ABWR supplied by General Electric, began operation in November 1996. Unit 7, a second ABWR, went critical (i.e., was turned on) in July 1997. Ten additional units are planned by 2010. Japan intends to generate over 50 percent of its electric power needs via nuclear power plants. The Taiwan Power Company is currently constructing two ABWRs, which are scheduled to come on-line in 2004 and 2005.

The ABWR is the first nuclear power plant expressly designed to meet the Nuclear Regulatory Commission's new requirement for "severe accidents." This means that the ABWR contains systems that prevent the release of radiation even in the unlikely event that the core and the plant are "severely damaged." Furthermore, the evolved systems have been designed to eliminate operator action and are thus referred to as "passive" reactors, because they use natural forces such as gravity or convection to work. These passive systems have been fully approved by the NRC. These ABWRs, along with the Westinghouse AP600, an ALWR also containing the passive system concept, as well as ABB-Asea Brown Boveri's System 80+, an NRC-certified plant with a spherical steel containment vessel enclosed in a concrete shielded building, provide additional safety via dual containment.

In the AP600, a large pool of water sits above the reactor. Should an accident occur, gravity drives the water into the reactor. In addition, new design has given it 60 percent fewer valves, 35 percent fewer large pumps, 75 percent less piping, and 80 percent less control cabling and ducting. Each of these new, next-generation power plants increase safety by redundancy, with multiple sets of systems providing backup for one another. Furthermore, with their greater efficiency, simplicity, and ease of operation, they are smaller, and with their modular construction techniques, construction time has been reduced to about 48–50 months, from the 70–120 previously required. Consequently, their cost has plummeted and become highly competitive. These new power plants should be more community friendly and acceptable. Of course, their use will be environmentally friendly as electricity production moves steadily away from fossil fuel plants.

Whether new generation or old generation, all nuclear power stations produce waste or spent fuel. What happens to it? And is it dangerous?

Used nuclear fuel cannot explode, and it doesn't burn. Remember, even when new, fresh nuclear fuel has too little U-235 to explode. And it is not flammable. Because it takes a month or more to open the reactor and remove spent fuel assemblies, this operation occurs once a year, perhaps once in two years. Plants are shut down and the oldest fuel assemblies are removed and replaced. The combined nuclear waste from the country's nuclear reactors totals some 2,000 metric tons annually.

Typically, a plant produces about 20 metric tons annually, all in solid form. Used fuel is stored at nuclear power plant sites, either in steel-lined, concrete vaults filled with water or in dry casks consisting of above-ground steel or steel-reinforced concrete containers with steel inner canisters. On-site storage is an interim measure, however. Although the NRC determined that used fuel could be stored at plant sites for one hundred years without adverse health or safety consequences, it also believes that disposal is necessary. The Nuclear Waste Policy Act of 1982 and its amendments of 1987 require or authorize the Department of Energy (DOE) to do the following:

- Locate, build, and operate a deep, mined geologic repository for high-level waste
- Locate, build, and operate a facility for interim storage of used fuel
- Develop a transportation system that safely links U.S. nuclear power plants, an interim storage facility, and a permanent repository

The repository, which was to have been completed by 1998, is at least twelve years behind schedule, and no site has been selected for an interim storage facility. The act's 1987 amendments designated Yucca Mountain in Nevada for study as a possible repository site, and the DOE is conducting a comprehensive scientific investigation of its usefulness as a repository.

Until a repository is ready to accept used fuel from nuclear power plants (in 2010 at the earliest), the United States will need a central facility to store the fuel. A centralized storage facility will provide added safety and security by using a single dedicated site, rather than leaving used fuel at more than seventy locations across the country. Under the Nuclear Waste Policy Act of 1982, and pursuant to contracts between utilities and the DOE, the federal government was responsible for removing used fuel from nuclear power plants beginning in 1998. However, the DOE has not yet selected a site for an interim storage facility.

Used nuclear fuel is transported from nuclear power plants to storage and disposal facilities either by rail, by truck, or, part of the way, by barge. Transportation containers used to ship high-level waste typically have walls one-foot thick, with shielding materials sandwiched between outer and inner metal shells. Those designed for truck transportation weigh between 25 and 40 tons and carry one to seven used fuel assemblies. Railroad containers weigh up to 125 tons, and carry more than twenty-five assemblies.

To ensure that the transportation containers retain their integrity in the event of an accident, they are designed to withstand a consecutive series of highly destructive tests: a 30-foot fall onto a flat, unyielding surface; a 40-inch drop onto a vertical steel rod; exposure to a 1,475° F fire for thirty minutes; and submerging under three feet of water for eight hours. The containers survived such tests intact.

The NRC studies showed that the engineering requirements create forces more destructive than would occur in actual accidents. Actual tests conducted to examine the accuracy of computer models and scale-model tests to analyze the ability of containers to withstand the most severe accidents drove casks into unyielding concrete walls at more than 65 mph, involved them in 80-mph train crashes, and exposed them to fully engulfing fires. The casks used in these brutal tests survived intact as well.

During the past thirty years, more than 2,900 shipments of used fuel have been safely completed in the United States, and many more in other countries. While vehicle accidents have occurred, there has not been a release of radioactive materials or a single injury attributed to the radioactive nature of the cargo. When the federal government finally opens an interim storage facility or a permanent repository, the number of used fuel shipments is expected to range from three hundred to five hundred per year.

Since the 1950s, scientific organizations around the world have examined the issue of radioactive waste management. Most organizations, from the National Academy of Sciences and the Office of Technology Assessment in the United States, to the International Atomic Energy Agency (IAEA) and the Organization for Economic Cooperation and Development's Nuclear Energy Agency (OECD/NEA), have reached the same conclusion, believing that the best and safest long-term option for dealing with high-level radioactive waste is deep geologic disposal.

What happens to spent but still weakly radioactive waste? And is it safe? The accumulated data, the open, public record, indicate that it is fair and reasonable to say that over the past fifty years, waste has been handled and managed in a responsible way. And yes, all criteria indicate they are safe. Remember too, that life is not risk free. Nothing can be absolutely safe. So, in the interest of additional confidence building and personal security, it may be useful to know that used nuclear fuel may be shipped only along specified highway routes. Shippers submit routes to the NRC for approval ahead of time. The NRC checks that a route conforms to U.S. Department of Transportation regulations, requiring the most direct interstate route and avoiding large cities when a bypass or beltway is available. NRC officials drive the route ahead of time if it has not been previously approved or used within the past few years. They will check for law enforcement and emergency response capability, as well as secure facilities for emergency stops. DOT regulations also require that the shipper notify the governor of each state on the route seven days before the trip.

But that isn't all. Specialized trucking companies handle used nuclear fuel shipments in the United States. These experienced, specially licensed companies haul all kinds of hazardous materials more than 50 million miles annually. Vehicles are state-of-the-art, equipped with computers that provide an instantaneous update on the truck's location and convey messages between driver and dispatcher through a satellite communications network. Drivers receive extensive training and must be certified. For their part, the DOT and NRC establish emergency preparedness requirements for radioactive materials. The Federal Emergency Management Agency and the DOE provide emergency response training for state and local law enforcement officials, firefighters, and rescue squads, covering preparedness planning and accident handling. In addition, DOE radiological assistance teams provide expertise and equipment, including mobile laboratories, to every region of the country. Also, according to a voluntary mutual assistance agreement, utilities respond to incidents in their area until emergency personnel from the shipper and shipping utility arrive. Short of stopping these transfers, little more can be asked of this industry.

A major impediment to the use of nuclear energy has been concern for waste disposal—the disposal of spent but still weakly radioactive fuel. Currently, federal law requires that spent fuel, fuel used only once, be disposed of as waste. Not so in England, Japan, and France, where radioactive fuel, fissionable fuel, is used and reused, meaning that their ultimate spent fuel is far less radioactive than ours, having had its fissionable content progressively reduced by successive reprocessing cycles.

The current and ongoing debate over the safety of using the Department of Energy's deep storage facility at Yucca Flats turns on the need for thousands of years of safe storage until the waste loses its radioactivity via natural decay. This debate could be short-circuited by reprocessing our huge backlog of waste. Reprocessing would extract the available and usable content of fissionable material, thereby substantially reducing the radioactivity of the final spent fuel. Its remaining radioactivity would then require hundreds of years of safe storage, rather than thousands, which would be far more readily accomplished. Furthermore, reprocessing extends the supply of nuclear fuel and does not produce material useful for nuclear weapons. Ergo, reprocessing would curtail the debate, allowing the country to get on with the business of bringing needed energy on-line.

Nevertheless, yet another question can be raised: Is it not germane to inquire why a large segment of the public came to fear nuclear power stations? Initially, nuclear power plants were called atomic energy plants, atomic reactors. And the Atomic Energy Commission was the governing federal agency. "Atomic" was easily identified and associated with atom bombs: the original cloud of the Trinity test that mushroomed skyward at White Sands, New Mexico, and the two that fell upon Hiroshima and Nagasaki. Three Mile Island and *The China Syndrome* followed, and finally there was Chernobyl to accentuate the negative. The perception then developed, abetted by the media and environmentalists, that because the nuclear power industry had obtained fuel from the military, bombs and power plants were intimately related and a nuclear power plant (no matter how egregiously false) could become a bomb at anytime. In fact, the nuclear power industry shot itself in the foot early on by purchasing reactor fuel on the cheap from the military when it had no need to do so. The utility industry, a hundred-billion-dollar industry, was and remains sufficiently well heeled to purchase whatever amounts of fuel it requires on the open market at competitive prices. Cheap fuel was not something they needed to stay in business. Nevertheless, by buying from the military, the perception was conveyed and gained wide currency among the public, who in its ignorance made the assumption that reactor = bomb. And why shouldn't it have? Which brings us to the second shot, in the other foot: allowing the public to believe, erroneously of course, that a power plant could be a bomb.

By being uncommunicative, by keeping the public in the dark, by not opening up to and educating folks about a new and remarkable source of energy, the public was allowed to believe the only thing it could imagine: nuclear plants could be a bomb that could explode at any time. The nuclear industry paid a heavy price for this blunder, and so has the country. This nation, and others, could have insulated itself against the political whims of oil-producing countries, against the economic instability produced by oil price fluctuations. It could have had clean energy with no releases of harmful particulates, or carbon dioxide (CO_2) to warm the atmosphere, decades ago.

The great advantage of nuclear power is its ability to deliver enormous amounts of energy from small amounts of fuel. Recall that a ton of U-235 produces the equivalent amount of energy as 2.5 *million* tons of fossil fuel. Think what that means in terms of environmental impact. By comparison, fossil fuels are notorious polluters. Consider too, that the United States and Canada possess about one-half of the uranium ore found in the Western world, and that it can be economically mined.

Demand for energy over the past two decades has literally skyrocketed. Populations everywhere have soared, and with it towns and cities are expanding at an accelerating pace. Development has changed the face of the national landscape. The demand for electricity has already exceeded the capacity to supply it, and blackouts and brownouts have become commonplace.

The need for energy and the need to free us from foreign oil supplies were major bones of contention during the presidential debates in 2000. Both candidates, Al Gore and George W. Bush, talked about drilling offshore and drilling for oil in Alaska. They talked about alternative energy sources—wind, solar, tide, hydro—and called for creative and imaginative thinking about them to develop the energy needed. But neither the vice president nor the governor ever ventured near nuclear energy, the one sure source that could easily supply the steadily increasing demand, cleanly, economically, and safely—the one source that could free us from foreign manipulation, reducing the ever-increasing levels of CO_2 and stopping global warming in its tracks.

The push for clean energy would lack urgency if worldwide energy needs had remained stable at the 1990 levels. Demand, however, has risen and will continue to rise substantially, driven by population increases everywhere, especially so in the underdeveloped, emerging nations. Of the world's 6 billion-plus people, 75 percent live in developing countries, where they so far consume less than 40 percent of the world's energy. A steadily growing and developing population can only compound the need.

The IPCC's Special Report on Emissions Scenarios (SRES) of 2000 presents a set of forty scenarios as projections of GHG emissions. Those forty reflect a range of assumptions on population growth, economic development, and technological progress, as well as international cooperation on energy use. The scenarios show that energy use will increase from between 1.7 to 3.7 times over the next fifty years. As they calculate it, demand for electricity will grow almost eightfold in the high-growth scenario, and double in the more conservative scenarios. Thirty-five of the forty scenarios include substantial reliance and increases in use of nuclear-generated power. They note, too, that renewable resources, including hydroelectric power, sustainable biomass, solar, geothermal, and ocean energy, while virtually inexhaustible, have low conversion efficiencies as well as low energy supply densities. The latter imply large land requirements that are generally unavailable, while solar and wind energy are unable to supply energy on demand due to the intermittent nature of wind and sun. Nuclear power generation, on the other hand, has virtually no GHG emissions, and the entire nuclear chain has among the lowest emissions per kilowatt-hour of any power-generating system, including renewables. Currently, nuclear power annually avoids GHG emissions equal to some 8 percent of the total global emissions of fossil fuels. It is not too late. The window of opportunity remains open with the new generation of power plants that are safer, more efficient, easier to operate, and less costly. With our newfound knowledge of radiation and its effects, the public may now be ready to move through the window. Perhaps, too, ionizing radiation as a symbol of destruction and lethal damage will yield to a more balanced and accepting view. Available electricity changed the world of the twentieth century; nuclear power could well be the energy revolution and solution of the twenty-first. President Bush, it is time for the N word.

CHAPTER 7

Hazardous Waste, Hazardous Thinking

Shortly after the publication of *Healthy People,* Surgeon General Julius Richmond's 1979 report to President Jimmy Carter,[1] which unequivocally stated that "the health of the American people has never been better," *Time* magazine published the first of two ghoulish covers dramatizing "The Poisoning of America." Noxious chemicals were everywhere, the articles claimed, and there was no place to hide. The first cover, on September 22, 1980, wasn't a strong enough dose. On October 14, 1985, the editors repeated the cover, an unprecedented occurrence. Both strikingly colorful covers were deadly dramatic. Dramatizing "those toxic chemical wastes," each displayed a person immersed in toxic wastes up to and including the tip of the nose. Below the surface, only a skeleton remained, though the 1980 cover still had birds wheeling in a blue sky and greenery on the far shore. By October 1985, the skeleton was up to its ears, and what remained of its face and hair was discolored. The trees had yellowed and a solitary bird flew overhead. Death and dying was the frightening message—one to be remembered.

But most of all, the covers were meant to deliver the message that we, all of us, were drowning in toxic waste and reaping its ill effects. The editors knew that between 1980 and 1985, in only five years, the ill effects had increased inordinately. They knew it, and they made certain the country knew it. Listen to the publisher: "If the cover of this week's issue looks familiar it is not because your imagination is playing tricks on you. Five years ago, *Time* used an almost identical image to illustrate a cover story on the environmental dangers of toxic wastes. The decision to reprise the earlier cover, an unprecedented step for the magazine, was prompted by the heightened sense of urgency about the problem." The ghoulish scene depicted by James Marsh in 1980 "has been slightly altered by the artist to account for the passage of time. The tide of pollution has edged higher and now threatens the victim's eyes. Skyscrapers have risen in the background, two trees have yellowed, and the cattails near the shore have died." Explains Marsh: "We wanted to show that aboveground things may look O.K., but beneath it's death."

The staffers who visited toxic sites were struck by the sometimes eerie nature of the newly created wastelands. Associate editor Kurt Andersen was most impressed by Times Beach, Missouri, which was evacuated in 1982–83 after being contaminated by dioxin. Says Anderson: "Times Beach looks as if a neutron bomb hit it. Houses are standing, windows are unbroken, some toys are still scattered around, but nobody walks the streets." Senior correspondent Peter Stoler and Chicago correspondent J. Madeline Nash experienced a strong sense of déjà vu as they updated their 1980 reporting. Stoler was reminded of John Brunner's 1972 science fiction novel, *The Sheep Look Up,* which described a world that was poisoning its air. "I thought it far-fetched," recalls Stoler. "Now I wonder if Brunner shouldn't have been more hysterical." Nash, who traveled from the Stringfellow Acid Pits in California to Burnt Fly Bog in New Jersey, was particularly disheartened by the Lone Pine landfill in New Jersey, "I had to wear a pair of protective boots," she says. "Around me were sticky rivulets of toxic ooze. There was an unmistakable scent of solvent in the air." Washington correspondent John Yang, who covered the bureaucratic side of the story, concludes, "It is a terribly complicated technical problem, as well as one fraught with emotion, just the kind of situation that guarantees anger and frustration."

Smelly, sticky, toxic ooze. You can feel it. Of course it was toxic. How could it not be? Oozy, sticky, and smelly must be toxic. How else would Nash know? Did the truth matter? Probably not. The magazine had made its point. The country was awash in toxic chemicals and it was exacting a heavy toll in lives and illness. *Time* knew this for a fact in the early 1980s. But did anyone else? The U.S. surgeon general sure didn't.

The year 1991 etches these covers and the message they conveyed in stark relief. Six years after the second cover, the National Academy of Sciences (NAS), the nation's most prestigious scientific body, published volume 1 in the series Environmental Epidemiology. Volume 1 bears the title *Public Health and Hazardous Waste.*[2] "Hazardous," not toxic. Indeed, there is a difference, and not a subtle one. These two terms are neither synonymous nor interchangeable. "Hazardous" means *possibility* of danger, a *chance* of risk, but "toxic" means *poisonous,* producing a deadly or injurious effect. These are very different concepts, unfortunately too often glossed over. What did the NAS have to say? "Part of our modern heritage," they inform us,

> is the increasing volume of waste created by all industrial societies. Today, there is also unprecedented concern over the potential consequences for public health and the environment of the exposure to wastes that are deemed hazardous under a variety of regulatory regimes. According to recent opinion polls, the American public believes that hazardous wastes constitute a serious threat to public health. In contrast, many scientists and administrators in the field do not share this belief. On the basis of its best efforts to evaluate the published literature relevant to this subject, the Committee cannot confirm or refute either view. A decade after implementation of Superfund (Comprehensive Environmental Response, Compensation and Liability Act, CERCLA, 1980), and despite Congressional efforts to redirect the program, substantial public health concerns remain and critical information on the distribution of exposures and health effects associated with hazardous-waste sites is still lacking.

That was their summary, and it bears repeating: "Substantial public health concerns remain and critical information on the distribution of exposures and health effects associated with hazardous-waste sites is still lacking."

But *Time* knew just how deadly they were, how mightily they affected public health! What else could "rivulets of ooze" mean? The editors were so sure that they socked it to the public a second time. But let's continue with the NAS's conclusion. To wit:

> Whether Superfund and other hazardous-waste programs actually protect human health is a critical question with respect to federal and state efforts to clean up hazardous wastes. To answer this question requires information on the scope of potential and actual human exposure to hazardous wastes and with the health effects that could be associated with these exposures. Based on its review of the published scientific/medical literature, the Committee finds that the question cannot be answered. Although billions of dollars have been spent during the past decade to study and manage hazardous waste sites in the U.S., an insignificant portion has been devoted to evaluate the attendant health risks. This has resulted in an inadequate amount of information about the connection between exposure and effect.

How's that? Can that be right? Not possible. Ten years of searching and billions of dollars later, and we still didn't know?

Yet *Time* had the answer in 1980, and the rivalets of ooze were toxic—a word never mentioned by the NAS. The bitterest of all pills is that *Time*'s message is the one that remains the lore of the land. *Time*, of course, never bothered to inform its readers of the NAS's findings. And who reads the NAS's reports anyway? Is it any wonder, then, that the country continues to hold tightly erroneous beliefs about risks to its health from chemical wastes? They'd be crazy not to: *Time* had spoken.

Time's reporting on the fact of toxic wastes fits nicely with its failure to give readers the message contained in *Healthy People*, the surgeon general's 1979 report. But then, why bother? It would be seen as contradictory reporting.

Hazardous Wastes: A Mini-Primer

It was in 1976 that Congress brought forth the Resource Conservation and Recovery Act (RCRA-PL 94–580), which directed the U.S. EPA to regulate hazardous waste because of its potential for harm. This piece of legislation was a "cradle-to-grave" law that placed the burden of proof of safety on the waste generator. Under RCRA, the generating industry or company was to be responsible for the waste from its creation until it no longer posed a threat. The RCRA stressed safe disposal rather than recycling or reductive treatments, and it established three key requirements governing their treatment, storage, and disposal: (1) For the land disposal requirement, hazardous waste generally must be treated to minimize threats to human health and the environment before disposal on land. (2) Under the minimum technology requirements, facilities that treat or dispose of waste, such as landfills, must meet certain design standards, such as installing a double liner under the landfill to protect soil and water from contamination. And (3) facilities that treat, store, or dispose of hazardous waste, including those carrying out cleanup activities, must obtain a permit to do so. A facility that has ongoing industrial activity and is requesting a permit to clean up a portion of the site must agree to clean up all parts of its property that are contaminated from past industrial operations. The EPA manages the cleanups at operating facilities that pose a high potential health or environmental risk under its "corrective action" program. It classifies hazardous waste as either "listed" wastes, meaning they were generated during specific industrial processes listed in its regulations, or "characteristic" wastes, meaning they possess one of four inherent qualities: ignitability, corrosivity, reactivity, or toxicity.

Although wastes are described as hazardous or toxic, a usable, clear, working definition has remained elusive. Nevertheless, hazardous waste was defined as "a solid waste or combination of solid wastes, which because of their concentration, or physical, chemical, or infectious characteristics, may cause an increase in mortality or an increase in serious illness . . . or pose a substantial present or potential hazard to human health or the environment when improperly treated, stored, transported, or disposal or otherwise managed." Obviously, lawyers have had their hands on this, allowing us to wonder about the meaning of "substantial" and "serious." It does not require a second reading to realize its almost total uselessness in the real world, except for its all-inclusiveness, which provides states with the power to control the disposal of most waste.

But it doesn't end there. Defining and identifying chemicals as toxic can be singularly difficult, as all substances can become toxic at sufficiently high doses and depending on who's imbibing. Recall the shape of the dose-response curve in the previous chapter, and recall, too, our man Paracelsus who insisted that what makes a poison is the dose. Thus, the question becomes: At what point does the shift from safe to hazardous to toxic occur? This concept is central to the problem and may be the shoal upon which the problem founders. It is appropriate to ask a dictionary for assistance. From my new *American Heritage Dictionary of the English Language* (4th edition, 2000), the noun *hazard* is defined as "a chance, an accident, a chance of being injured or harmed; danger." It also informs us that the adjective *hazardous* means "marked by danger, perilous, depending upon chance, risky." Risk appears central to the hazard problem. And risk implies probability and/or uncertainty. There is nothing definite about it. It does, however, raise the flag of prudence.

Toxic, also an adjective, means "capable of causing injury or death especially by chemical means." Poisonous. That's definite. Probability does not figure in this. Quite simply, hazardous and toxic are neither the same, similar, synonymous, nor interchangeable. Hazardous waste should be viewed in that context.

Although the U.S. EPA has defined what it believes is or constitutes hazardous waste, in fact, there is no universally accepted definition. Because every country and most states have developed their own definitions, it is difficult to determine how much waste any country generates. Without a level playing field, it is also difficult to know what wastes are involved. Guesstimates suggest a world total of 330 million tons annually, and some 57 million wet metric tons for the United States. Ten percent may fall under the rubrics *hazardous* or *toxic*, with petrochemicals and chemicals generally contributing 70 percent of the total. The EPA has also provided four adverbs—*ignitability, corrosivity, reactivity,* and *toxicity*—

to differentiate hazardous from nonhazardous solid waste. Briefly this is how the EPA describes them:

1. Ignitability (Code I). A substance is considered to exhibit this quality if a representative sample: a. Has a flash point less than 140° C as measured by the Pensky-Martin closed cup method. This applies to all liquids except those containing 24 percent alcohol by volume. b. Is a non-liquid capable of sustained and spontaneous combustion. c. Is an ignitable compressed gas or an oxidizing substance. Wastes that meet these criteria are designated "I" within the EPA hazard code and are identified by the designation D 001.

2. Corrosivity (Code C). Any substance, usually a liquid, with a pH of less than 2 (highly acidic) or greater than 12.5 (highly alkaline), or if it can be shown to corrode steel at a rate greater than 0.25 in./yr.

3. Reactivity (Code R). A solid waste is considered reactive if it violently combines with water, forming explosive mixtures, or if it is chemically unstable, forming toxic gases, or fumes on contact with water. In addition, if the substance or mixture could detonate if heated at standard temperature or pressure or under confinement, it is considered reactive.

4. Toxicity (Code T). A solid waste is considered toxic if, using prescribed chemical extraction procedures; the extract of a representative sample contains any of eight heavy metals or six pesticides in specified amounts. Toxicity is based primarily on responses observed in laboratory animals.

Each hazardous waste has been assigned an EPA identification number. For example, petroleum refinery waste, explosive propellants, and tannery waste are within the designation K 001–K 069. These numbers must be used in record keeping and with all notifications. Provisions also exist within the RCRA for waste to be removed from the list of hazardous substances, and wastes can also be declared nonhazardous. But the onus is upon the generator to show beyond a reasonable doubt that the wastes are safe and qualify for "delisting" or nonhazardous status.

With the above as our guide, it is fitting to inquire into the accumulated knowledge of health affects visited upon a tense and fearful public residing close to the thousands of waste sites around the country. Isn't this the concern raised by the National Academy of Sciences when it stated: "To answer this question requires information on the scope of potential and actual human exposure to hazardous wastes and with the health effects that could be associated with these exposures"? Indeed, what has been learned since 1991 that can help fill in the blanks for the people through the media, who are our only hope for getting messages to the greatest number of people?

The fallout from Love Canal (New York), Times Beach (Missouri), and other sites has increased public concern that birth defects, cancer, heart disease, and a spectrum of other ill effects may be related to proximity to waste sites. Nevertheless, it has yet to be demonstrated that exposure to waste chemicals of whatever type are sufficiently high to induce these adverse conditions. This is not a uniquely American phenomenon. Hazardous waste sites exist all over Europe, and the European Union is also seeking answers to the question of exposures and their potential for adverse effects. Accordingly, a multicenter study was mounted encompassing the United Kingdom, Belgium, Italy, and Denmark.

The study enrolled 1,089 babies with nonchromosomal congenital malformations and 2,366 births without malformations whose mothers resided within seven kilometers (three miles) of hazardous sites. From the data obtained, the authors inform us that "this study shows a raised risk of congenital anomaly in babies whose mothers live close to landfill sites that handle hazardous chemical wastes, although there is a need for further investigation of whether the association of raised risk of congenital anomaly and residence near landfill sites is a causal one." And they offer another significant observation. "In our opinion," they say, "the results of previous epidemiological multi-site studies do not greatly strengthen any conclusion of causality in our study."[3] Given so strong a dose of reality, a look at the studies in question is warranted.

The earliest study referred to occurred in New York State in 1992. With the availability of 917 waste sites in sixty-two New York State counties, a research team from Yale University and the New York State Department of Health evaluated 9,313 newborns with congenital malformations, comparing them to 17,802 healthy infants (the controls), all living near 590 waste sites. Even with the large number of participants, the odds-ratio (relative risk) for risk of bearing a child with a congenital malformation rose from 1.0 (unity) to 1.12, a 12 percent increase. What conclusion do the investigators draw from this? "Further research is needed to corroborate these findings, using environmental and biologic monitoring data to better define exposure status. Especially, the impact of active industrial exposures must be addressed, along with possible interactive effects of smoking, alcohol, and nutritional status. Confirmatory data from such studies would strengthen causal inferences regarding the tertogenicity of residential exposure to hazardous waste sites."[4] Obviously, they obtained a similar level of weak association, with an extremely weak odds-ratio.

In 1997, a group from the California Birth Defects Monitoring Program and UCLA's School of Public Health investigated the proximity to hazardous waste sites and the possibility of neural-tube defects, cleft palate, and heart defects. Not only were the investigators concerned with National Priority List sites (the sites the EPA considers most hazardous), but also residence within a quarter of a mile to a mile from such sites. They reported: "If the increased risks we observed for neural-tube defects (NTD's) and conotruncal heart defects among women living at this proximity are related to waste site exposures, these exposures would amount to less than 1–2 percent of the approximately 400 NTD's and 400 conotruncal cases that occur each year in California." And they further note: "Given the low prevalence of specific congenital malformations, however, the prospective assessment of potential exposures from hazardous waste sites may not be feasible."[5]

Using a case-control study design, a team from the Division of Occupational Health and Environmental Epidemiology of the New York State Department of Health sought to evaluate specific birth defects and exposure to solvents, metal, and pesticide contaminants from hazardous waste sites. Enrolling 473 central nervous system–defect births and 3,305 musculoskeletal –defect births to residents of eighteen counties, and comparing them to 12,436 normal births, they found no association between the mother's residential exposure and the risk of these specific defects. They suggested that in future studies investigators limit their research to sites with more intense exposures, which may show effects not seen at lower exposure levels.[6]

Taking a different tack, a Canadian team from the University of Quebec, the Nova Scotia Cancer Registry, and Dalhousie University sought to determine whether men who lived near a solid waste landfill in Montreal were at higher risk for developing cancer than individuals who lived at more remote locations. The landfill of their concern generated a rich mixture of volatile organic chemicals (VOCs), some of which are accepted and suspected human carcinogens. The researchers' data interpretation parallels the others. "The results of the analyses," they said, "suggest possible associations for liver cancer, kidney cancer, pancreatic cancer, and non-Hodgkins lymphomas, but the statistical evidence is not persuasive."[7] Indeed, this is a common and widely observed result of epidemiologic studies of human exposure to nearby landfill chemicals.

The diversity of sites, and the many different research teams with their individual methodologies, abets the idea of little to no adverse consequences from such exposure. It is therefore understandable why the multicenter European team would remark: "The results of previous epidemiological multi-site studies do not greatly strengthen any conclusions of causality in our study."[8]

What of the workers themselves at the listed sites, with their extreme proximity to those often-mixed wastes: how have they fared?

When she was a graduate student at Drexel University in Philadelphia, Chrysoula J. Komis, currently a visiting professor in the Industrial Hygiene Program at Temple University in Philadelphia, took on the study of worker exposure at hazardous waste sites. At the time, in 1990, she was concerned that over the previous decade a large growth industry had emerged to deal with assessment and remediation (cleanup) of the 30,000–50,000 abandoned and inactive waste sites, as well as the 1,118 sites on EPA's National Priority List. This new industry, employing, if the Occupational Safety and Health Administration (OSHA) is correct, over 65,000 workers, may be placing these workers at increased risk of exposure and illness given their intimate proximity to mixtures of chemicals both known and unknown.

Komis obtained and analyzed samples of a worker's breath and surrounding air before and after an eight-hour work day. These breath and air samples were subjected to mass spectrophotometric analysis to identify their chemical composition and concentration.

Few individuals, if any, could obtain greater exposure, and for longer periods, than workers at Superfund sites. For Komis, the question was: Do workers at hazardous waste sites "experience quantifiable internal exposures that place them at unusual risk of illness from low-level exposure to a range of potentially toxic chemicals"?

In addition to workers at Superfund sites, she was concerned about workers removing underground storage tanks—USTs—and their array of volatile organic chemicals, such as benzene, naptha, chloroform, gasoline, and chlorobenzene. Komis found that UST workers were at greater risk of exposure and of developing occupationally related illnesses than workers at Superfund sites. Although her chemical/breath sample data are suggestive that exposure to VOCs has the potential for initiating adverse health affects, none were observed.

It is possible that more time is needed for chronic illness to express itself. Possibly animal toxicity data, from which claims of human toxicity derive, are an inappropriate match for human illness, or the on-site levels of chemical exposures are insufficient to initiate illness. This study occurred a decade ago, and still there does not appear to have been a noticeable increase in illness among these workers. A major finding, however, was that UST workers knew little if anything about the potential hazards associated with their work, nor were they appropriately outfitted with protective equipment. Apparently their greatest risk was fire and explosion.[9]

Although the numbers of studies available for decision-making are small (a decided imbalance exists, created by the fact that negative studies often go unreported), the weight of evidence suggests far less hazard than has been assumed. Results are generally in a similar negative, or weakly positive, statistically insignificant direction. A reasonable person could be forgiven for thinking that with respect to hazardous waste, there has been more sound than fury.

In reviewing the toxicological hazard of Superfund hazardous waste sites, Johnson and DeRosa, of the Agency for Toxic Substances and Disease Registry (ATSDR), provide additional insights. They tell us "the hazard presented to the public by hazardous waste sites is a complex issue that requires examining each site on its own characteristics. Any examination must consider the extent of environmental contamination and possible contact with human populations, the toxicology of released substances, the nature and extent of potentially exposed vulnerable populations (e.g., children, pregnant women)." They go on to remark that, "of course, residence near a hazardous waste site does not necessarily translate to actual exposure to substances released from the site."[10] That seems to be confirmed by what the various epidemiological studies conclude.

Johnson and DeRosa also inform us that

> the threat posed by individual waste sites is classified in ATSDR's public health assessments according to the following five categories of health hazard: Urgent public health hazard: sites that pose an urgent public health hazard as the result of short-term exposures to hazardous substances. Public health hazard: sites that pose a public health hazard as a result of long-term exposures to hazardous substances. Indeterminate public health hazard: sites with incomplete information. No apparent public health hazard: sites where human exposure to contaminated media is occurring or has occurred in the past, but exposure is below a level of health hazard. No public health hazard: sites that do not pose a public health hazard.

The significant point to all this is given in the following statement. "A site," they say, "is assigned one of these categories on the basis of professional judgment, using weight-of-evidence criteria; the assignments are not risk-based derivations." This is essential to any understanding, as it runs counter to the reported epidemiological studies. Unfortunately, we do not know which site category the published epidemiological studies evaluated. The fact that assignments of hazard categories are made by "judgments" should come as a surprise to all but *Time* magazine, whose editors made their judgments a decade earlier and pronounced all sites toxic. They knew in 1980 what currently still remains either unknown, or mostly negative.

But let us continue to follow Johnson and DeRosa. "Cancer," they say,

> is a major health concern. It is a dread disease that is a major cause of death in the U.S. The extent to which environmental factors cause cancer is the subject of debate. If personal risk factors, like tobacco smoking, are included as environmental factors, then the "environment" is a major contributor to cancer mortality rates, because cigarette smoking is strongly associated with mortality from lung cancer. If, however, "environmental factors" are more narrowly defined to include only toxicants released into the general environment (excluding the workplace environment), then some investigators have indicated cancer mortality is only weakly associated with "environmental factors." Regardless of how one defines "environmental factors," prudent health policy advocates the prevention of exposure to carcinogenic substances, whether tobacco in the home, or asbestos in the workplace, or vinyl chloride in ground water.

A reasonable person could only agree that prudence does indeed dictate that prevention of exposure is primary. Nevertheless, a reasonable person cannot disregard how "environment" is defined, as it is essential to know where a problem actually resides, since entirely different preventive solutions will be required. If a problem is ambiently environmental, then governmental/industrial solutions are required; if a problem is personal/behavioral, then individual responses are in order. A reasonable person would want to be certain that preventive measures specific for the unique situation are applied, making it incumbent upon those rendering professional judgments as to what constitutes a hazard, and of its degree, to determine if *exposure* is in fact related to *adverse health effects*. Lacking that, we are left with opinions. That is why Johnson and DeRosa's following comment should come as no surprise.

> The relatively sparse data on cancer rates in populations residing near hazardous waste sites is somewhat surprising given that analysis of sites with completed exposure pathways shows the presence of several known or suspect human carcinogens. It is possible that the generally low exposures that characterize populations in completed pathways account for only a small increase in cancer rates, and therefore would be difficult to detect in cancer surveillance

systems. It is also possible that sufficient time has not elapsed between the releases of carcinogens into completed exposure pathways to cause an elevation
in cancer rates. As health assessments are tightly allied with completed pathways, it will be of use to know that it consists of five [*sic*] elements: a source of
contamination; an environmental medium (possibly ground water); a point of
exposure (drinking the water); and a receptor population-community residents and workers. All five elements must be present for a pathway to be considered completed.

This chain of events, leading to exposure and possibly an ill effect, has
seemingly tight links. But there is a missing link: the human epidemiologic
studies of the type described. This is the link that causes surprise for
Johnson and DeRosa.

If their suggestion that it may be too early to tell if cancer rates will increase because carcinogens may not yet be fully released, it is entirely
possible that a cancer explosion could be forthcoming around 2010 or
2020. But that also assumes that all the sites studied are "too young" to be
hazardous or toxic. They noted, too, that the low exposures may be too
difficult to detect by the tools currently available, which could be the case.
But it also leaves room for the real possibility that the low exposure levels
at many sites are noncarcinogenic and, as they remarked earlier, "residence
near a hazardous waste site does not necessarily translate to actual exposure to substances released from the site."

The idea that prudence dictates protecting the public is incontrovertible, but without human studies in hand and with only highly variable
animal data, was it necessary for environmentalists and the media to create
a cancer epidemic and public panic? Together the media and environmentalists created a monster. Such thinking is more hazardous than the
waste.

A closely related concern, another community issue, is whether incineration of hazardous waste is a threat to public health. Included in this
category are microbial contaminated hospital wastes and chemical and biological wastes. With the recent National Research Council's publication, *Waste Incineration and Public Health,* the most that can be said is
that "when operated properly by well-trained employees, modern waste
incinerators pose little risk to public health. But older designs, human
error, and equipment failure can result in higher than normal, short-term
emissions that need to be studied further." Their conclusion is that "no association has yet been made between emissions and disease. However,
given that ailments may occur infrequently or take years to appear and that

pollution may be present from other sources, it is difficult to determine if waste incineration can be blamed for local health problems."[11]

Isn't that reminiscent of the NAS's evaluation of hazardous wastes circa 1991? Of course, their comments are at variance with conventional community wisdom, including my own community's, where the belief is widely held that dioxin, a "notorious" poison, is produced in exceeding quantities, thus preventing reductions in ever-growing mountains of buried waste. Dioxin, another household word for fear, in both incinerator effluent stack gases and hazardous waste sites, may hold a key and is thus worth delving into.

Dioxin

Love Canal. Love Canal is the ultimate example of fear of dioxin. Soil samples taken from homeowner properties directly across from the canal yielded dioxin levels in the parts per billion (ppb) range. On a personal level, a dose is often defined by a pill, tablet, or capsule every four hours, or a teaspoonful three times a day. In soil sampling or animal feeding studies, especially when low levels are involved, scientists use milligrams per kilogram (mg/kg). A milligram is one-thousandth of a gram, and approximately 30 grams make an ounce. Sixteen ounces, 454 grams, give us a pound. A kilogram is the equivalent of 2.2 pounds. In scientific notation, milligrams per kilogram is equivalent to parts per million, ppm. Even smaller is the microgram, which is one-thousandth of a milligram. Micrograms per kilogram are referred to as ppbs, parts per billion, while nanograms, one-thousandth of a microgram, are parts per trillion, ppts. Understanding these minuscule amounts is essential if we are to make sense of any discussion of trace substances. It is necessary to understand that

> ppb is 1,000 times less than ppm, and
> ppt is 1,000 times less than ppb, which makes
> ppt 1,000,000 times less than ppm.

Of course it's confusing. It's just the reverse of dollar amounts where trillions are more than billions and billions more than millions. And parts per billion, trillion, and quadrillion are staggeringly tiny amounts of anything. Yet it is entirely understandable that homeowners at Love Canal were mortified to learn that they had dioxin on their property at levels of parts per billion. Billions! It sounds horrendous. Did anyone even attempt to explain the evident confusion? Not a soul. Not the media.

Soil samples from homes across from Love Canal contained levels of dioxin from 1 to 20 ppb. Recall, too, that it was the levels of dioxin obtained from feeding studies of guinea pigs that tagged dioxin as the most poisonous of chemicals. But the amount that felled guinea pigs was a thousand times greater than that found at Love Canal.

At this point, a brief digression is in order to deal with dioxin's paternity. At room temperature, dioxin is a colorless, crystalline solid. Chemists have isolated and identified 75 dibenzo-para-dioxins containing chlorine atoms. The 2,3,7,8-isomer appears to be the most toxic to animals, but the lethal dose varies considerably from species to species. The discussion that follows deals solely with 2,3,7,8-tetrachlorodibenzo-p-dioxin, TCDD. The lethal dose required to kill 50 percent of guinea pigs was 1 ppm. It was 22 ppm for male rats, 45 for female rats, 70 for monkeys, 114 for mice, and 5,000 for hamsters, a tremendous variation and a great inconsistency. Which, if any of these values, is predictive of adverse *human* health effects?

Studies of chemical workers immediately suggest that they are a unique population, working daily, as they do, either directly with or near the chemical. Their exposure, their daily doses, are normally far higher than exposures received by the general population. That's an essential point. A report published in the *Journal of the National Cancer Institute* by a team from the National Institute for Occupational Safety and Health (NIOSH) found that among a cohort of 5,132 chemical workers at twelve chemical plants in the United States that produced TCDD-contaminated products, including Agent Orange, from 1942 to 1984, forty-two years of regular contact, most of it directly to the skin, there were no increases in diabetes, a weak positive trend in heart disease with increasing high exposure levels, and a statistically significant increasing trend for all cancers combined with increasing exposure to dioxin levels. The researchers tell us that "excess cancer was limited to the highest exposed workers, with exposures that were 100 to 1000 times higher than those experienced by the general population and similar to the TCDD levels used in animal studies." They also found that "no new soft-tissue sarcomas were observed, and that mortality from non-Hodgkin's lymphoma, another cancer thought to be related to TCDD exposure, was unremarkable." The salient point here was the exposure level necessary to induce cancer development: 100–1,000 times greater than levels found in air inhaled by the public.[12]

NIOSH conducted another study, this one to determine the long-term adverse cardiovascular effects of occupational exposure to TCDD. At the completion of this study, the investigators found that heavily exposed workers, many of whom had persistently elevated blood-TCDD levels, "had no significantly increased risk for any of the cardiovascular outcomes (cardiac arrhythmias, hypertension, abnormal peripheral arterial flow) we investigated."[13] Let's take this a step further.

Trichlorophenol. The morning of July 10, 1976, was not unlike other Saturday mornings in Meda. Fifteen miles north of Milan, Italy, with a population of less than 20,000, Meda was a quiet, rural community. One hundred sixty of its citizens worked for ICMESA (Industrie Chemische Meda Societa Anonima), a subsidiary of the pharmaceutical firm of Givaudin and Hoffman-LaRoche.

The Meda plant produced TCP, trichlorophenol, for use in making hexachlorophene. Plant workers knew that the safety valve of the 10,000-liter reactor vessel had not been provided with protective devices, but production had proceeded smoothly for years, so it wasn't given a second thought.

Between noon and 2 P.M., a runaway reaction began in the reactor. Although the plant was shut down for the weekend, the reactor had been charged with ingredients needed for production of a batch of TCP. An unusual amount of pressure developed within the reactor. Without the protective units, the rupture disk burst, and hot gases, vapor, and particulates exploded into the air above the plant. Dense white clouds formed, and the prevailing winds carried the chemical mist to the southwest. Although the incident occurred in Meda, Seveso became the epicenter of the chemical rain. By Monday, children began to complain of red, burning skin lesions. Rabbits, cats, birds, poultry, and frogs were dying. But it wasn't until July 19, the following Monday, that ICMESA acknowledged that 2,3,7,8-tetra-chlorodibenzo-p-dioxin (TCDD), the most potent of the more than twenty tetrachloro isomers, had been expelled along with TCP and sodium hydroxide. Given an almost complete lack of organization, the people were exposed for approximately three weeks before the first groups of children were evacuated. And for some thirty days after the release, the only clinically observable signs were florid skin lesions approximating second and third degree burns. Two months later, chloracne (a skin eruption resembling acne but due to contact with chlorine or its compounds) appeared. New cases occurred well into the spring of 1977. For some children, chloracne persisted through 1979.

Because available laboratory animal data indicated that birth defects were a prominent sequel of TCDD exposure, obstetricians and pediatricians in the entire province of Lombardy were alerted. Although Italian law mandates reporting of birth defects, Italy is well known for its underreporting. However, during 1977, thirty-eight defects were reported from eleven cities: seven in Seveso and sixteen in Meda. Of the three zones of contamination—high, medium, and low—Seveso was in the high zone and Meda in the medium. With so large a surge in reporting, something untoward appeared to have occurred. But the reporting was curious. Meda, with less than half the exposure, had more than twice the number of defects. And doublings of defects were reported from Bergamo, Como, Brescia, and Cremona in the northeastern reaches of Lombardy, in the opposite direction of the path of the drifting chemical cloud.

Unfortunately, but of inestimable value, because of the fear of birth defects that the publicity generated, thirty medically induced abortions were performed, four among women of Seveso. None of the embryos had any type of malformation. Is TCDD fetotoxic? Lab *animal* data are clear on this: it is. But is TCDD fetotoxic for humans? It has yet to be demonstrated. By 1984, eight years after the accident, examinations showed that birth defects, spontaneous abortions, deaths, and tumors were not induced by the heavy "rain" of TCDD and TCP. Especially pertinent was the determination that levels of TCDD averaged 20 ppm in Seveso.

As eight years may be too brief for effects, subtle or not so subtle, to express themselves, the accident became an ongoing study for Italian scientists. In 1998, twenty-two years later, researchers at the University of Milan reviewed the long-term effects of heavy dioxin exposure. They noted that "the amount of TCDD released has been the subject of conflicting estimates," and "the results reported . . . do not provide conclusive evidence of long-term effects on the exposed subjects of the Seveso accident. For this reason, the follow-up period for the mortality and cancer incidence studies has been extended . . . and molecular epidemiology studies have been initiated." We can expect to hear from them again in another five and ten years. By the years 2003 and/or 2008, more definitive results may be forthcoming. However, they did find that TCDD blood plasma levels obtained from both men and women in the most contaminated zone were at the parts per trillion, ppt, and ppq, parts per quadrillion (femtogram/

kilogram) level.[14] What is the message inherent in such microscopic numbers? That is the essential question.

Still Bottoms. On May 26, 1971, Russell Bliss, an independent oil salvage contractor, stopped at Shenandoah Farms near Moscow Mills, southwest of St. Louis, to apply a coat of oil to their horse arena. The oil was in fact undiluted still bottoms, waste from chemical distillation, containing TCDD at a concentration of 350 ppm; 350,000 ppb! By May 29, horses became ill and dead birds were found on the arena floor. By the middle of June, insects, worms, rats, mice by the bucketful, hundreds of birds, a dozen cats, and four dogs were found dead in or near the arena. Of eighty-five horses that had used the arena, forty-three had died. Twenty-six pregnant mares aborted and foals exposed in utero died at birth or shortly after. Not a species within the principal animal phyla was spared except one: people. For one six-year-old girl the arena was her "sandbox." Three younger children and a number of adults were regularly in and out. Other than transient headaches, bloody noses, chloracne, hematuria, and diarrhea, all had uneventful recoveries.

Bliss also played a major role in contaminating Times Beach, Missouri. The dusty roads in and around the town were also oiled with his TCDD-contaminated still bottoms. But Times Beach sits astride the flood plain of the Meramec River. The years 1982 and 1983 were flood years, and the Meramec responded by overflowing its banks and inundating the town. Although insoluble in water, dioxin was spread, albeit unevenly, throughout the place. The U.S. EPA responded by declaring Times Beach a disaster area. The town was shuttered, abandoned, and its people dispersed on the basis of lab animal data. Mind-boggling. I have already noted earlier in this chapter how *Time* magazine brought Times Beach to its readers: "Times Beach looks as if a neutron bomb hit it. Houses are standing, windows are broken, some toys are still scattered around, but nobody walks the streets." Did *Time* do anything to inform, edify, or bring a modicum of sanity to the marketplace of ideas? Not a whit. It is worth noting that to date there have been no documented cancer cases among the dislodged population. That's another media shortcoming—no follow-up. Past events are barely, if ever revisited to bring, new, up-to-date information to readers. What's past is past. Forgetaboutit.

Agent Orange. The U.S. Air Force began using 2,4,5,T in Vietnam in 1962. At that time, the defoliant was "coded" as Agent Green. The drums containing the chemical had a green band painted around them. It was not until 1965 that "Orange" came into use, following agents Pink, Purple, Blue, and White. Agent Green contained TCDD as a contaminant. Estimates suggest a level of 66 ppm. Agent Purple, a newer product, contained 33 ppm. From 1965 to 1970, Agent Orange was used. It contained 2 ppm. In Vietnam, both airborne crews and nonflying personnel were used to prepare and broadcast the defoliant over the landscape. Some of the groups received daily exposures of 2 ppm.

The exposed personnel were enrolled in Project Ranch Hand, an epidemiological study initiated by the Air Force to ascertain long-term adverse health effects of their TCDD exposure. Over the ensuing twenty years, controversy has been the only consistent outcome. Epidemiologic data, however, suggest no excess mortality, tumors, heart disease, diabetes, or birth defects. Most recently, a medical team at Brooks Air Force Base in San Antonio, Texas, reexamined Ranch Hand Veterans and analyzed their blood, obtaining dioxin levels of from 0 to 618 ppt (median 11.9 ppt). They concluded that the risk of cancer at sites other than the skin within twenty years of service was increased in Ranch Hand Veterans with elevated dioxin levels, but the pattern was inconsistent with that of another study, suggesting that the excessive risk may not have been caused by dioxin exposure. "Overall, we found no consistent evidence of a dose-response gradient and no significant increase in cancer risk in the high dioxin exposure category, the subgroup of greatest a priori interest."[15] It is worth comparing the 2 ppm TCDD dose obtained in Vietnam with the Seveso accident, which exposed children and adults to approximately 20 ppm; with chemical workers exposed to 10–100 ppm; and with Times Beach at over 350. Then consider the thousand times less—parts per billion—found around homes abutting Love Canal.

There is a dilemma in all the numbers. Chemists can devise analytic methods sensitive enough to measure parts per billion, trillion, and quadrillion (quadrillion is a billion times less than a million). In fact we have arrived at a time when molecules can be measured. But to what purpose? What does that do to zero? Does zero exist? When is *nothing* present? If ill effects are not found at parts per million, then parts per billion or trillion become meaningless. That should have been the message for homeowners at Love Canal. Numbers matter. Where was *Time* magazine and the media generally when they were truly needed? The message of the numbers should go out to those concerned about dioxin in incinerator stack gas effluents, where levels of parts per quadrillion and less have been reported. Indeed, where are the messengers?

Having broached the subject of Love Canal, let us pick up that thread.

Back to Love Canal. Love Canal and Niagara Falls enjoy worldwide reputations: Niagara Falls for newlyweds and lovers; Love Canal for dread. Niagara's reputation is well deserved. Love Canal's may not be. Nevertheless, its tarnished image and reputation gained in the late 1970s lingers.

William T. Love had a noble idea: to build a power-producing canal and offer free energy to attract industry for a model city to be built on the shore of Lake Ontario. His canal would tap the unrelenting force of Niagara Falls as it raced into the rapids before dropping 180 feet into the Niagara River. With his remarkable powers of persuasion, he raised sufficient funds in 1892 to organize a development company. However, President Grover Cleveland's second administration was not three months old when a series of bank failures and a general industrial collapse inaugurated the Panic of 1893. Love's canal was an early casualty. Had the Depression not done him in, alternating current surely would have. The discovery of electricity meant that factories were no longer required to be located near falling water to produce the required electric power.

Love's 16-acre canal, or ditch, 3,000 feet long, 60 feet wide, and 10 feet deep, would not long remain empty. Enter Elon Hooker. Also quick to see the benefits that proximity to the Falls bestowed in the way of cheap electric power, Hooker established the Electrochemical Company for the production of chlorine and sodium hydroxide. The company thrived and the city of Niagara Falls and the canal prospered. In 1942, permission was given to Hooker Chemical to dispose of its chemical waste in Love's canal. In 1947, the city sold the canal to Hooker. From 1942 to 1953, the canal was used as Hooker's primary chemical waste disposal site. Over 20,000 tons of chlorinated hydrocarbons, fatty acids, alkalis, and other chemicals (two hundred have since been cataloged) were buried there in metal and fiber drums or as sludge. By 1953, the ditch was full. It was capped with clay, covered with soil, and shortly thereafter became the neighborhood's grassy playing field. An elementary school and housing followed soon.

Between 1957 and 1977, intimations of trouble were broadcast. In May 1977, a survey showed that a number of the homes adjacent to the canal had chemical residues in their basements and that the city's storm sewers contained PCBs (polychlorinated biphenyls). Excessively heavy rains in 1976 and 1977 caused flooding, and leaking drums were popping to the surface. Samples of the chemical sludge were positive for dioxin. Toward the end of April 1978, New York State Health Commissioner Robert Walen stated that the conditions at Love Canal were a serious threat to health. On August 2 he issued the following order: Love Canal Chemical Waste Landfill constitutes a public nuisance and an extremely serious threat and danger to the health, safety, and welfare of those using it, living near it, or exposed to the conditions emanating from it, consisting of, among other things, chemical wastes lying exposed on the surface in numerous places and pervasive, pernicious, and obnoxious chemical vapors and fumes affecting both the ambient air and the homes of certain residents living near the sites. He then declared "the existence of an emergency" and recommended the immediate evacuation of pregnant women from the area. That was the beginning—of the crisis. From the time he gave that order, confusion and anger reigned. Fear was rampant, fanned by community activists and their media advocates. Few knew who or what to believe. Trust in government vanished. Then Congressman Al Gore, in his halcyon days, referred to Love Canal at a congressional hearing as "a very large cancer cesspool."[16]

There was blame aplenty to go around. A substantial portion can be laid at the media's doorstep, particularly the *Niagara Gazette* and its one-man disaster area, Michael Brown, who, rather than attempting to provide balanced reporting, became prosecutor, judge, and jury, and his verdict was guilty. For him and Lois Gibbs, a community activist, Love Canal was the sole and immediate cause of irreparable harm to the residents. Not only did they pronounce sentence on the canal, but on waste sites from Maine to California and states in between. Brown, in his infamous book, *Laying Waste: The Poisoning of America by Toxic Chemicals*[17] (did *Time* magazine get its ideas from him?), along with his magazine articles, "The Poisoning of America" and "A Toxic Ghost Town," both in *The Atlantic*,[18] single-handedly gained Love Canal the international notoriety it has yet to shake. The residents preferred to believe, preferred to put their trust, in know-nothing advocates who were loud in their denunciation of the governor, the state health commissioner, and the Department of Health.

Both Michael Brown and Lois Gibbs accepted the anecdotal accounts of the residents as revealed truth and disseminated them to a shocked, but absorbing world. Brown went on to make a career of denouncing the canal. Why book publishers and magazine editors placed him before a larger public is a question yet to be answered. But he was not alone. Responding to his sensationalism, ABC-TV went him one better, with its

"Killing Ground," a so-called documentary giving Love Canal pride of place as the opening segment of its hour-long diatribe of anecdotal mischief, with individuals ascribing to the canal whatever ailed them.

However, whatever it was that emerged from Love Canal between 1978 and 1981 was not anything remotely resembling credible scientific/medical studies or reliable information. To this day, there has never been a case of cancer, heart disease, or birth defect attributable to the canal.

But other things did emerge. On May 21, 1980, President Jimmy Carter declared Love Canal an emergency and provided funds for relocating seven hundred families. If anything positive emerged, it was Superfund. In December 1980, Congress enacted CERCLA, which provided a pot of funds for waste-site remediation. That money became Superfund.

As the twentieth century faded into the twenty-first, new occupants moved into refurbished homes around the canal. But Love Canal is not over yet. It is not over until the Fat Lady sings. And the Fat Lady is currently working diligently to provide answers, the first reliable set of answers to be surrendered by Love Canal. In this instance, the Fat Lady is the New York State Department of Health and its Division of Environmental and Occupational Epidemiology (directed by Alice D. Stark). It was awarded a grant by the Agency for Toxic Substances and Disease Registry (ATSDR) in 1997 to conduct a follow-up health study of the families who lived near the canal prior to 1979. With the passage of four decades (since chemicals first began to appear), more than adequate time has elapsed for adverse health effects to become expressed. But is there anyone, anywhere, who doesn't believe that Love Canal was the inciting cause of needless cancers, birth defects, heart disease, and more? How could they not, given the media's excesses?

The Love Canal Follow-up Health Study, its official title, will be searching for cancer cases, deaths from various causes, and reproductive outcomes, as well as analyzing blood samples collected two decades ago (for PCBs, dioxin, and other long-lived chemicals) among previous Canal residents. Their vital data and illness rates will be compared to those of other Niagara County residents and upstate New Yorkers generally.

The blood sera samples, a probable mine of information, have been categorized as likely to be exposed to Love Canal chemicals, possibly exposed, and not likely to have been exposed. Excitement and expectations are running high. In addition to the blood, the investigators have some

13,000 soil and sediment samples that were taken in 1978, along with extensive personal interviews also obtained at that time. They have also tracked the people who lived there and searched the New York State Cancer Registry for unbiased determination of cancer in those individuals still living in the state. They have also checked cancer registries in other states to determine if cancer occurred in those now living out-of-state. Similarly, the study team is searching for adverse reproductive effects in children born to parents in the canal area, and are looking at grandchildren as well. Children are expected to have had a higher potential for exposure than adults who lived in the same house simply because children tend to spend more time playing outside, contacting canal chemicals or handling contaminated soil.

By September 2000, the study had traced every former resident of the canal area who had been interviewed by the Department of Health two decades ago, and the team actually located 96 percent of them. They matched them against the New York State Vital Records death certificate files and the National Death Index, looking at both immediate and underlying causes of death, and compared them to other residents of Niagara County and New York State generally. Preliminary results of the mortality study have been made public and are less than spectacular. The death rates (adjusted for age and sex) of Love Canal residents are about the same as upstate New Yorkers and slightly lower than other Niagara County residents. When the causes of death are grouped and compared to Niagara County and upstate New York, some causes appear more often among Love Canal residents and some less often. Since the overall rate is the same or lower than for other New Yorkers and Niagara County residents, it is to be expected that, when organizing the deaths into groups, some will be higher and some will be lower by chance alone. Again, stay tuned.

The Millennium Calls for Change

Change is sorely needed. Coverage of science and medicine by the media needs a makeover, an overhaul. Where to begin? With the published literature, for openers. Articles published in medical and scientific journals are a means of communication among researchers to keep them up-to-date and to show the various ways investigators have approached the same or similar problems. Most importantly, researchers show one another how they set up their experiments and analyzed and interpreted their data. Comments are anticipated and expected. This is the way each area of investigation progresses. Journal articles were never meant to be reading material for the general public. Judah Folkman of Boston's Children's Hospital, said it best: "Mouse experiments do not belong on the front pages of the *New York Times*."[19] Indeed they do not. False hope, premature hope, is the last thing the public wants or needs.

Unfortunately, over the past decade the newspapers, television, and radio have become infatuated with medical issues but haven't understood the need for review and consensus. For them, a publication is a conclusive work rather than what it really is: a work in progress.

In their zeal to inform us, they've created an epidemic of anxiety, year after persistent year of alarm. With these unending sources of fear, could it be otherwise? Thus, over the past few years alone, we've been treated to an extraordinary range of potential causes of cancer. Among the putative hazards of life in our neighborhoods are asbestos, dioxin, hot dogs, breast implants, pesticides, coffee, liquor, hair dryers, mouthwash, dietary fat, magnetic fields, and cellular phones. The litany of complaints is long and seemingly endless. Tentative reports become facts once the press gets hold of an article. And the many caveats laced into a publication are lost on their way to the pressroom.

In fact, the search for links between environment and illness has yielded little. That's firm. What, then, should the public, the reader, believe? Nothing. Nothing? Right. Nothing at all? Right again. Nothing, until confirmation and consensus have been attained. And, yes, it could take 5, 10, 20 years to nail down a causal relationship. If that lacks appeal, if it is too amorphous, let the sage advice of the Swiss psychologist Jean Piaget be our guide. "The great danger today," he wrote, "is of slogans, collective opinions, ready-made trends of thought. We have to be able," he cautioned, "to resist, individually, to criticize, to distinguish between what is proven and what is not." That's the key: to be able to distinguish between works in progress and completed pieces. That's the message to take away, to carry with you.

The controversy over electromagnetic fields—the high-power lines—continues, as do the issues of radon in homes, chemical wastes, pesticides, and the many others noted earlier. These issues are too important to be left to TV, radio, and newspapers, the scoundrels at whose doorsteps must be placed our current pandemic of mediagenic diseases. To our detriment, the media work both sides of the street, creating hysteria on the one hand, too often without adequate proof, while raising expectations prematurely, racing to be first with the latest developments before they're ripe. No, it isn't the scientists who deserve our ire. Their publications are meant only to inform one another. Blame for this sorry state of affairs must be heaped on the media, which foist works in progress on an unsuspecting public.

How gullible, how accepting are we? Let's find out. Nathan Zohner, a fourteen-year-old, and, at the time, a freshman at Eagle Rock Junior High, won top prize at the Greater Idaho Falls Science Fair. His award-winning project had two parts to it. First, he explained the scientifically proven dangers of dihydrogen monoxide:

- It can cause excessive sweating and vomiting.
- It is a major component of acid rain.
- It causes severe burns when in gaseous form.
- Accidental inhalation can kill you.
- It has been found in the tumors of terminal cancer patients.

Nathan then asked fifty people at the Fair whether they would support a ban on dihydrogen monoxide. The result: 43 favored a ban, 6 were unsure, and 1 person was opposed. Why was he opposed? He knew that dihydrogen monoxide is also H_2O—water. Zohner's project was titled, "How Gullible Are We?" His conclusion: "I'd say they're extremely gullible. They need to pay more attention." The moral: scary-sounding names can turn everyday phenomena into bogeymen for the uninformed.

Steve Allen, of blessed memory, was a funny guy. He had been making us laugh for decades. The Public Broadcasting System (PBS) celebrated his seventy-fifth birthday with an hour of clips from a number of his past TV shows. They were howlers. On one, he took a microphone out to Broadway and Forty-second, stopping men and women, shoving a mike under their noses and asking the question: "If a man running for President goes on TV and openly admitted that he was a practicing heterosexual, would you vote for him?" "Good God, no." "Well, I believe a person's private life is his own. It shouldn't disqualify him from office." "A what! Oh, no, never." And on and on. The audience was doubled over laughing. So was I. Hilarious, yes, but sad, too, very sad. The Zohner Effect again. On a summer's day, are Broadway and Forty-second Street, or Idaho Falls, cross-sections of America?

The Zohner Effect raises yet another concern. Informing the public is at the heart of all environmental issues. But the public and the scientific "community" are clearly out of sync with respect to their estimations of the real risks to life and health. Each has a different understanding. The playing field is clearly not level. Let's pursue this.

Seventeen years after a 1979 report of a possible link between electromagnetic fields (EMFs), high-power lines, and childhood leukemia, the National Academy of Sciences reviewed over five hundred published papers dealing with this association and concluded that "the current body of evidence does not show that exposure to these fields presents a human health hazard." They noted, too, that neighborhoods with concentrations of power lines are often more heavily populated and poorer, areas where cancer rates are also often higher than in more affluent areas. Is it necessary to be reminded that wealthier is healthier?

To their credit, the NAS unanimously recommended further investigation to pry out the true cause of risk. Will that transpire? More than likely. Will it lay the EMF issue to rest? Not likely. Why? This contentious, high-anxiety issue has been battered about for over two decades, generating more heat than light, because the Paul Brodeurs of this world can turn a healthy profit by preying upon the fears of an uninformed citizenry with such screeds as *Currents of Death* and *The Great Power-Line Coverup*.[20] These books unabashedly escalate public anxiety and worry. Indeed, they read well and have high visibility while National Academy reports languish. The result: mediagenic disease. Why? Wiggle room. There's always wiggle room. Consider this. Over the past three decades, survey upon survey documented declines in Europe's stork population. Simultaneously, other surveys found the European birth rate to be declining. What are we to make of this? For those who believe storks deliver babies, this can be worrisome. For nonbelievers, the decline of both storks and babies requires further elucidation. Separating chance occurrence from actual risks is the domain of epidemiology. As we shall see, epidemiologists using a variety of investigative tools seek to relate cause with effect. But this business is not for the faint of heart. Why? The cigarette smoke/lung cancer relationship will be our guide to fuller understanding. But first, a brief divertissement to epidemiology.

A Brake for Epidemiology

For physicians, the question is: "What?" What's troubling this person, and what needs to be done to restore her to health? For epidemiologists, the question is: "Why?" Why are these people ill with this condition at this time? Epidemiology is the medical/public health science that searches for causes—the investigation of possible risk factors that may answer the "why" question. The epidemiologist knows that disease, illness, or whatever condition may be does not distribute itself randomly in populations. There are good and sufficient reasons why these people, but not those, are ill with a specific ailment at a specific time. While the physician deals with individuals, with cases, the epidemiologist deals with both, cases and the population from which they sprang. For it is only from group or population data that judgments about causality can be made, and it is only from group data that information generalizable to individual cases can be obtained. Uncovering the factor or factors that provoke a troubling condition is the enterprise at hand.

Earlier (in chapter 2), I asked what the causes of Lyme disease, Legionellosis, bovine spongiform encephalitis, and Hantavirus pulmonary syndrome were. Was it, I asked, a microbe, or was it a series of events that combined to produce each? Knowing the correct cause or causes is essential for the application of appropriate preventive or control measures. Was the nuclear-power generating plant at Three Mile Island the cause of cancer in residents living nearby? Did residents of Love Canal incur increased numbers of cancers and birth defects as a consequence of their proximity to Love Canal? Are electric blankets the cause of cancers in children? Do electromagnetic fields, radiation from high-power lines, cause cancer? How would we know if any or all of these relationships are in fact causal? Do cell phones affect the brain? Is a newly prescribed medication better than the one being currently used? Does stretching before exercise prevent muscle and bone injury? Again, how would we know? Why make changes? Why not? How can we avoid or minimize the application of useless, even harmful therapy, or maximize the benefit? Perhaps most important, how can we reduce uncertainty and fear.

Because of the relatively short time lapse between introduction of a pure culture of a potentially pathogenic microbe into susceptible animals and the subsequent occurrence of illness, the determination of cause is, in many cases, relatively straightforward, given the application of the Koch-Henle postulates. However, for noninfectious conditions such as lung cancer or heart disease and exposure to a risk factor such as cigarette smoke, the elapsed time before appearance of a lung lesion or a coronary event, the latency period, could be twelve, twenty, or thirty years. Obviously, a different approach to establishing causality, a cause-effect relationship, is needed.

The critical concept is that of population: groups of people, rather than individuals as seen by physicians in their offices. It is only with data obtained from groups of people—sizable groups, along with comparison control groups—that pertinent information can be derived. The objective is to make a strong statement, such as "A causes B"—a goal fraught with traps for the unwary. How for example, will the data be obtained? With the data on hand, the question becomes, Could this condition have occurred by chance alone? With six-billion-plus people in the world, two conditions could be present in numbers of people on the basis of chance alone. Alternatively, if chance is ruled out, could something else, suspected or unsuspected, account for the observations? Are we measuring what we think we're measuring? All observations must overcome the presumption that they are the product of chance or inaccuracy. The major issue in any epidemiological study is the determination of whether a true association exists between the variable studied, for example, between smoking and lung cancer, fluoride and dental caries, blood-lead-level and IQ attainment, breast cancer and organochlorines.

Causation and Association

Two key operational concepts are *causation* and *association*. An exposure, or independent variable, is said to be a cause of an illness when it is a necessary prerequisite for the illness: that it precedes the illness, and that the relative frequency of the illness increases in its presence and decreases in its absence. Causation is not the subject of speculation or conjecture; a set of internationally accepted criteria has been established to aid in its determination. By contrast, association simply means there is some numeric relationship between an illness or condition, the dependent variable, and a risk factor, the independent variable. It neither means nor implies causation. In fact, there may be no relationship. In the case of variables that appear to be related as, for example, the decline in the West German birth rate between 1965 and 1976 and the nearly identical rate of decline in the numbers of brooding storks in West Germany during the same period, while statistically accurate, any apparent association could not rationally be defended as proof that a decline in the number of storks caused the decline of West Germany babies—or even that the two phenomena are closely related. A false or fictitious association can result from chance occurrence or from inherent bias. Because bias can mask or exaggerate an association, and because it is here that so many journalists and commentators fail their readers and listeners, bias requires elaboration.

Bias

Bias is any systematic error resulting in an incorrect estimate, over or under, of the strength of an association between exposure and risk of disease. The validity (correctness of measurement or labeling) of any study depends on the accuracy with which enrolled subjects are assigned to one of four possible categories: diseased, absent or present, and exposed, absent or present. This may seem simple enough, but many conditions do not show overt symptoms or signs so that under- or overdiagnosis can put the wrong people in wrong categories. While cancer of the lung is well defined, pelvic inflammatory disease is less so, and misclassification can be substantial. Additionally, if we wanted to know what percentage of the population has heart disease at any given time and we conducted a field survey by asking passersby if they had heart disease, we would obtain a number, but it would be seriously flawed because of the number of people with heart disease too ill to get up and walk the streets. We have a bias problem as the "field" sample selectively eliminates a number of people with heart disease. Results will be underestimated. Similarly, opinion sampling prior to the 1948 presidential election, by its reliance on telephone surveys, was biased, resulting in the prediction that Thomas Dewey would defeat Harry Truman. Phone subscribers in 1948 were far more likely to be Republican than Democratic in their political affiliation, and the researchers failed to detect and correct for this bias. Telephone surveys also favor those with phones and those who do not have to work and can be at home to answer the survey questions. Fewer responses will come from poorer families.

Perhaps even more distorting of data and its interpretation is the question of who gets into a study. *Selection bias* refers to ways participants are accepted into a study. The group chosen for comparison with the cases—the controls—can be a major source of bias. The characteristics of the population using a health service can suggest an association that is artifactual and certainly noncausal. So, for example, when Leo Buerger first described Buerger's disease (thromboangitis obliterans), he suggested that the condition occurred frequently among Polish and Russian Jews, and that hospitals in New York City provided a good opportunity to study the condition. In fact, Buerger was an attending physician at Mount Sinai Hospital in New York City, which, at the time, catered almost exclusively to Polish and Russian Jews. Consequently, any condition described by Buerger might readily appear to be common among Polish and Russian Jews, simply because they were there in large numbers.[21]

Selection bias invalidated a grand experiment undertaken in Scotland in 1930. The Lanarkshire Milk Experiment concluded that schoolchildren given supplemental milk gained more weight than those who did not receive the milk. Seventy years ago, the effects of milk consumption were not at all known. In the experiment, three-quarters of a pint of raw milk was given daily to five thousand children. Another five thousand received an equal amount of pasteurized milk (a new idea in the 1930s). Both received Grade-A tuberculin-tested milk. Ten thousand children were enrolled as controls, receiving no additional milk. All twenty thousand were weighed and their height was measured at the beginning and end of the study, which lasted four months.

The two groups that received the milk gained more weight and height than the controls. But the study had begun in mid-February and ended in June. Children were weighed with their clothes on. It was later learned that sympathetic teachers had selectively placed the poorer children in the milk groups. The poorer children also had fewer winter clothes, so they weighed less in February. In June, the weight difference of the rich and poor children disappeared. The poorer children looked as if they had gained more weight than they had.[22]

Yet another source of unreliability comes from *information bias*, the differences in the way data on exposure or outcome are obtained from cases and controls. So, again, bias results when members of the exposed and nonexposed groups report their exposures with a far different degree of completeness or accuracy. Mothers whose pregnancy results in an infant with a birth defect are more likely to recall medications and injuries, which can readily lead to false associations between a potential risk factor and a congenital anomaly.

Measurement and observer bias occur all too frequently, as in measuring height with shoes on, or weight with clothes on, or blood pressure taken with blood pressure cuffs that are too large or too small, or when two different observers read the same X-ray differently. Subjective perceptions can result in low reliability. *Interview bias* occurs when an interviewer asks questions differently of members of the case and control groups, eliciting responses of a different kind and degree. And self-reporting creates additional problems, for example, people who underreport the number of alcoholic drinks consumed daily or weekly, or the participants who overreport the number of sexual encounters during a week or month. Self-reporting of weight, food consumption, and blood pressure can be badly underreported.

The epidemiological landscape is afflicted with yet another source of bias. *Publication bias* can skew our full understanding of a subject if only certain data are published. Journal editors prefer positive to negative findings: they make for better headlines. And researchers often fail to submit negative or equivocal results, believing they are uninteresting or that they will be rejected. The lack of negative findings affects the balance and consistency of research. As conclusions about risk are often based on the balance of published results, the lack of negative data can yield false attribution of health effects where none actually exist.[23]

So, for example, the Naval Shipyard Workers Study, "Health Effects of Low-Level Radiation in Shipyard Workers" (cf. pp. 204–205), a particularly well designed and conducted study with appropriate numbers of participants to obtain good statistical power, was a collaboration between the Department of Energy, which funded the $10 million study, and the Department of Epidemiology at the School of Public Health at Johns Hopkins University. Although the Department of Energy required a final report from the investigating team, which it obtained, the decision to publish the study's methods and results in a peer-reviewed scientific/medical journal was left to Genevieve Matanoski, the study's principal investigator. Since 1991, when the report was given to the Department of Energy, she has had little interest in getting the information, the data, to the scientific community or the public generally: in this instance, data showing that low levels of gamma radiation are not detrimental to human health. An unfortunate decision on her part.

Given the intensity of the backlash against nuclear energy, this finding would have been a major contribution to public understanding and scientific knowledge. Lack of information, positive or negative, can be a significant omission in the decision-making process. And taxpayers may well ask what the point is of giving away their tax dollars for studies from which they reap no benefit.

It is also unfortunate that NIOSH did not pursue, as it had planned, a follow-up study to determine the continuing state of health of the shipyard workers, who were young men at the time of the study and found to be in good health. A follow-up study would have added even greater confidence about low levels of radiation if the results had continued to show ongoing good health. Of course there is still time.

Bias occurs not only where it is expected, but also where it is not expected. Thus, all investigations require confirmation, and until that is forthcoming, all results must be considered preliminary. That's another take-away message. And as if that were not trouble enough, studies are further undermined by confounding. *Confounding* is the confusing (mixing) of the effect of particular exposure on the studied disease with a third factor, the confounder. When a confounder is at work, what looks like a causal relationship between an exposure and an illness is something else altogether—the confounder. The *confounder* is a variable associated with the exposure and independent of that exposure and is itself a risk factor for the disease. A study showing that families owning cappuccino makers have healthier babies may be flawlessly executed and produce "statistically significant" results. No competent epidemiologist, however, would accept such a study as proof that the presence of a cappuccino maker in the home improves infant health. Obviously, it is the more affluent families that can afford cappuccino makers; affluence and health are directly related. In this instance, the socioeconomic status of the study participants has acted as a confounder. Confusing two supposedly causal variables contributes so mightily to study error that it deserves yet another example. Gray hair has been associated with the risk of myocardial infarction, or heart disease. Age, however, increases both the amount of gray hair and the risk of heart disease. Indeed, group differences in age can and do confuse or confound comparisons of two populations. Confounding can lead to either apparent differences between groups when they do not exist, or no differences when they do exist. As we have seen, studies can determine that consumption of vegetables rich in beta-carotene and Vitamin C, for example, protect against cancer. More veggies, less cancer. But is it due to the carotene, fiber, or something else in the vegetables? Or are the test subjects who eat more veggies younger, less likely to smoke, more likely to exercise and eat less fat? Eating vegetables and being cancer free may readily be confounded by a number of other possible risk factors. The sources of bias and error are many and frequent. And we shall see why the media's reporting of only published conclusions, which are often given to overstatement and more certainty than the data permit or inherent bias warrants, can be so misleading to a public looking to the media for assurance. But first, what types of studies provide the data?

Testing Hypotheses

Two types of analytical studies can be called upon to test hypothesized associations: retrospective and prospective. The *retrospective* study begins at the end. Participants are classified on the basis of the state of the disease, and test subjects have already had the disease in question. The task is to track back in an attempt to discover the risks and the exposures the participants may have encountered that could have caused their condition. These "cases" are compared to a control group free of the condition but resembling the cases as closely as possible. The essence of this type of study is interviewing: questions, questions, questions. And the question at issue is: Was past exposure to a potential risk factor greater among the cases than among the control group? Indeed, the objective of every epidemiological study is to find a group with a higher incidence of a specified condition than another group.

The case/control study was developed ostensibly to study rare events, or those that take years to develop. By contrast, the *prospective* or cohort study begins with healthy people in both the test and control groups, the presumption being that the illness being studied does not exist among either of the collected cohorts. A cohort is a defined group sharing such common experiences as birth in the same year or within a five-year period, living in the same town, or having a similar occupational history. The test group has an exposure to a potential risk factor and is observed for months or years to determine the number of new cases, new illnesses, that occur over the test period. The unexposed group, the controls, is also followed prospectively, allowing the determination of the frequency with which each group develops the condition being studied. The number of new cases, the incidence within each group, is counted to obtain absolute incidence rates. A ratio of the two incidence rates can then be calculated to yield a "Relative Risk" (RR), a measure of the strength of the association. Numbers less than 1 suggest a negative relation, possibly a protective benefit, as in the event of an administered vaccine. Numbers greater than 1 imply an increased risk among the exposed. Relative risks of less than 3 or 4 are widely considered weak associations, possibly the result of inherent systematic bias.

The resulting numbers can be a source of controversy, debate, and anxiety. Large numbers, generally over 10, indicate great strength of association. Twenty and higher would suggest a direct cause-effect relationship. Unfortunately, such numbers occur infrequently. Most often it is the low numbers between 1 and 3 that prevail, to become the source of media and environmentalist angst. Furthermore, as case-control studies assemble those who have already had an illness, it can never determine cause, which requires that exposure preceded the illness. Accordingly, the RR obtained is only estimated. Again, unfortunately, this detail is conveniently overlooked as published articles overstate their findings. It is from the prospective study in which exposure precedes disease and groups remain at continuing risk that absolute, excessive risk potentially caused by the exposure in question can be obtained. Unfortunately, there are all too few of these studies. Why? Because they are costly and require a good deal of time, often years, to complete. The Framingham Heart Study is currently in its forty-sixth year and requires sophisticated personnel to administer and conduct.

To bolster the RR and help determine if the suggested association is simply that or goes beyond to a direct causal effect between exposure and disease, A. B. Hill, Sir Austin Bradford Hill, an outstanding British physician, in an effort to make inferences regarding causality more objective and less sensitive to individual interpretation, contributed a set of criteria to be met before causality is inferred. Hill's criteria, listed below, have become widely adopted.

1. *Strength*. A large relative risk increases the likelihood of a causal association. (If bias is minimal to nonexistent, and the number is 25, a direct cause-effect association is all but certain.)
2. *Consistency*. If the association has been confirmed by other studies under differing methodological conditions, and with different populations, the likelihood that the association is causal increases.
3. *Specificity*. If the association is specific to one risk factor and one disease, the chance of a causal association increases.
4. *Temporality*. The exposure must occur before the disease.
5. *Biological gradient*. If a dose-response relationship between exposure and illness can be demonstrated, the association is likely to be causal. (This is one of the strongest criteria. Lung cancer increases with increased numbers of cigarettes smoked. The converse holds that with cessation of exposure, or reduction in dose, the condition abates or ceases.)
6. *Plausibility*. The association does not fly in the face of current biological knowledge, understanding that the period in which we live limits and increases our state of knowledge.
7. *Coherence*. The association fits with what is already known about the natural history of the disease. (Lung cancer in men occurred some 30 years after they began smoking. The same pattern exists with women who took up the habit 30 years after men did.)

The extent to which these criteria are met determines the degree of confidence in accepting an association as causal. In this regard, Hill's words are prescient. "All scientific work," he wrote, "is incomplete whether it be observational or experimental. All scientific work is liable to be upset or modified by advancing knowledge. That does not confer upon us a freedom to ignore the knowledge we already have, or to postpone the action that it appears to demand at a given time."[24]

There are two ways to test a hypothesis about etiology: experimental and observational. Epidemiologic studies, whether retrospective or prospective, are observational. That's the rub. In observational studies, researchers can only wait and see. For the prospective study, they wait to count each new incident as it occurs and ascertain that the case meets previously established criteria. For the retrospective study, they ask lots of questions and hope for appropriate responses. Creativity plays little part in these studies. Creativity comes into play in what is referred to as the "gold standard" of epidemiological studies: the experiment, the intervention, the randomized clinical trial. These are prospective, but the investigator controls the type and degree of exposure as well as who is exposed. The randomized clinical trial obtains the highest-quality data with the least bias. These studies are being used to determine the efficacy and safety of medications, surgical procedures, and dietary regimens. For the most part, epidemiologists do not have the luxury of such trials, as human experimentation is ethically and morally reprehensible, as well as legally untenable—another reason why bias, confounding, and chance must be scrupulously guarded against. Observational studies are all they have. Their limitations are severe, but few appreciate this fact.

Chance

A further point, chance, requires additional comment, as too many publications receive undue attention because media folks are tuned into statistical significance, confidence limits, and p-values. This triad is the contribution of statisticians who attempt to determine if the numbers gathered, the data, could have occurred by chance alone. After all, with over 6 billion people in the world, the chance of finding some in which two conditions exist simultaneously is not all that rare. Confidence limits, intervals, or levels account only for random variation in the data. It tells nothing about the plethora of systematic errors, the biases, the confounding inherent in the study. "What people want to do when they see a 95 percent confidence interval is say, I'll bet there's a 95 percent chance the true value is in there. Even if they deny it, you see them behaving and discussing their study results as though that's exactly what it means."[25] If a study's confidence interval is given as 1.73–1.98 and is accompanied by a p-value of 0.5, the authors are stating that the result could have occurred by chance less than 5 percent of the time. The confidence interval seeks to provide a range of values within which the "true" value may lie, with a certain probability. Such bracketing, and the conclusion that it represents revealed truth, calls to mind John Paulos's cautionary tale. Paulos, chairman of the mathematics department at Philadelphia's Temple University, understood this problem as well as anyone. As he tells it: "Three statisticians went duck hunting; as a duck approached their blind, one fired; his shot sailed just over the duck. The second fired, and his shot flew just below the duck. The third statistician jumped up and yelled, we got it!"[26] Media writers might insinuate this tale into their word processors.

It is of utmost importance to understand that statistical significance has nothing to do with either clinical or biological significance. Observations can differ significantly or correlate highly but still be absurd or irrelevant from a medical point of view. This brings us to those oft-used nonsense terms *correlated* and *linked*, which mean no more than a simple numerical association. Neither has any special or unusual meaning beyond the dictionary definition of a relationship between two or more things. If the public were given to understand that "linked" and "correlated" were simply being used as synonyms for a statistical association and no more, that would be a step in the right direction And if the RR were also tacked on to news accounts, along with its meaning, so that the public comes to treat and understand it as they do temperature, humidity, and the chance of rain or snow, I suspect anxiety would diminish tenfold. Why? Follow me.

Reporting the Results of Studies

The point of all this is to highlight the essential fact that, yes, there is inconsistency between and among investigators researching the same problem. There has to be. It would be highly unusual if there wasn't, given the nature of the investigation and the fundamental fact that people do differ. Remember that random selection of the population is necessary if the sample is to mirror the population at large. Recall, too, that all studies use samples drawn from the general populations. Since no study can utilize the entire population, samples must be used, and these samples must resemble the population at large as closely as possible if findings are to be generalizable: otherwise the study would be meaningless. But what is the general population? How is a study done, say, at the University of Arizona, utilizing sample populations from the Southwest, to be compared with one done in Minnesota or Iowa; or one done in Nepal or Goa? That alone should give pause. In pulling a study together and pursuing it, each research team, wherever it is, will have its own built-in set of biases. That's the way science works. There will be differences and inconsistencies until a consensus is achieved. That's a key.

It is the media that fail the community, not the scientists. It is the media, the writers, and the commentators who fail to comprehend the problems, the complexities inherent in all studies, and simply report conclusions without caveats. The unvarnished fact is that most published studies are and remain nothing more than simple numeric associations. It is the rare study that comes up causal. Smoking and lung cancer is the outstanding and model example.

If we use a RR of 3 or more as a cutoff for possible causal relationships, and forgetting for the moment the 95 percent confidence limits and Hill's criteria, what do we find? In terms of reported cancer risks, consuming olive oil only once a day or less had an RR of 1.25; that having shorter or longer than average menstrual cycles yielded an RR of 2; that ever having used a sun lamp produced an RR of 1.3 for melanoma; that eating yogurt at least once a month had an RR of 2 for ovarian cancer; that a high-cholesterol diet produced an RR of 1.65 for rectal cancer in men; that lengthy occupational exposure to dioxin yielded an RR of 1.5 for cancer of all sites; that eating red meat five or more times a week accounted for an RR of 2.5; that use of phenoxyherbicides on lawns turned up an RR of 1.3 for malignant lymphoma in dogs.[27]

Not to be overlooked are the many studies of electromagnetic fields (EMFs), the high-power lines, which from 1979 to the present have purported to show a causal relationship for both adult and childhood cancers. So, for example, in homes above 2mG (milligauss), summary risk ratios for all childhood cancers yield 1.1; brain tumors, 0.7; and leukemia, 2.7. For adult workers, all electrical occupations combined, the RR is 1.11, and the summary ratio of sixteen adult studies for brain cancer with occupational exposure to EMFs is 1.24.[28] Furthermore, a recent statement by Michael H. Repacholi of the World Health Organization and Anders Ahlbom of Sweden's Karolinska Institutet on the link between EMFs and childhood cancer, referring to a new study currently underway in Japan, is instructive. "This study," they say, "in conjunction with those being done in Germany and Italy, may be the last hope of finally resolving the vexing issue of whether there is truly an increased risk of childhood cancer from exposure to magnetic fields, or whether the weak association is occurring by chance."[29] And on it goes. All are nothing more than simple associations that have been passed off to the public as of great concern to its well-being, when in fact they were of little to no value except as anxiety-producing bits of unnecessary news.

False alarms abound. But worse, they are never extinguished, removed from the public's mind. Once written or commented upon, they are as if fixed in concrete, with science and scientists taking the hit. Even the scientifically illiterate media heap scorn upon scientists for their lack of certainty and seeming endless inconsistency, the unkindest cut of all. It's time for the media to take its rightful place, front and center, at the head of the misinformation line. They've earned it. We can't expect environmentalists to give us a balanced view of life, but surely we should expect more of the media.

Clustering

Leaving this topic without a word about clustering would be incomplete, given the media's and the public's affinity for it. Clustering, a term used when a number of cases occur close together in space and time, seems to the public to be certain evidence of the presence of ambient environmental toxins. It does stir the imagination. More formally, the National Centers for Disease Control and Prevention (NCDC) defines clusters as "an unusual aggregation of health events, real or perceived." Distinguishing true clusters from chance clusters can be difficult, but the types of cancers included in a cluster help sort this out. When a chemical, a carcinogen, is found in the air, soil, or water, it is usually associated with and confined to increased numbers of cancer of one, or at most two, anatomic sites. When lung, pancreas, breast, colon, or prostate is included, it is more than likely that a local toxic phenomenon is not involved.

The NCDC abandoned routine investigation of clusters—some sixteen hundred are reported annually to state health departments—because of the excessive cost in time, money, and personnel required, with little to nothing to show for their efforts. Of sixty-one clusters reported to the NIOSH, none proved meaningful in either epidemiological or general terms.[30]

The theory of random sampling suggests that clusters could be expected to occur simply by chance alone. Indeed, Raymond R. Neutra of the California Department of Health Services maintains that probability theory suggests that 17 percent of the 29,000 towns and census tracts in the United States will have at least one of the eighty recognized types of cancer elevated in any given decade, producing 4,930 chance clusters. Making the problem even more difficult for investigators is the fact that so many clusters include fewer than ten cases, which is next to impossible to deal with epidemiologically.

All too often, cases are included that were diagnosed before the afflicted individuals moved to the neighborhood, or the cases are found by community activists looking for them. Geographic boundaries are then drawn around them, as was the case with the Texas sharpshooter who first fired at the side of a barn, then painted a bull's eye around the hole. This gerrymandering produces seemingly causally related cases, but is in fact a community determinant.

Before a cluster can be shown conclusively to exhibit a cause-effect relationship, investigation should show, must show, that the suspect cases had been exposed to suspected environmental agents and had greater exposure than those free of the disease. Legionnaires' disease, Legionellosis, offers a sound example of a real or true cluster in which knowledge of the space-time clustering of cases aided identification of the causal microbe and its cooling tower reservoir. When the causal agents were discovered and removed, the case numbers dropped precipitously. It is, therefore, reasonable to expect that until a risk factor or factors are known and removed, a cluster should continue to enlarge. This has yet to occur in any reported cancer cluster.

Clustering was well known and readily identifiable at church picnics, club meetings, and corporate outings where illness occurred within 6–24 hours after eating and the offending infectious organism and those who ate and didn't eat the suspected food were identifiable. Many clusters of *Cyclospora*-induced gastrointestinal illness around the country were found to be due to contaminated raspberries imported from Guatemala.[31] Here, again, the time elapsed between exposure and illness was comparatively short: days. Indeed, clusters definitely do occur, the inciting risk factors are identified, and further illness is prevented or controlled. But these incidents usually have larger numbers of cases within well-defined boundaries, identifiable exposures, and agents—the salient factors lacking in most clusters of perceived ambient environmental cancer threats.

If locally perceived and reported cancer clusters have taught us anything, it is that misclassification, gerrymandering, and the Texas sharpshooter have joined forces and are working overtime. Unfortunately, the media appear to have learned nothing from the many perceived clusters.

So, for example, it has yet to be shown that Love Canal was the cause of cancer and birth defects in neighborhood families, yet to the American public, Love Canal stands as a monument to environmental degradation: a media event if ever there was one. The public, with little knowledge or understanding of the underlying issues, knows only what they read in the papers, which offer no more than superficial but emotional anecdotes attributed to community members. Weeks pass, the issue fades, but the idea of an environmental toxin has been impressed, and abides. Scientists get a bad rap for doing little to solve the problem, while the media remain heroes for airing the issue. It's time for a change.

Cigarette Smoke and Lung Cancer Revisited

With this grounding in epidemiology, it's back to the lung cancer/cigarette relationship. The available circumstantial evidence—and it *is* circumstantial, but nonetheless strong enough to establish a conclusion by inference—indicates that cigarette smoke causes lung cancer. Nevertheless, not everyone who smokes gets lung cancer. But the risk of getting it increases substantially with the number of cigarettes smoked. Here, again, the dose makes the poison. This is certain. But no direct cause-effect relationship exists to back it up. That's our dilemma.

How has the cigarette smoke/lung cancer connection been studied? Retrospectively, for the most part, using an epidemiologic case and control study design. This was done for good reason. It's simpler and relatively inexpensive. In this type of study, investigators select a group of people who have the condition in question (the cases). They check how frequently they were exposed to a hypothesized risk factor compared to a group of similar individuals without the condition (the controls). Here, the cases that concern us are individuals with lung cancer, and the risk factor is cigarette smoke; the controls are individuals free of lung cancer. Both groups are interviewed to determine the frequency of their past use of cigarettes. The preferred outcome would be the more cigarettes smoked, the greater the frequency of lung cancer; and, in the lung cancer-free group, little or no smoking. Literally hundreds of studies of this type have been reported. Other studies have looked at sections of lung tissue obtained from lung cancer cases, comparing them with tissue sections of individuals with no lung cancer. The object here is to determine if in fact there are differences, the types of cellular and tissue changes that took place, and if they can be ascribed to cigarette smoke.

Many of the studies were performed on animals, including training dogs to smoke (they not only learned to smoke, but dearly loved the opportunity). Their lung tissue, after heavy smoking, was remarkably similar to the human lung tissue of heavy smokers. In other studies, a variety of animal, human, and bacterial cells were subjected to clouds of smoke in closed containers to determine the effects of smoke. It was from the thousands of studies conducted in dozens of countries that the conclusion was reached that smoking not only is a risk factor for lung cancer, but that the risk is increased proportionately with the number of cigarettes smoked. The evidence is strong, yet it is circumstantial, indirect, and consequently offers a window of opportunity to anyone wishing to call the relationship into question. The tobacco companies love this window, placing ads in newspapers and magazines regularly, attempting to convince smokers and potential smokers that without an established direct cause-effect relationship, the body of indirect circumstantial evidence is nonsense and should be dismissed. But many smokers, to their detriment, bought the argument. Was there no way to circumvent this window and obtain a direct, unimpeachable cause-effect response? Yes and no.

I posed this question regularly to medical, nursing, and graduate students in my epidemiology courses. It was not an easy question and took a while to get the hang of it. As they asked questions and became more creative, they generally came up with a solution, but they agreed it was impossible. And therein lies the conundrum. Why impossible? First of all, if we are to demonstrate unequivocally that smoking is a cause of lung cancer (I say *a*, rather than *the*, because lung cancer can be induced by more than a single risk factor), we must be certain that our study participants inhale smoke, and only smoke; otherwise we are back on square one trying to disentangle smoke from other risks. How do we assure such a circumstance? Again, comparing groups of people is essential. No surrogates, no animals, no retrospective interviews and faulty memories to contend with, and no inherent bias.

One of the groups must be smokers, another nonsmokers. Of course we must begin our study with people who have never smoked, and they must be made to smoke. Each group must have sufficient numbers to assure reliable conclusions. How many? Do we know the number of people expected to get lung cancer annually? Data from past years suggests about fifty per 100,000 people. That can translate to five per 10,000. For us, five are too few. Fifty is a reasonable number, especially if we develop a strong, tight study design. Undoubtedly, there would be objections from those claiming that fifty are too few, that one hundred would be better. It's something to ponder. At a minimum, our study will require enrolling 100,000 people who smoke. For the sake of cost and efficiency, I would be willing to go with 50,000 controls, the nonsmokers. So, we are now looking at a study with 150,000 participants. Actually, I would prefer another 50,000 in the smoking group because it would be nice to establish groups of smokers by number of cigarettes smoked per day: half a pack, one, two, and three packs. This would yield a dose/response curve that would add immense strength to the cause-effect relationship. Is 200,000 any more burdensome than 150,000? It's worth thinking about.

How will we choose our participants? This is vital. Volunteers? Researchers have learned to be wary of volunteers. They simply do not reflect the population as a whole. We need an appropriate cross section of the general population. We could assign numbers randomly, but would those selected participate? And consider this. Smoking-related lung cancer has a latency period of fifteen to forty years. This means that from the initial insult, the initiation of smoking, an interval of fifteen to forty years may elapse before a single case of lung cancer appears.

We must also have both male and female participants, roughly of equal numbers, and none of our enrollees can yet have had their first cigarette. What does this imply? Knowing as we do that smoking often begins at age 12, possibly 11, our "subjects" should be no older than 10, and guaranteed not to have smoked. Are the dimensions and difficulties of this study, as well as its complexity beginning to take shape? Let's go on. We've only just begun.

We need at least 100,000 boys and girls ages 9 to 11 who have never smoked. We must assign them to a smoking or nonsmoking group. In this, they have no choice. We must also be certain that the smokers smoke and the nonsmokers do not. And how many cigarettes must the smokers smoke every day, and for how many years? Evidence gathered over the years suggests a minimum of twenty a day—one pack—for five to ten years.

Before the study gets under way, we must establish our endpoint. What will our clinical criteria be for lung cancer? Criteria of a positive finding must be agreed upon in advance by all physicians who will read chest X-rays. This prior agreement will preclude bias and confounding. And if this study is to yield unequivocal results, we must be certain that smokers smoke the cigarettes assigned, and that the nonsmokers do not inhale a single cigarette. Can we be certain of this? Another question: Where is this study to be undertaken? That's a key! Can each participant live at home, attend school, carry on a normal social life, and promise to smoke or not to smoke as is required by the test group? No. Not possible. This study is too important to trust to anyone's word; there are too many temptations lurking about. What if someone forgot he or she had a cigarette, or didn't feel like having one today? We must have assurances, but how can they be obtained? The only possible way to do so would be to lock up all the participants, and the only practical way to do this is in small groups around the country, with assigned monitor-supervisors. This incarceration would have to continue well into each participant's adulthood: none could leave before age 50. By then, our fifty lung cancer cases should have appeared.

By now you've concluded, as we did, that such a study is both morally and ethically reprehensible, and logistically and practically impossible. It would never fly in a democratic society and, more than likely, not even be possible in any dictatorship in today's world. And rightly so. It's mad. Why? Because the information to be obtained, a direct cause-effect relationship that cigarette smoke causes lung cancer, is not worth the effort to achieve it, given the exceptionally strong circumstantial evidence already in place.

But—and this is the mother of all but's—without this type of study, however, the questions related to radon in homes, leukemia and electromagnetic fields, cigarettes and lung cancer, and many other such issues can never be finally and directly settled. That window of opportunity will be used, is used, frequently to advantage: it is the cigarette manufacturer's dream come true. It also keeps the pot boiling on a number of other illnesses said to be environmentally related.

This is the kind of problem we must worry about: people purposefully trying to deceive us. Unfortunately, no manner of study design or testing can provide the absolute certainty that we want. The media and purveyors of horror stories such as *The Hot Zone* and *The Coming Plague*, which are microbiologically and immunologically flawed, create fear and helplessness, and provide not a shred of understanding. But they do sell, and therein hangs the tale: in the bottom line.

Most of us cannot judge or estimate the frequency of serious, lethal events. In study after study, judgments show consistently biased opinions, overestimation of minor causes of death, and underestimation of major causes. In addition, we tend to exaggerate the frequency of specific illnesses. So, for example, a listing by the general public of the most and least risky activities would show major differences with such a list developed by scientists. Why? Public judgments are severely colored by the media, not only because of what they don't tell us, but because for the past quarter century they have been in crisis mode and report harm disproportionately to its actual occurrence. The engine driving the media is that *bad news sells*. It is exceptionally difficult to alter or modify perceptions because people want their news simple. But the issues of concern are far from simple, and worse, we tend to ignore evidence that is contradictory to our cherished, preferred beliefs. The print media—magazines and newspapers—which more often than not mislead, remain the preferred founts of information.

The dominant perception for most of us, which contrasts sharply with views of professional scientists, is that we face far more risk today than in the past, and that future risks will be even greater. The past, so the myth goes, was a better, less risky time. That we have emerged from a past of widespread illness and a brief life span is rarely acknowledged, let alone credited. The richest, longest-lived, healthiest country is also the most worried, the most anxious.

What happened to us in the twenty-five years between 1950 and 1975? A new generation grew up: a generation made to fear the world, made to fear their environment; air, water, soil, and food despoiled, polluted, contaminated. The unshakable myth: technology, in the form of a military/industrial complex, is the noxious cause of high death and illness rates. Such instilled beliefs exist cheek by jowl with the incontrovertible facts of life and death that proclaim that we have never been healthier, and that a polluted environment, however defined, has little to do with our health. In fact, *we place ourselves at risk of illness and premature death by our personal and individual behavior*. But this becomes much too personal: better to assign blame to impersonal culprits, and the environment will do nicely. Personal behavior has been given short shrift. The crisis-producing media, preferring harm to health, continues to hold the public in thrall.

The risk playing field, as noted earlier, is uneven between scientists and the generally public. Scientists judge risks on the basis of numbers, on yearly fatalities and illnesses; the public assesses risk on perception of catastrophic potential and threat to children and grandchildren. Consequently, the two groups are at opposite ends of the risk spectrum, and, perhaps most important, the public estimates risk, however benign, as unacceptably high. Zero risk, absolute safety, is the common goal; an outcome alien to scientists as unrealistic, uneconomic, unnecessary, and unattainable. Above all, however, the yawning chasms between the groups are the actual figures for annual illnesses and death. For example, the 1979 accident at Three Mile Island, which produced no deaths, no illnesses, no attributable cancer cases, almost became the nail in the coffin of the nuclear power industry. TMI was, if nothing else, a media event of monumental proportions. It demonstrated the overarching importance and effectiveness of the media's ability to establish nationwide perceptions. Mediagenic disease was created there, as was public policy. Twenty years down the road, TMI remains one of the salient environmental noncatastrophes of the century. But that message has still not gotten wide distribution. Why not? How would the media explain their earlier excess? It would make a nifty story, especially in color, with a lot of red faces.

Furthermore, the amount of print journalism devoted to causes of death from illicit drug use, airplane crashes, motor vehicle accidents, toxic agents, and homicide, for example, is staggeringly disproportionate to the actual number of deaths attributable to these causes. As shown in chapter 1, the distortion is seen as important simply because of the amount of space devoted to this kind of hype. The information provided may be true, but only partially so. Consequently, the public has a skewed understanding of what risks are actually most harmful and which, in fact, are the least. Chicken Little may be the world's most famous alarmist, but she does have a number of claimants in the media vying for the title who have tried, often successfully, to make hypochondriacs of us all.

It is worth recalling James Lovelock's warning. Lovelock, guru of the Greens, attacked the Friends of the Earth at their 1989 annual meeting in London. He lambasted them for hounding the nuclear and chemical establishments without warrant. According to Lovelock, these industries were not the enemies. "Most of us," he said, "are hypochondriacs in one way or another. . . . Few actions are more despicable than the manipulation of this fear by corrupt scientists for their short-term personal advantage." He warned the Friends to be suspicious of "those who try to frighten you by implying that nuclear installations are responsible for the leukemia clusters observed in their vicinity or who exaggerate the dangers of chemicals like dioxin." This was not the message the Greens expected of their champion, which may explain the almost total lack of media coverage. But it was an overdue message. Indeed, it is time to throw off our "mind-forged manacles."

The past quarter of a century has been a miserable period in which the media and environmentalists prospered, and the public suffered. The media has had a simple motive—profit—while they were speaking and writing with little knowledge of their subject. Environmentalists, a mixed bag, had their own agenda. While their desire for clean air and water is laudable, was it necessary to create a fictitious cancer epidemic? Why is it necessary to turn the people into a nation of fearful hypochondriacs? But the public, too, must share a measure of blame for their almost total belief and reliance on others for decision-making. Absolute truth is unattainable; but approximate truth, which closely identifies with reality, is surely obtainable and far better than the chaff currently passing for wisdom.

Change is overdue. It is time to move on, to start over. An about-face on the part of both print and electronic media, as well as the public, would induce a sea change of portentous magnitude. Can this come about? Indeed it can. We need only rouse the Sleeping Giant! Have you been had? You bet you have!

The Sleeping Giant

To break the hold of the mass media and the environmentalists, we need to become a people who ask questions—sophisticated, probing questions. Needed, too, is a greater degree of skepticism topped with a dollop of cynicism. To hear more people say, "How's that?" or "Run that by me again," would indicate that change is in the air, would do wonders for our national discourse, and would begin to lower the daily doses of blather. But probing questions require insight, background, and the knowledge to make connections. Can this be attained? It can and, yes, there is a remedy for this twentieth-century disease. The remedy is SL: scientific literacy.

I propose a national campaign of scientific literacy that requires that all students demonstrate an understanding of the workings of science, religion, and pseudoscience. Such demonstration must put the media and environmentalists on notice: prepare for hard, searching questions. Be prepared to explain and defend your advocacy. In this new environment, the media will also prosper as they acquire scientific literacy. Unnecessary advocacy will plummet because there will be no profit in it, and because they will know better.

Informing the public is at the heart of all environmental concerns. No one knew this better than Thomas Jefferson. "If we think," he wrote, "the people are not enlightened enough to exercise their control with a wholesome discretion, the remedy is not to take it from them, but to inform their discretion."[1] Inform them indeed, adequately and appropriately. But the information must fall upon fertile, well-watered ground if it is to blossom into the fruit of knowledge.

Even though formal education is almost universal, too many students leave high school and university without a smidgen of understanding of how new scientific and medical information is gathered, organized, and interpreted, and how conclusions are drawn. Many of these graduates become our journalists, newscasters, TV commentators, talk-show hosts, magazine and newspaper columnists—in a word, our opinion makers. They quote, paraphrase, or rework conclusions of published articles, but what of the study itself—was it methodologically sound? That's crucial. Too many are unprepared to give their listeners or readers the full story, the type of information needed for rational decision-making.

Three problems afflict us: lack of accurate, trustworthy information, conflicting information, and continuous exposure to misinformation. Result: mental pollution, a mediagenically induced malady, the offspring of medical/scientific news dispensed by scientific illiterates. Commentators and writers with not a clue as to the effects of experimental confounding, bias, sample size, plausibility, appropriate controls, statistical techniques, and researchers' overstatement of conclusions are constitutionally unable to differentiate good science from poor.

No TV, radio station, magazine, or newspaper worthy of the name would countenance the use of the untutored to dispense and interpret news about fashion, finance, foreign affairs, politics, or sports. Science alone is left to anyone not otherwise occupied. The mighty weapon of scientific literacy is needed to overhaul and bring needed sanity to a communications media hell-bent on alarming the public.

Schools should be required to reevaluate and reconfigure their curricula to include scientific literacy. Help with the necessary expertise will be available nationwide. In fact, it is already in place, waiting to be tapped. And let's be clear about it, SL neither means nor requires that everyone become a scientist. It does require that schools inculcate habits of critical thought, the ability to evaluate and analyze information, as well as comprehend the processes of science and how they differ from religion and pseudoscience. So, come along with me on this journey of discovery. As that Marx fellow suggested, "We have nothing to lose but our chains." Mental chains. Is there anything worse?

Follow me as I offer examples of good and not-so-good science. And follow me as we examine different truths: scientific and religious truths (and pseudoscience), which have been with us since early humans gazed at the heavens and wondered. I then consider the identifying traits of each and make the case for teaching them in our public schools. Finally, we arrive at our destination: the unveiling of the grand plan for the twenty-first century—a nationwide blooming of scientific literacy.

Real Science and Scientists

Pellegra and Joseph Goldberger

For the *Encyclopaedia Britannica,* Joseph Goldberger does not exist. Is it because his nomination for the Nobel Prize in Medicine was rebuffed five times? His celebrated medical sleuthing should have placed him among that esoteric pantheon.

Goldberger grew up on the hard streets of New York's Lower East Side. He studied at City College and graduated from Bellevue Hospital Medical College. Private practice in Wilkes-Barre, Pennsylvania, did not go well, but other uses for his considerable talent lay ahead. The parallel between Goldberger and his contemporary Arthur Conan Doyle was taking shape. Goldberger joined the U.S. Public Health Service (USPHS) in 1899. His medical detective career was about to unfold.[2]

Pellagra was rife in the Mediterranean countries, but especially so in Italy, where it had been described for over two hundred years, and whence it obtains its name. By 1914, over 25,000 cases, with a fatality rate over 40 percent, had been reported in the United States. During the Reconstruction era, pellagra was rampant in the Confederate states and unusually severe in Mississippi, Arkansas, Alabama, and Georgia. In 1911, the state of Illinois Pellagra Commission ended its investigation with these conclusions: "a) according to the weight of evidence, pellagra is a disease due to infection with a living microorganism of unknown nature; b) a possible location for this infection is the intestinal tract; c) deficient animal protein in the diet may constitute a predisposing factor in the contracting of disease."[3] In 1913, in its first progress report of its studies in Spartenburg County, South Carolina, the Thompson-McFadden Pellagra Commission arrived at a similar conclusion. For them, "The supposition that the ingestion of good or spoiled maize is the essential cause of pellagra is not supported by our study; and pellagra is in all probability a specific infectious disease communicable from person to person by a means at present unknown."

Pellagra is not pleasant. It begins with loss of appetite, muscle weakness, lassitude, poor digestion, and diarrhea, followed by dark blotches on skin that is exposed to sunlight; mental confusion develops, with loss of memory, resembling insanity. Death is the end stage. These symptoms are often referred to as pellagra's 4 D's: dermatitis, diarrhea, dementia, and death. For the USPHS, pellagra was a top priority; control and prevention were of utmost importance. Surgeon General Rupert Blue tapped

Goldberger to investigate—a natural choice given his experience and success with typhus, diphtheria, measles, and the itch mite.

For three months, Goldberger visited institutions, including orphanages and mental asylums, throughout Mississippi, Georgia, and Louisiana, looking for an infectious connection. But his findings were always the same. The D's were limited to the children. Those between the ages 6–12 were at greatest risk; those under 6 and over 12 much less so. Given their identical living conditions, how could they be spared? But there was an even more startling fact: nurses never got the disease. Neither did the physicians, cooks, or clerks. Furthermore, the illness appeared to be confined to rural areas, and to the poorest families. In the cities, neither poor nor rich were affected. If, as all commissions had assumed, the disease was infectious and transmissible, such remarkable gaps made no microbiological sense. In June 1914, three months into the project, Goldberger wrote to Surgeon General Blue describing his observations. In part, his letter reads, "The inference may therefore be safely drawn that Pellagra is not an infection but that it is a disease essentially of dietary origin."[4] He had a theory; now he had to prove it.

He enlisted the cooperation of two orphanages and a mental asylum. Between them, the two orphanages contributed 209 cases. At the Georgia State Sanitarium, 72 child inmates, 36 colored and 36 white, were enrolled, for a total of 281 cases of pellagra. He was assured that nothing but the diet would be changed. No change in the water supply, no change in overcrowding, and no change in general hygienic conditions, which were poor at best.

How did the diets change? Milk intake was greatly increased. Every child under 12 received a 7-ounce cup of fresh, sweet milk at least twice daily. Buttermilk was added and served daily at the midday meal. Eggs, not part of the regular diet, were given to each child under 12. Fresh meat, normally served once a week, was increased to 3–4 times a week. Beans and peas, which had been served only during the summer and fall, were made an important part of every midday meal. The carbohydrate component was also modified. Breakfast cereal was changed from grits to meal, partly to increase the corn partly to increase milk consumption To further reduce carbohydrate intake, corn syrup and molasses were entirely excluded for weeks, then later allowed in small amounts during evening meals.

While waiting for the diets to take effect, Goldberger and his crew set about determining the communicable nature of pellagra. He, his wife, and fourteen Public Health Service colleagues attempted to infect themselves.

From seventeen florid cases, they obtained blood, urine, feces, scaly skin from pellagrous lesions, and nasopharyngeal (mucus) secretions. And in Goldberger's words, "Blood was administered by intramuscular or subcutaneous injection; secretions by application to the mucosa of the nose and nasopharynx (in and around the throat); scales and excreta by mouth. Both urine and feces were ingested by 15 of the volunteers, 5 of whom also took blood, secretions and scales." He called the experiments "filth parties." And the outcome? "During a period of between five and seven months none has developed evidence justifying a diagnosis of pellagra. These experiments furnish no support for the view that pellagra is a communicable disease; they materially strengthen the conclusion that it is a disease essentially of dietary origin, brought about by a faulty, probably deficient diet."[5] What of the diet studies?

Of the 281 pellagrous children who entered the study, 244 remained in it for the full year. Of these, only one had any signs of pellagra at the study's completion. Goldberger could report that "in orphanage M there has been no pellagra in this institution this year." And at Orphanage B, "in only 1 of those 105 pellagrins following the change in diet, has there been recognized evidence justifying the diagnosis of a recurrence." As for the Georgia State Asylum, "none of this group of 72 patients has presented recognizable evidence of a recurrence of pellagra."[6] The numbers were overwhelming. One case among 244. Based on these numbers alone, most epidemiologists would venture that this was an example of a direct cause-effect relationship.

Even with these numbers, lady luck was standing by, and Goldberger knew how to deal with her.

The first instance (there were two, surely a surfeit) occurred at the Georgia State Asylum. "Although not specifically planned, conditions at the GS Sanitarium have been such as to provide a control group of pellagrins in both the colored and white female service. This permitted the making of a direct comparison of the results observed in the wards in which diet was modified, with those not modified. Of 17 colored female pellagrins, 9 (53%) have already presented recurrences. Among the 15 white females, 6 or 40 percent have had recurrences this year. Again the differences are strikingly impressive."[7]

The second bit of luck was perhaps serendipitous. After the study's discontinuance at one orphanage, the administrator decided that since the "study" was over, it was time to return to the traditional diet. Over the ensuing nine months, approximately 40 percent of the inmates developed the

D's. When Goldberger learned of this, the diet was changed again. Fourteen months later, the orphanage was free of pellagra. Most epidemiologists would trade their eye-teeth for such on and off switching. It also gave Goldberger another idea. Why not reverse the experiment? Can pellagra be produced in healthy men by feeding them a diet of the type associated with a high incidence of the disease? He was able to do this. Setting out to deliberately give people a disease, as noted earlier, would be considered unethical today and could not be done.

The Rankin Farm, eight miles east of Jackson, part of the Mississippi State Penitentiary, offered a site. Twelve white, adult male convicts volunteered for the study. They were segregated and kept under special guard. Of the twelve, eleven remained for the length of the study. One hundred eight convicts were available as controls, five of whom would be especially observed for the entire period of the study; all would continue on the normal prison fare. For two months prior to the diet change, the volunteers were observed for possible pellagra or its occurrence.

The deficiency diet consisted of biscuits, grits, cornbread, white rice, potatoes, pork fat, cabbage, collard and collard greens, turnips and turnip greens, sugar, syrup, salt, and pepper. After seven months, 6 of the 11 (54%) developed pellagra. Those on the standard diet remained pellagra free. Again, very impressive numbers. It was better to be a well-fed prisoner than an inmate at an orphanage.

Over the next several years, Goldberger and coworkers conducted animal feeding studies to identify the nutritional factor responsible for the deficiency. He postulated the existence of a previously unknown factor he dubbed P-P: Pellagra Protective factor.

With his untimely death in 1928, he would never learn that niacin, one of the B-complex vitamins, readily convertible in the body to active nicotinamide, was in fact the P-P factor. Subsequently, with niacin-enriched bread and cereals, pellagra was eradicated. Goldberger's work was a scientific tour de force, a triumph of scientific procedures, an open mind, observation, questioning, reasoning, rethinking, testing prevailing belief, experimenting to obtain new information, collecting and interpreting data, and finally coming to a conclusion. It doesn't get much better.

Against entrenched professional opinion, Goldberger proved that pellagra was neither infectious nor transmissible, but rather an illness induced by a vitamin-deficient diet. Ultimately, he made it a thing of the past.

Not worth a Nobel Prize, nor a line in the *Britannica*?

Ignaz Semmelweis and Puerperal Fever

Ignaz Semmelweis was a student at the University of Vienna's Medical School, well before Alfred Nobel had any inkling of the havoc that dynamite and other explosives would wreak. Upon graduation, Semmelweis specialized in obstetrics and took a position as an assistant in the First Division Maternity Ward of the Vienna General Hospital.

Nineteenth-century maternity clinics—especially charity clinics—were "houses of death." Childbed fever (puerperal fever) was rampant and fatal in more than 50 percent of the cases. To reduce their chances of contracting this horrendous bacterial infection yet qualify for postpartum care, women in labor often wandered the streets until giving birth in a doorway or field. Then, with their baby, they walked to a nearby hospital. Risky, absolutely, but also safer than delivery in many clinics. It was in this world where Semmelweis assumed his duties. Fortunately, he was assigned to the First Division. Had he been appointed to the Second, it is uncertain he would have risen to the challenge.

The First Division, for women in labor, was to be avoided: there was real danger there. Women knew it and tried every stratagem to avoid assignment there. In 1846, for every one hundred deliveries in the wards, there were twelve deaths in the First Division but only two in the Second.

In an attempt to fathom puerperal fever, with its chills, fever, pain, respiratory distress, and death, Semmelweis autopsied hundreds of women who had died in both wards but found nothing to explain the different rates. He also began considering the accepted theories such as overcrowding, which many believed produced harmful miasmas. The high mortality in the First was believed to be the consequence of foul air. Semmelweis found that as most women avoided the pernicious First, the Second ward was the most crowded, yet had the most births and fewest deaths.

Another belief held that rough treatment by medical students was the cause. Semmelweis observed students and midwives and found that although both performed similarly, the midwives in the Second Division still had far fewer deaths. In his desperation, he turned to the religious practices on the wards. From his notes we learn that "the hospital chapel was so located that when the priest was summoned to administer the last rites in the Second Division he could go directly to the room set aside for ill patients. But when summoned to the First, he had to pass through five other rooms with women in labor, but not ill, to get to the sick, and in so doing he was always preceded by a sexton ringing a bell. The frequency of his call, and the constant ringing of the bell, it was theorized, so demoralized the women in labor that they fell ill and died of a deep depression." Semmelweis was so disturbed by this that he "appealed to the compassion of the servant of God and arranged for him to come by a less direct route, without bells, and without passing through other rooms. Thus, no one outside the room containing the ill patients knew of the priest's appearance."[8] Did the death rates change in any way? Not a bit.

In March 1841, Semmelweis went off to Venice for a brief vacation. On returning, he was shocked to learn that Professor Jacob Kolletschka, his friend and mentor, had died of a wound inflicted during dissection of a cadaver. Most electrifying was the fact that at his autopsy, which Semmelweis attended, he noticed that the infected lesions resembled those found on women who had died of childbed fever. He tells us that "the cause of Prof. Kolletschka's death was known; it was the wound by the autopsy knife that had been contaminated by cadaverous particles. Not the wound but contamination of the wound by cadaverous particles caused his death."[9] (Recall that it was not until 1876 that microorganisms were shown to cause human illness.) Semmelweis had his epiphany. He knew that he and other obstetricians, and his students, had been autopsying cadavers just before examining women in labor and after delivery. They were all infecting (contaminating) the women. He was mortified. Midwives had no contact with cadavers. The women who wandered in from the street carrying their just-delivered infants had no need to be examined, so they were not affected. He found, too, that mortality rose and fell with the number of autopsies performed. He had identified the cause of the staggering mortality rates in the First Division, and he knew what to do. All physicians and students coming from the autopsy rooms were required to wash their hands with soap, followed by rinsing in a chlorine solution, before entering the maternity wards. The deaths dropped precipitously. This is a shining example of how the synthesis of observation and experiment can provide an unambiguous answer to a scientific-medical conundrum. Here we see the power of an open mind, willing to try new ways, in the face of narrow-minded but powerful opinion, and we also see the many false paths that often must be taken before arriving at the truth—an essential key.

The Medical Community and Kaposi's Sarcoma

The following investigation could conceivably be nominated for a prize, but not the Nobel. It stumped the medical community: stopped them cold—temporarily.

It began in June 1981, when a triad of uncommon meanness descended upon young, promiscuous, homosexual men: Kaposi's sarcoma, *Pneumocystis carinii* pneumonia, and a spate of opportunistic infections. The National Centers for Disease Control sounded the alarm. An epidemic appeared to be in the making. Otherwise healthy young men, primarily in metropolitan areas, were presenting with malignant tumors of muscle, blood vessels, and fibrous tissue; their arms and legs were pocked with purple-brown spongy patches, and a rare type of protozoan-induced pneumonia was mercilessly afflicting them. But these unusually sexually active young men were also recreational drug users. The leading candidate was amyl nitrate: poppers. As vasodilator and muscle relaxants, poppers had a long history of use in the gay community. Sociologists and psychiatrists had documented its destructive behavioral effects long before AIDS further darkened the landscape.

Enhancement of orgasm, euphoria, and, above all, relaxation of all muscles including the anal sphincter contributed to its popularity. The original poppers came in small glass spheres that were crushed, popped, and inhaled. With rapid sphincter relaxation, they made anal intercourse easy while heightening orgasm.

Paper after paper published in a range of respected medical journals reported independent significant statistical associations between amyl nitrate use and Kaposi's sarcoma.[10] By 1982, an international ban on poppers was being proposed as a means of preventing a drug-induced AIDS epidemic.[11] Before an official ban was put forward, a curious event occurred. A virus was discovered: HIV—human immunodeficiency virus—was isolated and found to be the cause of AIDS. Amyl nitrate was forgotten by scientists (but not by the gay community, which continues to use it liberally) in their dash to understand this new and complex human pathogen. How could such confounding occur? As mentioned in an earlier chapter, in epidemiological parlance "confounding" refers to the concurrent exposure of two or more intimately linked risk factors. The confounder is the factor whose known effect is falsely believed to be the cause of the disease. In this instance, amyl nitrate use and homosexual intercourse occurred simultaneously, confounding the cause of the immunodeficiency syndrome. Until the virus was isolated and shown to be both infectious and communicable, amyl nitrate was erroneously assumed to be the likely causal factor. Fortunately, the virus was rapidly isolated and shown to be causal, while amyl nitrate was allowed to die on the vine. Nevertheless, the amyl nitrate–HIV/AIDS relationship remains a classic case of a rare but remarkable example of excessively strong confounding that misled the medical community albeit temporarily.

Johannes A. G. Fibiger and a False Alarm

Johannes Andreas Grib Fibiger was the twentieth recipient of the Nobel Prize in Medicine. Professor Fibiger was a pathologist at the Anatamo-Pathological Institute of the University of Copenhagen. He won this coveted, prestigious award for his hypothesis that a parasitic roundworm, *Spiroptera*, a nematode, was the cause of stomach cancer.

But 1926 was not a good year for the Nobel. Listen to him:

> By transmission of *Spiroptera neoplastica* to black and white rats, and white mice, the development of neoplasia can be induced on the fundus of the stomach, and in rats in the tongue also. These neoplasms possess exactly the same histological structure as malignant epitheliomata (keratinizing squamous-cell carcinomata) in man and animals. They grow invasively into connective tissue and muscle tissue, and produce metastases in lymph nodes, peri-neural lymphatic spaces, the lung, and the periosteum. They continue their growth whether or not the Spiropterae (as observed in the tongue) disappear entirely or only partly. They are transplantable, and when transplanted grow invasively into organs and tissue. Neither the metastases nor the transplanted tumors contain Spiropterae, which have no share in their developmental growth. That these tumors are true carcinomata cannot, thus, be doubted, and the fact that they may occur in younger animals does not diminish our right to range them among the true malignant neoplasms.[12]

Fibiger's critics noted a litany of errors. He failed to use control animals; he failed to report the number of rats with stomach cancer without worms; he mistook hyperplasia for cancer; he used wild rats, which prevented others from reproducing his work.[13] It took decades to demonstrate that worms played no part in stomach cancer. But his work serves a purpose; it reminds us of the many blind alleys down which scientists can wander in the search for truth, and be misled. But in time, the errors are redressed.

The Role of Religion and Pseudoscience

The foregoing examples notwithstanding, good science, poor science, and confounding are the stuff of science. Each in their way seek verifiable truth. And bad or good, all share common attributes.

For scientists, amateur or professional, whatever their interest, their objectives, methods, and results are open and public, subject to inspection, evaluation, and criticism by others. No scientists, however great their celebrity, are above questioning. Their collected data are obtained by observation, testing, and experimentation. Furthermore, it is the rare or odd subject that is ever formally closed, ever completed. Knowledge begets knowledge. New knowledge is expected to replace "old." Researchers expect and anticipate that their work will be scrutinized by other scientists, and whatever the object of study, from Aardvark to Zymurgy, it is certain to be researched by a plethora of investigators from Stockholm to Shanghai to San Francisco, employing procedures of their own devising and with unique populations, all of them seeking verifiable data that can be generalized to entire populations. Faulty work eventually gets demolished by the work of others, while work well done gains adherents and strength, as new evidence supports it. To all this, there is but a single caveat: investigations are limited to objects and events of the natural world. That's fundamental and essential—the natural world, as opposed to the spiritual world.

Which brings us to the fact that there are other truths, poetic and religious, for example. Poetic truth is a representation, an expression of the emotions of all aspects of our lives. Religious truth deals with a divine or supernatural power considered to control human destiny. And although there is more than one truth, they need not be conflicting, nor need one supplant or supersede the other: we live by, and with, more than a single truth. Nevertheless, contrary to scientific truth, which seeks only to relieve nature of her "secrets," religious truth emanates from revelation of the spiritual world. For scientists, the world is tentative, provisional, and in shades of gray. Proof arrives via observation and experiment, maximized for objectivity by design. The work thrives on controversy but advances by consensus. Religious truth by its nature is absolute, black or white, it is or it isn't. And it is personal, emotional, preconceived and subjective. Faith is the only requirement for the acceptance of proof. Controversy is intolerable, as Copernicus and Galileo knew. St. Augustine captured and framed its essence 1,600 years ago, and it still holds true today. "Nothing is to be accepted," he declared, "save on the authority of scripture, since that authority is greater than all the power of the human mind."[14] Clear, precise, absolute.

Straddling both scientific and religious truth is pseudoscience: untested, unproven, accepted unquestioningly. UFO's, dietary supplements, extraterrestrials, crystal power, channeling, Ayurvedic medicine, polywater, and Chinese herbal cures are current examples.

Creationism

Creationism, with all the trappings of both religion and pseudoscience, deserves attention, given its resurgence. Creationism, the acceptance of the Bible as literal human history, is wholly at variance and incompatible with the concept of Darwinian evolution. Nevertheless, across the country there is increasing agitation to teach creationism in public schools along with evolutionary biology. Is creationism science, or is it religion? Does it matter? Perhaps.

Most disconcerting is its number of adherents. Recent surveys suggest that close to half our population and some 25 percent of college students believe that we humans did not evolve but were created by God, some ten thousand years ago, at about the time the last ice age was retreating from North America and northern Europe. Many people had assumed that a literal interpretation of the Bible had abated as new scientific discoveries occurred and accumulated. Is the Earth the center of the universe, and does the Sun orbit the Earth? Was the Earth created in seven days?

The concept of evolution saw the light of day in the mid-nineteenth century. Until then, the Western world generally accepted as literal fact the account of creation as laid out in the biblical book of Genesis. According to Genesis, the world had been created relatively recently. From it we also learned, and were taught, that life was suddenly created and that every living thing—all the flora and fauna—was created separately and distinctly, and that the many thousands of different species have remained fixed and unchanged over the long centuries. And most importantly, Genesis teaches that humankind was created by God, in his image. Evidence and proof are unnecessary. Faith is sufficient.

But this account, this history, was not to remain unchallenged. Charles Darwin, an English naturalist, whose geologic and biologic studies suggested that all species, including humans, were changeable and divergent, not at all fixed. "Descent with modification" was Darwin's new and bold idea. He proposed, too, that species had branched and evolved through natural selection. This essential concept implies that, given competition for food, for example, those individuals best adapted to their unique environment are most likely to survive, reproduce, and pass their unique traits on to their prodigy. Over thousands of years, this process is subtly slow as new species emerge to exhibit a variety of accumulated changes. Consequently, those best fitted to their respective environments have the best chances of survival. In a word, evolution.

But the mechanism, the means by which the effects, the changes, the modifications wrought by natural selection are produced, had to await the work of the Austrian monk and botanist, Johann Gregor Mendel. With all the fanfare given—quite appropriately, by the way—to the Genome Project, we could be forgiven for forgetting that it was Mendel who discovered the gene, in 1860. Working in the garden of his Augustinian monastery in Brno (pronounced burr-no) on pea-breeding experiments, he discovered that differences among varieties of peas—color, size, shape, and texture— were due to pairs of genes, the units of heredity. It was he who discovered that genes were the means through which traits were passed from parents to offspring. Curiously enough, it was a cleric who changed the world forever, by showing the way of natural selection.

Furthermore, essential to evolution is the concept of branching and the descent from a common ancestor of a single and unique origin. Common ancestry implies a falling away of special creation. Nevertheless, and be that as it may, we humans remain unique among all organisms, all species. Our intelligence, history, continuity, and culture set us apart from our closest hominid, the ape. It is the falling away of special creation, the implication that God may not be required for the descent of man, that so enflames creationists. And, if that isn't irritation enough to them, there is chance and randomness, which show themselves in curious ways. Who, for example, would have designed blood vessels and nerves traversing the inside of the retina of our eyes, creating a blind spot at their point of exit? Surely not a grand architect, but chance and randomness could. And who would have designed a human whose urine and earwax would turn purplish black on contact with air depending on what he or she ate? Those so afflicted are accumulators of homogentisic acid, and their disease, Alcaptanuria, is an inborn error of metabolism. These people lack a gene on chromosome 3 that codes for an enzyme, which normally breaks down the acid. Alcaptanuria clusters in families and is expressed when inherited from both parents.[15] Again, chance and randomness at work. Part of the grand design?

Evolution for creationists is synonymous with godlessness. Consequently, evolution, they say, must be denounced as scientific atheism. In addition, geological, archeological, paleontological, and biological evidence of evolution have no place at the creationist table. For creationists, evolution is false, wrong, an evanescent theory. Echoing St. Augustine, Henry Morris, the head of the Institute for Creation Research, is clear about man's origins. Listen to him: "If man wishes to know anything about creation (the time of creation, the duration of creation, the order of creation, the methods of creation, or anything else), his sole source of true information is that of divine revelation. God was there when it happened. We were not there. Therefore, we are completely limited to what God has seen fit to tell us and his information in this written word. This is our textbook on the science of creation."[16] Clear enough—and entirely at odds with current science. Yet in the same breath, creationists demand that "creationist science" be taught in our public schools alongside evolutionary biology. This issue is so profoundly consequential and urgent that I will embrace it momentarily. But first let us consider the concept of theory, which so annoys and challenges creationists.

Theory

Ideas, hunches, theories, have been about for as long as individuals wondered about the world around them. The sixteenth and seventeenth centuries were hotbeds of new theories, and of planetary, celestial thinking. In 1543, the year of Copernicus's death, his book, *De Revolutionibus Orbium Caelestium—On the Revolutions of the Heavenly Spheres*—was published.[17] It put forth the hypothesis, the theory that the planet Earth traveled around the Sun—a heretical notion, given Church doctrine that the Earth was the center of the universe, and all heavenly bodies circled the Earth. His book was labeled antibiblical and intolerable.

Staring incredulously through his twenty-power telescope, Galileo saw the satellites circling Jupiter and became a convert to the Copernican idea. From that moment on, it was the telescope that "spoke directly to the senses" and short-circuited the Church's jurisdiction over the heavens.[18] At his heresy trial, Galileo tried to thread an uneasy passage, balancing simultaneously biblical truth and Copernican theory. There is only one truth, he told the Inquisition, but it is communicated in two forms: the language of the Bible and the language of nature. Both are God's language. The Inquisitors didn't buy it. The theory was too dangerous, too threatening to their authority. And too many people were getting into the act. Johannes Kepler, another star gazer, put it this way: "My aim is to show that the celestial machine is to be likened not to divine organism, but rather a clockwork."[19]

Galileo had in fact shot himself in the foot, as it were, by remarking that "by denying scientific principles one may maintain any paradox."[20] And Leonardo da Vinci let it be known "that experience does not even err, it is only your judgment that errs in promising itself results which are not caused by your experiments."[21] People were thinking. Ideas were blossoming. But the star gazers could not prove, could not verify their theories; not the way Dr. Goldberger could. The results of his controlled trials were observable, repeatable, and verifiable. Theory was proven by objective evidence.

Fast-forward to the twenty-first century and a closer look at theory. I have a theory, a hunch, that holds that today's extreme, aggressive sports—snowboarding, skateboarding, BMX biking, bungee jumping, and sky-diving—are the province of those youngsters, like my grandson, Zach, who at an earlier time would have been one of our pioneers: our Daniel Boones, John Fremonts, the Bowie brothers, Lewis and Clark, and the Pony Express riders. And, if Boone, Fremont, and the Bowies were to return today, they would doubtlessly be skateboarders, skydivers, and BMX bikers. My theory maintains that with no frontiers left to open or conquer, our energetic men and women who would have taken trails West require outlets befitting their pent-up energy that only extreme sports can satisfy. That's a theory, my theory. Does it have any validity? Only testing will provide an answer. Will it ever be tested? It's anyone's guess. At this juncture it remains a hunch. Someone else could well theorize an entirely different reason or explanation for the extreme sport craze—we could even be treated to a half-dozen or more. Whether good or bad, all would be theories, and, until tested, theories they'll remain.

With that as our prelude, we can ask: How did the Grand Canyon form? An intriguing and compelling question—one that creationists have a ready answer for. Nevertheless, in June 2000, some one hundred scientists gathered at Grand Canyon Village to sort out their differences, which center around four different and conflicting theories.[22] Will there be a resolution and a unifying theory, backed by verifiable evidence showing how the canyon was cut so deeply? Not in my lifetime. But eventually there will be one. Ideas about how the canyon formed are a grand example of theories in search of support. Is the hand of God involved? Can that become theory number five?

The Grand Canyon is not alone as a subject for theorists. *Longisquama insignis* was an Archosaur, an "old" snakelike critter, old, very old. If its dating is sound, it roamed Central Asia some 220 million years ago, a time that creationists simply do not recognize. Anything beyond ten thousand years ago is anathema to them; it was never there.

For *Longisquama*, "roamed" may be the wrong mode of travel. *Longisquama* had not only feathers, but it also had four legs. Did it walk, glide, or fly? Do feathers mean it was birdlike, and did dinosaurs evolve into birds, or was this saurian not a dinosaur at all?[23] It looks as if natural selection and branching evolution are at work, but at this moment there are still many questions and few answers. It will be years before *Longisquama*'s paternity is ironed out. But that's what it's all about: searching for answers to nature's many puzzles and clues. The search is open, subject to criticism, suggestion, evaluation, testing, and verification. Given time and resources, the process works.

Whether the Earth is round or flat is beyond theory. Support and strength for a globular Earth come from a variety of sources that increase its strength appreciably. Although space probes and satellites have sent back images showing Earth to be spherical, the ancient Greeks were aware of Earth's globular shape well before cameras were sent into space. Aristotle (c. 350 B.C.) reasoned that the Earth was round because it always cast a round shadow on the Moon during an eclipse. Only a round Earth would do that. Had the Earth been flat, its shadow would have been a narrow band, and such a band had never been seen. That the Earth was round was also known to early sailors. Watching other ships as they did, it was evident that as ships approached from across the sea, at the horizon, it was the ship's top rigging that was first to come into view. Columbus was well aware of these observations as he prepared to sail west to the Indies. During the International Geophysical Year of 1957–1958 firm data on the bulging of the Earth at the equator was substantiated by *Vanguard I*, proving Isaac Newton's prediction which he had based on his calculation of the tremendous effects of a spinning Earth. Later, when the *Apollo 8* astronauts came up from behind the Moon, the view of the Earth they saw, to which so many of us were also treated shortly after, was half a globe. That the Earth is round is well beyond theory. The observable fact that so many can see both the takeoffs from Earth and landings on the Moon and Mars is also firm proof that our theory— our knowledge of planetary motion and gravitational forces—is correct: prediction is the task of theory, and correct prediction, the ultimate test.

We can plot, in advance, where the Moon will be on a certain day, and we can send a spacecraft on a trajectory with sufficient power to overcome the Earth's gravitational field, permitting the vehicle to enter space and head for a point at which the Moon's orbit will bring it at the time the craft arrives. It has been done six times. This tells us that our understanding, our calculus, is correct. For sure, a man-made spacecraft may malfunction, the vehicle may explode, or veer off course, but none of that denies our basic knowledge.

For physicists and mathematicians, "theory" is not so specific. For them, firm support exists for both the special and general theories of relativity; referring to either principle as a theory raises no doubts. And the truth of particle physics was amply demonstrated early in the morning on July 16, 1945, at Alamagordo in the New Mexico desert. The mushroom cloud was proof of that.

Climatologists may disagree about the uncertainty and degree of predicted global warming, but that's because experiments are impossible. There is only one Earth, and it is too large to bring into a laboratory for study, too large to be subjected to a battery of tests. Consequently, the testing must be done with computers via mathematical modeling. Models are designed to explain and predict. Individual scientists use different models with differing assumptions and accordingly obtain different results. But regularly and frequently, they come together to exchange data and information and alter their models. In time the differences will narrow. Science is not errorless, nor are scientists infallible, but errors have a relatively short life, and conclusions are only tentative. The process begins with theory, and it remains for researchers to prove or disprove.

Creationists have framed their own responses to these many issues—responses that are personally satisfying. They are skeptical of scientific truth. Skepticism is good, and to a point required. Total skepticism is neither called for nor necessary. Will the genetic code ever be shown not to be derived from a four-letter alphabet? That red blood cells do not pick up oxygen from the alveoli of the lungs and discharge carbon dioxide? That tuberculosis can occur in the absence of the tubercle bacillus? No. And even though we were not present at the beginning, as creationists enjoy reminding us, we have the tools to know a good deal about the beginning—either beginning. Given a little time, things do fall into place.

Still, creationists cannot be denied their agile imaginings. They have, without a penny's worth of testing, searching, experimentation, or proof of any kind, in the manner of Procrustes, fit their evidence, their singular point of view, to the Genesis story. No mean feat. Creationist arguments are not only without proof, but negative, seeking only to discredit scientific estimates. Yet, given the incomplete and temporary state of our knowledge, scientific truths about evolution are themselves but best estimates, not absolute truths, but far closer to the facts than the creationist accounts. Nevertheless, they are entitled to their views, so there are, then, at least two worldviews of our origins, two sets of truths: evolution and creationism. Should one prevail? Is one superior, preferable to the other? Perhaps. Is it necessary that one supersede the other? At first blush these questions may appear answerable by a simple "yes" or "no." A moment's reflection, however, prompts one to ask: Should an educated person not be knowledgeable, conversant, with creationist tenets? Should fundamentalist Christians spend their lives not knowing (appreciating) the difference between scientific truth and literal biblical interpretation? There is but one answer for everyone: know both!

Earlier, I had urged that the twenty-first century not be saddled with the baggage of the twentieth. Lifting this burden requires a more critically thinking population: a population more critical of what is said, heard, and read; a population ready to examine the facts for themselves, rather than passively accept others' thoughts and biases. This should be twenty-first-century thinking. Accordingly, I propose that our public schools, from the elementary grades to university, restructure some of their curricula—not necessarily with additional science courses, but with instruction in scientific literacy (SL): critical thinking, logical thinking, independent thinking. SL must be an educational goal for the twenty-first century that enlightens students about the processes and methods underpinning science, pseudoscience, and religion.

While scientific literacy and critical thinking are necessary and desirable, this dynamic duo will not spring full-grown, like Topsy, from the dull, mundane dispensing of facts by so-so teachers. Side-by-side teaching of scientific truth and religion/pseudoscience will only arise from devising hypotheses, designing and executing experiments, and examining evidence in the classroom, along with encouraging questions, questions, questions. The senses can be easily fooled. Magicians have built their professions on it. Avoiding this too common pitfall requires a fair degree of objectivity that scientific literacy can provide. But the key remains with, and falls to, excellent teachers. Without them, we can expect continuing conflict.

The fact that creationism is not a science should not automatically bar it from science classes. Good science can be differentiated from poor science and pseudoscience (which is not erroneous science), and in teaching both, it becomes evident that society—everyone—understands and accepts that there are different types of truth. Students and adults should be versed in both, knowing that each is separate and distinct, and that each has a place and function. This kind of education is preferable to indoctrination. I hasten to add that science seeks only to explain how things occur, not why: *why* things occur is the province of philosophers. Furthermore, scientific truth and religious truth need not be at war. Each trods a different path to a different truth, and there is room for both. A paraphrase may help: Render unto science that which is science's, and render unto religion that which is religion's.

With further critical examination of such popular pastimes such as astrology, UFOs, psychic surgery, aromatherapy, auras, crystal power, and the like, they will become more mundane and lose their novelty. Color them ordinary. Informed discussion of community concerns such as food irradiation, genetically modified foods, pesticides and cancer, indoor and outdoor air pollution, food safety, and emerging diseases will surely become less frightening. They will be confronted from a strong base of knowledge, and more of us will be adequately positioned to comment intelligently and make reasoned, considered decisions rather than emotional ones. As a society, we will be less prone to deception and bunkum. Decision-making will be broader based rather than the province of a noisy few who have their own agendas.

Furthermore, with the advent of SL, our lives will be opened to horizons not previously contemplated. With less to worry about now that the issues are understood, stress and anxiety will fall away, and we will become more interesting individuals as our ability to participate in discussions of serious issues increases. Environmentalists will find it increasingly difficult to press their special and unwarranted pleadings. As Marie Curie said: "Nothing in life is to be feared, it is only to be understood. Now is the time to understand more, so that we may fear less." A worthy prescription. Understanding more and fearing less is the essence of scientific literacy.

The Grand Plan

There is good news to proclaim. But how is scientific literacy going to spread? It is time to rouse the Sleeping Giant, to liberate the enormous potential of our nationwide educational infrastructure.

University presidents hold the key. Presidents of state universities and other university systems will move the process. The presidents will pass a strong, unambiguous message to their vice presidents and provosts for academic affairs that all faculty members be encouraged to aid the SL movement; that participation in this meritorious effort would be valued equally with teaching, research, and publishing; and that they would be looking for evidence that this all-university program would be up and running in the near term. And most important, funds to support this effort will be readily available. Such a message would be electrifying.

In turn, vice presidents and provosts for academic affairs will convey the presidents' directives to deans and department chairs, who will convey this salutary communiqué to department members, many of whom have been thirsting for so promising an opportunity. Foundations, industry, and an array of government agencies will provide funding for courses, conferences, resource development, and workshops.

Elementary and secondary schools will rise to the challenge, knowing that they will have ready access to university faculty for help in curriculum development, as well as courses providing the basic information needed to advance their own classroom skills and backgrounds.

University faculty who are excellent teachers will thrive in this new environment. In addition to working closely with elementary and high school teachers, they will be involved in public education.

From personal experience, I know that professional organizations have tried to offer discussions on current issues for the public at their national meetings, with little success. There was little enthusiasm for it on the part of researchers, who looked upon annual meetings as their private preserve, forums to demonstrate their prowess as researchers and accumulate points with chairmen and deans. But those who did get involved were not taken seriously; after all, the public was hardly the audience of concern there. But this will change—for the better. Supported with full backing, conferences will get the space, resources, and press. This time around, open meetings will be advertised and properly marketed. The public will know a conference is in town and they're invited. But these are annual affairs. Locally, universities and colleges will regularly offer programs to the public dealing with new medical discoveries, environmental issues, new scientific inventions and technologies, nuclear energy and more. And the people will come: from the National Science Foundation's biennial surveys, we know of the public's keen interest in these topics.[24] However, it is also known that many people have little or no grasp of how science proceeds, how scientific information is obtained. Pseudoscience is much easier to deal with, and no less interesting. The fact that it is underpinned by anecdotal evidence, information passed from person to person, usually of personal accounts, recommendations, and personal witness, as opposed to information obtained by controlled and published studies, appears to matter little. The Greeks had a word for this: *anekdotos*, unpublished, unverified, and so it remains. SL will provide the needed education to think more rigorously as it explores the essential character of evidence: the grounds for belief or disbelief, the information on which to base proof and establish truth or falsity.

We know, too, that TV science shows such as *Magic School Bus, Zoom,* and *Bill Nye's Science* have shot to the top of the charts. Yes, these are for children, but parents and grandparents become wrapped up in them, too, as they are hungry for solid information about their world. The time is ripe. The public presentations will in fact be two-way streets: the public, obtaining information of a type and scope unique for them, and the faculty being asked questions they've never previously been asked. Both will grow; both will profit. A new and uplifting town-gown relationship will ensue. Universities and colleges will acquire a new and sorely needed respectability, to the extent that their annual budget requests sail smoothly through their state legislatures.

But this is only part of it. Universities and colleges will also offer week-long and weekend workshops, short courses, for media personnel so they can upgrade their science backgrounds while permitting them to vent their frustrations about the availability and willingness of researchers to discuss their work. Again, a two-way street from which greater understanding and cooperation will emerge. The power to question is tremendous power.

The National Institutes of Health, which, at the request of Congress, instituted an Office of Alternative Medicine, will set up an Office of Science Education for the Public. Faculty members, teachers, and administrators will find that status, recognition, and advancement can and will obtain from their commitment to this national effort, as it does for bench scientists. But when President George W. Bush signs into law legislation authorizing the Department of Education to offer grants of one million dollars to each state university participating in this program, this seed money will not only secure the program and free up faculty members on a part-time basis, it will provide this national effort with the cachet necessary to succeed. Our aroused Giant will be a win-win undertaking. Scientific literacy is the new road to Wellsville. "SL" will be our new drummer, returning us to a less stressful, anxiety-filled life. Happiness may just become infectious and communicable, and the endless negative media hype will cease.

Within two decades the country will be breathing easier. The Luddites and the Cassandras among us will be on the run. The twenty-first century will be the century of scientific literacy for all. And it began because a university president had a vision. Who will be the first to nudge the Giant?

Notes

Chapter 1. Top of the Charts

1. U.S. Dept. of Health, Education, and Welfare, Public Health Service, *Healthy People: The Surgeon General's Report on Health Promotion and Disease Prevention*, Pub. no. 79-55071 (Washington, D.C.: Government Printing Office, 1979).

2. Reuel A. Stallones, "The Rise and Fall of Ischemic Heart Disease," *Scientific American* 243 (5) (1980): 53–59.

3. D. M. Lloyd-Jones, M. G. Larson et al., "Lifetime Risks of Developing Coronary Heart Disease," *The Lancet* 353 (1999): 89–92.

4. R. Hitt, Y. Young-Xu et al., "Centenarians: The Older You Get, the Healthier You've Been," *The Lancet* 354 (1999): 652.

5. I. L. Horon and D. Cheng, "Enhanced Surveillance for Pregnancy-Associated Mortality—Maryland, 1993–1998." *JAMA* 285 (2001): 1455–1459.

6. Centers for Disease Control, "HIV/AIDS Surveillance Report," Year-end Edition, 1 (2) (1999): 1–47. Cf. B. Schwartländer, G. Garnett, N. Walker, and R. Anderson, "AIDS in a New Millennium," *Science* 289 (2000): 64–67.

7. W. Cates, Jr., "Estimates of the Incidence and Prevalence of Sexually Transmitted Diseases in the United States," *Sexually Transmitted Diseases* (suppl.) 2 (4) (1999): 52–56.

8. A. Jemal et al., "Recent Trends in Lung Cancer Mortality in the U.S.," *Journal of the National Cancer Institute* 93 (4) (2001): 277–283.

9. Women's Heart Health Initiative, American Medical Women's Association, Alexandria, Virginia, 1995 (info@amwa-doc.org).

10. L. Thompson, "Trying to Look Sunsational? Complexity Persists in Using Sunscreens," *FDA Consumer* 34 (4) (2000): 15–21.

11. F. Noonan, J. A. Recio et al., "Neonatal Sunburn and Melanoma in Mice," *Nature* 413 (2001): 271–272.

12. R. A. Weinberg, *One Renegade Cell: How Cancer Begins* (New York: Basic Books, 1998).

13. World Health Organization, *Preventing Cancer*, Technical Report Service, 276 (Geneva: World Health Organization, 1964).

14. T. H. Maugh II, "Cancer and Environment: Higginson Speaks Out," *Science* 205 (1979): 1363–1366.

15. R. Doll and R. Peto, "The Causes of Cancer: Quantitative Estimates of Avoidable Risks of Cancer in the United States Today," *Journal of the National Cancer Institute* 66 (6) (1981): 1196–1265.

16. D. Trichopoulos, F. F. Li, and D. J. Hunter, "What Causes Cancer?" *Scientific American* 275 (3) (1996): 80–87.

17. F. Laden and D. J. Hunter, "Environmental Risk Factors and Female Breast Cancer," *Annual Review of Public Health* 19 (1998): 101–123.

18. P. Lichtenstein, N. V. Holm, E. Pukkala, A. Skytthe et al., "Environmental and

Heritable Factors in the Causation of Cancer: Analyses of Cohorts of Twins from Sweden, Denmark, and Finland," *New England Journal of Medicine* 343 (2) (2000): 78–85.

19. S. Begley, "Stop Blaming Your Genes," *Newsweek,* July 24, 2000, 53.

20. P. G. Kopelman, "Obesity as a Medical Problem," *Nature* 404 (2000): 635–643.

Chapter 2. Our Microbial World

1. Hippocrates, *The Genuine Works of Hippocrates*, trans. Francis Adams (Baltimore: Williams and Wilkins, 1939), 19–42.

2. J. H. Cassidy, *Charles V. Chapin and the Public Health Movement* (Cambridge, Mass.: Harvard University Press, 1962).

3. R. Dubos, *Man Adapting* (New Haven: Yale University Press, 1965).

4. M. R. Frieje, *Spas, Hot Tubs, and Whirlpool Baths: A Guide to Disease Prevention* (Tucson: University of Arizona Press, 2000). Cf. L. M. Prescott, T. P. Harley, and D. A. Klein, "Legionnaires' Disease and Pontiac Fever," in chap. 37, "Human Diseases Caused Primarily by Gram-Positive and Gram-Negative Bacteria," in *Microbiology*, 3d ed. (Dubuque, Iowa: Wm. C. Brown Publishers, 1996), pp. 744–745.

5. R. S. Ostfeld, "The Ecology of Lyme Disease," *American Scientist* 85 (1997): 338–436.

6. R. S. Lane and G. B. Quistad, "Borreliacidal Factor in the Blood of the Western Fence Lizard (*Sceloporus occidentalis*)," *Journal of Parasitology* 84 (1) (1998): 29–34.

7. J. C. Butler and C. J. Peters, "Hantavirus and Hantavirus Pulmonary Syndrome," *Clinical Infectious Diseases* 19 (1994): 387–395.

8. Centers for Disease Control, Special Pathogens Branch, "Viral Hemorrhagic Fevers Fact Sheet: Ebola Hemorrhagic Fever," August 22, 2000.

9. Z. Hujalek and J. Halouzka, "West Nile Fever: A Re-emerging Mosquito-borne Viral Disease in Europe," *Emergent Infectious Diseases* 5 (5) (2000): 1–5.

10. T. Solomon and M. J. Cardosa, "Emerging Arboviral Encephalitis," *British Medical Journal* 321 (2000): 485–486.

11. D. W. Chen, "New Epidemic Proving Fatal to Foxhounds," *New York Times*, August 8, 2000, 1.

12. Dubos, *Man Adapting*.

13. M. A. Graber and A. Nugent, "Peptic Ulcer Disease: Presentation, Treatment, and Prevention," *Emergency Medicine* 31 (November 1999): 66–70.

14. K. Schwarz, "Über Penetrierende Magen und Jejunalgeschure," *Beitrage für Klinischen Chirurgie* 67 (1910): 96–101.

15. N. Uemura, S. Okamoto, S. Yamamoto et al., "Helicobacter pylori Infection and the Development of Gastric Cancer," *New England Journal of Medicine* 345 (2001): 784–789.

16. B. J. Marshall, "Treatment Strategies for *Helicobacter Pylori* Infection," *Gastroenterological Clinics of North America* 22 (1) (1993): 183–202.

17. P. Brown, "On the Origin of BSE," *The Lancet* 352 (1998): 252–253.

18. M. R. Scott, R. Will et al., "Compelling Transgenic Evidence for Transmission of BSE Prions to Humans," *Proceedings of the National Academy of Science* 96 (26) (1999): 15137–15142.

19. L. Tan, M. A. Williams et al., "Risk of Transmission of BSE to Humans in the United States," Report of the Council on Scientific Affairs, *Journal of the American Medical Association* (hereafter *JAMA*) 281 (24) (1999): 2330–2338.

20. J. B. Muhlestein et al., "Randomized Secondary Prevention Trial of Azithromycin in Patients with Coronary Artery Disease," *Circulation* 102 (2000): 1755–1760.

21. S. Murakami et al., "Bell Palsy and Herpes Simplex Virus: Identification of Viral DNA in Endoneural Fluid and Muscle," *Annals of Internal Medicine* 124 (1, pt. 1) (1996): 27–30.

22. T. Anttila, P. Saiku et al., "Serotypes of *Chlamydia trachomatis* and Risk for Development of Cervical Squamous Cell Carcinoma," *JAMA* 285 (2001): 47–51.

23. B. Lorber, "Are All Diseases Infectious?" *Annals of Internal Medicine* 125 (10) (1996): 844–851.

24. J. B. Twitchell, *Twenty Ads That Shook the World* (New York: Crown Publishers, 2000).

25. G.A.W. Rook and J. L. Stanford, "Give Us This Day Our Daily Germs," *Immunology Today* 19 (3) (1998): 114–116.

26. T. M. Ball, J. A. Castro-Rodriguez et al., "Siblings, Day-Care Attendance, and the Rise of Asthma and Wheezing during Childhood," *New England Journal of Medicine* 343 (8) (2000): 538–543.

27. D. P. Strachan, "Hay Fever, Hygiene, and Household Size," *British Medical Journal* 299 (1989): 1259–1260.

28. S. Illi, E. von Mutius et al., "Early Childhood Infectious Diseases and the Development of Asthma Up to School Age: A Birth Cohort Study," *British Medical Journal* 322 (2001): 390–395.

29. Rook and Stanford, "Give Us This Day."

Chapter 3. Food, Glorious Food

1. Dietary Supplement Health and Education Act of 1994. Public Law 103-417 (S. 784), October 25, 1994, *U.S. Code and Administrative News*, no. 3.

2. "Little Accord in a Round Table of Diet Experts," *New York Times*, February 25, 2000, and A. Underwood, "The Battle of Pork Rind Hill," *Newsweek*, March 6, 2000, 50–52.

3. F. Ruschitzka et al., "Acute Heart Transplant Rejection Due to St. John's Wort," *The Lancet* 355 (2000): 548–549.

4. S. C. Piscitelli, A. H. Burstein et al., "Indinavir Concentrations and St. John's Wort," *The Lancet* 355 (2000): 547–548.

5. *Food Safety: Improvements Needed in Overseeing the Safety of Dietary Supplements and "Functional Foods"* (Washington, D.C.: U.S. General Accounting Office/ RCED-00-156, July 2000).

6. B. N. Ames et al., "Dietary Pesticides (99.99% All Natural)," *Proceedings of the National Academy of Science* 87 (1990): 7777–7781.

7. *Unsubstantiated Claims and Documented Health Hazards in the Dietary Supplement Marketplace* (Rockville, Md.: Department of Health and Human Services, Public Health Service, FDA, July 1993).

8. G. M. Lord, R. Tagore et al., "Nephropathy Caused by Chinese Herbs in the UK," *The Lancet* 354 (1999): 481–482.

9. E. Gertner et al., "Complications Resulting from the Use of Chinese Herbal Medications Containing Undeclared Prescription Drugs," *Arthritis & Rheumatism* 38 (3) (1995): 614–617.

10. T.K.Y. Chan, J. C. Chan et al., "Chinese Herbal Medicines Revisited: A Hong Kong Perspective," *The Lancet* 342 (1993): 1532–1534.

11. T. E. Towheed and T. P. Anastassiades, "Glucosamine Therapy for Osteoarthritis," *Journal of Rheumatology* 26 (11) (1999): 2294–2296.

12. K. B. Bouker and L. Hilakivi-Clark, "Genistein: Does It Prevent or Promote Breast Cancer?" *Environmental Health Perspectives* 108 (2000): 701–708.

13. V. Smil, "Magic Beans," *Nature* 407 (2000): 567.

14. A. Vincent and L. A. Fitzpatrick, "Soy Isoflavones: Are They Useful in Menopause?" *Mayo Clinical Proceedings* 75 (2000): 1174–1184.

15. G. Beaubrun and G. E. Gray, "A Review of Herbal Medicines for Psychiatric Disorders," *Psychiatric Services* 51 (7) (2000): 1130–1134.

16. H. K. Berthold et al., "Effect of a Garlic Oil Preparation on Serum Lipoproteins and Cholesterol Metabolism: A Randomized Controlled Trial," *JAMA* 279 (23) (1998): 1900–1902.

17. C. Stevenson et al., "Garlic for Treating Hypercholesterolemia: A Meta-analysis of Randomized Clinical Trials," *Annals of Internal Medicine* 133 (2000): 420–429.

18. J. Waggoner, "Ginseng Therapy for Farmlands," *New York Times,* December 1, 1999.

19. "If Germany Okays an Herb, Is It Safe in the U.S.?" *Tufts University Health and Nutrition Letter* 18 (10) (December 2000): 2, 4–5.

20. Centers for Disease Control, Division of Bacterial and Mycotic Infections, "Foodborne Infections: How Many Cases of Food-borne Disease Are There in the United States?" (http://www.cdc.gov/ncidod/dbmd/diseaseinfo/foodborneinfections_g.htm # mostcommon), March 29, 2000.

21. Ibid.

22. B. P. Bell, M. Goldoft et al., "A Multistate Outbreak of *Escherichia coli* O157:H7— Associated Bloody Diarrhea and Hemolytic Uremic Syndrome from Hamburgers," *JAMA* 272 (17) (1994): 1349–1353.

23. "What Is Food Net? CDC's Emerging Infections Program," Foodborne Diseases Active Surveillance Network (FoodNet) (http://www.cdc.gov/ncidod/dbmd/foodnet/what_is htm), July 20, 2000.

24. I. Nachankin, "Campylobacter jejuni," Part III, chap. 9, in *Food Microbiology: Fundamentals and Frontiers,* ed. M. P. Doyle, L. R. Beuchat, and T. J. Montville (Washington, D.C.: AMS Press, 1997); Centers for Disease Control, Division of Bacterial and Mycotic Infections, "Campylobacter Infections" (*http://www.cdc.gov.ncidod/dbmd/diseaseinfo/campylobacter_g.htm*), April 6, 2000.

25. T. W. Hennessey, C. W. Hedberg et al., "A National Outbreak of Salmonella Enteritidis Infections from Ice Cream," *New England Journal of Medicine* 334 (20) (1996): 1281–1286.

26. T. J. Török, R. V. Tauxe et al., "A Large Community Outbreak of Salmonellosis Caused by Intentional Contamination of Restaurant Salad Bars," *JAMA* 278 (5) (1997): 389–395.

27. C. P. Salmon, M. G. Knize et al., "Minimization of Heterocyclic Amines and Thermal Inactivation of *Escherichia coli* in Fried Ground Beef," *Journal of the National Cancer Institute* 92 (21) (2000): 1773–1778.

28. J. Rocourt and P. Cossart, "Listeria Monocytogenes," in *Food Microbiology: Fundamentals and Frontiers*, ed. M. P. Doyle, L. R. Beuchat, and T. J. Montville (Washington, D.C.: ASM Press, 1997).

29. C. B. Dalton, C. C. Austin et al., "An Outbreak of Gastroenteritis and Fever Due to Listeri Monocytogenes in Milk," *New England Journal of Medicine* 336 (2) (1997): 100–105.

30. U.S. Food and Drug Administration, Center for Food Safety and Applied Nutrition, "Yersinia enterolitica," in *Bad Bug Book: Foodborne Pathogenic Microorganisms and Natural Toxins Handbook (http://vm.cfsan.fda.gov/~mow/chap5.html)*, March 8, 2000.

31. Centers for Disease Control, Division of Parasitic Diseases, "Toxoplasmosis. Parasitic Disease Information" (http://www.avma.org.care4pets/antoxo.htm# danger), September 4, 2000.

32. B. L. Herwaldt, M. J. Beach, and the Cyclospora Working Group, "The Return of Cyclospora in 1997: Another Outbreak of Cyclosporiasis in North America Associated with Imported Raspberries," *Annals of Internal Medicine* 130 (3) (1999): 210–220.

33. U.S. Senate, Permanent Sub-Committee on Investigations, Committee on Government Affairs, "Food Safety: Federal Efforts to Ensure the Safety of Imported Foods Are Inconsistent and Unreliable," Report.

34. Ibid.

35. U.S. Department of Agriculture, "Irradiation of Meat Food Products; Final Rule," *Federal Register* 64 (246), December 23, 1999. Cf. "Safety of Irradiation to Control Microorganisms in Poultry," *Federal Register* 62 (232), December 3, 1997.

36. J. F. Diehl, *Safety of Irradiated Foods* (New York: Marcel Dekker, 1990).

37. P. Huang, T. Weber et al., "The First Reported Outbreak of Diarrheal Illness Associated with Cyclospora in the United States," *Annals of Internal Medicine* 123 (6) (1995): 409–414.

38. C. W. Hedberg, K. L. MacDonald, and M. T. Osterholm, "Changing Epidemiology of Food-borne Disease: A Minnesota Perspective," *Clinical Infectious Diseases* 18 (1994): 671–682. Cf. M. T. Osterholm, "Cyclosporiasis and Raspberries: Lessons for the Future," *New England Journal of Medicine* 336 (22) (1997): 1597–1598.

39. American Medical Association, Council on Scientific Affairs (Reference Committee E), "Irradiation of Food," Report 4 (I–93) , Chicago (adopted 1992).

40. American Dietetic Association, "Position Paper: Food Irradiation," *Journal American Dietary Association* 100 (2) (2000): 246–253.

41. "Irradiation in the Production, Processing and Handling of Food (Safe Use of Ionizing Radiation for the Reduction of Salmonellian Fresh Shell Eggs)," *Federal Register* 65 (141), July 21, 2000.

42. Caudill Seed Co., Inc., "Filing of Food Additive Petition (Safe Use to Control Pathogens in Alfalfa)," *Federal Register* 65 (64605–07), October 30, 2000.

Chapter 4. Food, Cancer, Heart Disease

1. J. Higginson and C. S. Muir, "Environmental Carcinogenesis: Misconceptions and Limitations to Cancer Control," *Journal of the National Cancer Institute* 63 (6) (1979): 1291–1298. Cf. T. H. Maugh II, "Cancer and Environment: Higginson Speaks Out," *Science* 205 (1979): 1363–1366; R. Doll and R. Peto, "The Causes of Cancer: Quantitative Estimates of Avoidable Risks of Cancer in the United States Today," *Journal of the National Cancer Institute* 66 (6) (1981): 1196–1265. Cf. R. Doll, "The Pierre Denoix Memorial Lecture: Nature and Nurture in the Control of Cancer," *European Journal of Cancer* 35 (1) (1999): 16–23; D. Trichopoulos, F. P. Li, and D. J. Hunter, "What Causes Cancer?" *Scientific American* 275 (3) (1996): 80–87.

2. D. C. Farrow and D. B. Thomas, "Cancer," in *Maxcy-Rosenau-Last, Public Health and Preventive Medicine*, ed. R. B. Wallace, 14th ed. (Stamford, Conn.: Appleton and Lange, 1998), 909–928.

3. B. N. Ames, M. K. Shigenaga, and T. M. Hagen, "Oxidants, Antioxidants, and the Degenerative Diseases of Aging," *Proceedings of the National Academy of Science* 90 (1993): 7915–7922.

4. J. W. Fahey, Y. Zhang, and P. Talalay, "Broccoli Sprouts: An Exceptionally Rich Source of Inducers of Enzymes That Protect against Chemical Carcinogens," *Proceedings of the National Academy of Science* 94 (1997): 10367–10372.

5. N. T. Telang et al., "Inhibition of Proliferation and Modulation of Estradiol Metabolism: Mechanism for Breast Cancer Prevention by the Phytochemical Indole-3-Carbinol," *Proceedings of the Society of Experimental and Biological Medicine* 216 (1997): 246–251.

6. K. Steinmetz and J. D. Potter, "Vegetables, Fruit, and Cancer Prevention: A Review," *Journal of the American Dietary Association* 96 (10) (1996): 1027–1039.

7. W. J. Blot, "Vitamin/Mineral Supplementation Cancer Risk: International Chemoprevention Trials," *Proceedings of the Society for Experimental Biology and Medicine* 216 (1997): 291–296.

8. C. H. Hennekens, J. E. Buring, and R. Peto, "Antioxidants, Vitamins—Benefits Not Yet Proved," *New England Journal of Medicine* 330 (15) (1994): 1080–1081.

9. I. D. Podmore, H. R. Griffith et al., "Vitamin C Exhibits Pro-Oxidant Properties," *Nature* 392 (1998): 559.

10. P. Palozza, "Prooxidant Actions of Carotinoids in Biological Systems," *Nutrition Revue* 66 (9) (1998): 257–265.

11. *Dietary Reference Intakes for Vitamin C, Vitamin E, Selenium, and Caratenoids* (Washington, D.C.: National Academy Press, April 2000).

12. G. E. Goodman, "The Clinical Evaluation of Cancer Prevention Agents," *Proceedings of the Society for Experimental and Biological Medicine* 216 (1997): 253–258.

13. A. L. Waterhouse et al., "Antioxidants in Chocolate," *The Lancet* 348 (1996): 834.

14. A. R. Goldbohm, M.G.L. Hertog et al., "Consumption of Black Tea and Cancer Risk: A Prospective Cohort Study," *Journal of the National Cancer Institute* 88 (1996): 93–99.

15. M.G.L. Hertog, E.J.M. Feskens et al., "Dietary Antioxidants, Flavinoids, and Risk of Coronary Heart Disease: The Zutphen Elderly Study," *The Lancet* 342 (1993): 1007–1011.

16. A. Jha, M. Flather et al., "The Antioxidant Vitamins and Cardiovascular Disease: A Critical Review of Epidemiologic and Clinical Trial Data," *Annals of Internal Medicine* 123 (1995): 860–872.

17. R. M. Hoffman and H. S. Garewal, "Antioxidants and the Prevention of Coronary Heart Disease," *Archives of Internal Medicine* 155 (1995): 241–245.

18. *Harvard Health Letter* 25 (12) (October 2000): 2–3, 6–7.

19. K. Klipstein-Grobush, J. M. Geleijnse et al., "Dietary Antioxidants and Risk of Myocardial Infarction in the Elderly: The Rotterdam Study," *American Journal of Clinical Nutrition* 69 (1999): 261–266.

20. K. B. Michels, E. Giovannuci, K. J. Joshipura et al., "Prospective Study of Fruits and Vegetable Consumption and Incidence of Colon and Rectal Cancer," *Journal of the National Cancer Institute* 92 (21) (2000): 1740–1750.

21. R. L. Weinberg, *One Renegade Cell* (New York: Basic Books, 1998).

22. Ames, Shingenaga, and Hagen, "Oxidents, Antioxidents, and the Degenerative Diseases of Aging."

23. U.S. EPA, Office of Pesticide Programs, *What Is a Pesticide?* (*http://www.epa.gov/pesticides/citizens/antimic.htm*), November 17, 1999.

24. J. Dich, S. H. Zahm et al., "Pesticides and Cancer," *Cancer Causes and Control* 8 (1997): 420–443.

25. B. N. Ames and I. T. Gold, "Environmental Pollution, Pesticides, and the Prevention of Cancer: Misconceptions," *FASEB Journal* 11 (1997): 1041–1052.

26. M. A. Benarde, *Our Precarious Habitat: Fifteen Years Later* (New York: John Wiley, 1989).

27. S. Ishiwata, "On a Severe Softening of Silkworms (Sotto Disease)," *Dainihan Sanbshi Kaiho* 9 (114) (1901): 1–5.

28. E. Berliner, "Über die Schlafsucht der Mehlmottenraupe (*Ephestia kühniella* Zell.) und ihren Erreger *Bacillus thuringiensis* n.sp.," *Zeitschrift für Angewan. Entomologie* 2 (1915): 29–56.

29. K. A. McGrath, ed., *World of Biology* (Detroit: Gale Group, 1999), 501–509.

30. J. E. Losey, L. S. Rayor, and M. E. Carter, "Transgenic Pollen Harms Monarch Larvae," *Nature* 399 (1999): 254.

31. "University of Maine Research on Maize (Corn) Cross-Pollination," University of Maine Cooperative Extension, Orono, News Release, January 26, 2000.

32. C. L. Wraight, A. R. Zangerl et al., "Absence of Toxicity of *Bacillus thuringiensis* Pollen to Black Swallowtails under Field Conditions," *Proceedings of the National Academy of Science* 97 (14) (2000): 7700–7703.

33. Ibid.

34. M. Sears, "Bt Corn Pollen Does Not Hurt Monarch Butterfly Larvae," University of Guelph, Institute of Food Science Technology, London, U.K., March 2000 (http://www.ifst.org/genedh.htm).

35. A. M. Shelton et al., "Field Tests on Managing Resistance to Bt-engineered Plants," *Nature Biotechnology* 18 (2000): 339–342.

36. F. Gould, "Testing Bt Refuge Strategies in the Field," *Nature Biotechnology* 18 (2000): 266–267.

37. "Monarch Butterflies iii." Biopesticide Regulation Registration. Preliminary Risk-Benefit Analysis. U.S. EPA, Washington, D.C., September 19, 2000.

38. M. J. Crawley, S. L. Brown et al., "Transgenic Crops in Natural Habitats," *Nature* 409 (2001): 682–683.

39. "Food Fight: The Truth about Genetically Modified Organisms," *Green Peace Magazine* (Spring 2000), 14–15.

40. National Research Council, *Field Testing Genetically Modified Organisms: Framework for Decisions* (Washington, D.C.: National Academy Press, 1989).

41. National Research Council, *Genetically Modified Pest-Protected Plants: Science and Regulation* (Washington, D.C.: National Academy Press, 2000).

42. J. A. Nordlee, S. L. Taylor et al., "Identification of a Brazil-Nut Allergen in Transgenic Soybeans," *New England Journal of Medicine* 334 (11) (1996): 688–692.

43. Ibid.

44. R. A. Goldberg and C. Koppell, *Pioneer Hi-Bred International: Developing an Environmental Statement and Strategy* (Cambridge, Mass.: Harvard Business School, 1992).

45. D. D. Metcalf, J. D. Ashwood et al., "Assessment of the Allergenic Potential of Food Derived from Genetically Engineered Crop Plants," *Critical Reviews of Food, Science, and Nutrition* 36 (1996): S165–S168.

46. IFT Expert Report on Biotechnology and Foods, "Human Food Safety Evaluation of rDNA Biotechnology-Derived Foods," *Food Technology* 54 (9) (2000): 53–61.

47. S. H. Sichever et al., "Prevalence of Peanut and Tree Nut Allergy in the U.S. Determined by a Random Digit Dial Telephone Survey," *Journal of Allergy and Clinical Immunology* 103 (4) (1999): 559–562.

48. H. S. Skolnick et al., "The Natural History of Peanut Allergy," *Journal of Allergy and Clinical Immunology* 107 (2001): 367–374.

49. J. Christensen, "Golden Rice in a Grenade-Proof Greenhouse," *New York Times,* November 21, 2000, F1, 5.

50. C. S. Smith, "China Rushes to Adopt Genetically Modified Crops," *New York Times,* October 7, 2000, A3.

51. J. Tu, G. Zhang et al., "Field Performance of Transgenic Elite Commercial Hybrid Rice Expressing *Bacillus thuringiensis* delta-Endotoxin," *Nature Biotechnology* 16 (2000): 1101–1105.

52. T. H. Tai, D. Dahlbeck et al., "Expression of the Bs2 Pepper Gene Confers Resistance to Bacterial Spot Disease in Tomato," *Proceedings of the National Academy of Science* 96 (1999): 14153–14158.

53. C. Lewis, "The Coming of Biotech Animals," *FDA Consumer* 35 (2001): 15–20.

54. S. Thompson, "Are Bioengineered Foods Safe?" *FDA Consumer* 34 (1) (2000): 18–23.

55. *Safety Aspects of Genetically Modified Foods of Plant Origin,* Report of a Joint FAO/WHO Expert Consultation on Foods Derived from Biotechnology (Geneva: FAO of the UN and WHO, 2000).

56. K. A. Goldman, "Bioengineered Food—Safety and Labeling," *Science* 290 (2000): 457–459.

57. M. Kato et al., "Caffeine Synthase Gene from Tea Leaves," *Nature* 406 (2000): 956.

Chapter 5. Troubled Air

1. J. T. Houghton, *Climate Change: 1995. The Science of Climate Change* (Cambridge, U.K.: Cambridge University Press, 1996).

2. B. Brown and L. Morgan, *The Miracle Planet* (New York: Gallery Books, 1990).

3. M. A. Benarde, *Global Warning: Global Warming* (New York: John Wiley, 1992).

4. G. P. Patterson et al., "Greenhouse Gases in Intensive Agriculture: Contributions of Individual Gases to the Radiative Forcing of the Atmosphere," *Science* 289 (2000): 1922–1925.

5. J. E. Lovelock et al., "Halogenated Hydrocarbons in and over the Atlantic," *Nature* 241 (1973): 194–196.

6. F. Möller, "On the Influence of Changes in the CO_2 Concentration in Air on the Radiation Balance of the Earth's Surface and the Climate," *Journal of Geophysical Research* 68 (1963): 3877–3886.

7. A. Ravel and V. Ramanathan, "Observational Determination of the Greenhouse Effect," *Nature* 342 (1989): 758–761.

8. W. T. Sturgis, T. J. Wallington et al., "A Potent Greenhouse Gas Identified in the Atmosphere: SF5CF3," *Science* 289 (2000): 611–613.

9. S. A. Arrhenius, "On the Influence of Carbonic Acid in the Air upon the Temperature of the Ground," *Philosophical Magazine* 41 (5) (1896): 237–276.

10. R. Revelle and H. Suess, "Carbon Dioxide Exchange between the Atmosphere and Ocean, and the Question of an Increase in Atmospheric CO_2 during the Past Decades," *Tellus* 9 (1957): 18–27.

11. C. D. Keeling et al., "Measurements of the Concentration of Carbon Dioxide at Mauna Loa Observatory, Hawaii," in *Carbon Dioxide Review*, ed. William C. Clark (Cambridge, U.K.: Cambridge University Press, 1982), 377–389.

12. Intergovernmental Panel on Climate Change, *IPCC Special Report: Emissions Scenarios. Summary for Policy Makers*. Special Report of Working Group III, United Nations Environmental Program (Nairobi, Kenya: United Nations Office, 2000).

13. Ibid.

14. U.S. EPA, Global Warming, Regional Impact Report, Human Health, chap. 8. North America. 8.3.9 (http://www.epa.gov/global warming/publications/reference/IPCC/Chap 8/ america 15.html/, August 15, 2000).

15. Ibid.

16. D. J. Rogers and S. E. Randolph, "The Global Spread of Malaria in a Future, Warmer World," *Science* 289 (2000): 1763–1766.

17. Ibid.

18. J. Pelley, "Deadly *E. coli* Outbreak Focuses Canadian Privatization Debate," *Environmental Science and Technology* 34 (August 1, 2000): 336A.

19. U.S. EPA, Regional Impact Report.

20. P. Krugman, "Sins of Emission," *New York Times,* November 29, 2000, A35.

21. A. C. Revken, "Effort to Cut Warming Lacks Time and Unity," *New York Times,* November 26, 2000.

22. J. Motavalli, "Pneumatic Car: Environmental Bonanza or Lots of Hot Air," *New York Times,* November 24, 2000, F1.

23. B. G. Ferris, F. E. Speizer et al., "Effects of Sulfur Oxides and Respirable Particles on Human Health," *American Review of Respiratory Diseases* 120 (1979): 767–779; D. W. Dockery, C. A. Pope, et al., "An Association between Air Pollution and Mortality in Six U.S. Cities," *New England Journal of Medicine* 329 (24) (1993): 1753–1759; J. Kaiser, "Panel Backs EPA and Six Cities Study," *Science* 289 (2000): 711.

24. A. J. Cohen and C. A. Pope III, "Lung Cancer and Air Pollution," *Environmental Health Perspectives* 103 (suppl. 8) (1995): 219–224.

Chapter 6. Clean Energy: Power from Atoms

1. *Sources and Effects of Ionizing Radiation*, UNSCEAR 2000 Report to the General Assembly with Annexes, vol. 1 (Geneva: United Nations, 2000).

2. Ibid.

3. Ibid.

4. W. J. Schull, *Effects of Atomic Radiation: A Half-Century of Studies from Hiroshima and Nagasaki* (New York: Wiley-Liss, 1995).

5. "The TMI-2 Cleanup—Challenging and Successful," *Backgrounder* (Middletown, Pa.: GPU Nuclear, 2000).

6. M. C. Hatch, J. Beyea et al., "Cancer Near the Three Mile Island Nuclear Plant: Radiation Emissions," *American Journal of Epidemiology* 132 (1990): 397–412.

7. S. Jablon et al., "Cancer in Populations Living Near Nuclear Facilities: Survey of Mortality Nationwide and Incidence in Two States," *JAMA* 265 (11) (1991): 1403–1440.

8. S. Rambo, "No Radiological Health Effects. Case Dismissed, by U.S. District Court Judge, Harrisburg, June 1996," cited in *Backgrounder*, GPU Nuclear, Middletown, Pa., 2000.

9. E. O. Talbott, A. O. Youk et al., "Mortality among the Residents of the Three Mile Island Accident Area: 1979-1992," *Environmental Health Perspectives* 108 (6) (2000): 545–551.

10. *Sources and Effects of Ionizing Radiation.*

11. Ibid.

12. B. L. Cohen, "Test of the Linear No-Threshold Theory of Radiation Carcinogenesis for Inhaled Radon Decay Products," *Health Physics* 68 (1995): 157–174.

13. P. E. Tyler, "Living in the Shadow of Chernobyl's Reactor," *New York Times,* June 4, 2000, 1, 10.

14. W. Hufmann et al., "Lung Cancer Incidence in a Chinese High Background Area—Epidemiological Results and Theoretical Interpretation," *Science of the Total Environment* 45 (1985): 527–534.

15. W. J. Blot, Z. Y. Xu et al., "Indoor Radon and Lung Cancer in China," *Journal of the National Cancer Institute* 82 (12) (1990): 1025–1030.

16. Z. Wang, J. D. Boice, Jr., et al., "Thyroid Nodularity and Chromosome Aberrations among Women in Areas of High Background Radiation in China," *Journal of the National Cancer Institute* 82 (6) (1990): 478–485.

17. K. N. Nair, K.S.V. Nambi et al., "Population Study in the High Natural Background Radiation Area in Kerala, India," *Radiation Research* 152 (1999): S145–S148.

18. G. Jaikrishan, V. J. Andrews et al., "Genetic Monitoring of the Human Population from the High-Level Natural Radiation Areas of Kerala on the Southwest Coast of India. I. Prevalence of Congenital Malformations in Newborns," *Radiation Research* 152 (1999): S149–S153.

19. V. D. Cheriyan, C. J. Kurien et al., "Genetic Monitoring of the Human Population from High-Level Natural Radiation Areas of Kerala on the Southwest Coast of India. II. Incidence of Numerical and Structural Chromosomal Aberrations in the Lymphocytes of Newborns," *Radiation Research* 152 (1999): S154–S158.

20. R. Rajendran et al., "Prevalence of Oral Submucous Fibrosis in the High Natural Radiation Belt of Kerala, South India," *Bulletin of WHO* 70 (6) (1992): 783–789.

21. K. Magnus, A. Engeland et al., "Residential Radon Exposure and Lung Cancer: An Epidemiological Study of Norwegian Municipalities," *International Journal of Cancer* 58 (1994): 1–7.

22. C. Hill and A. Laplanche, "Overall Mortality and Cancer Mortality around French Nuclear Sites," *Nature* 347 (1990): 755–757.

23. S. C. Darby and R. Doll, "Fallout, Radiation Doses near Dounreay, and Childhood Leukemia," *British Medical Journal* 294 (1987): 596–602.

24. L. D. Dodds, D.J.T. Marrett et al., "Case-Control Study of Congenital Anomalies in Children of Cancer Patients," *British Medical Journal* 307 (1993): 164–168.

25. E. Roman et al., "Cancer in Children of Nuclear Industry Employees: Report on Children Aged under 25 Years from Nuclear Industry Family Study," *British Medical Journal* 318 (1999): 1443–1450; Cf. also 1453–1454.

26. G. M. Matanoski, "Health Effects of Low-Level Radiation on Shipyard Workers," Final Report, June 1991 (Washington, D.C.: Department of Energy, DE-ACO2-79EV 10095).

27. E. S. Gilbert, S. A. Fry et al., "Analysis of Combined Mortality Data on Workers at the Hanford Site, Oak Ridge National Laboratory, and Rocky Flats Nuclear Weapons Plant," *Radiation Research* 120 (1989): 19–35.

28. E. S. Gilbert et al., "Updated Analysis of Combined Mortality Data for Workers at the Hanford Site, Oak Ridge National Laboratory, and Rocky Flats Weapons Plant," *Radiation Research* 408 (1993): 408–421.

29. *Climate Change and Nuclear Power* (Vienna: International Atomic Energy Agency, 2000).

Chapter 7. Hazardous Waste, Hazardous Thinking

1. *Healthy People: The Surgeon General's Report on Health Promotion and Disease Prevention* (Washington, D.C.: U.S. Department of Health, Education, and Welfare, 1979) DHEW [PHS] pub. no. 79-55071.

2. National Research Council, *Environmental Epidemiology*, vol. 1, *Public Health and Hazardous Wastes* (Washington, D.C.: National Academy Press, 1991).

3. H. Dolk, M. Vrijheid et al., "Risk of Congenital Anomalies near Hazardous-Waste Landfill Sites in Europe: The EUROITAZLOAN Study," *The Lancet* 352 (1998): 423–427.

4. S. A. Geschwind et al., "Risk of Congenital Malformations Associated with Proximity to Hazardous Waste Sites," *American Journal of Epidemiology* 135 (11) (1992): 1197–1207.

5. L. A. Croen et al., "Maternal Residential Proximity to Hazardous Waste Sites and Risk for Selected Congenital Malformations," *Epidemiology* 8 (4) (1997): 347–354.

6. E. G. Marshall et al., "Maternal Residential Exposure to Hazardous Wastes and Risk of Central Nervous System and Musculo-skeletal Birth Defects," *Archives of Environmental Health* 52 (6) (1997): 416–425.

7. M. S. Goldberg et al., "Risks of Developing Cancer Relative to Living near a Municipal Solid Waste Landfill Site in Montreal, Quebec, Canada," *Archives of Environmental Health* 54 (24) (1994): 291–296.

8. Dolk et al., "Risk of Congenital Anomalies."

9. C. J. Komis, "Exposure Assessment of Workers at Hazardous Waste Sites Based on Concurrent Environmental Monitoring and Breath Sampling" (Ph.D. diss., Drexel University, 1993).

10. B. L. Johnson and C. T. DeRosa, "The Toxologic Hazard of Superfund Hazardous Waste Sites," *Reviews of Environmental Health* 12 (4) (1997): 235–251.

11. National Research Council, *Waste Incineration and Public Health: Report of the Committee on Health Effects of Waste Incineration* (Washington, D.C.: National Academy Press, 1999).

12. K. Steenland et al., "Cancer, Heart Disease, and Diabetes in Workers Exposed to 2, 3, 7, 8-Tetrachlorodibenzo-p-dioxin," *Journal of National Cancer Institute* 91 (9) (1999): 779–786.

13. G. M. Calvert et al., "Evaluation of Cardiovascular Outcomes among U.S. Workers Exposed to 2, 3, 7, 8-Tetrachlorodibenzo-p-dioxin," *Environmental Health Perspectives* 106 (suppl. 2) (1998): 635–643.

14. M. T. Landi, D. Consonni et al., "2, 3, 7, 8–Tetrachlorodibenzo-p-dioxin Plasma Levels in Seveso 20 years after the Accident," *Environmental Health Perspectives* 106 (5) (1998): 273–277; P. A. Bertazzi et al., "The Seveso Studies on Early and Long-Term Effects of Dioxin Exposure: A Review," *Environmental Health Perspectives* 106 (suppl. 2) (1998): 625–632.

15. N. S. Ketchum et al., "Serum Dioxin and Cancer in Veterans of Operation Ranch Hand," *American Journal of Epidemiology* 149 (7) (1999): 630–639.

16. House of Representatives, Hazardous Waste Disposal, Part I. Hearings before the

Sub-Committee on Oversight and Investigations of the Committee on Interstate and Foreign Commerce, 96th Congress, ser. No. 96–48, 1979.

17. M. H. Brown, *Laying Waste: The Poisoning of America by Toxic Chemicals* (New York: Pantheon Books, 1980).

18. M. H. Brown, "Love Canal and the Poisoning of America," *The Atlantic* (December 1979), 33–47; M. H. Brown, "A Toxic Ghost Town," *The Atlantic* (July 1989), 23–28.

19. C. Kalb, "Hype, Hope, Cancer," *Newsweek,* December 28–January 5, 1999, 73.

20. P. Broduer, *Currents of Death* (New York: Simon and Schuster, 1989); P. Broduer, *The Great Power Line Coverup* (Boston: Little, Brown, 1993).

21. R. M. Page, G. E. Cole, and T. C. Timmreck, *Basic Epidemiological Methods and Biostatistics* (Sudbury, Mass.: Jones and Bartlett Publishers, 1995).

22. V. M. Montori et al., "Publication Bias: A Brief Review for Clinicians," *Mayo Clinical Proceedings* 75 (2000): 1284–1288.

23. D. B. Altmann, "Statistics and Ethics in Medical Research: Collecting and Screening Data," *British Medical Journal* 281 (1980): 1399–1401.

24. A. B. Hill, "The Environment and Disease: Association or Causation," *Proceedings of the Royal Society of Medicine* 95 (1965): 213–222.

25. G. Taubes, "Epidemiology Faces Its Limits," *Science* 269 (1995): 164–169.

26. J. A. Paulos, *A Mathematician Reads the Newspapers* (New York: Basic Books, 1995).

27. Geschwind et al., "Risk of Congenital Malformations."

28. L. A. Sagan, *Electrical and Magnetic Fields: Invisible Risks?* (Amsterdam: Gordon and Breach, 1996).

29. M. H. Repacholi and A. Ahlbom, "Link between Electromagnetic Fields and Childhood Cancer Unresolved," *The Lancet* 354 (1999): 1918.

30. K. J. Rothman, "Keynote Presentation: A Sobering Start for the Cluster Busters' Conference," *American Journal of Epidemiology* 132 (1990): S6–S13.

31. R. Soave et al., "Cyclospora," *Infectious Disease Clinics of North America* 12 (1998): 1–12.

Chapter 8. The Sleeping Giant

1. W. D. Ruckelshaus, "Science, Risk, and Public Policy," *Science* 221 (1983): 1023–1028.

2. R. P. Parsons, *Trail to Light: A Biography of Joseph Goldberger* (Indianapolis: Bobbs-Merrill, 1943).

3. J. Goldberger, "The Etiology of Pellagra: The Significance of Certain Epidemiological Observations with Respect Thereto," *Public Health Report* 29 (1914): 1683–1686.

4. J. Goldberger, "Pellagra: Causation and a Method of Prevention, a Summary of Some of the Recent Studies of the U.S Public Health Service," *JAMA* 66 (1916): 471–476.

5. J. Goldberger, C. H. Waring, and W. F. Tanner, "Pellagra Prevention by Diet among Institutional Inmates." *Public Health Reports* 38 (1923): 2361–2368.

6. Ibid.

7. Ibid.

8. K. C. Carter and B. R. Carter, *Childbed Fever: A Scientific Biography of Ignaz Semmelweis* (Westport, Conn.: Greenwood Press, 1994).

9. Ibid.

10. R. O. Brennan and D. T. Durack, "Gay Compromise Syndrome," *The Lancet* 2 (1981): 1338–1339.

11. T. J. McManus et al., "Amyl Nitrate Use by Homosexuals," *The Lancet* 1 (1982): 503.

12. J. Fibiger, "On *Spiroptera carcinomata* and Their Relation to True Malignant Tumors: With Some Remarks on Cancer Age," *Journal of Cancer Research* 4 (1919): 367–387.

13. P. D. Stolley and T. Lasky, "Johannes Fibiger and His Nobel Prize for the Hypothe-

sis That a Worm Causes Stomach Cancer," *Annals of Internal Medicine* 116 (9) (1992): 765–769.

14. D. J. Futuyama, *Science on Trial* (New York: Pantheon Books, 1983).

15. R. M. Nesse and G. C. Williams, *Why We Get Sick: The New Science of Darwinian Medicine* (New York: Vintage Books, 1996).

16. H. Morris, *Studies on the Bible and Science* (Grand Rapids, Mich.: Zondervan Publishing House, 1974). Cf. "Creationism in Schools: The Decision in *McLean v. the Arkansas Board of Education*," *Science* 215 (1952): 934–944.

17. D. J. Boorstin, "Into 'the Mists of Paradox,'" in *The Discoverers*, vol. 1 (New York: Harry N. Abrams, 1991), 438–454.

18. Boorstin, "Caught in the Crossfire," in *The Discoverers*, 484–490.

19. D. J. Boorstin, *The Discoverers*, vol. 1 (New York: Random House, 1983), p. 108.

20. M. Zeilik, *Astronomy: The Evolving Universe*, 5th ed. (New York: John Wiley, 1988), 53.

21. Boorstin, *The Discoverers*, vol. 2, p. 517.

22. S. Blakeslee, "Making Sense of Grand Canyon's Puzzles," *New York Times*, June 6, 2000, "Science Times," 1.

23. T. D. Jones, J. A. Ruben et al., "Nonavian Feathers in a Late Triassic Archosaur," *Science* 288 (2000): 2202–2205.

24. National Science Foundation, *Science and Engineering Indicators 2000*, vol. 1 (Arlington, Va.: National Science Board, 2000) (NSB-00-1).

Index

About the Author

Recently retired as professor and director of the Environmental Issues Center, Temple University, Dr. Benarde was also acting chairman, Department of Community and Preventive Medicine, Hahnemann Medical College and Hospital, Philadelphia.

In addition to authoring eleven books, and extensive lecturing, Dr. Benarde was featured, for two years, on the ABC-TV series *Environment and Health*.

Prior to joining the Hahnemann faculty, Dr. Benarde was a member of the Rutgers University faculty, where he taught epidemiology and public health. During this period, he was the recipient of a WHO Fellowship that took him to the University of London's School of Hygiene and Tropical Medicine to study epidemiology and international health problems.

You've
Been Had!

PREVIOUS BOOKS BY THE AUTHOR

Global Warning, Global Warming

Our Precarious Habitat . . . Fifteen Years Later

Asbestos: The Hazardous Fiber

Our Precarious Habitat

Beach Holidays: Portugal to Israel

The Chemicals We Eat

Race Against Famine

The Food Additives Dictionary

Disinfection

You've
Been Had!

How the Media and Environmentalists Turned America into a Nation of Hypochondriacs

Melvin A. Benarde

RUTGERS UNIVERSITY PRESS
NEW BRUNSWICK, NEW JERSEY, AND LONDON

280400

MAY 2 3 2003

Library of Congress Cataloging-in-Publication Data
Benarde, Melvin A.
    You've been had! : how the media and environmentalists turned America into a nation of
hypochondriacs / Melvin A. Benarde.
        p.   cm.
Includes bibliographical references and index.
ISBN 0-8135-3050-4 (cloth : alk. paper)
    1. Environmental health.   2. Environmental health—Responsibility.   3. Quacks and quackery.
4. Consumer education.   5. Mass media in health education.   I. Title.

RA440.5 .B46 2002
615.9'02—dc21

                                                                            2001048401

British Cataloging-in-Publication information is available from the British Library.

Manufactured in the United States of America

Design by John Romer